AF426492

Patterns
vol.1

m²ft architects
(Flavio Martella, Maria Vittoria Tesei)

A project by m²ft architects.

Editing, review and graphics:
Flavio Martella
Maria Vittoria Tesei

First printing, 2021.

ISBN 9798622837135

We are visual beings. We live and eat images, every day, every minute. The access to the digital layer has allowed our lives to be continually referenced to new images, new visual boundaries, new graphic narratives. A constant stimulus that is creating a new mass graphic culture where everyone can contribute on something.

The search for the newness creates continuous variations of the existing. Small changes that do not seem to bring much, but instead make all the difference of the case, allowing you to go from the banal to the unique. As when in architecture it is sufficient to change the arrangement of the facade bricks to radically transform the appearance of the building and create something new. But that building could have been different as many times as it would have been possible to do with bricks. We live in a world mediated by patterns.

This prompted us to investigate the potential of continuous reiteration, of imperceptible change, of the series. We have therefore created a collection of patterns that are constantly growing and changing, as indeed is the era in which we live.

This is an assembly of patterns that can serve as an inspiration to other agents of this visual world. A collection that takes references from history, events and our personal experiences, but which is not ordered according to these starting points. It is deliberately messy, chaotic and dense, trying to remove any reference and push for the formulation of new series.

ENJOY!

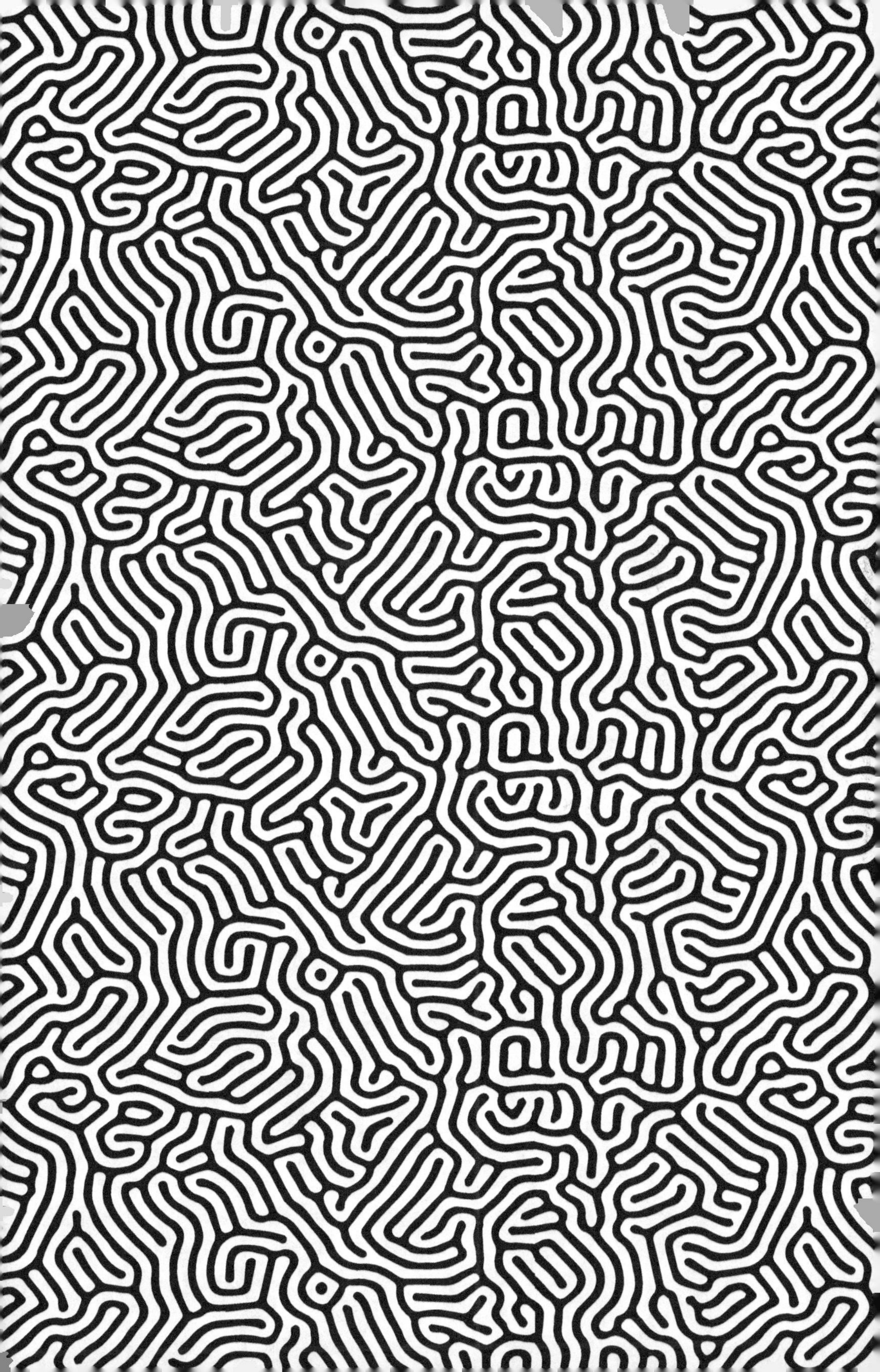

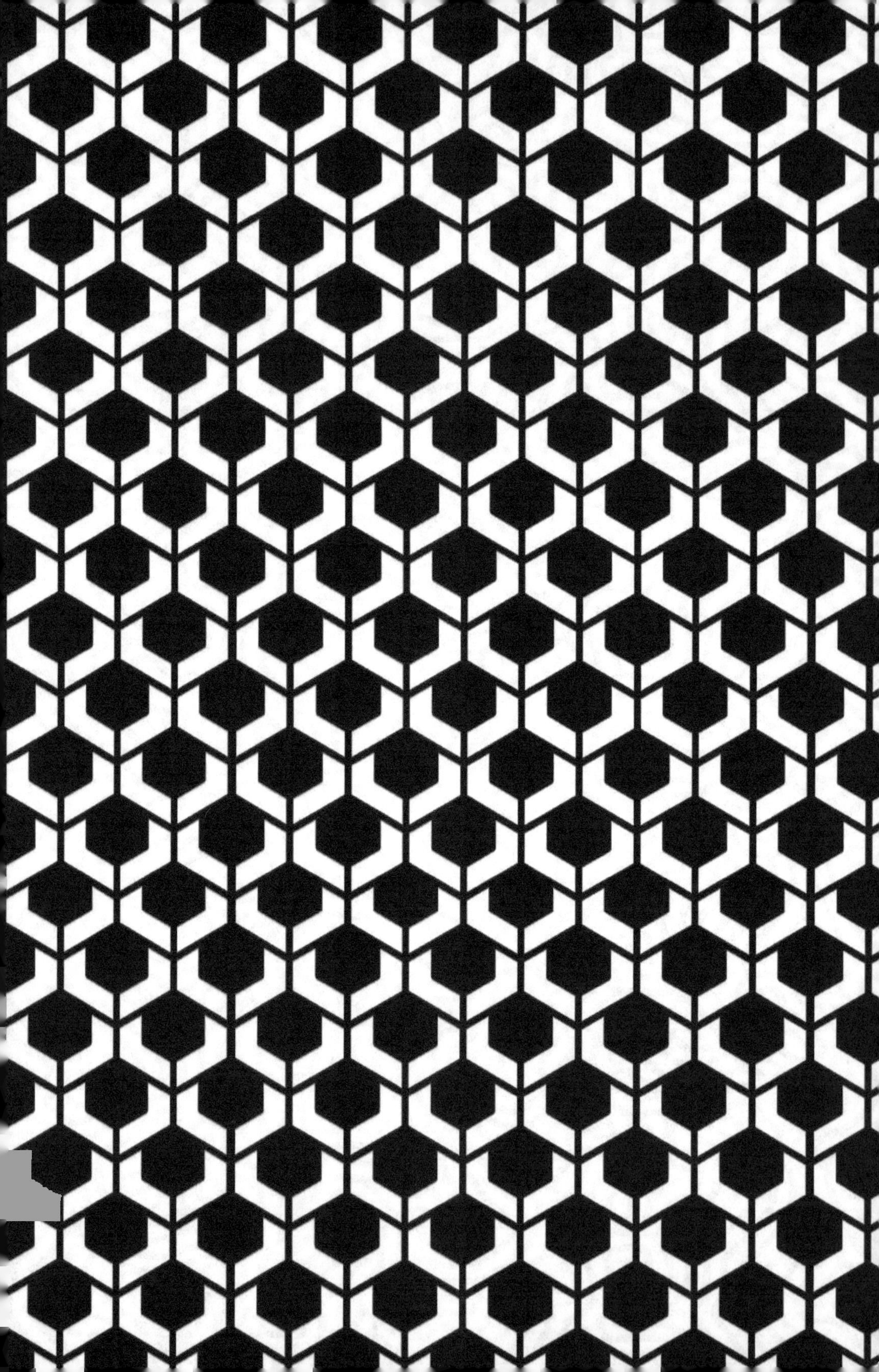

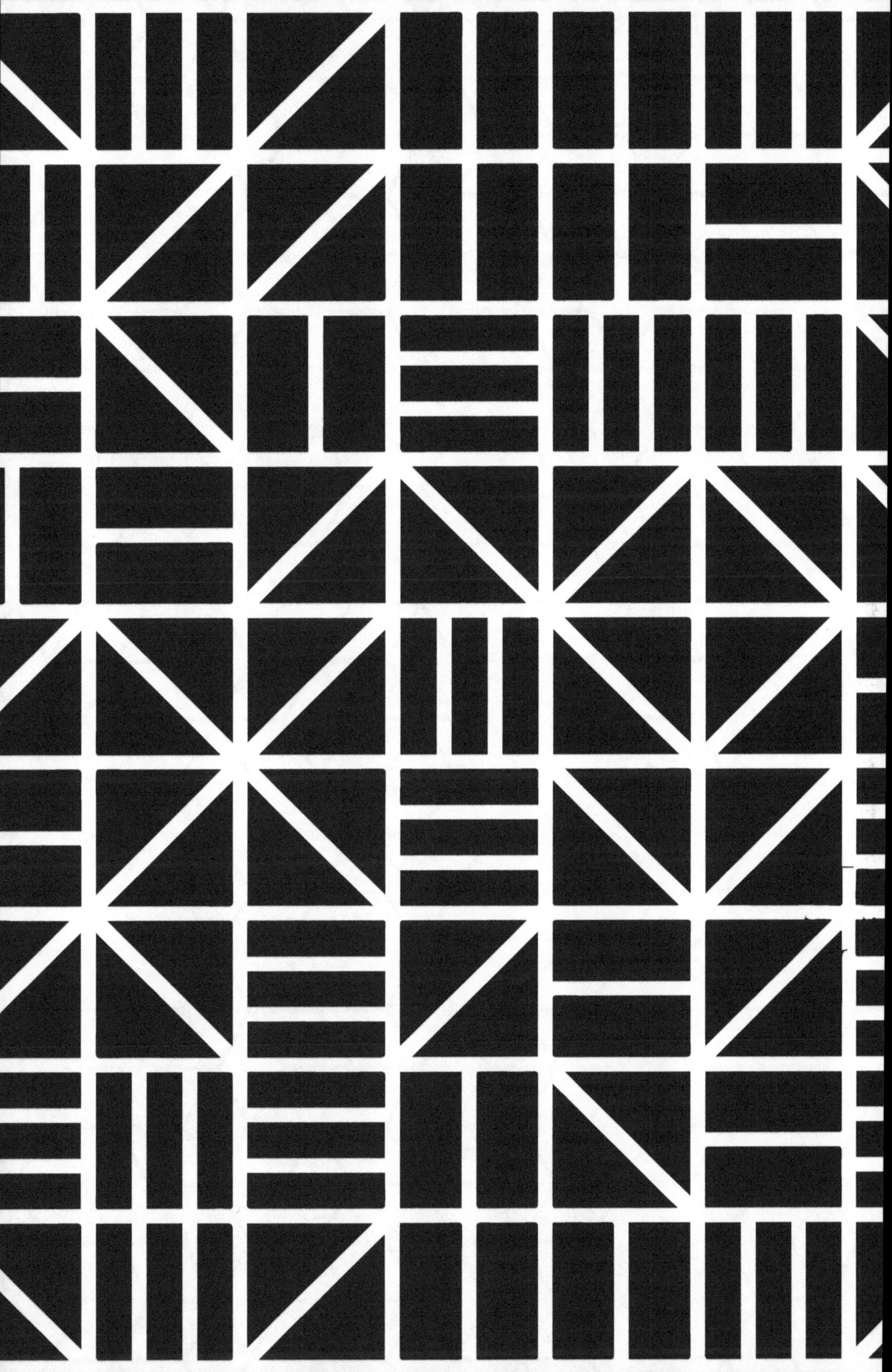

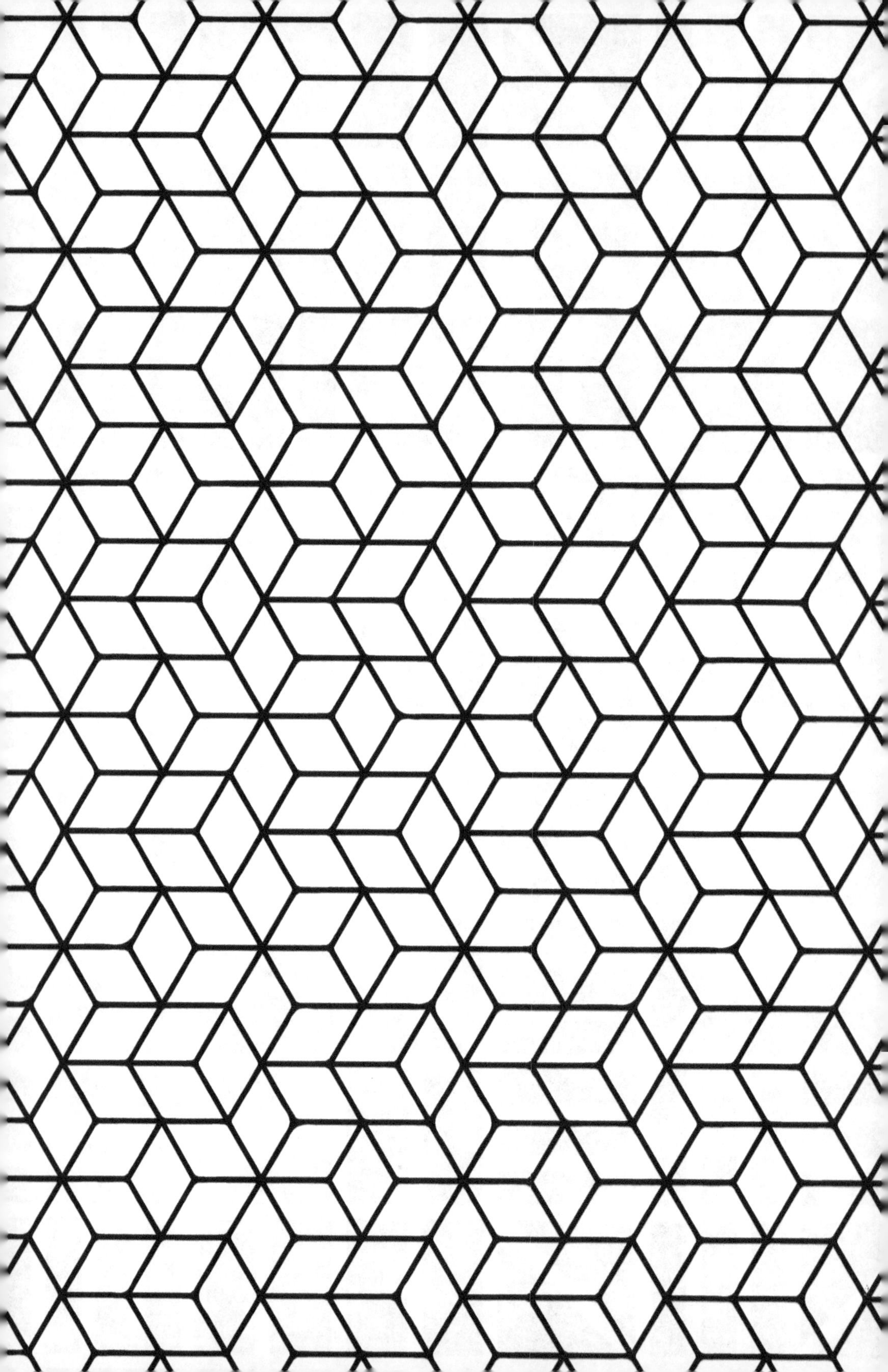

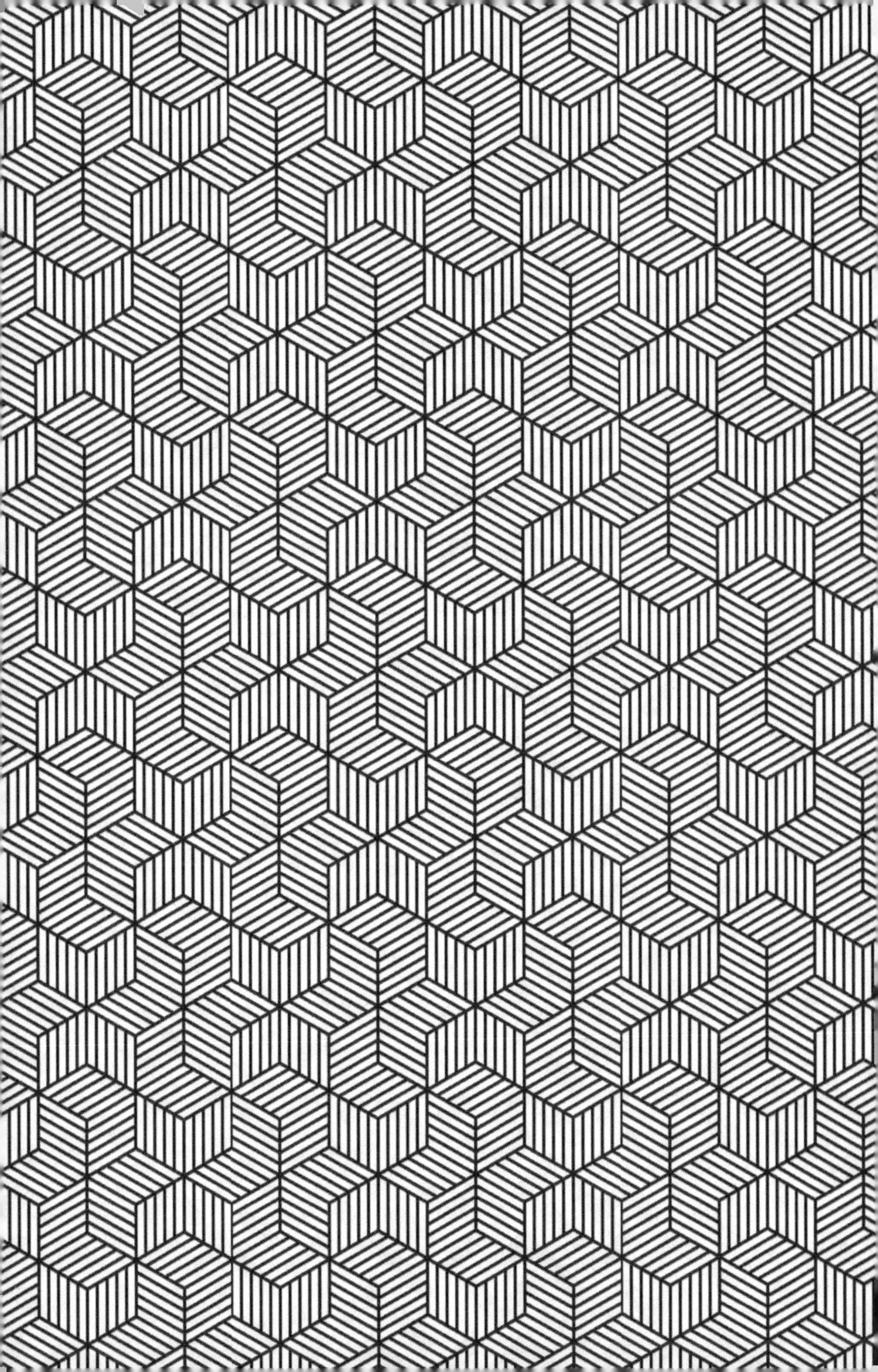

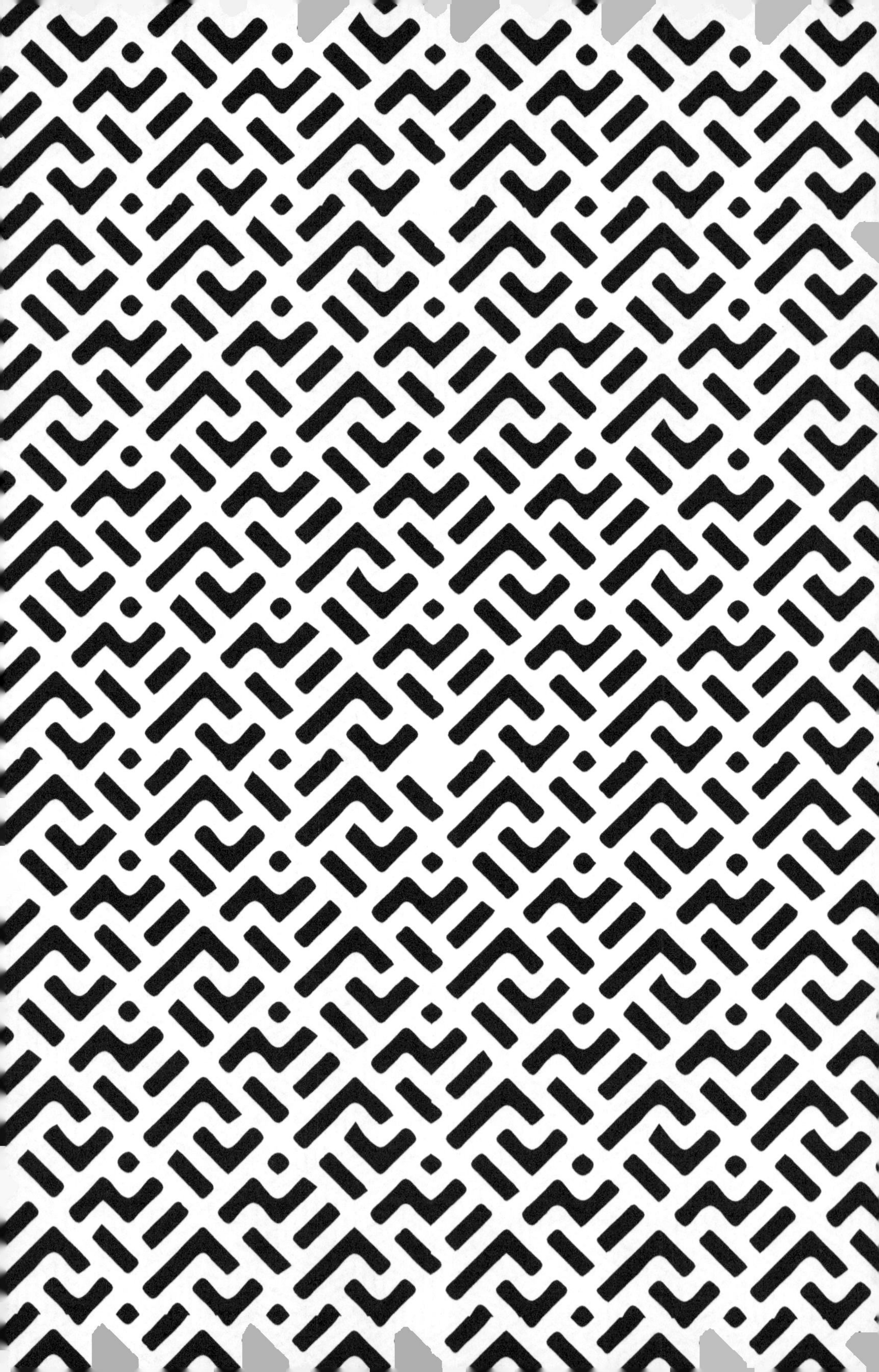

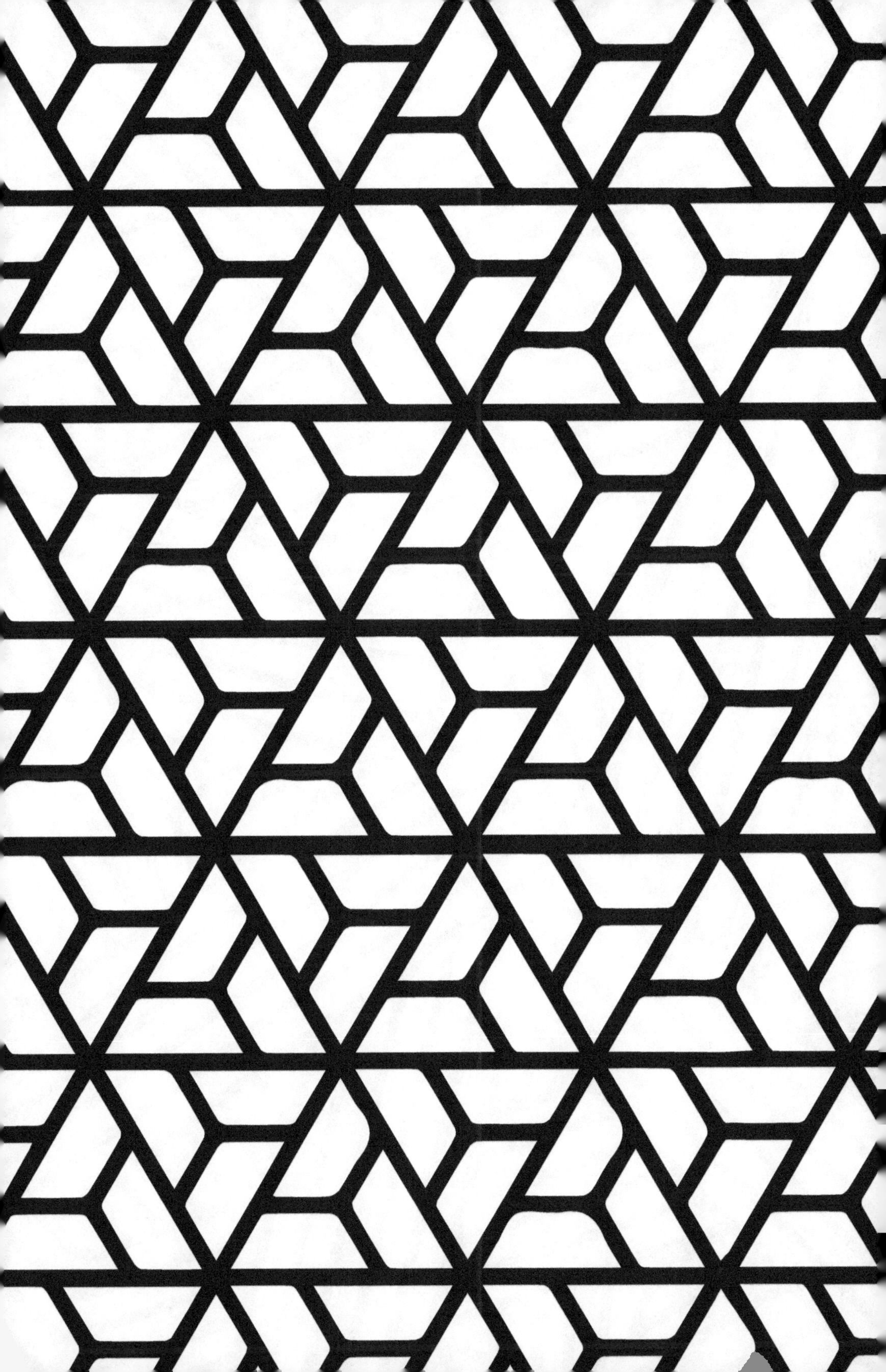

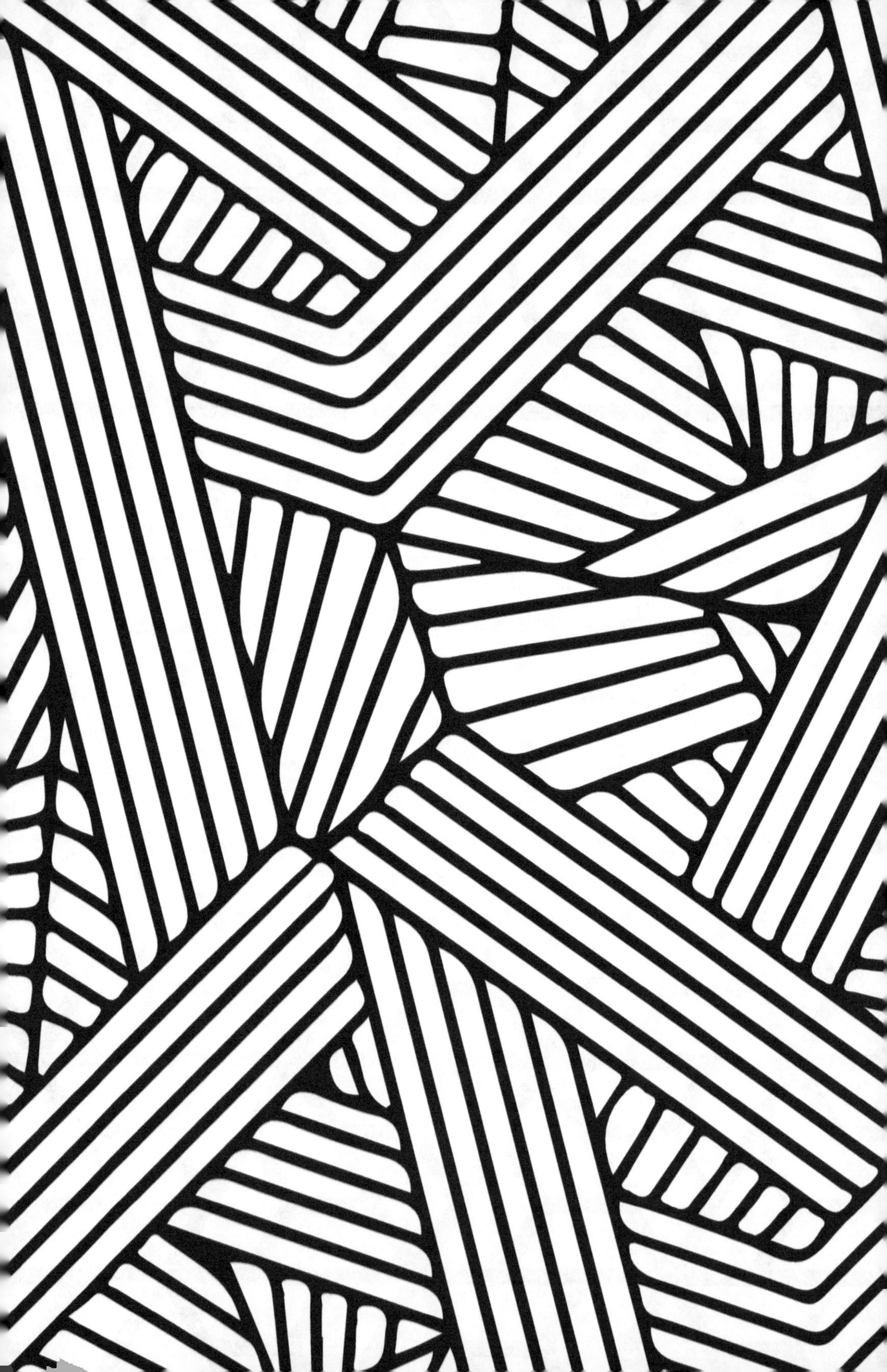

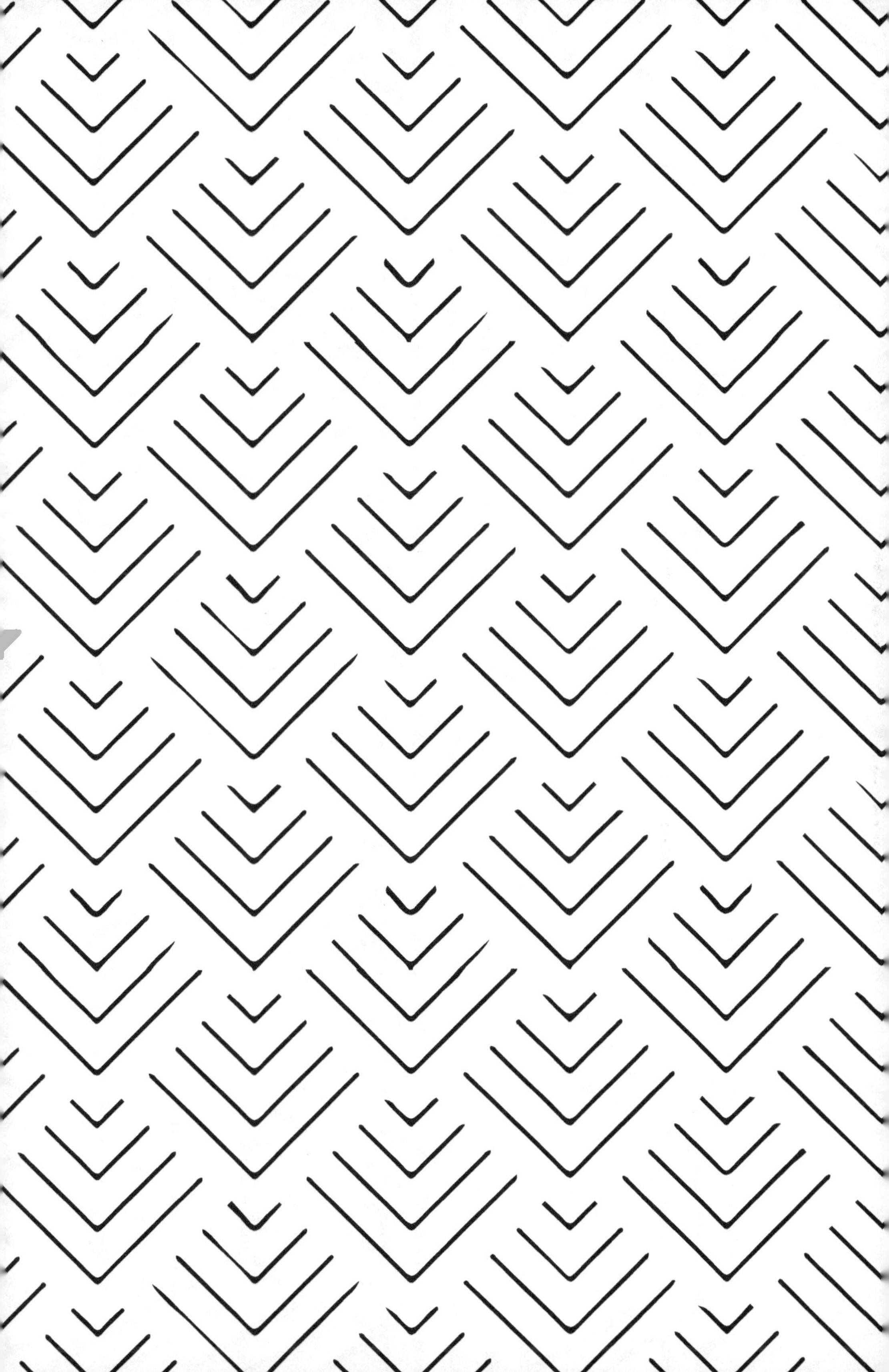

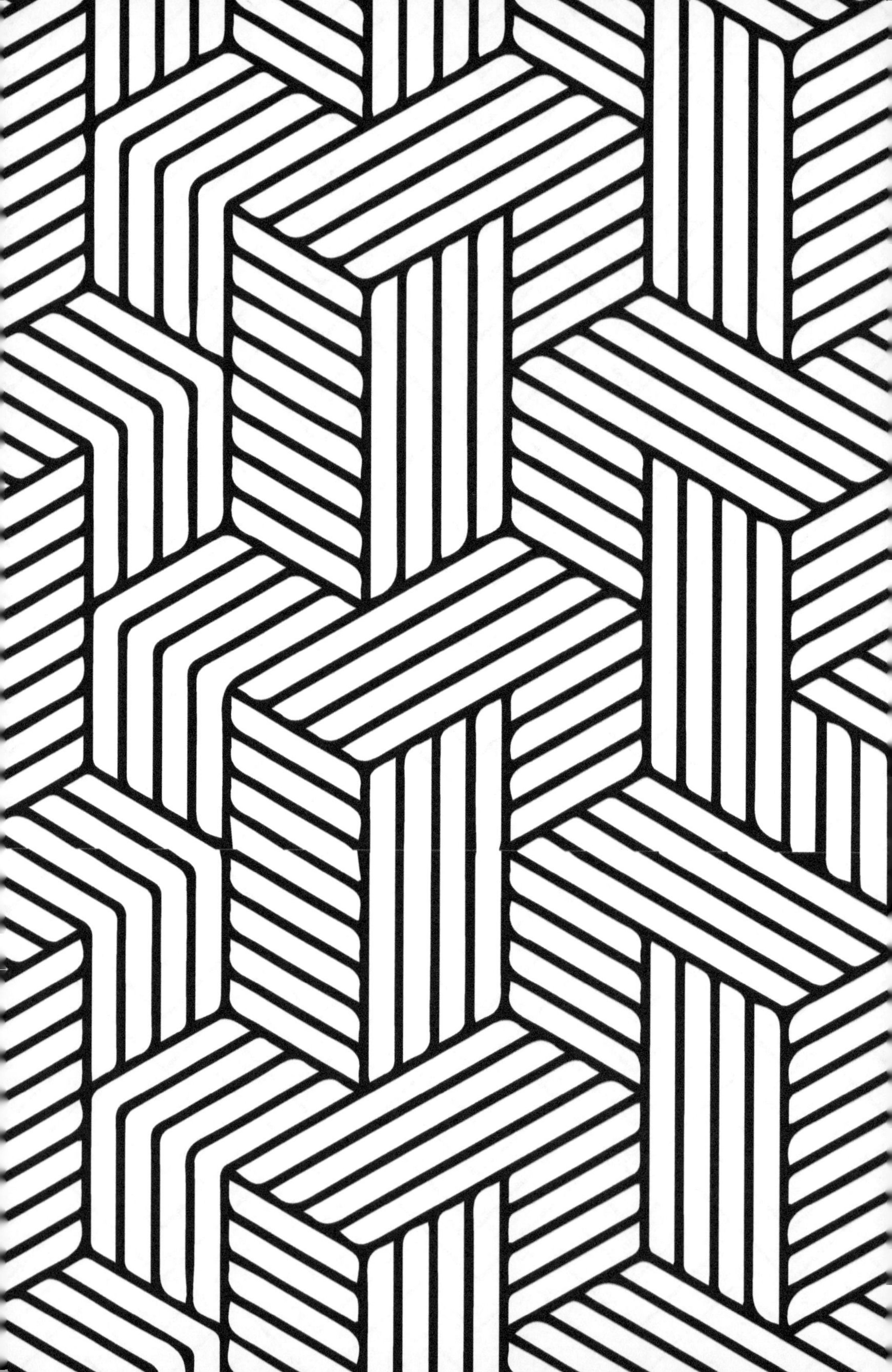

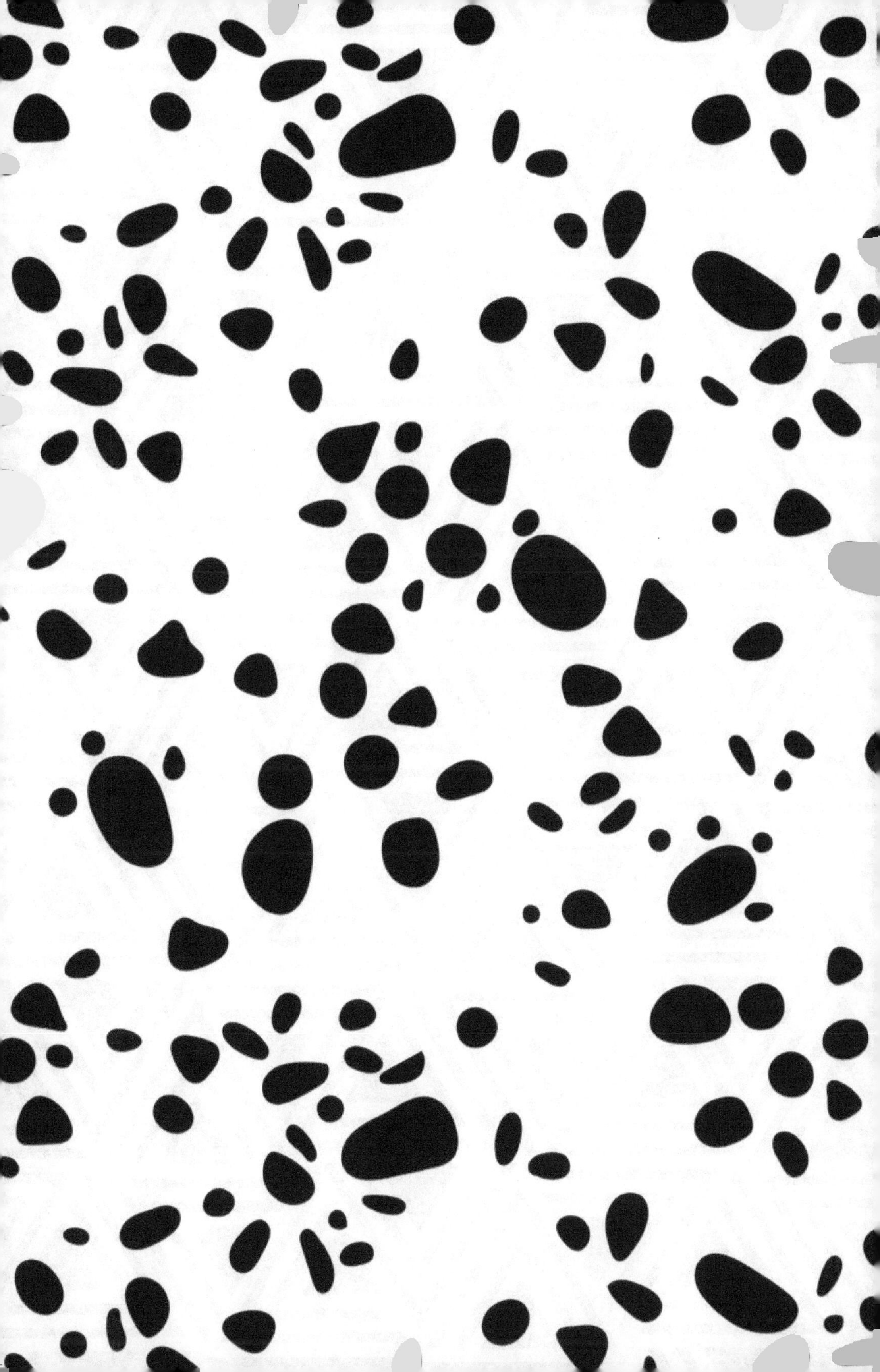

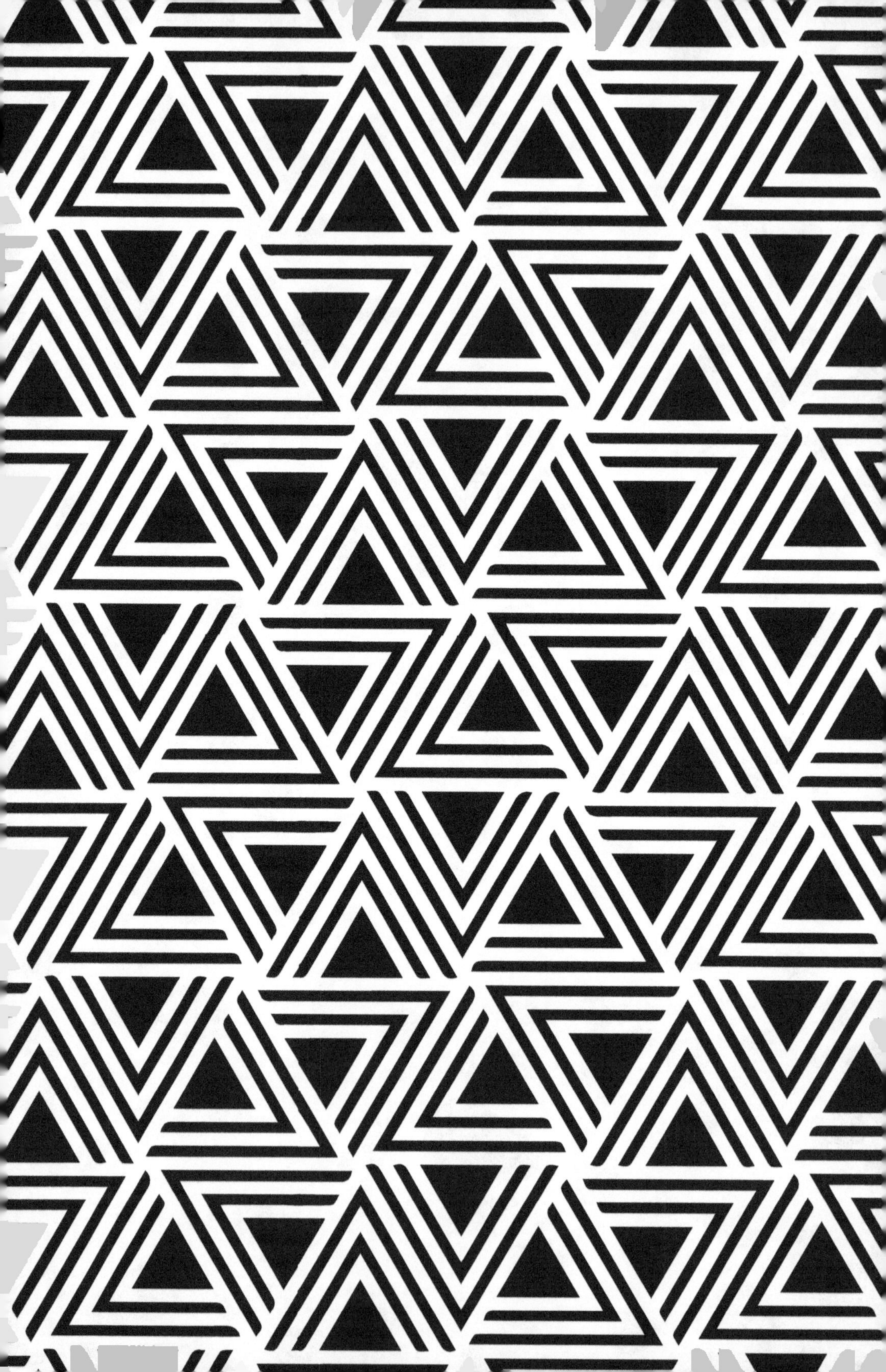

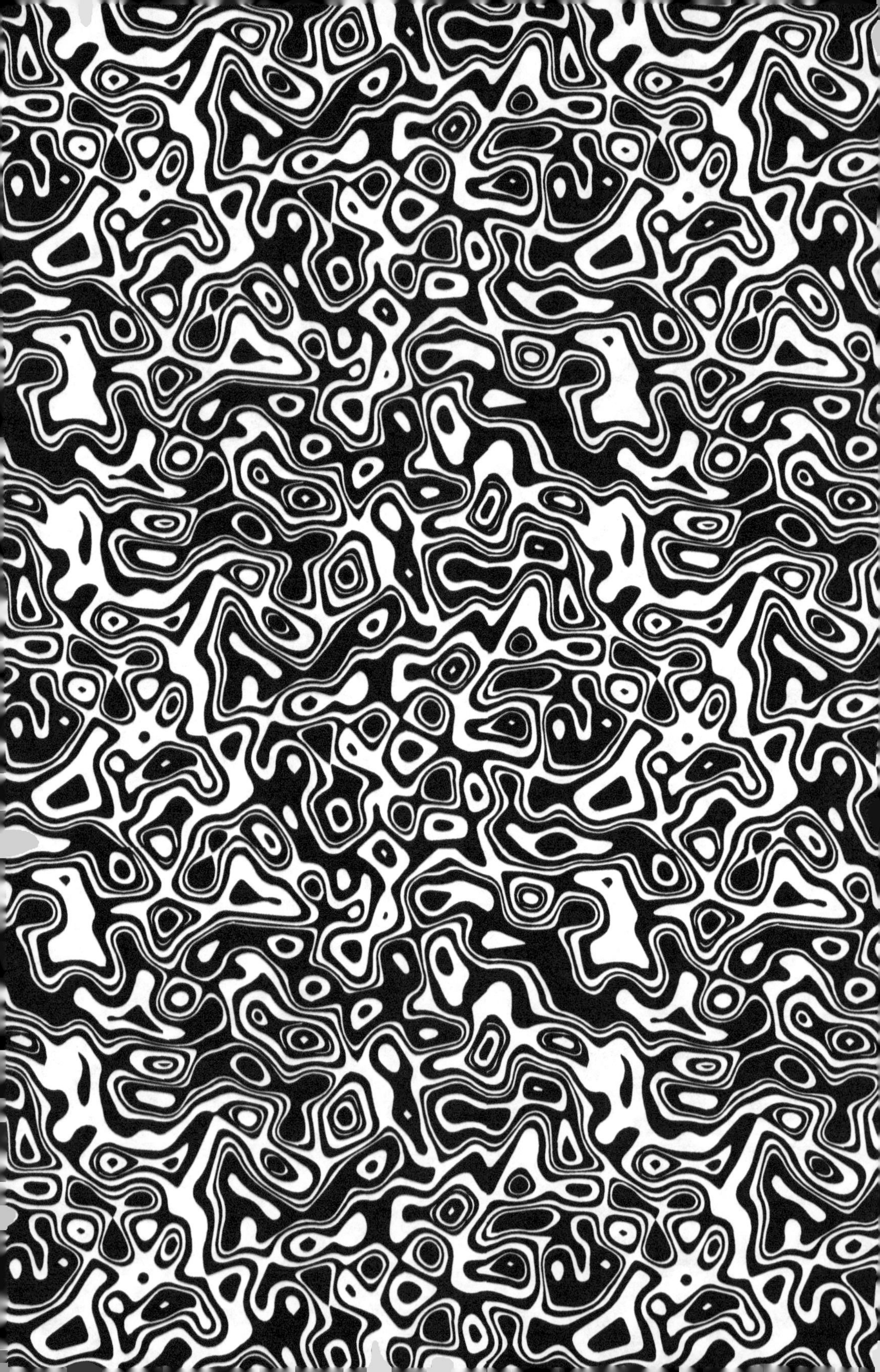

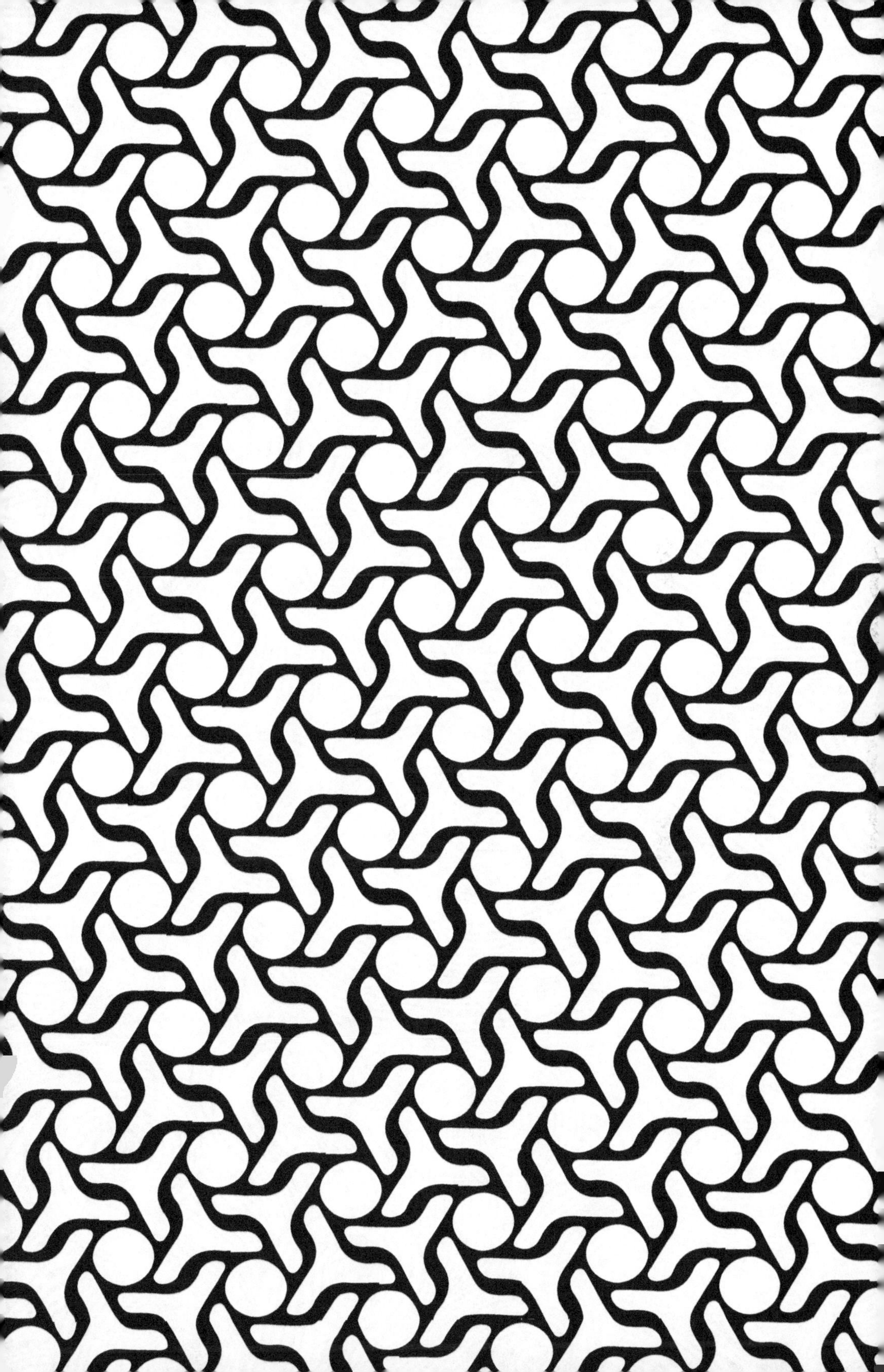

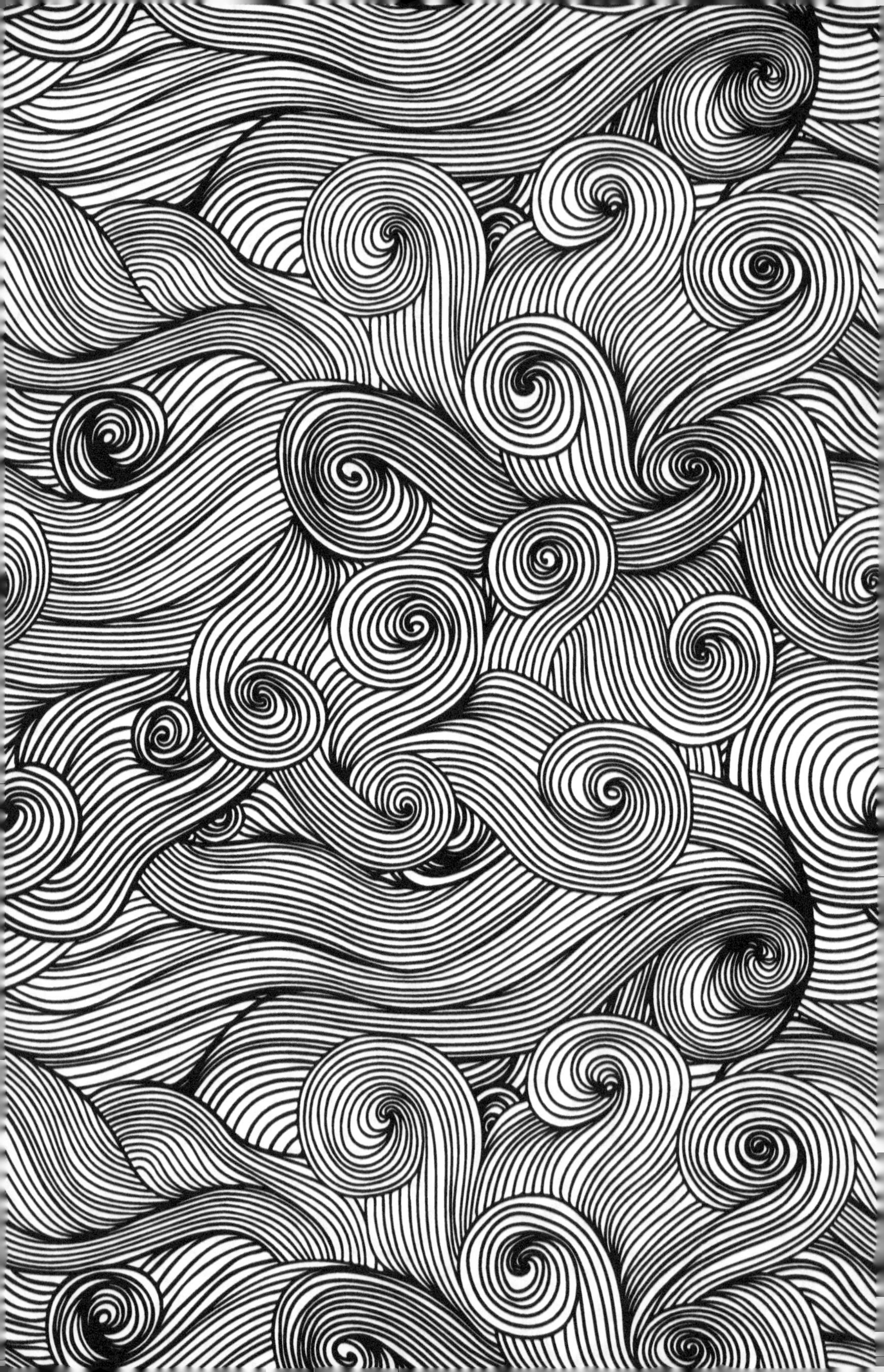

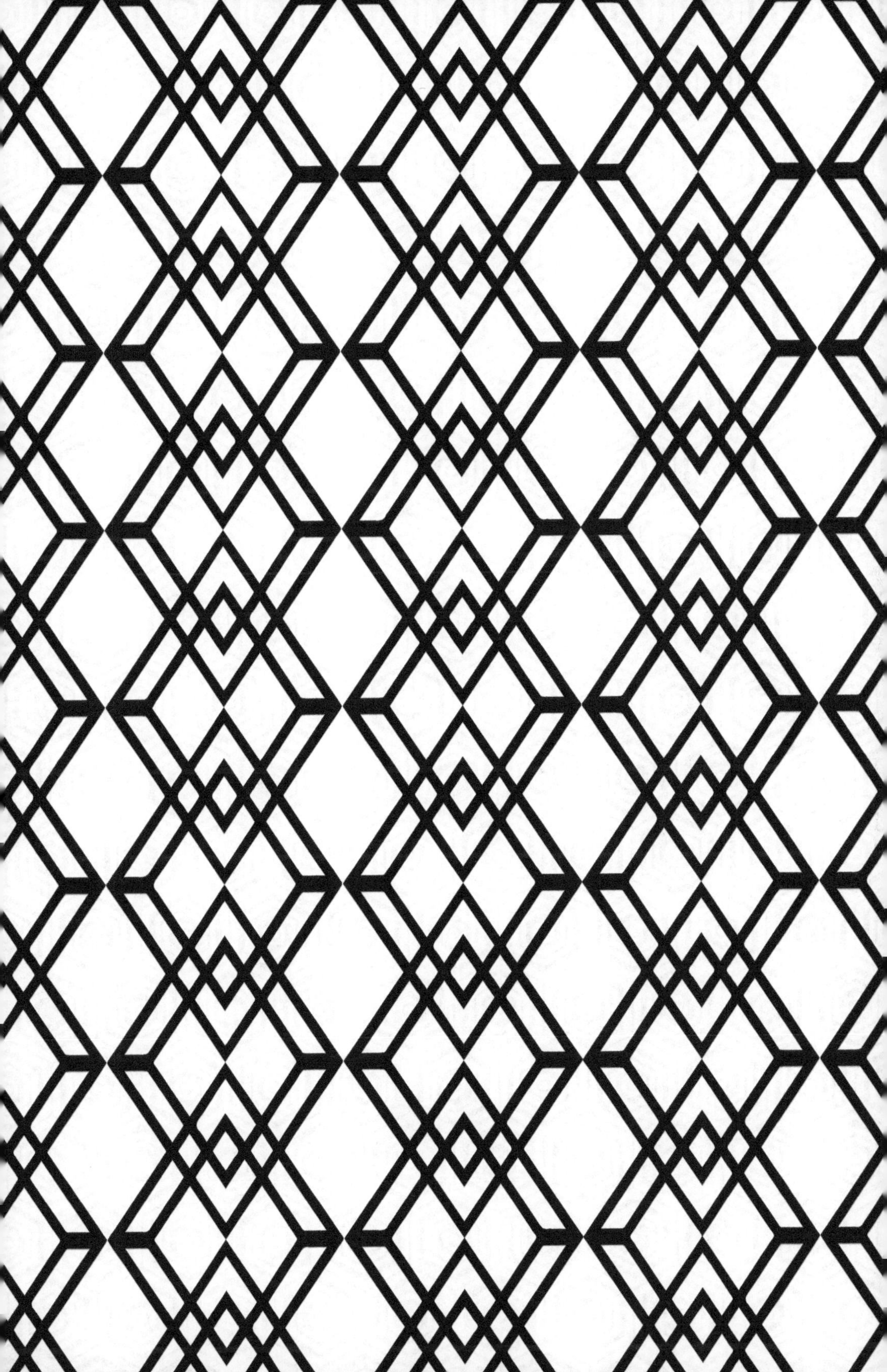

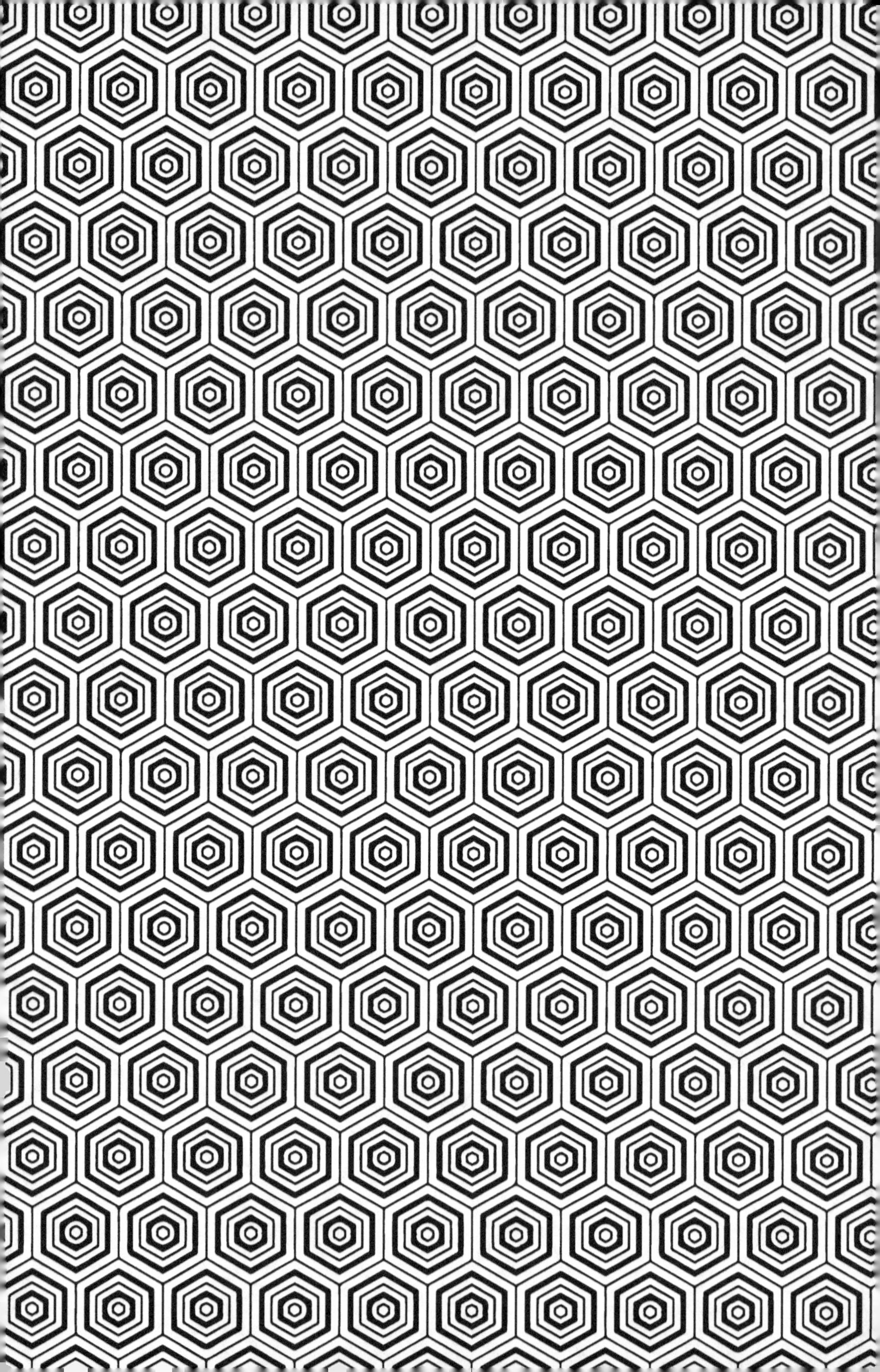

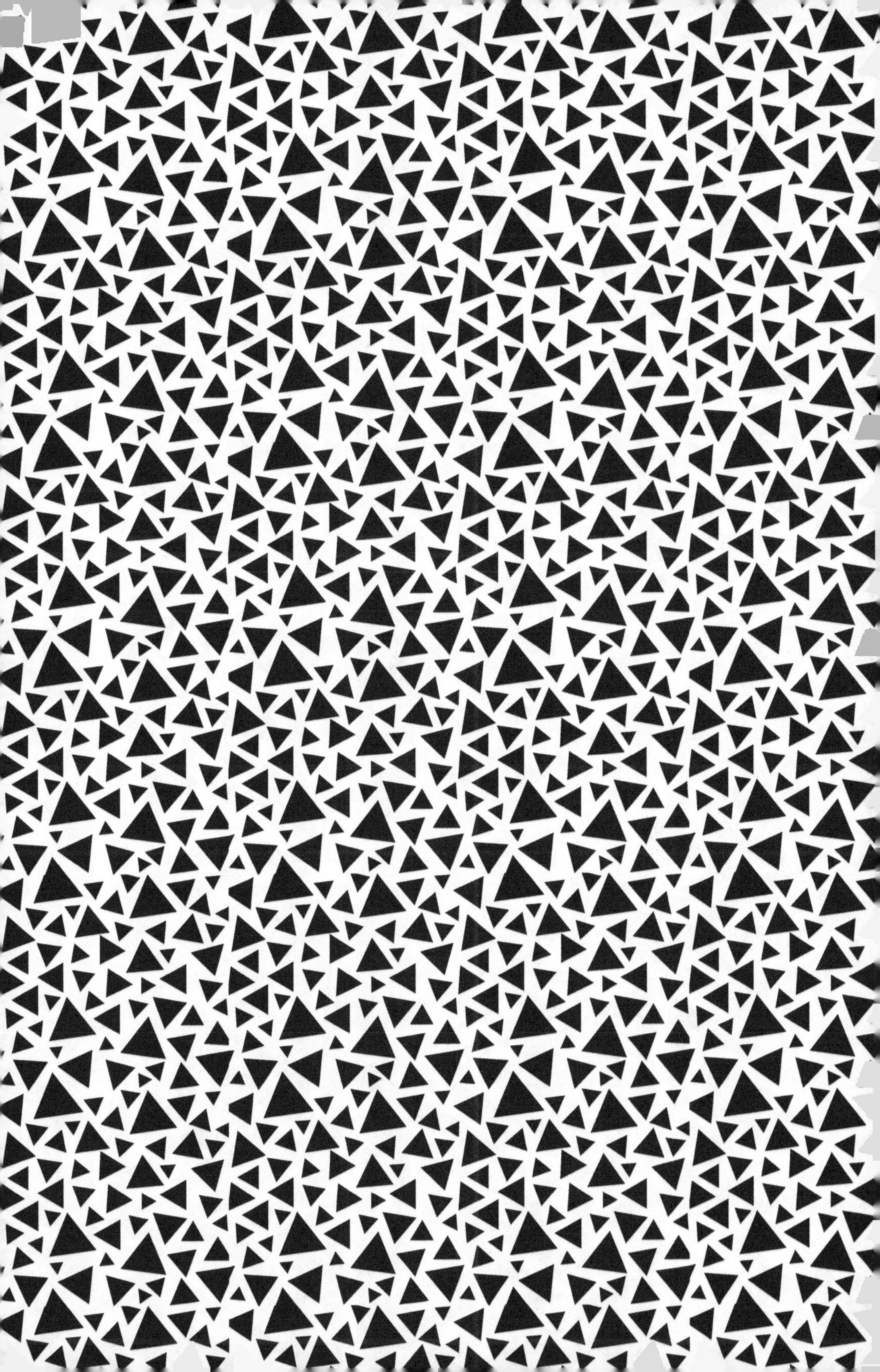

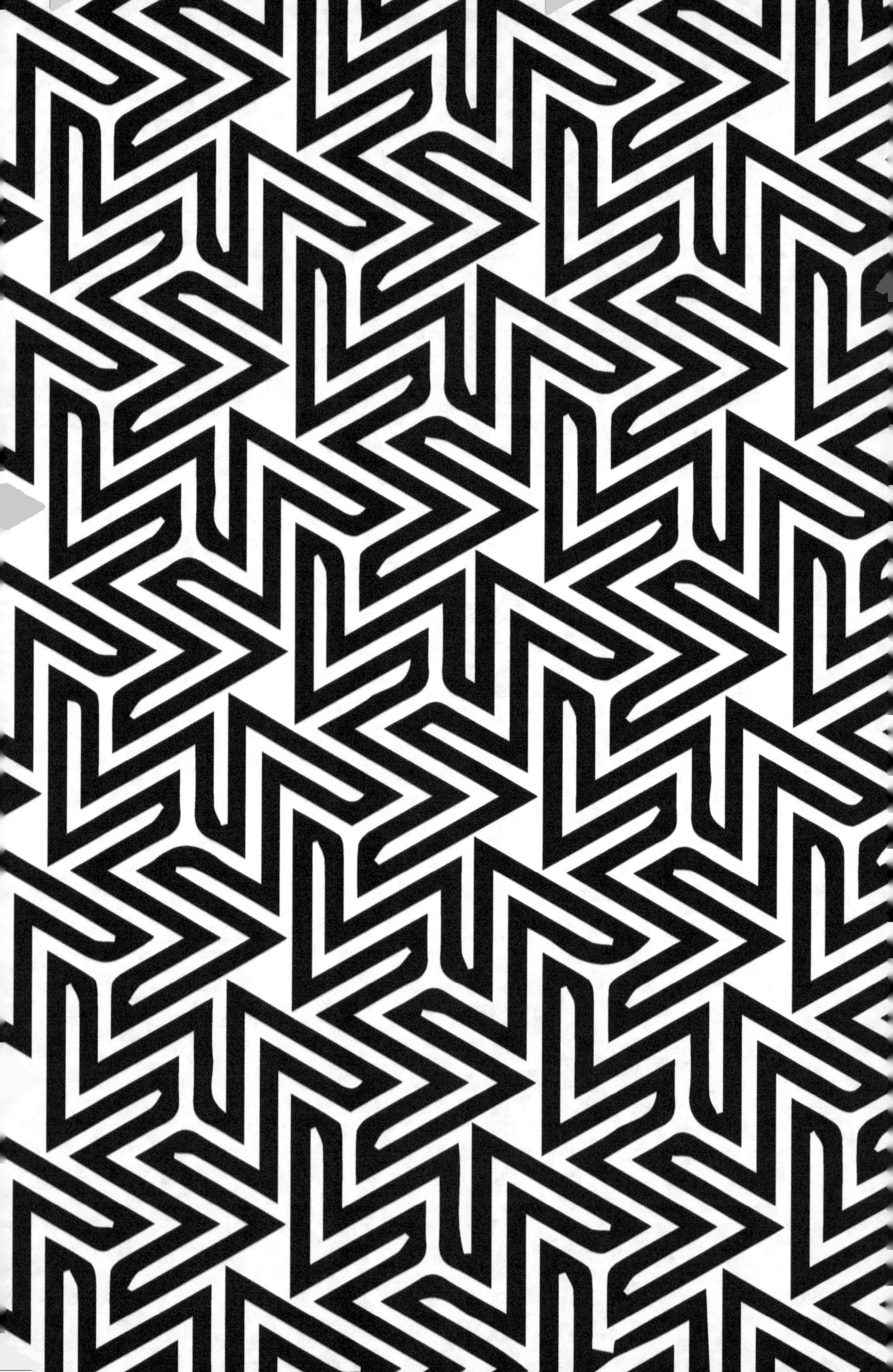

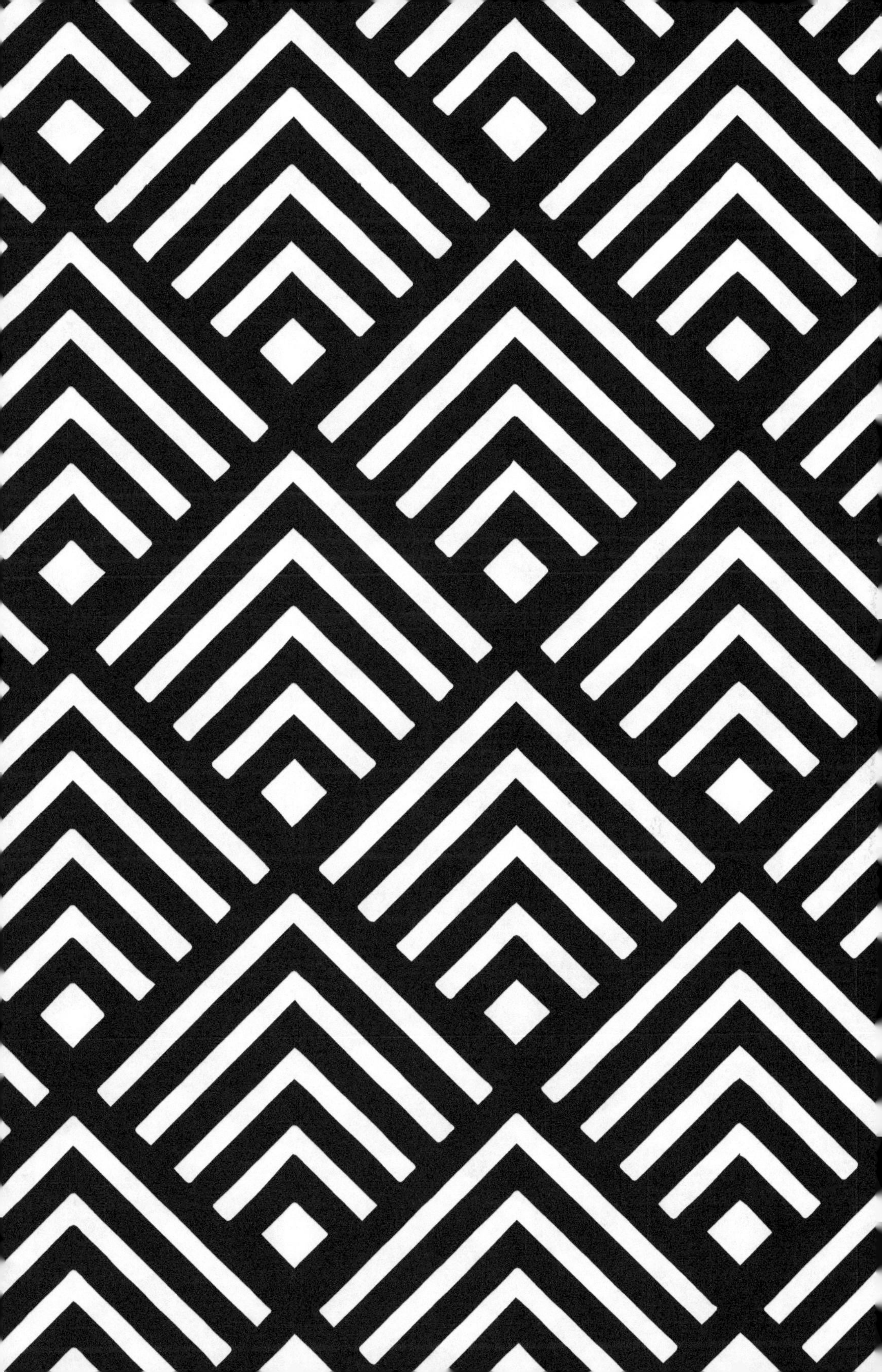

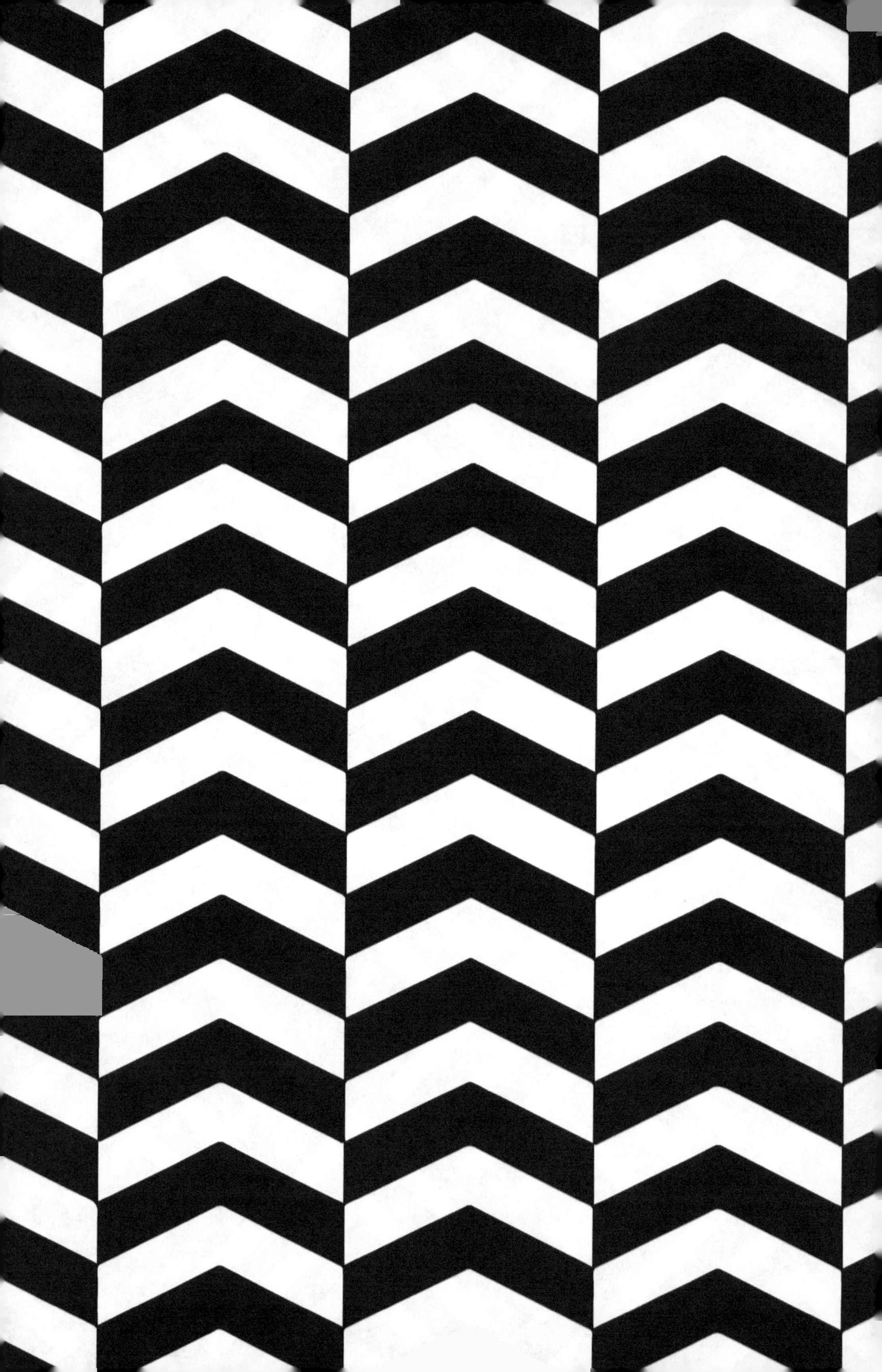

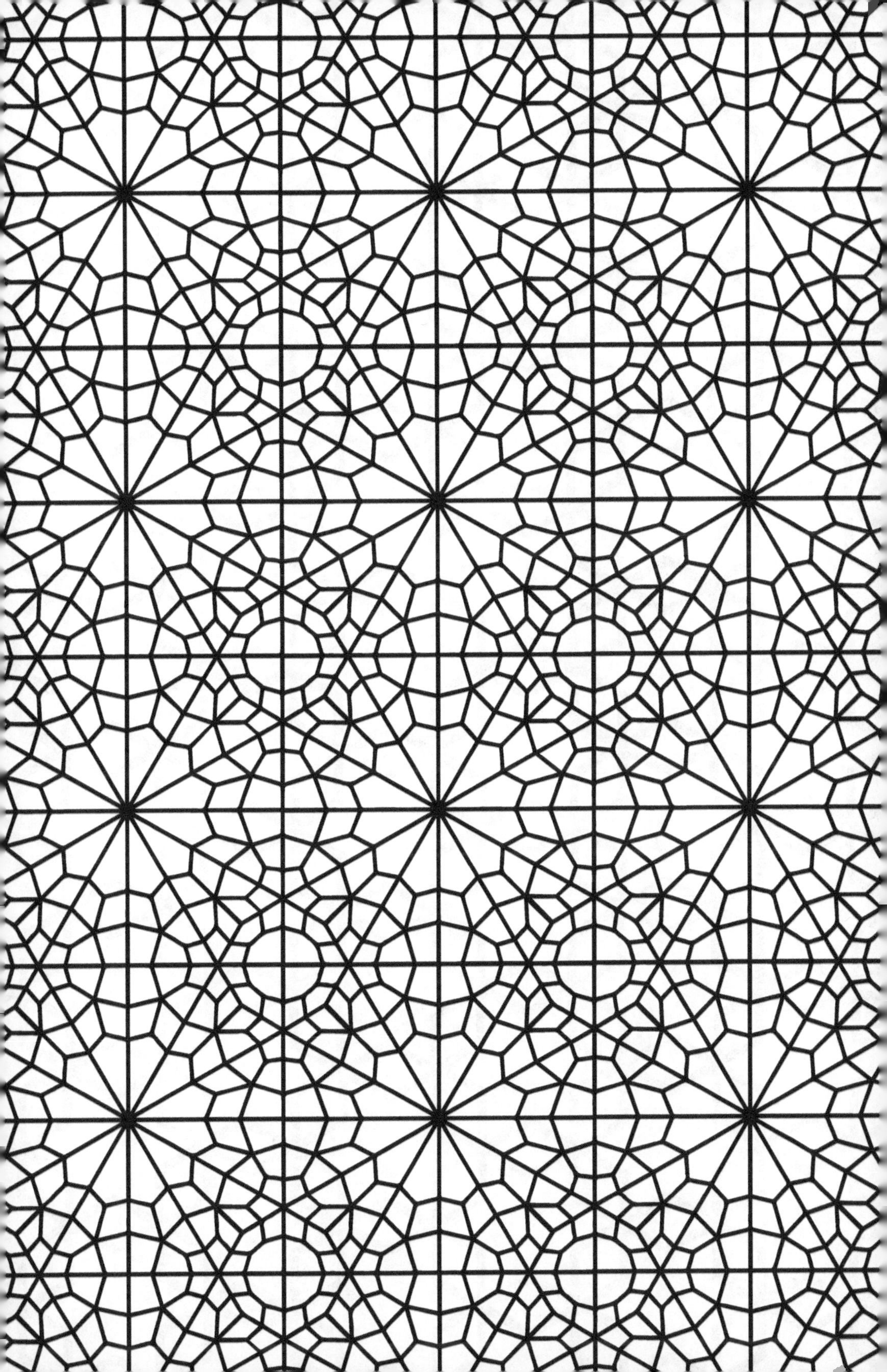

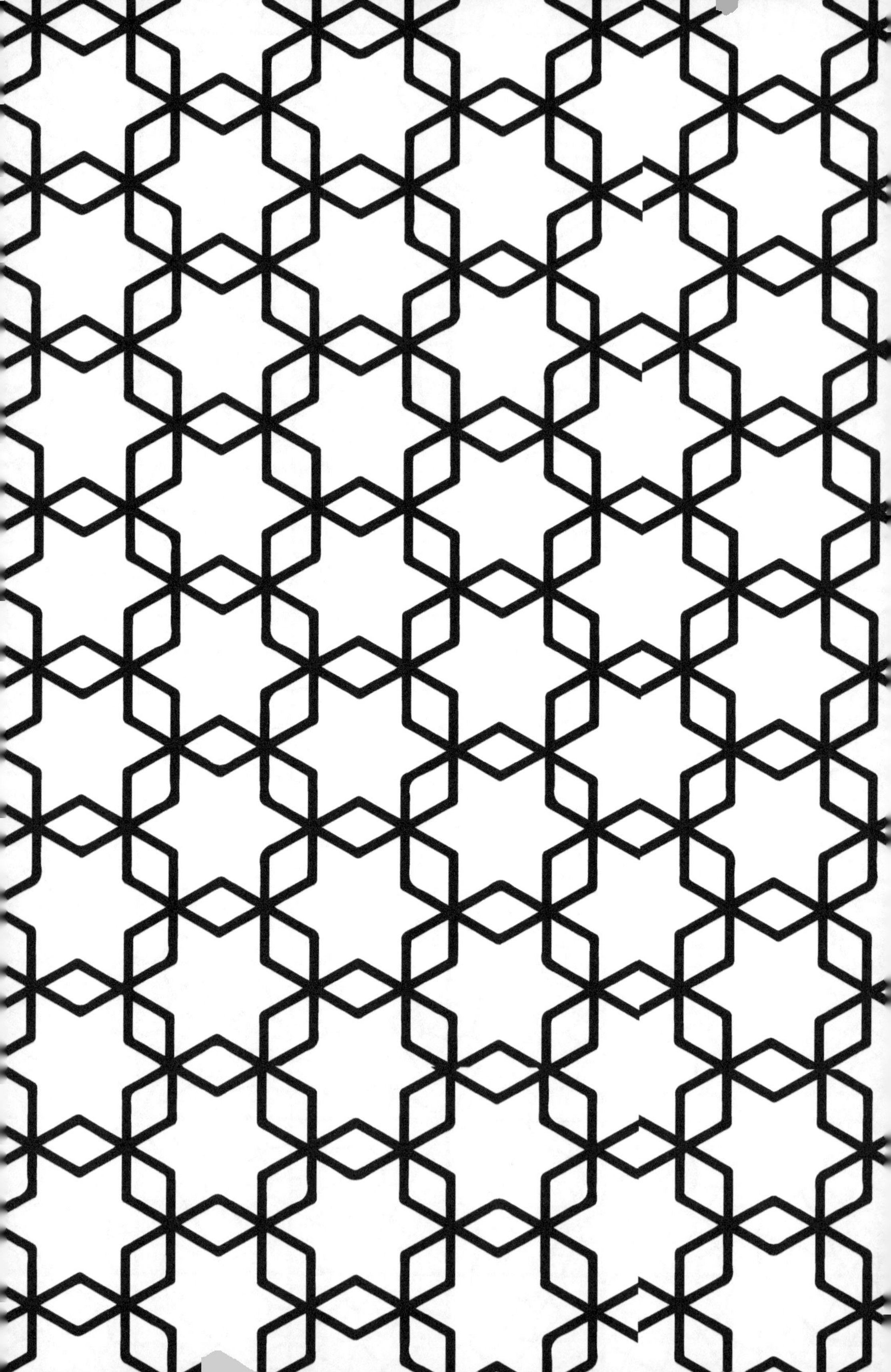

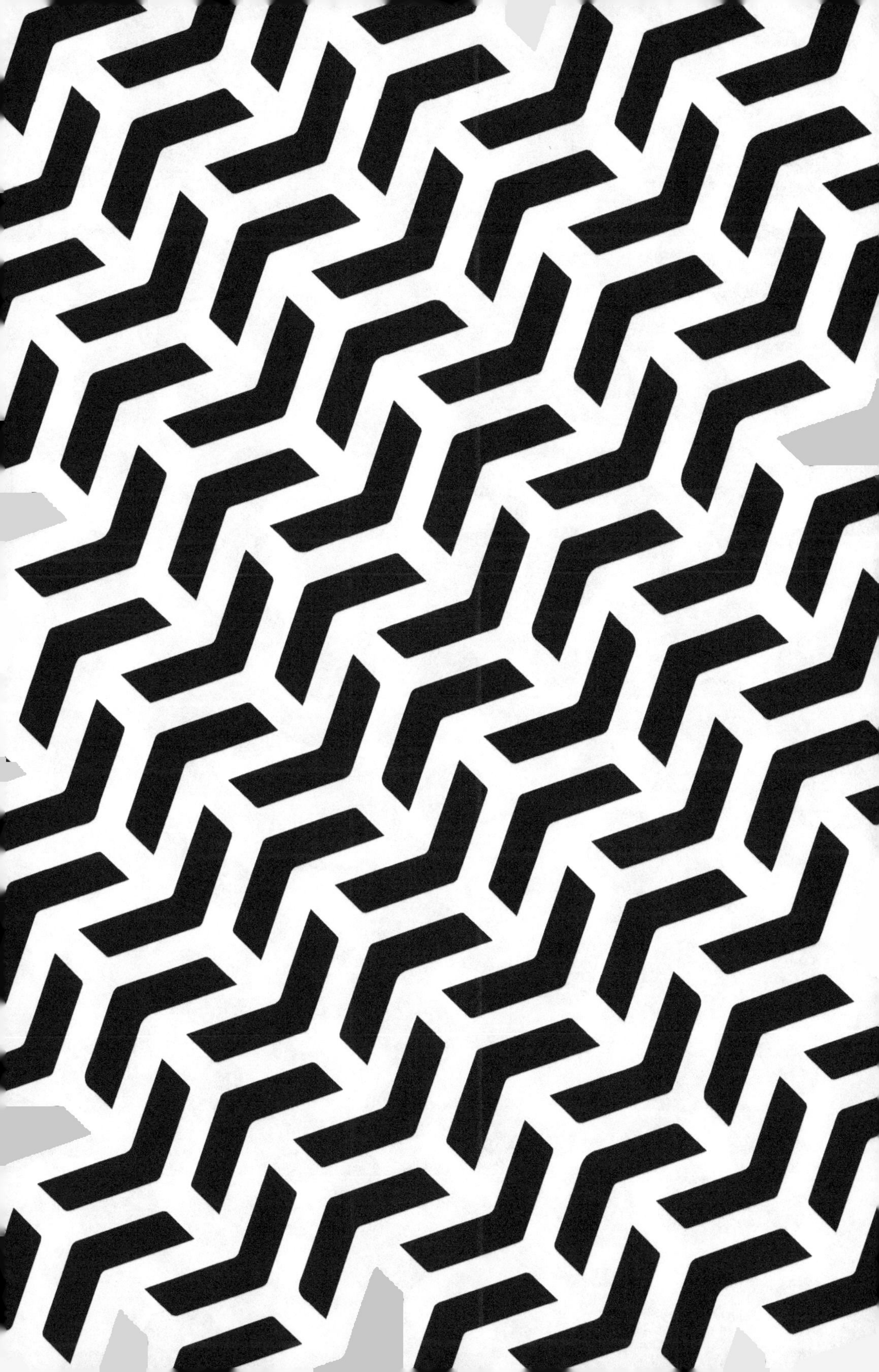

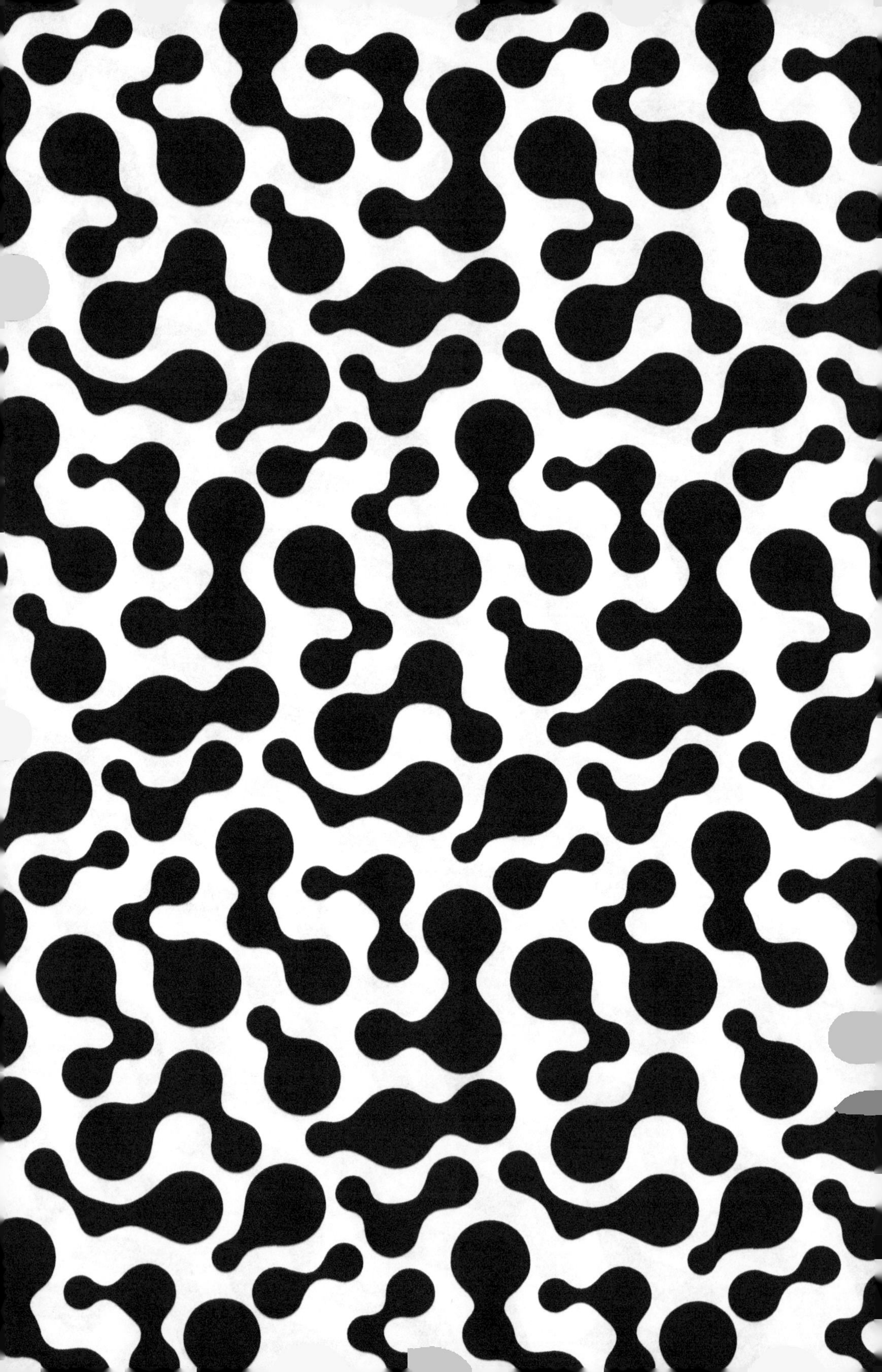

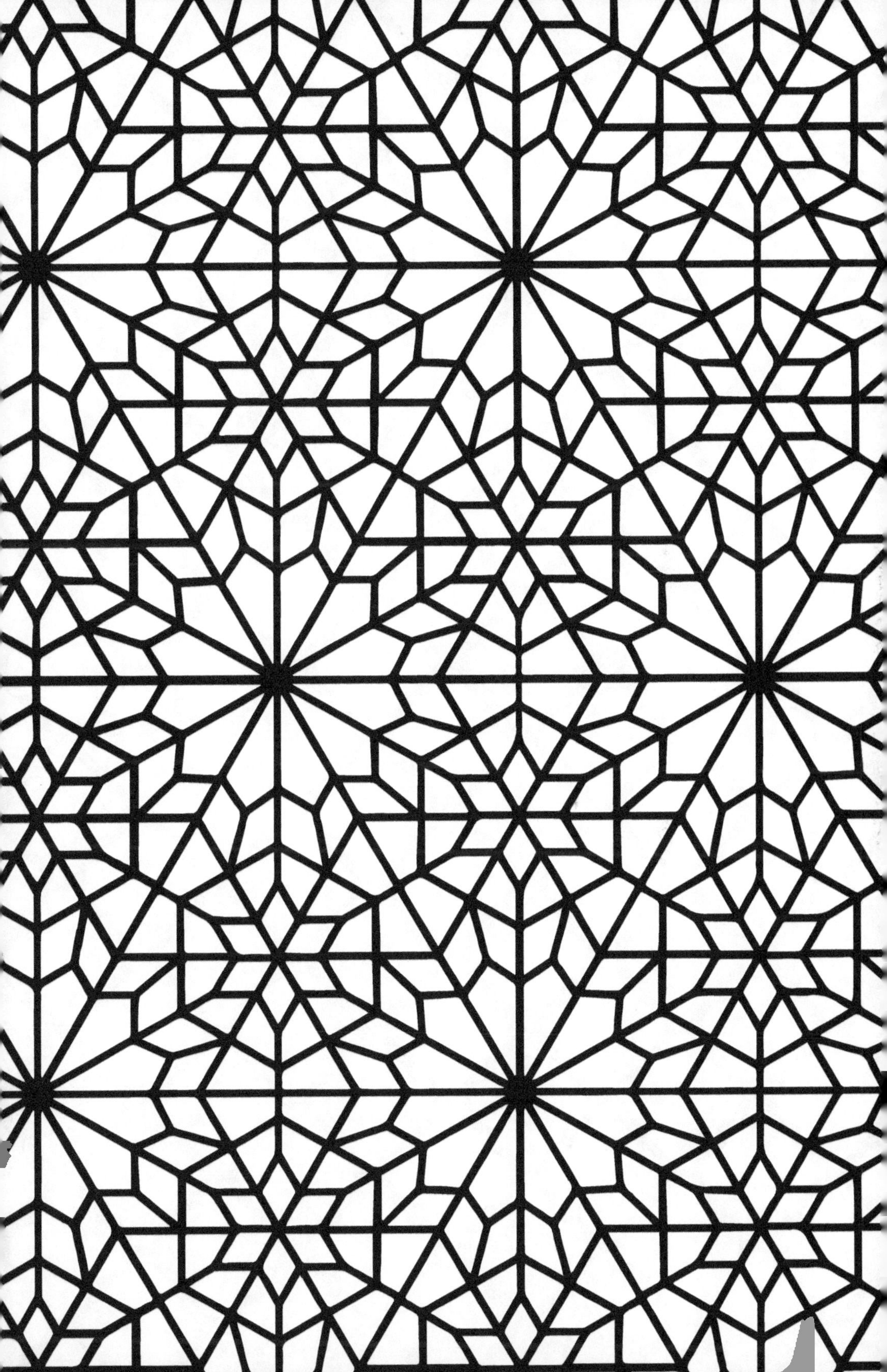

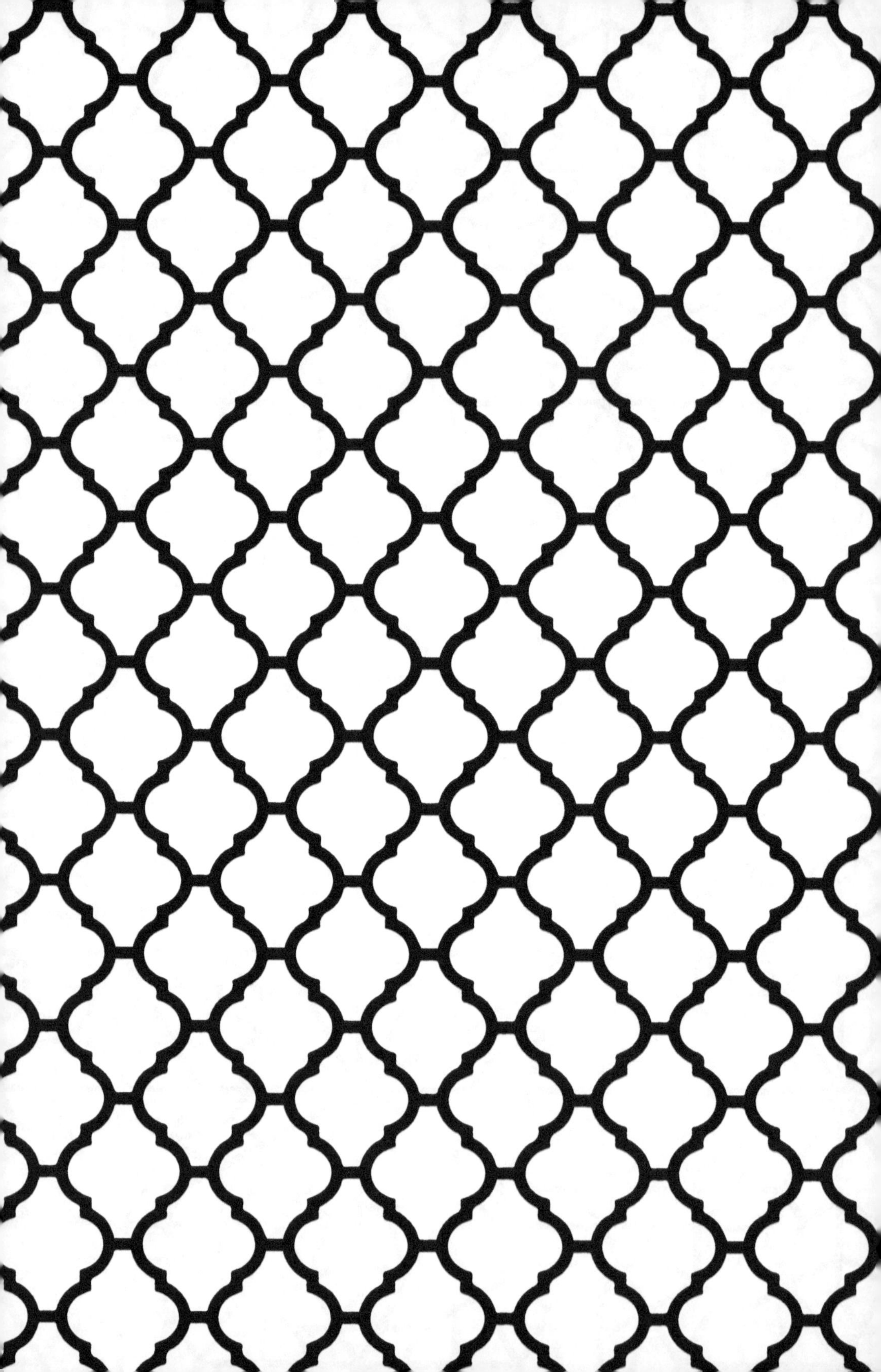

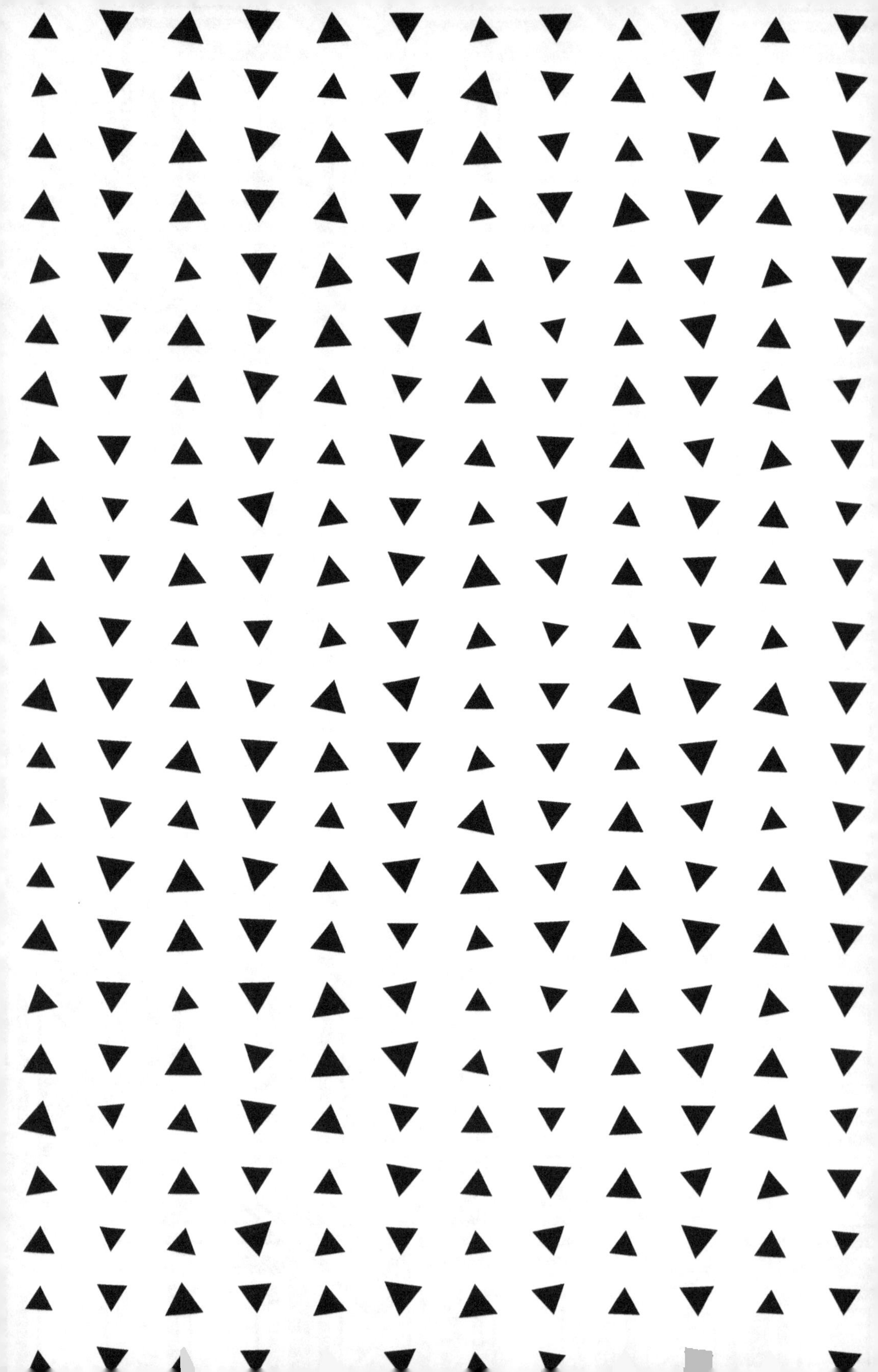

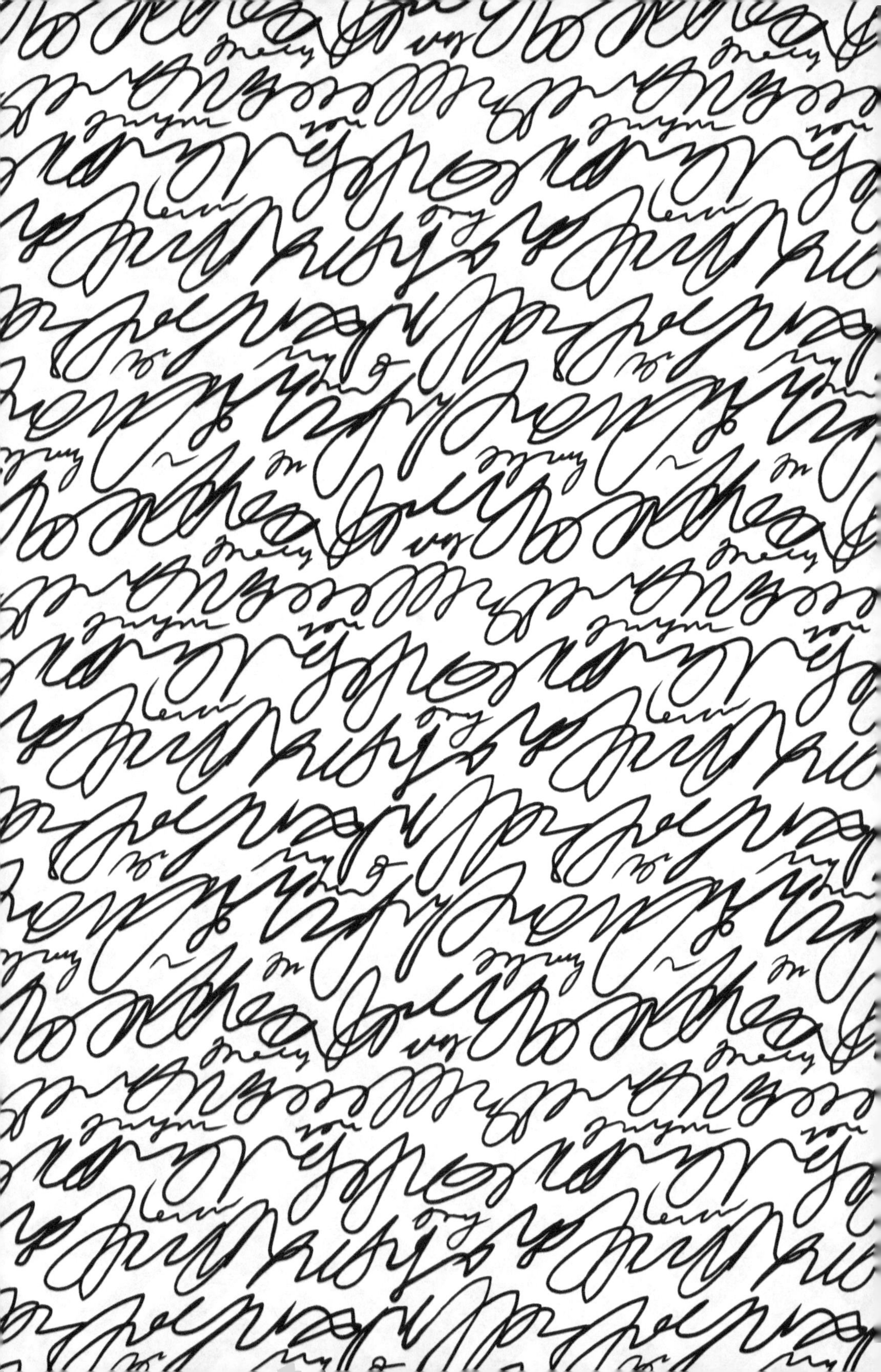

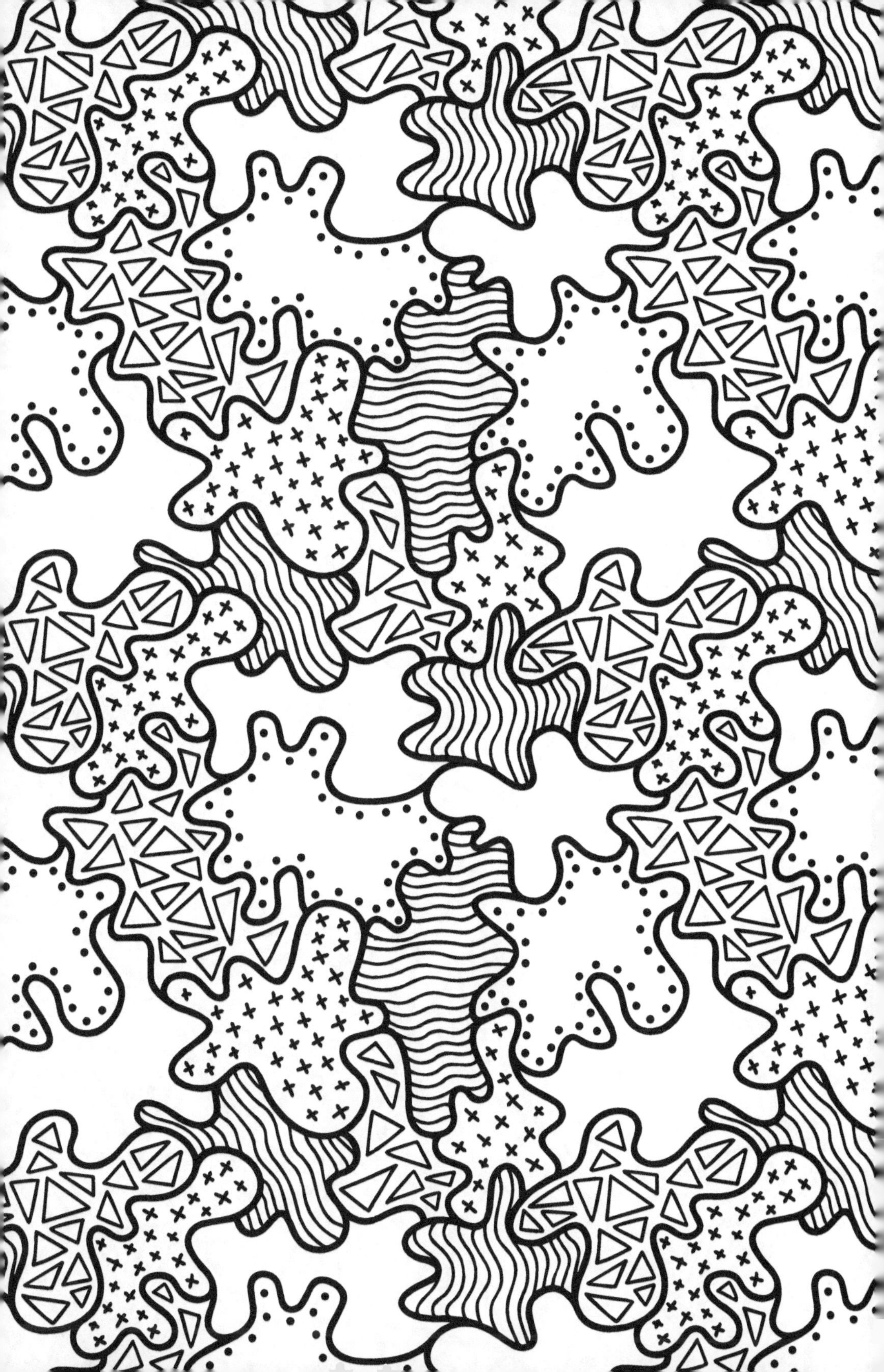

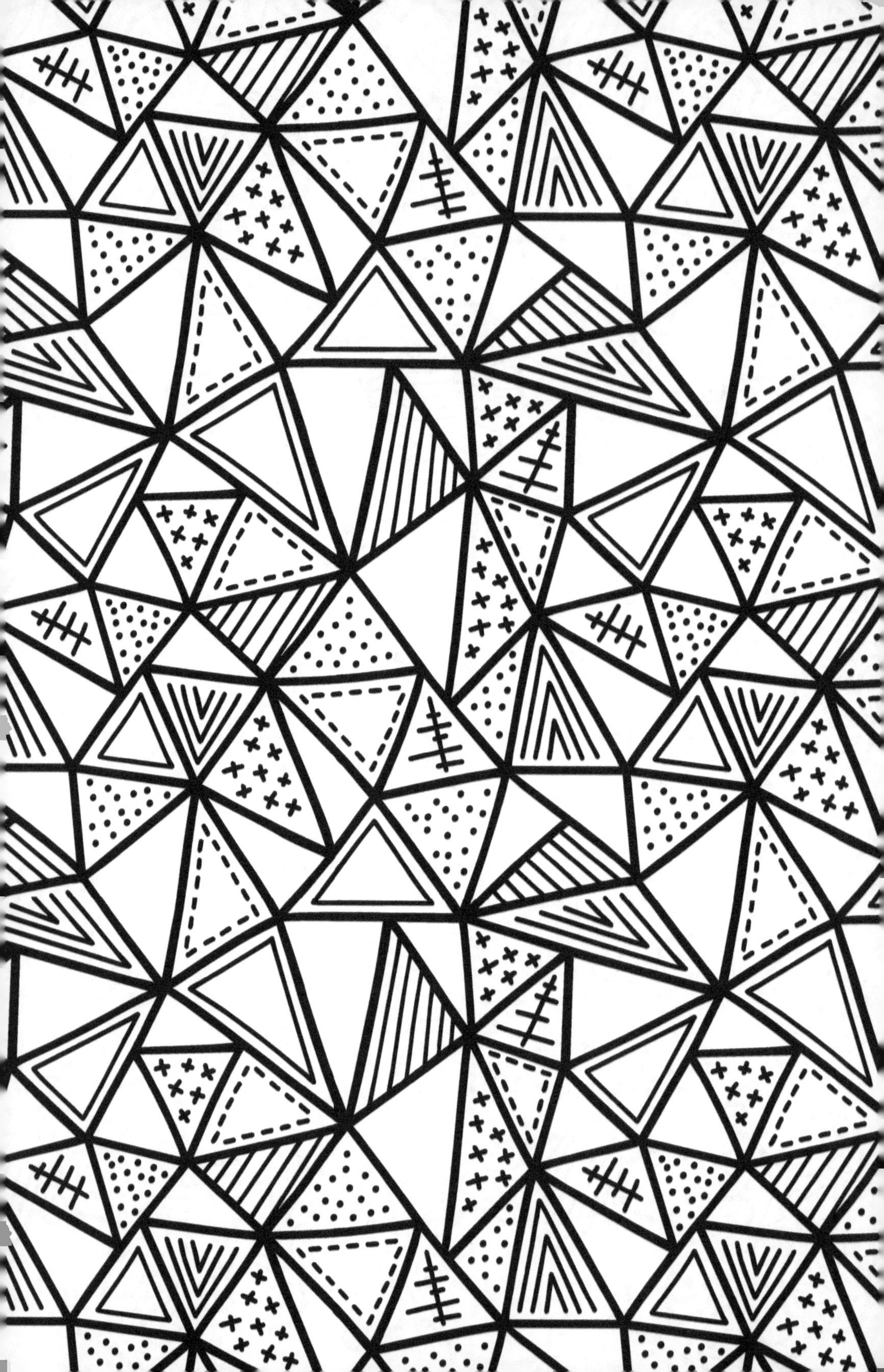

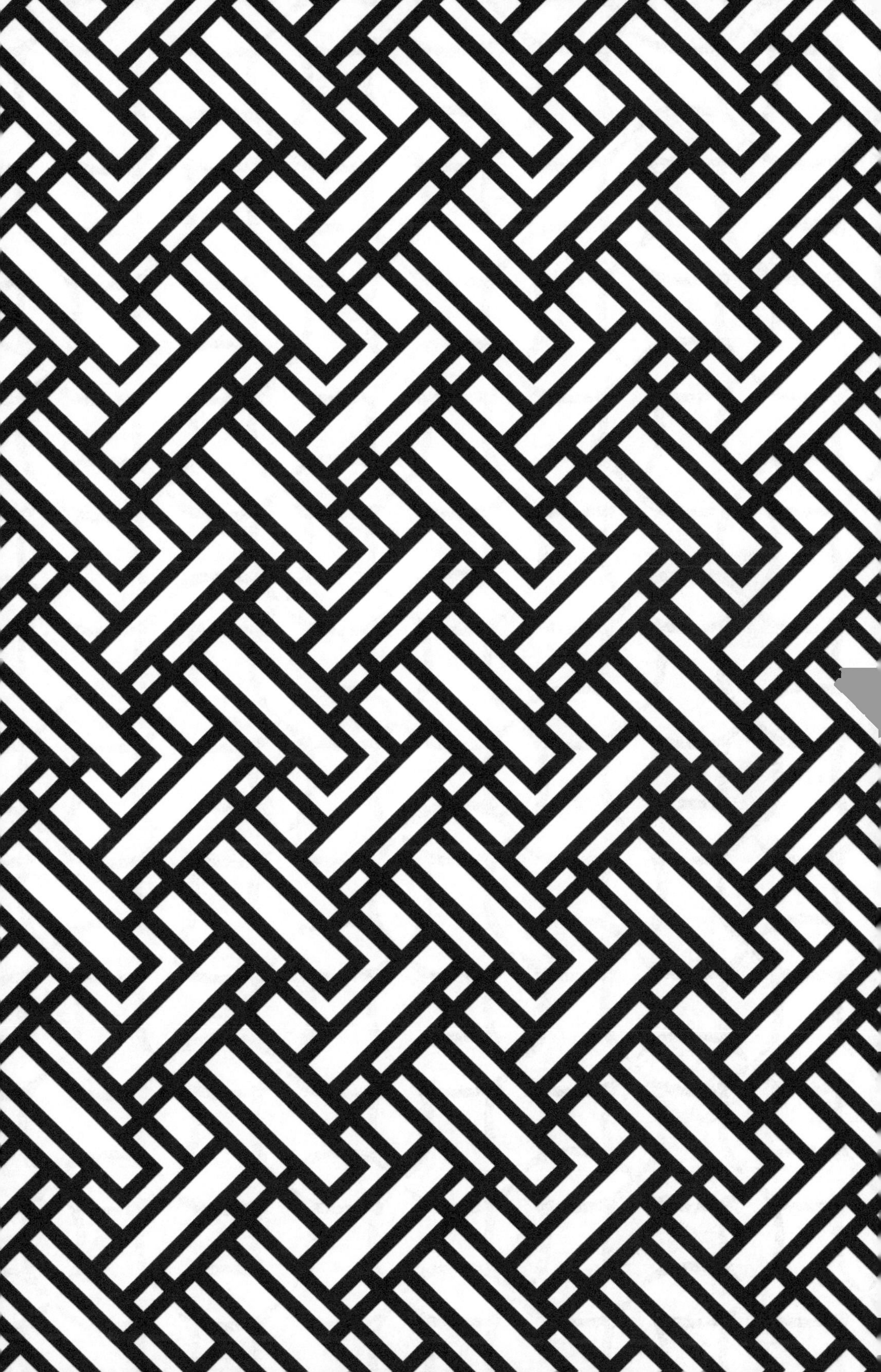

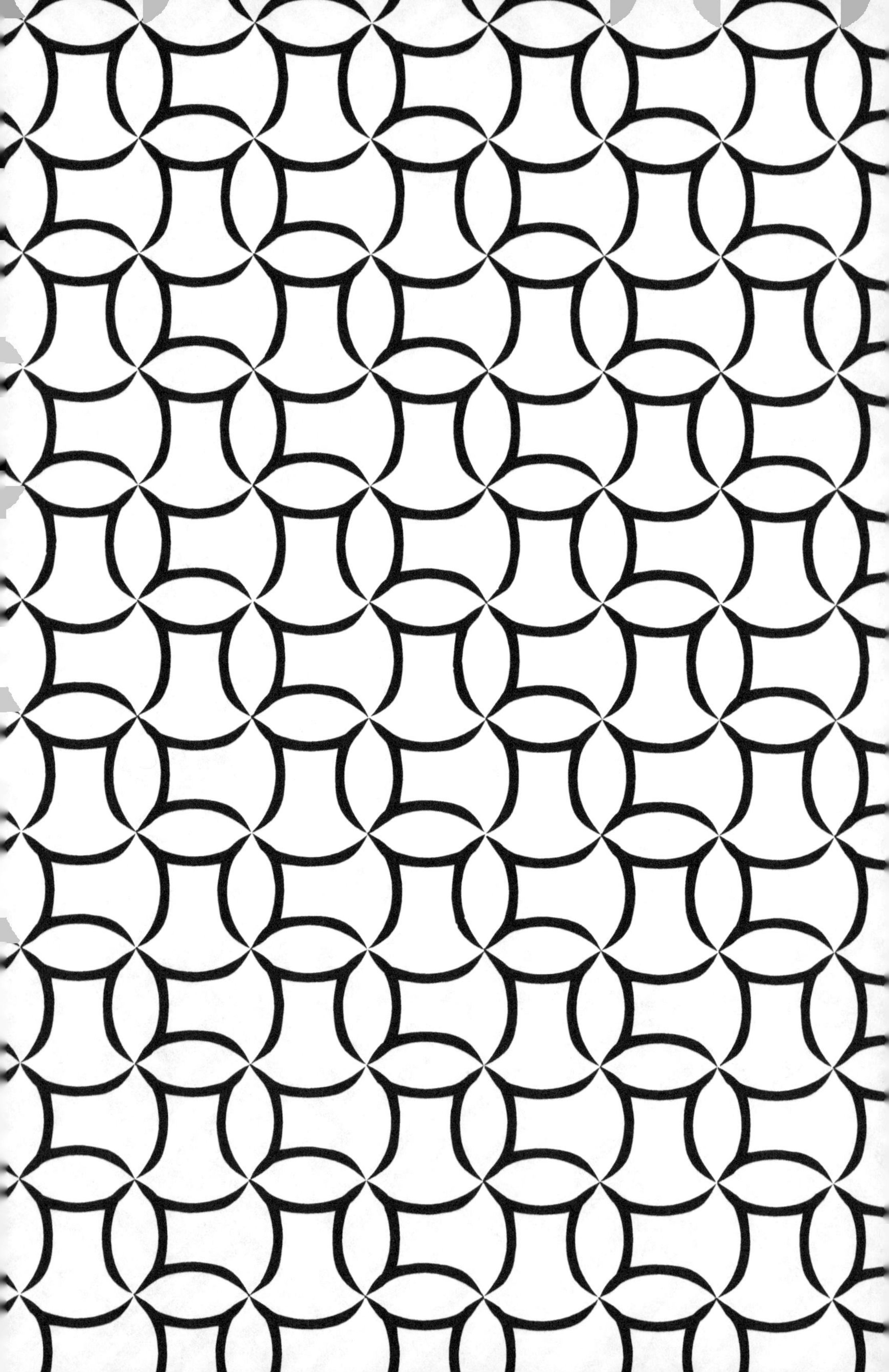

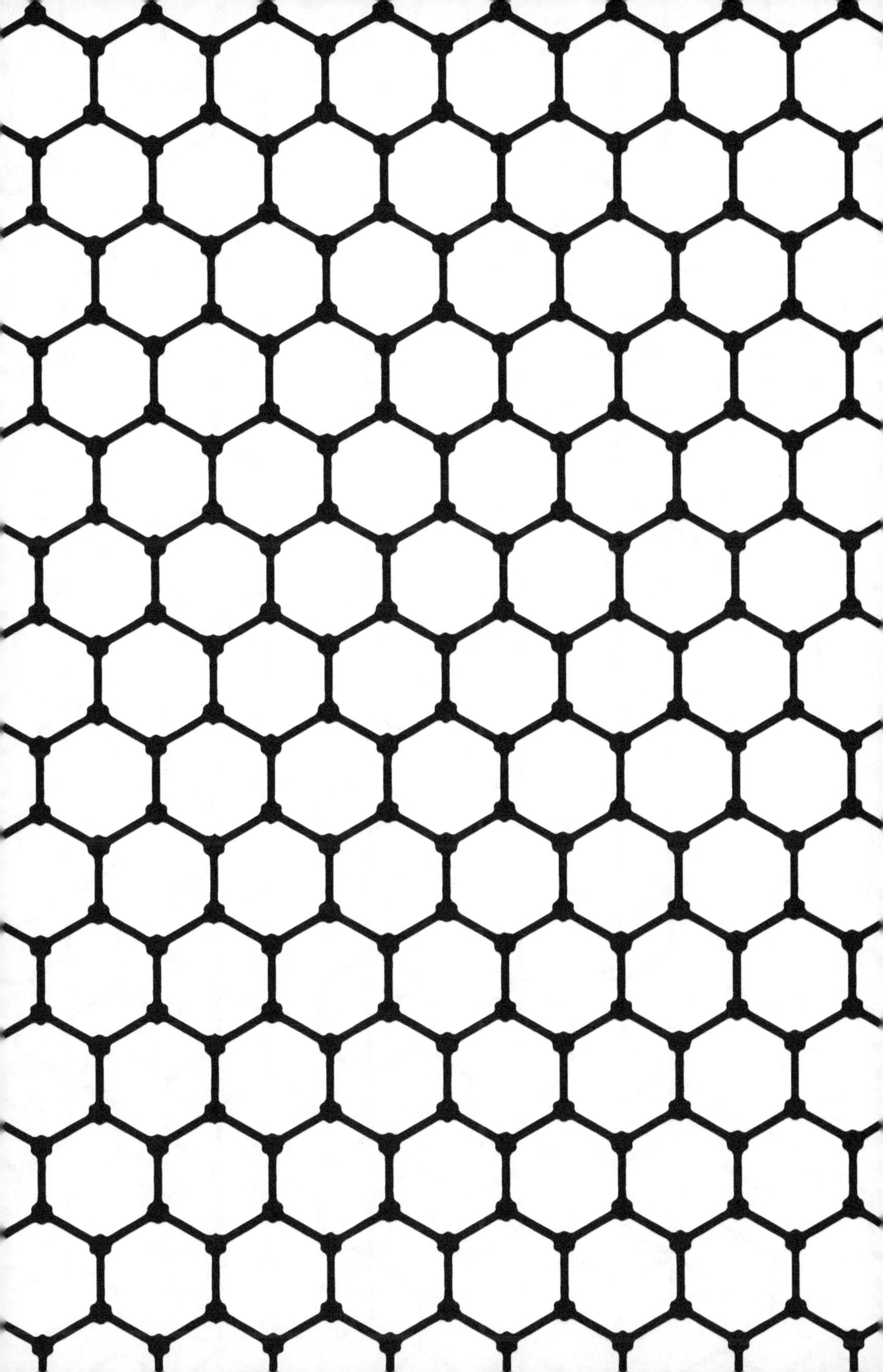

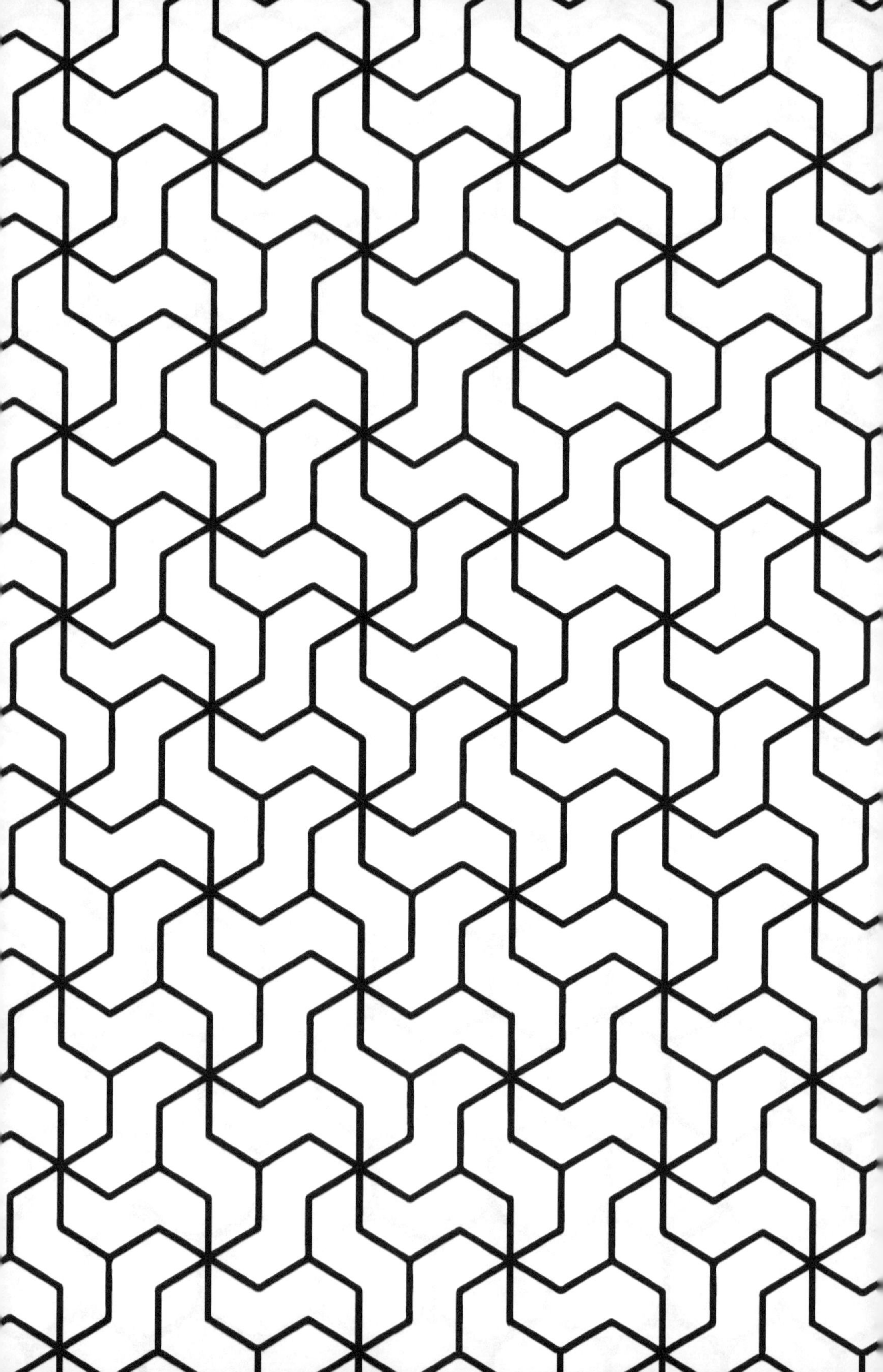

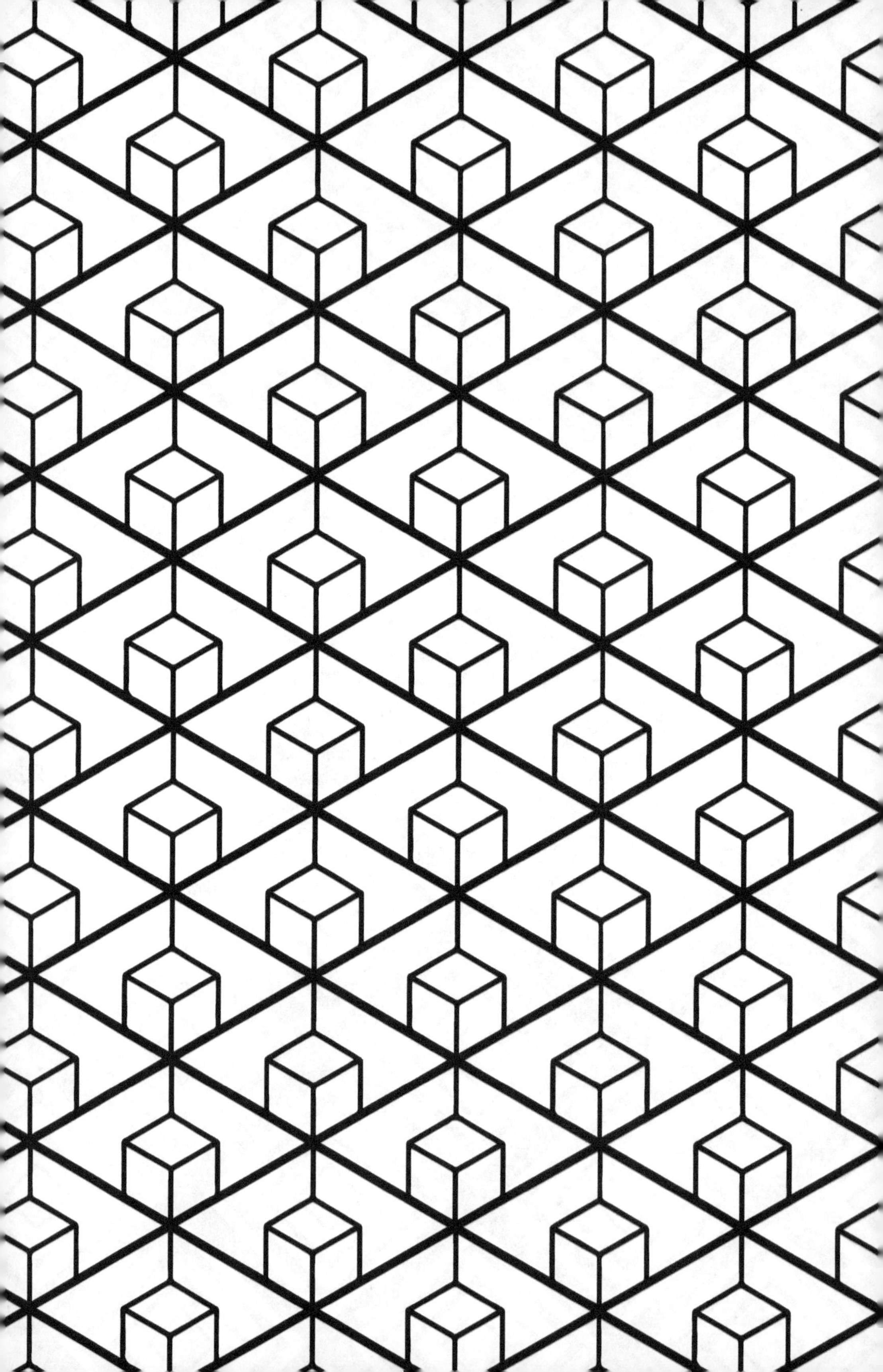

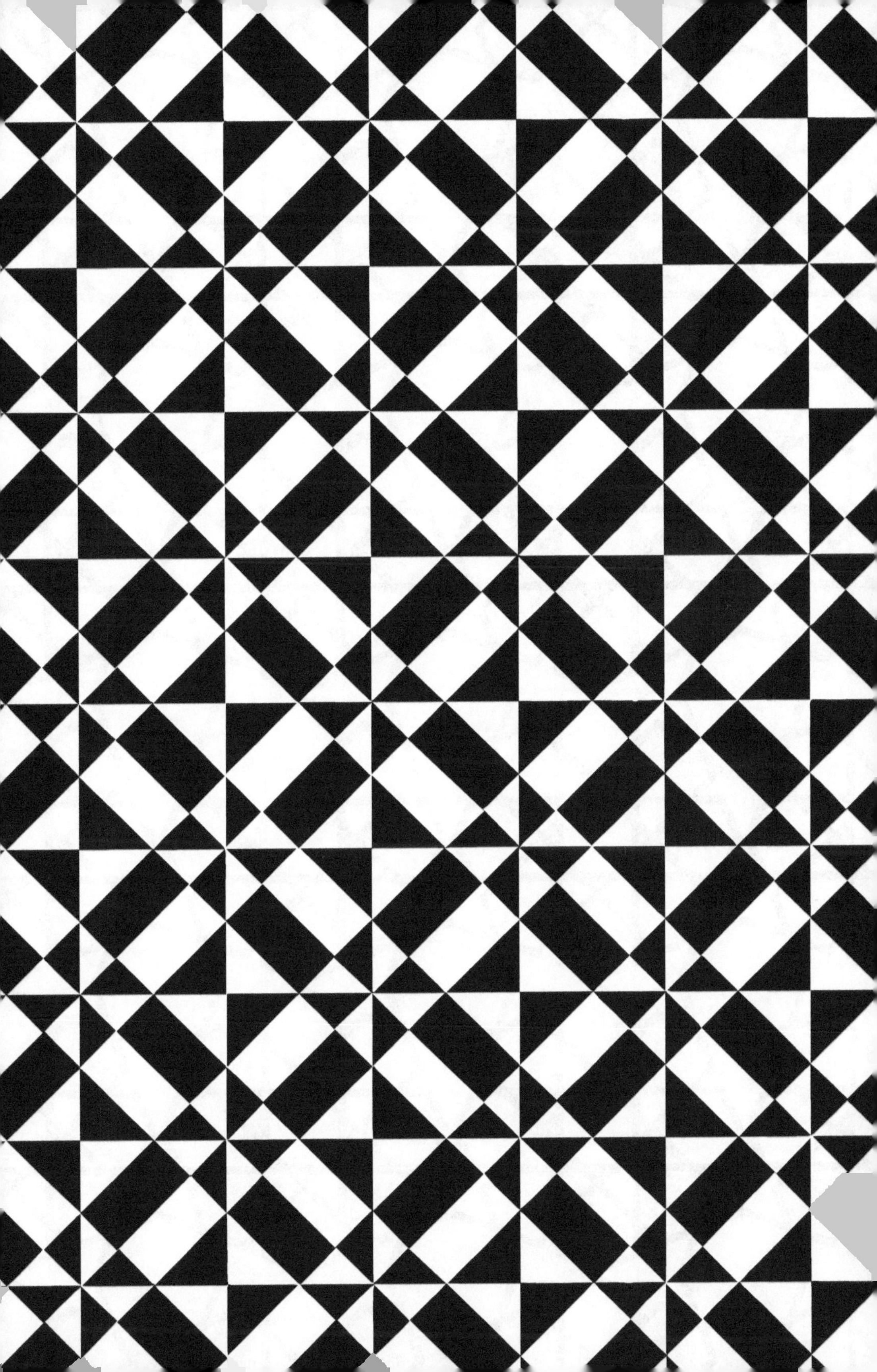

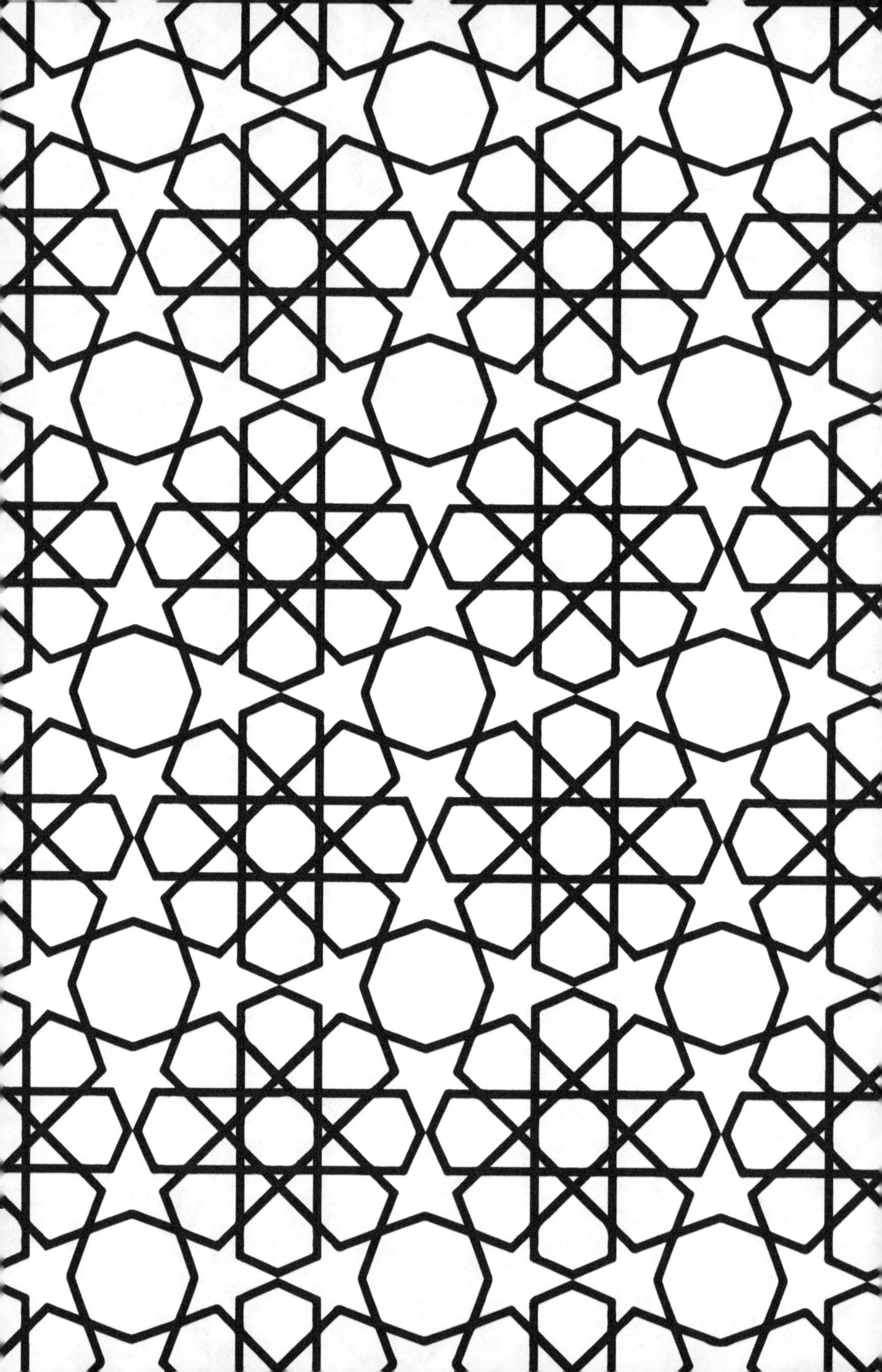

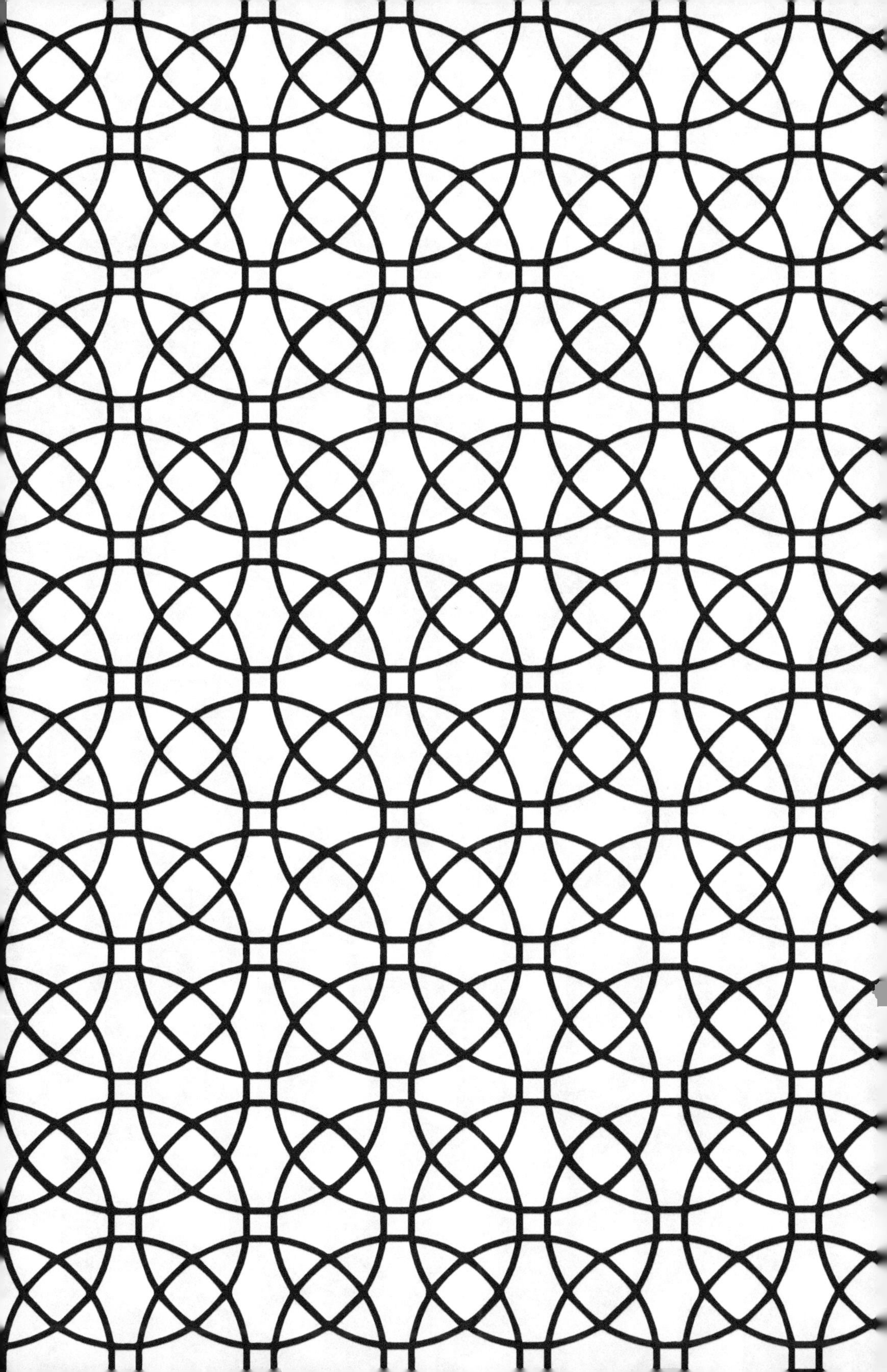

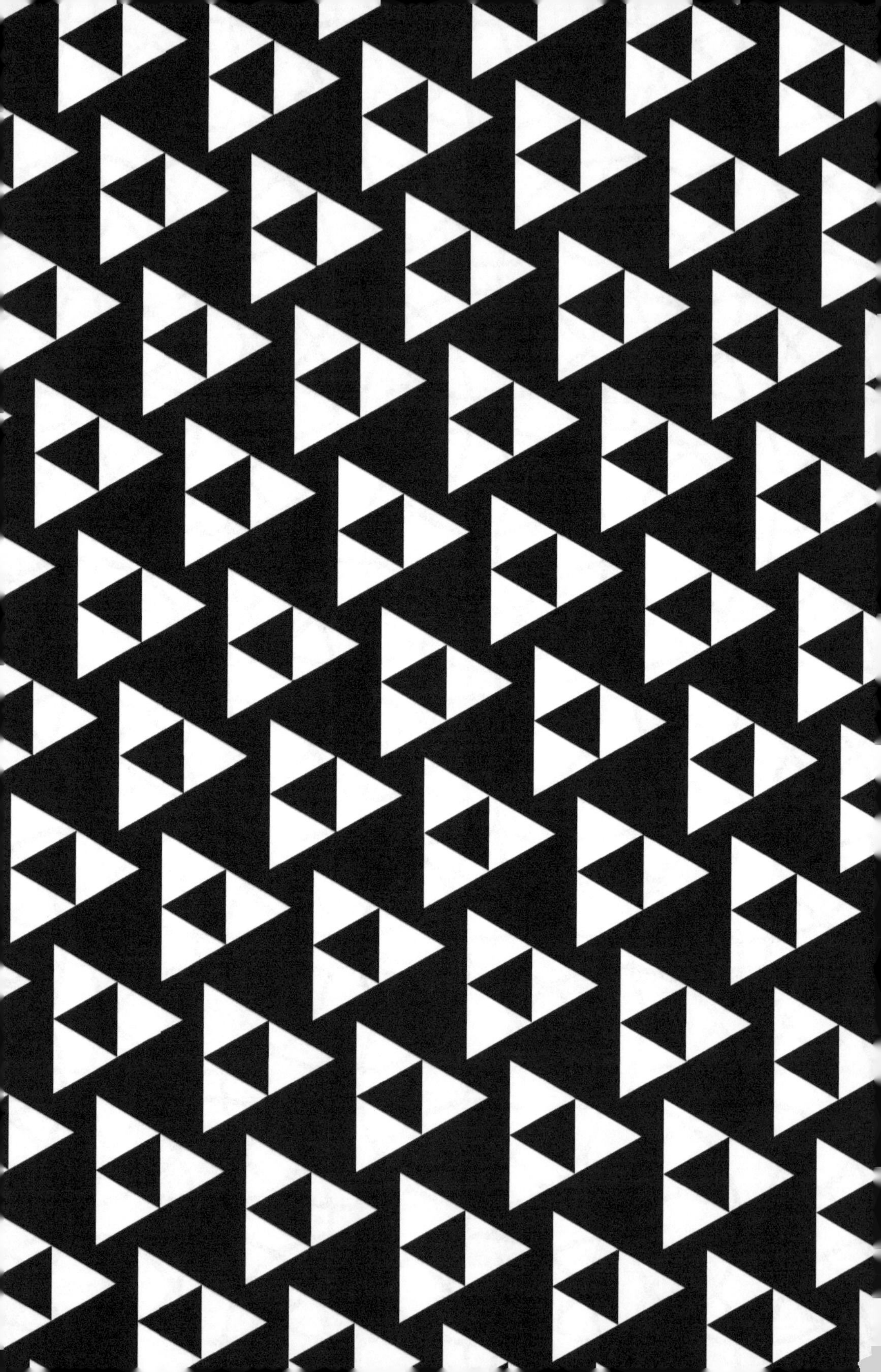

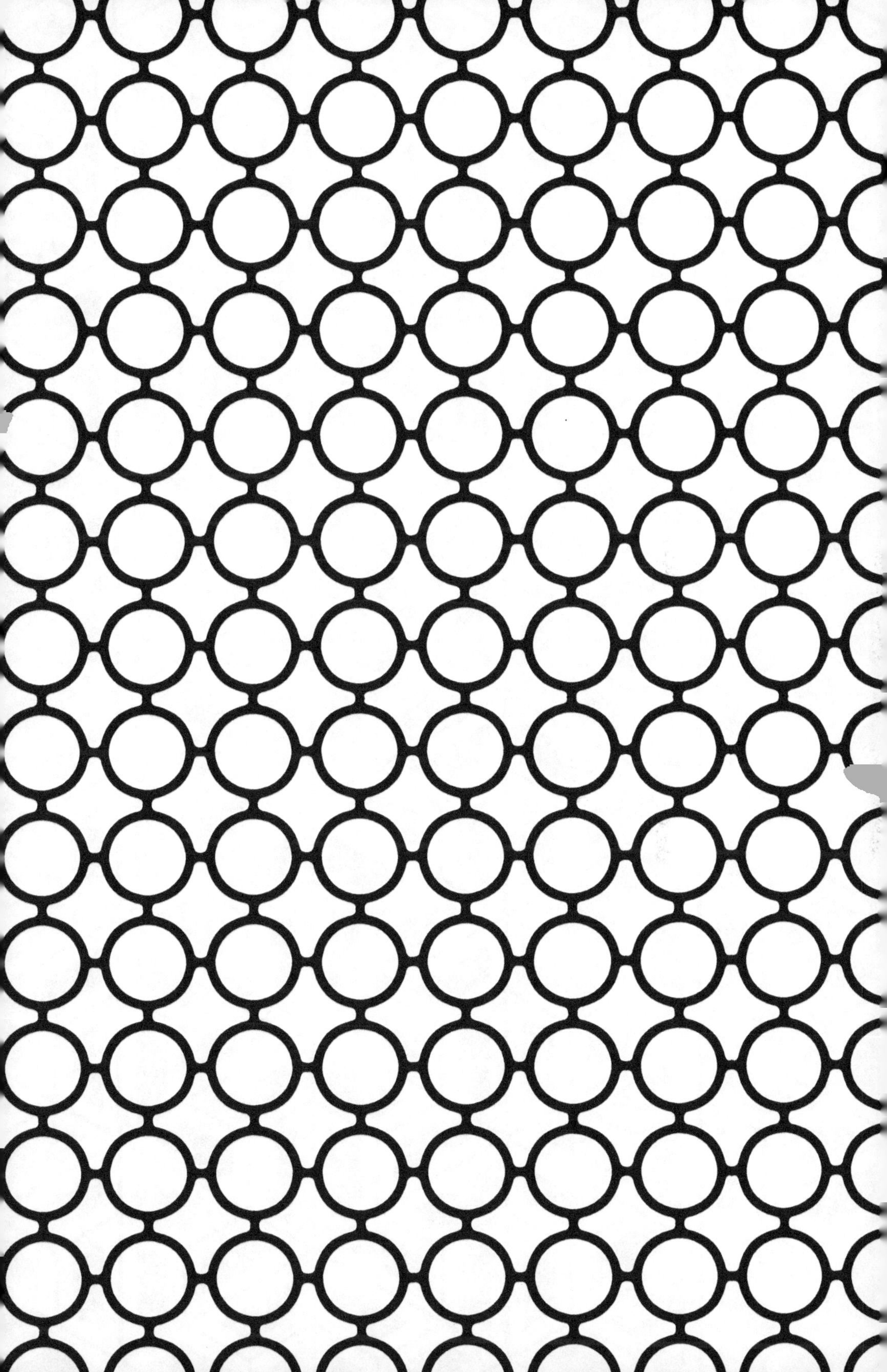

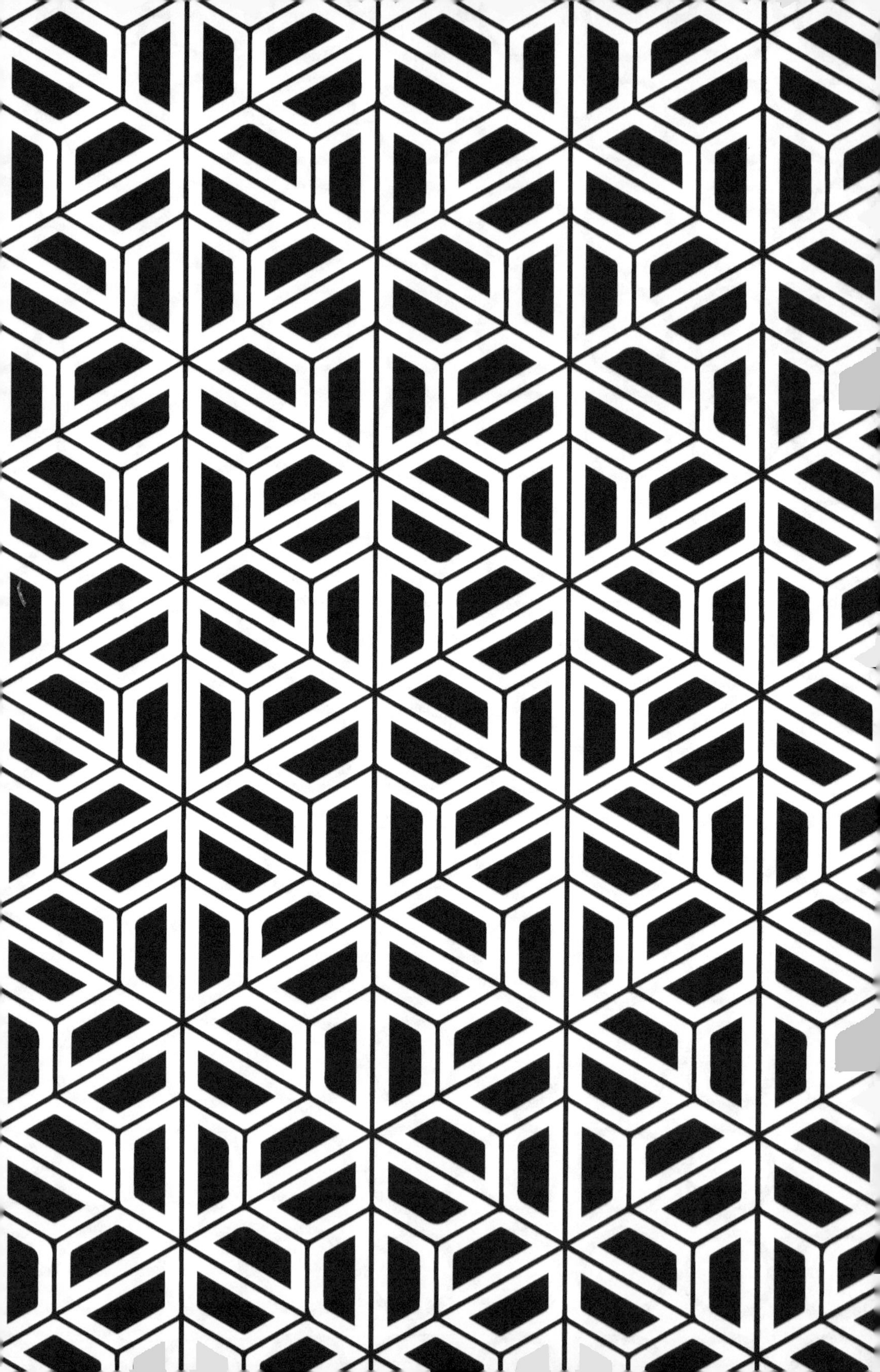

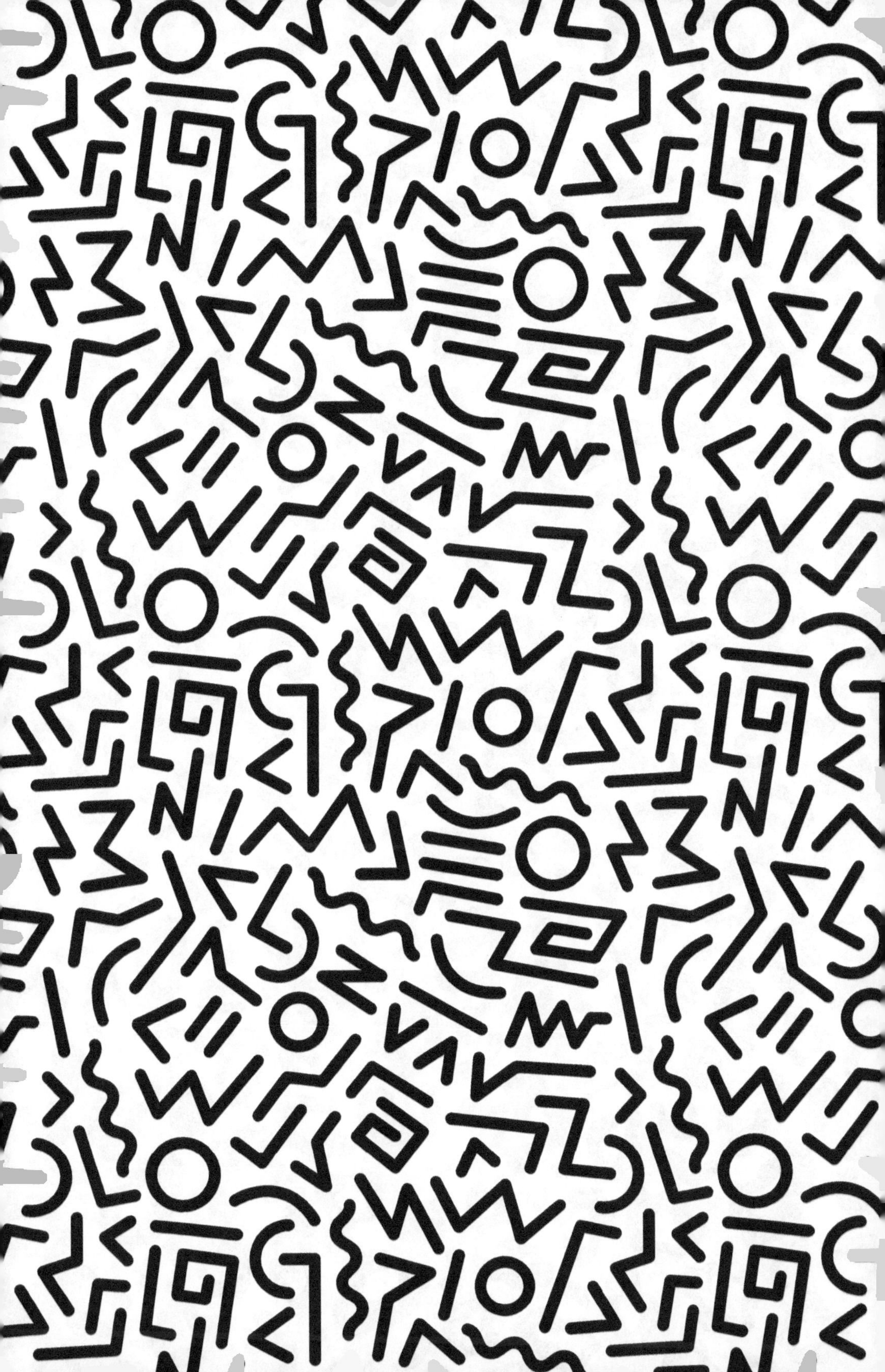

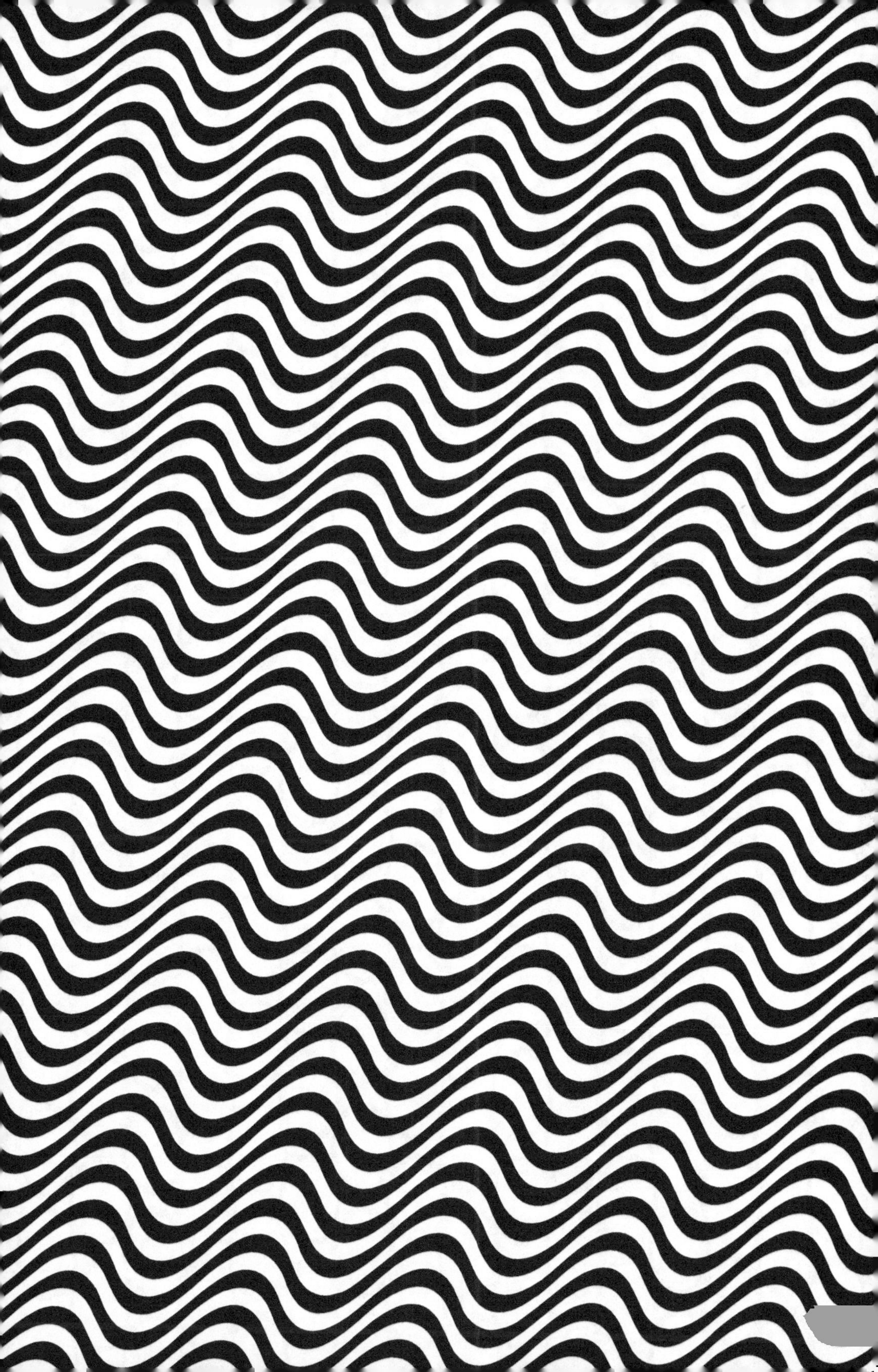

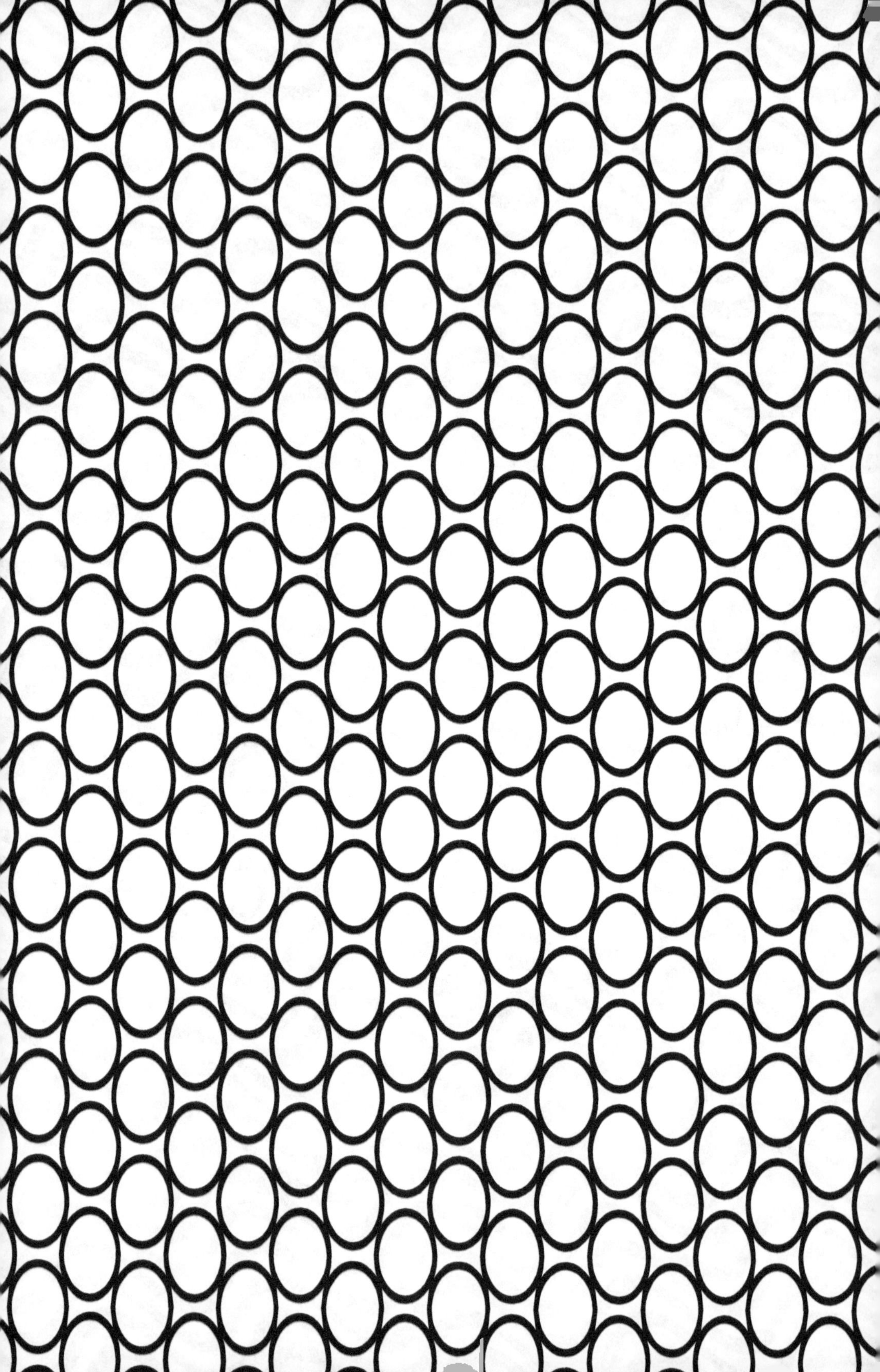

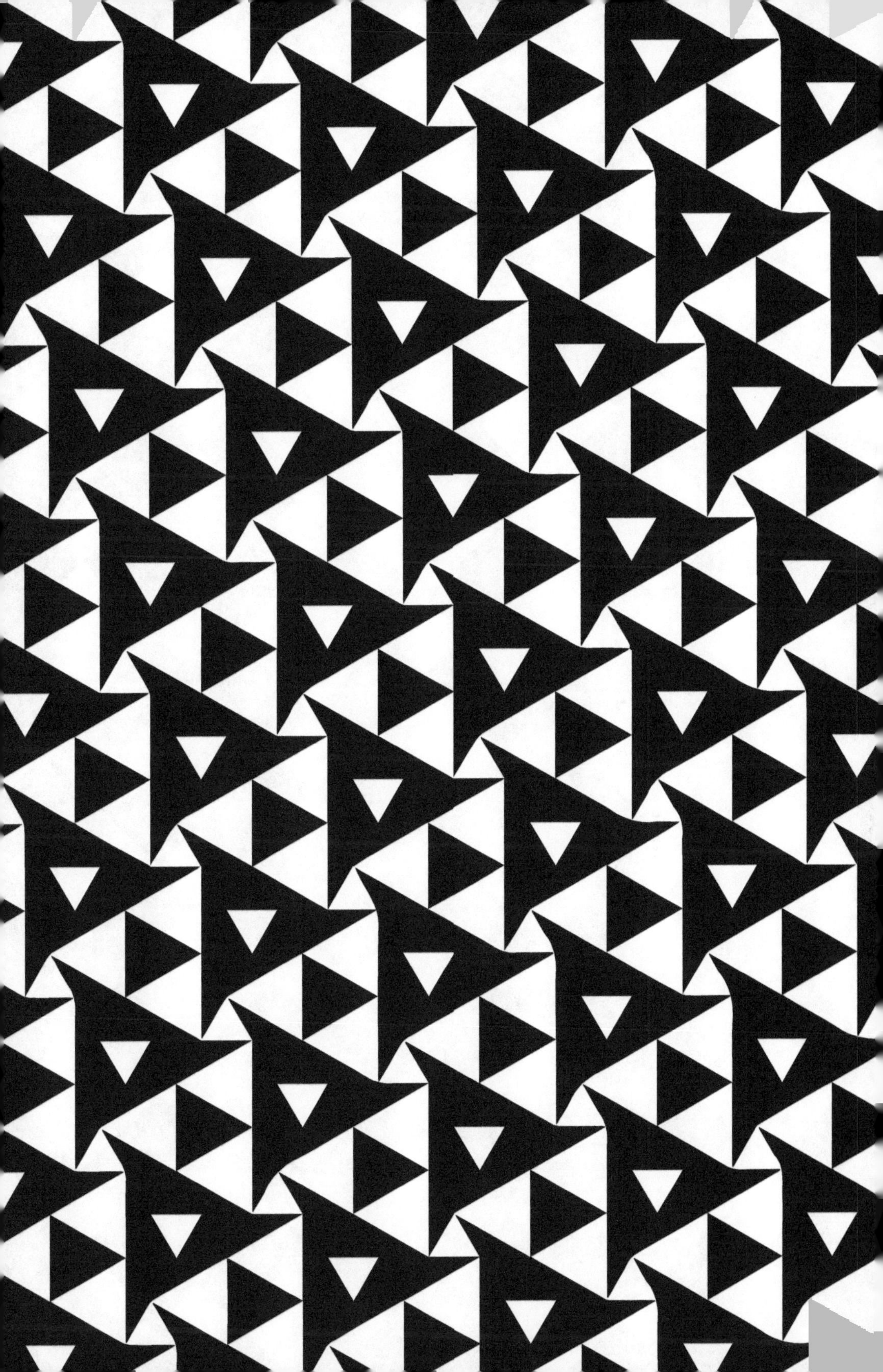

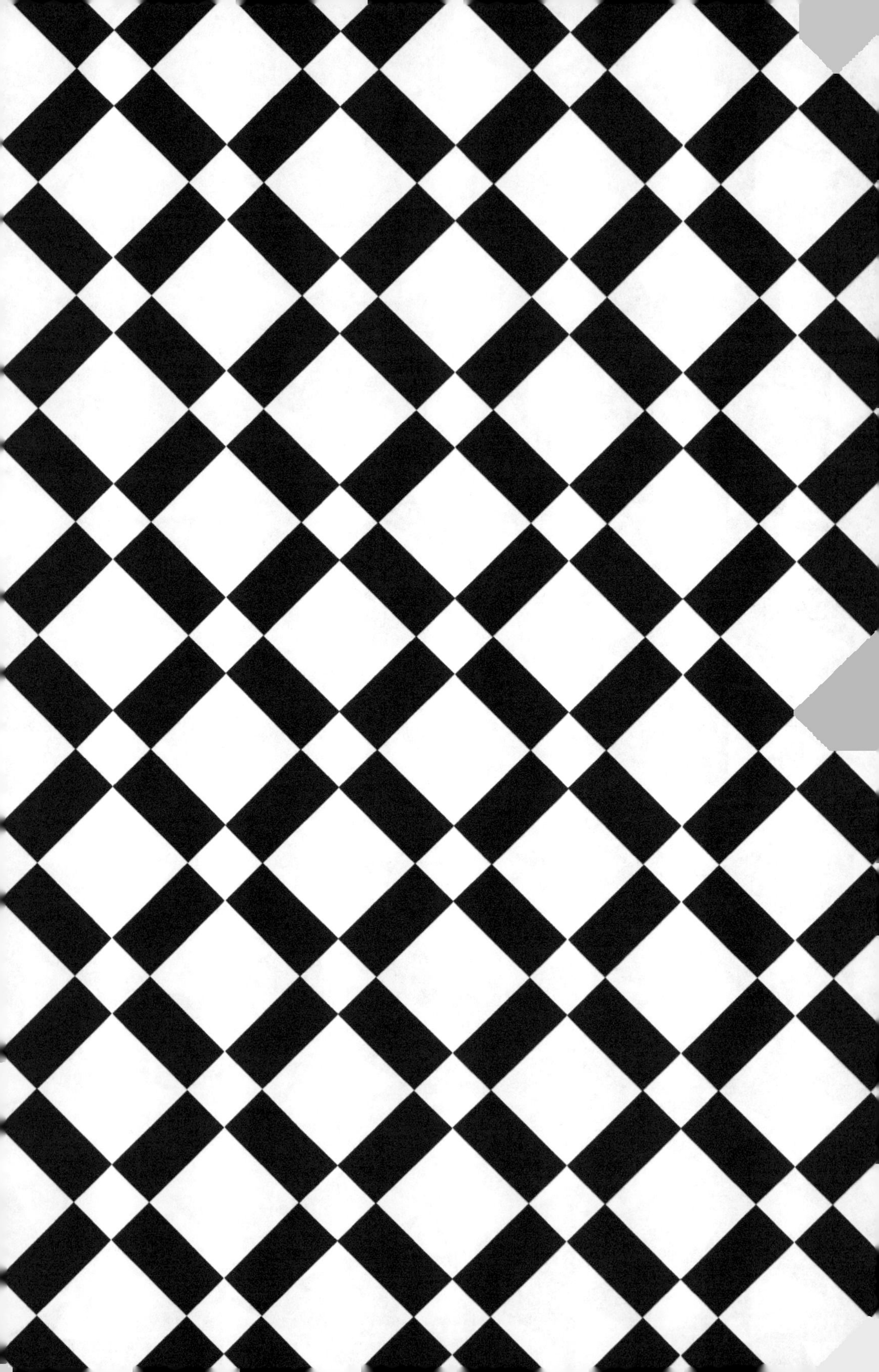

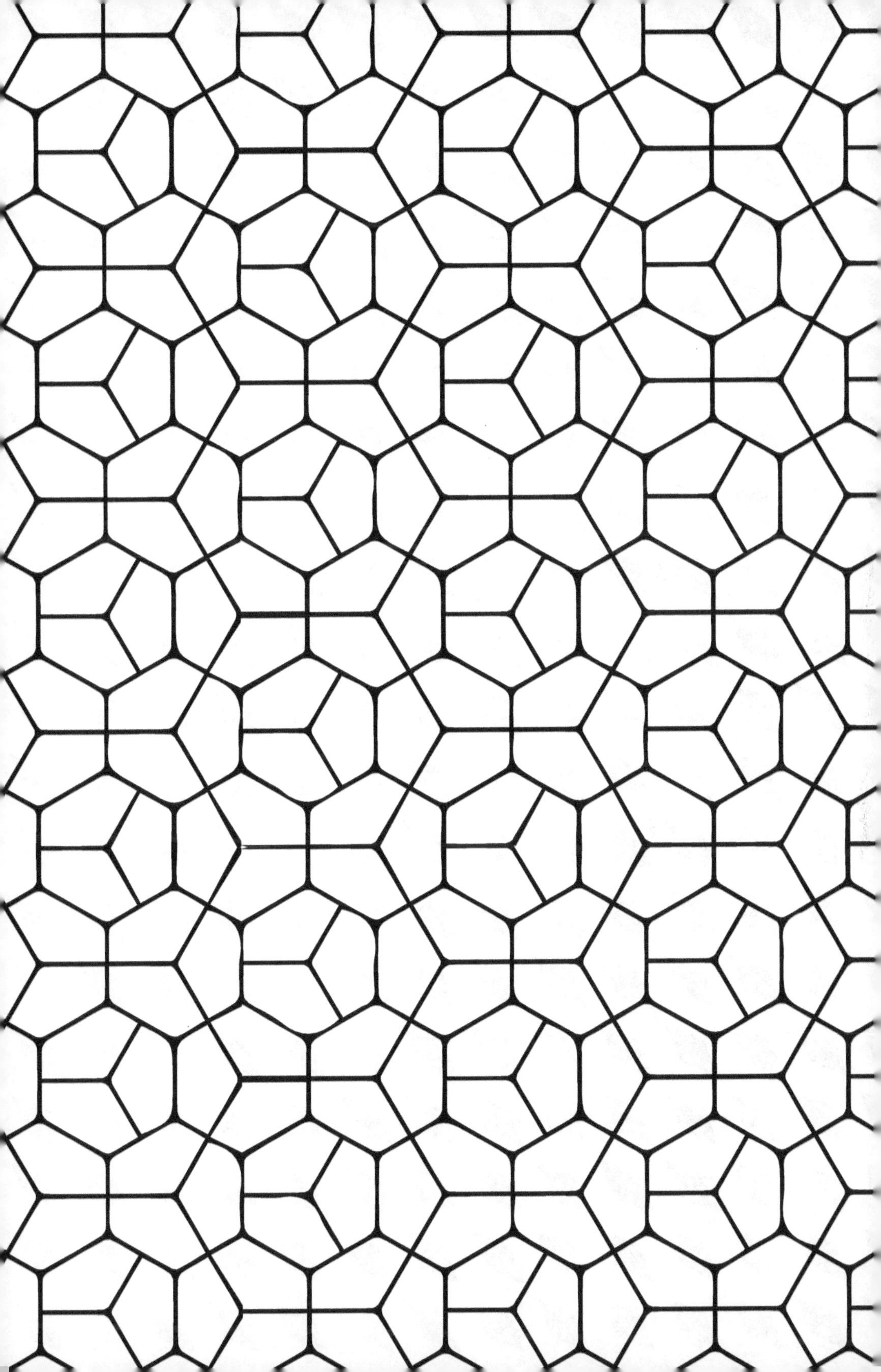

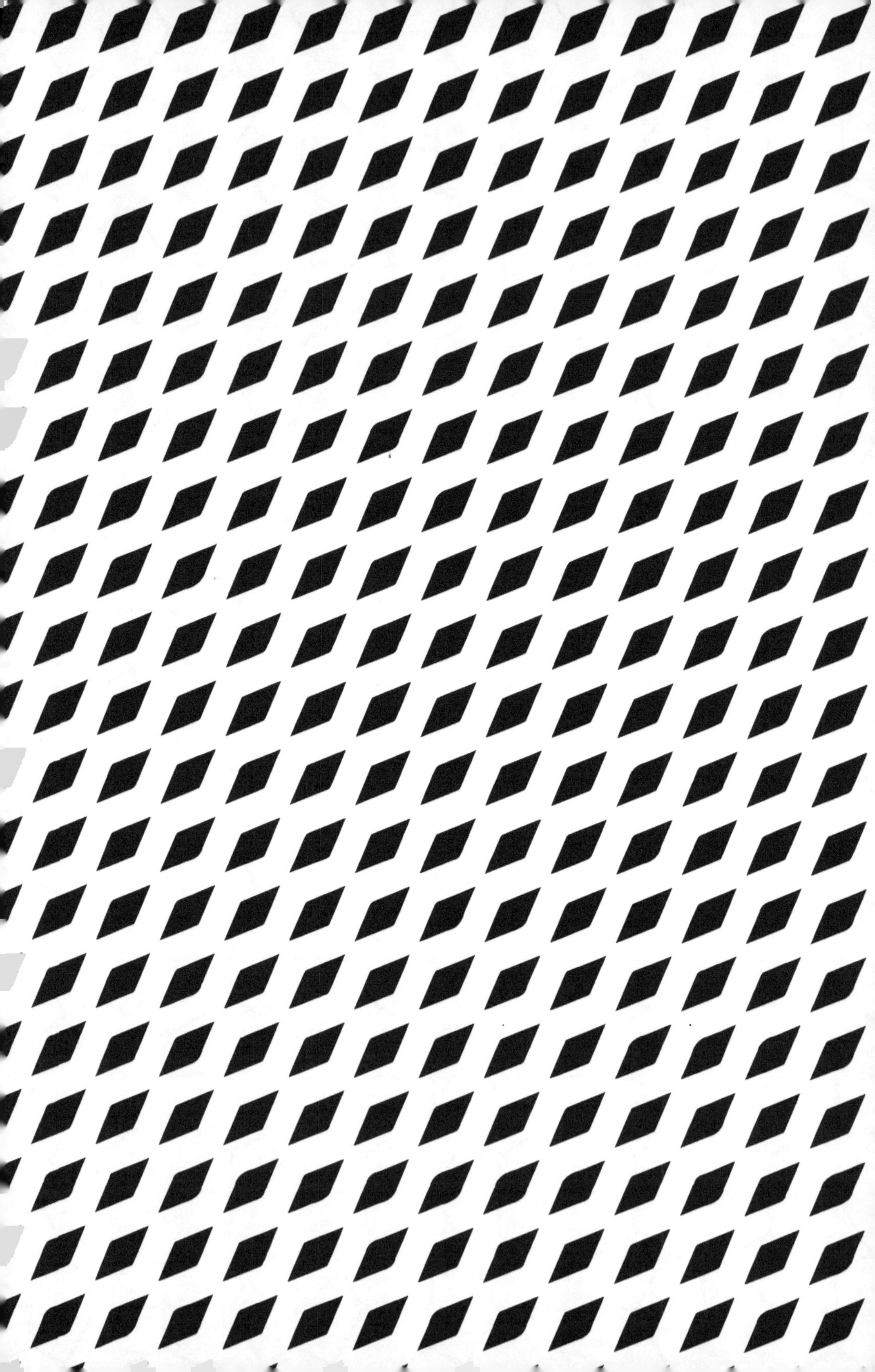

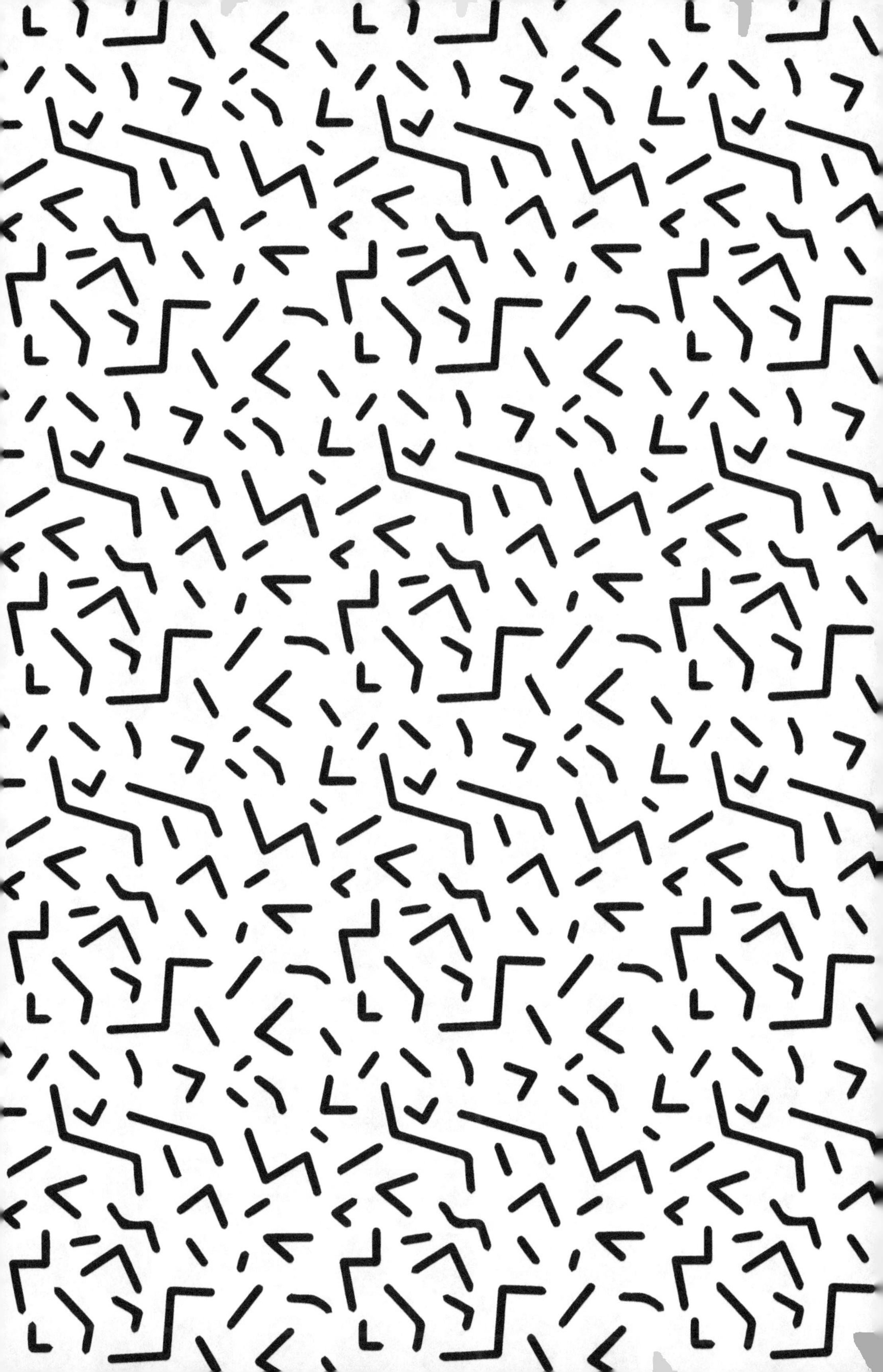

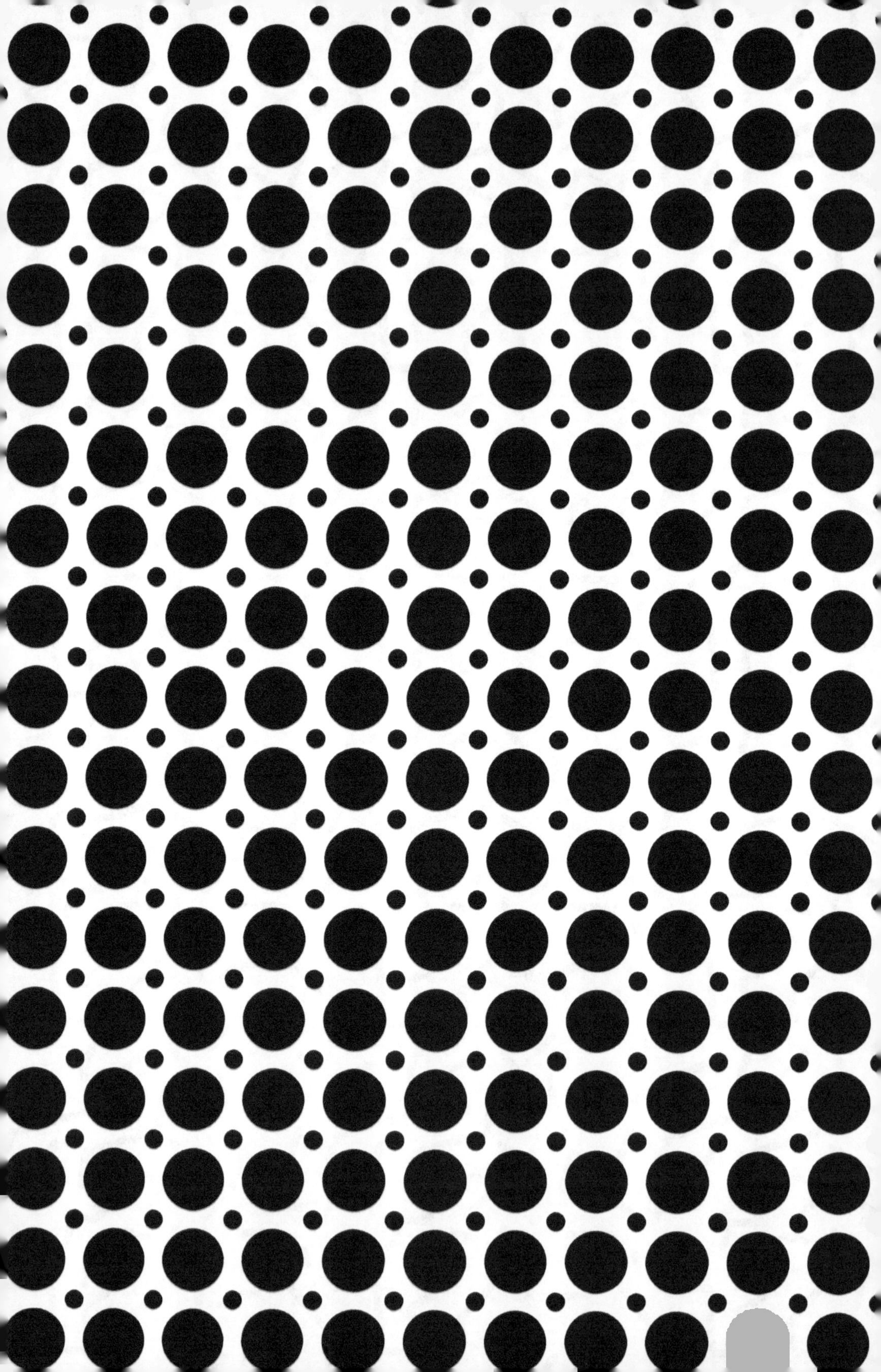

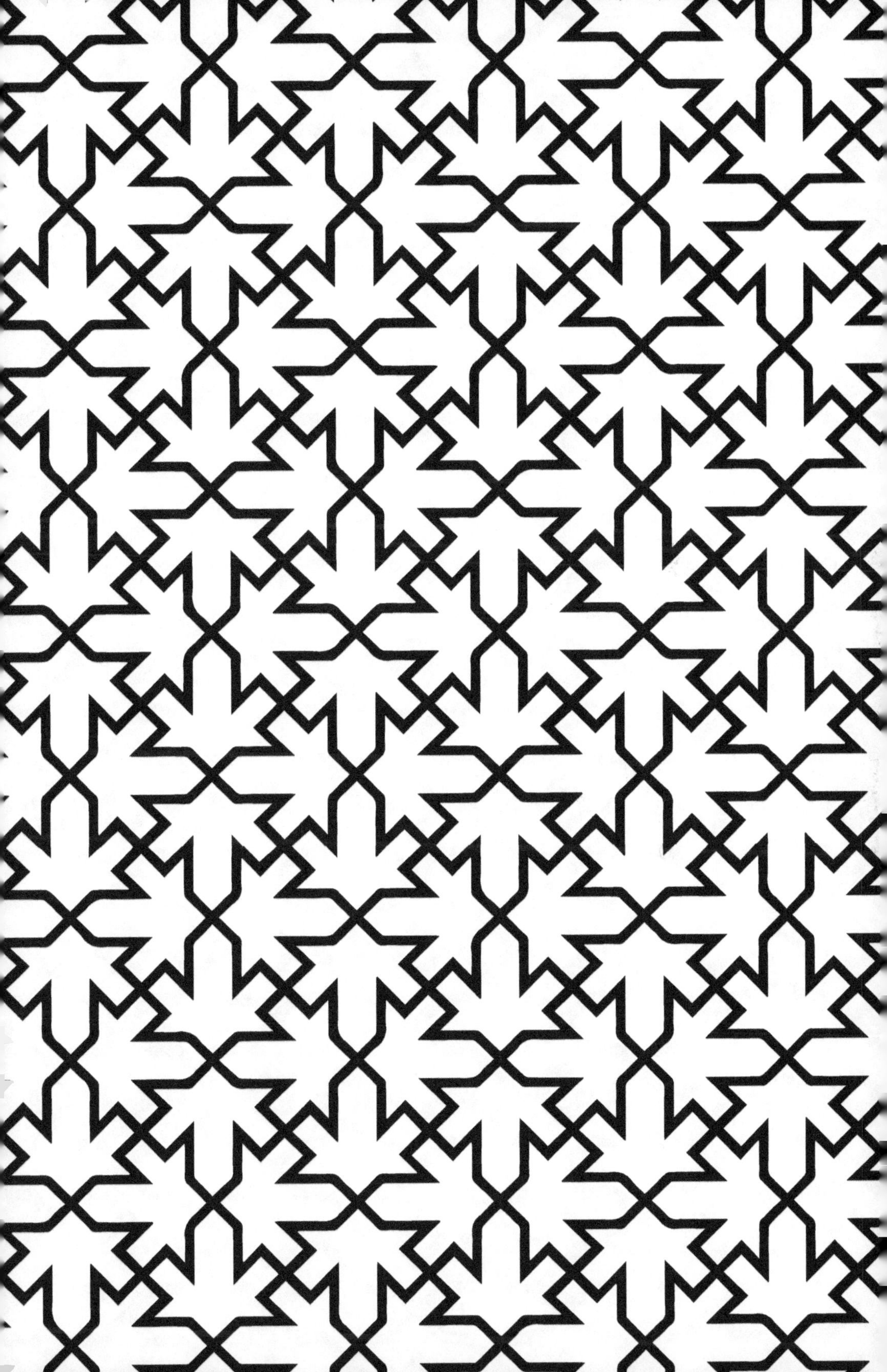

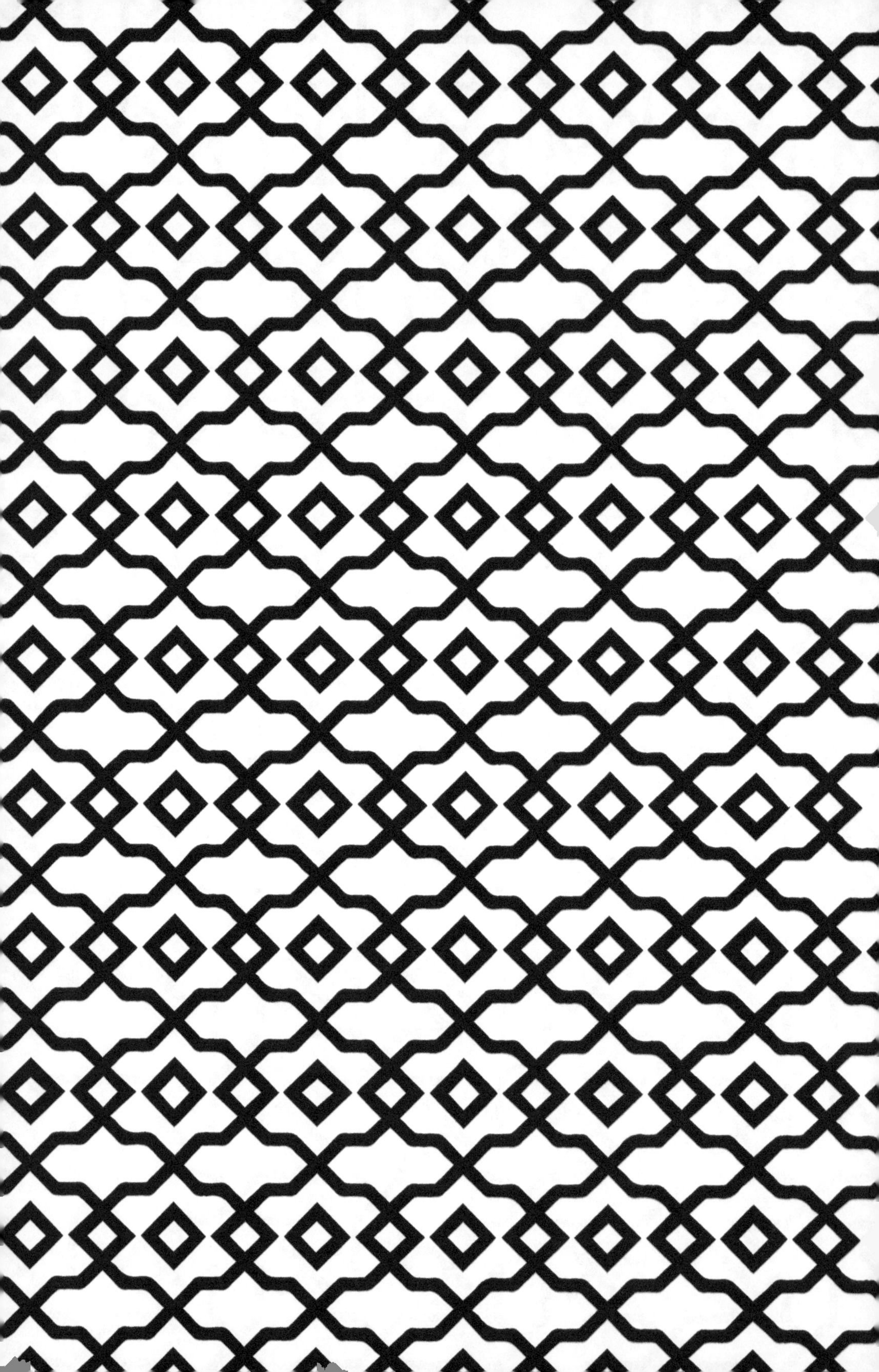

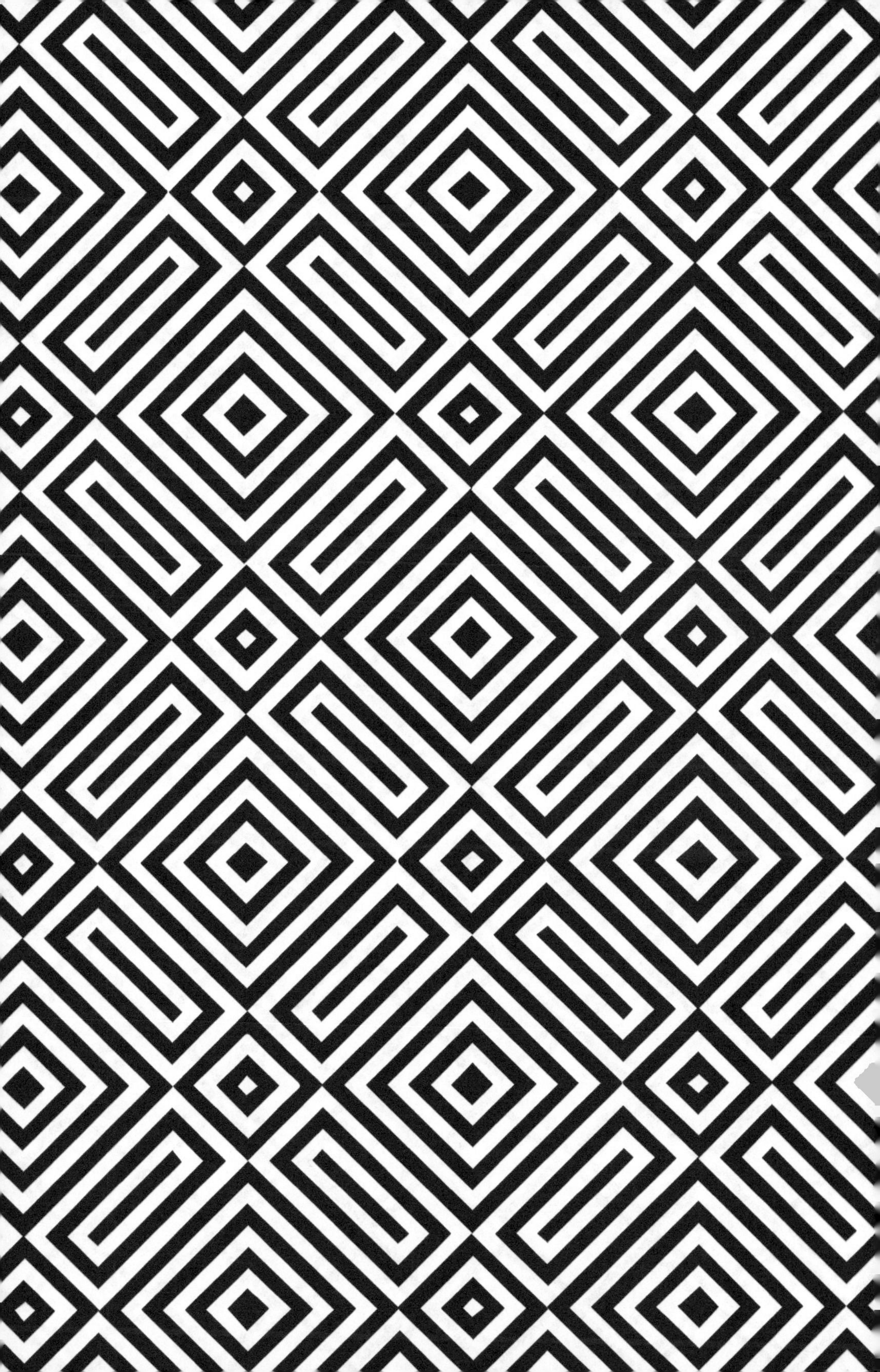

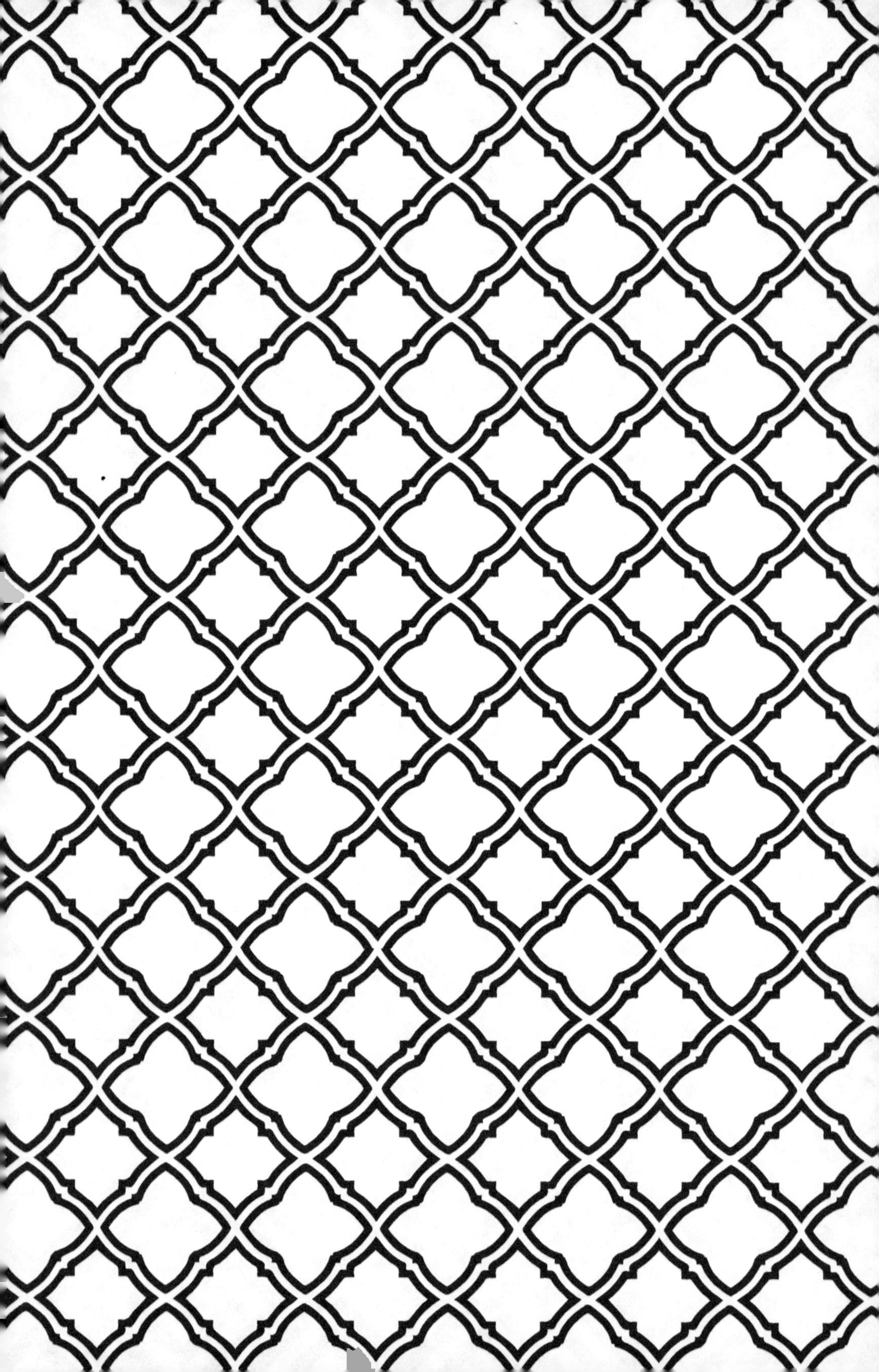

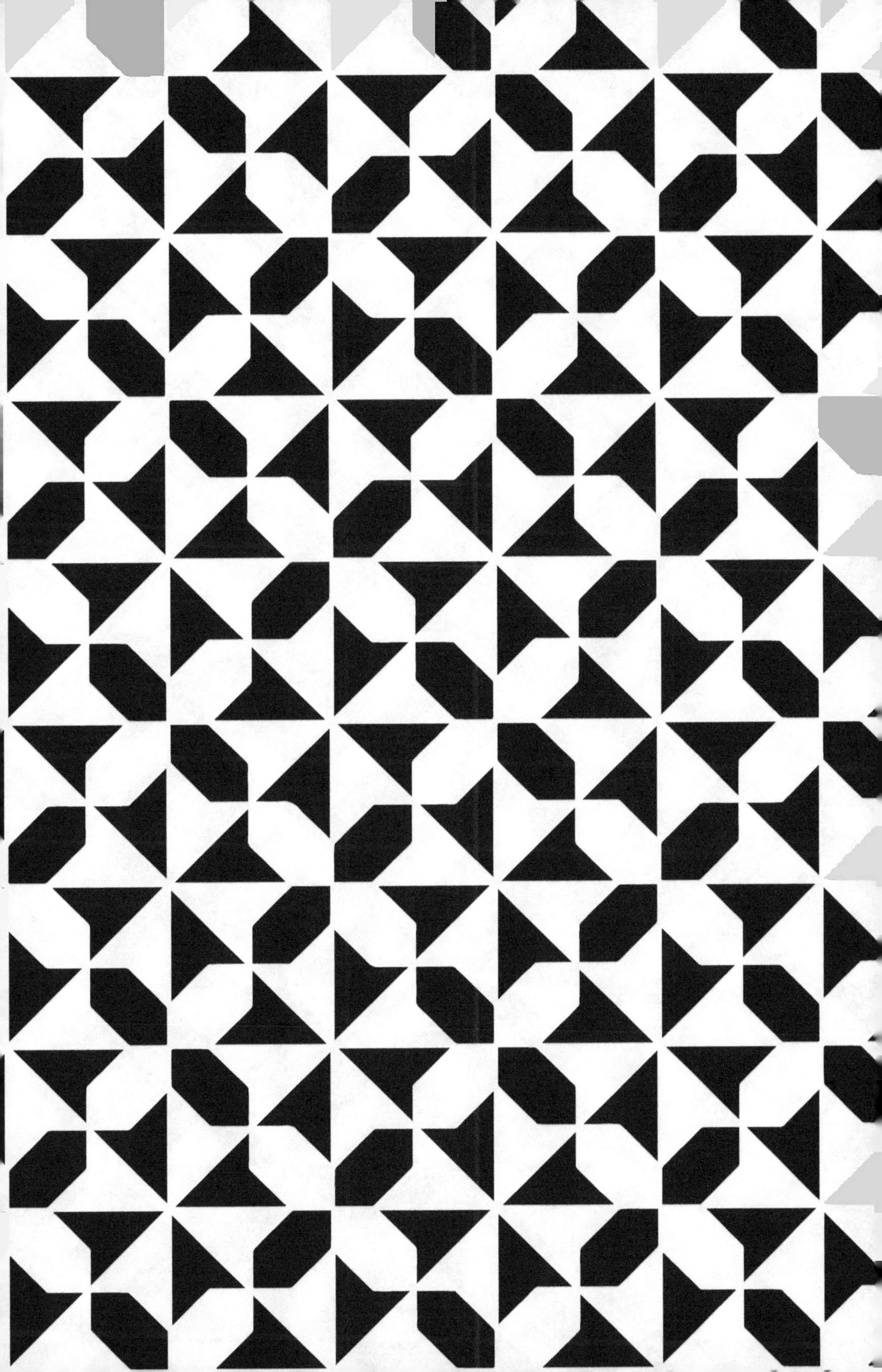

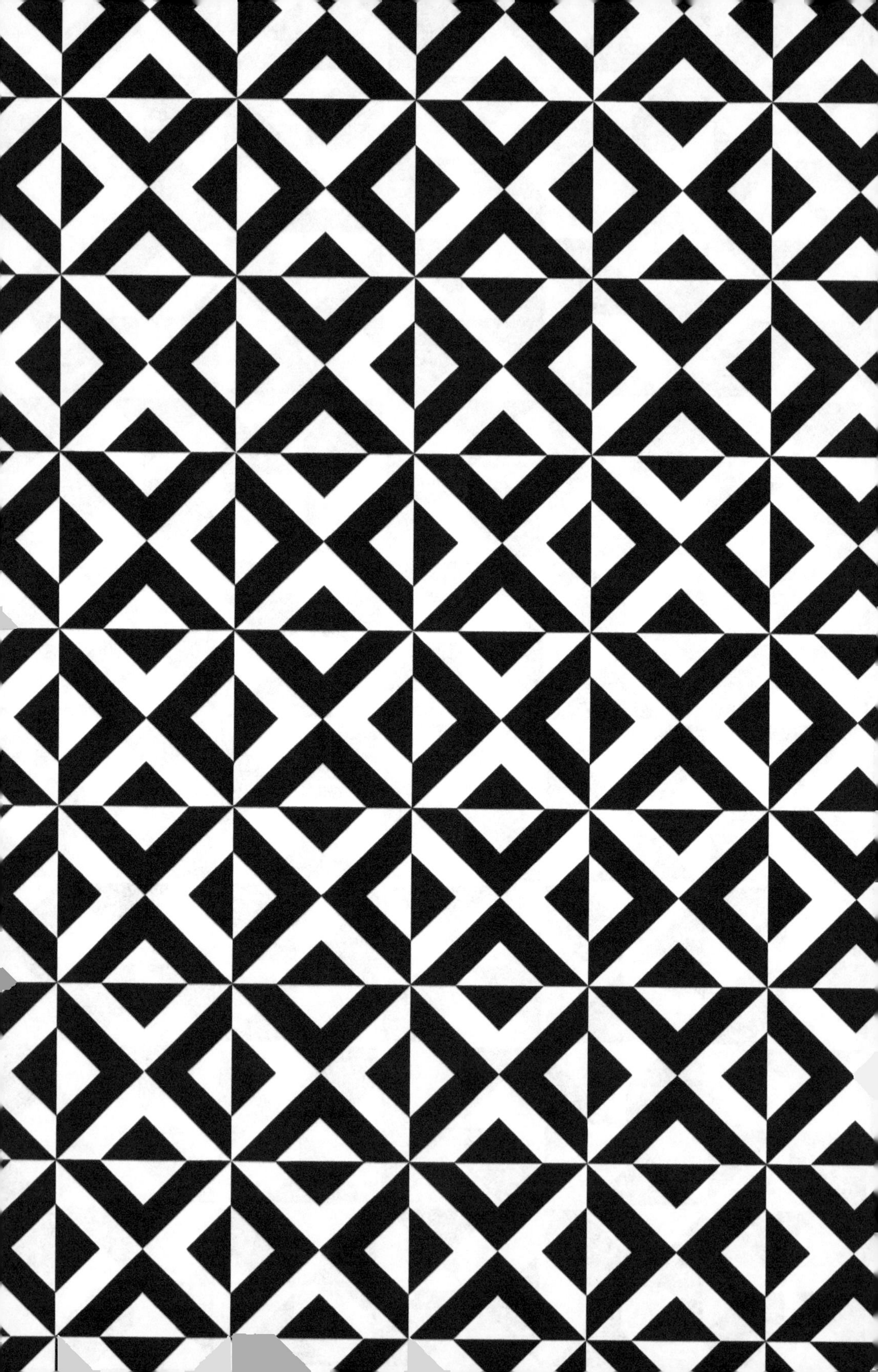

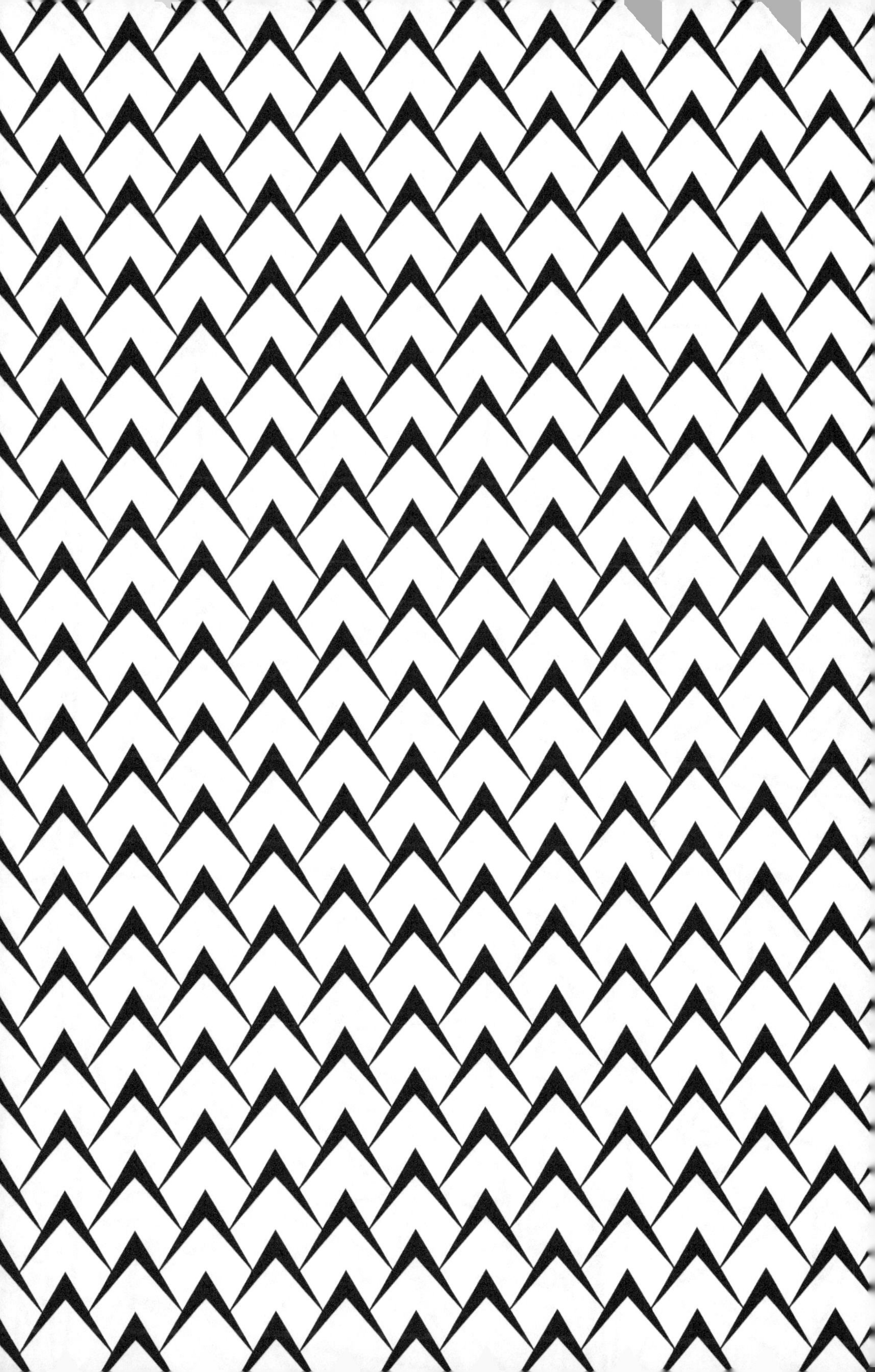

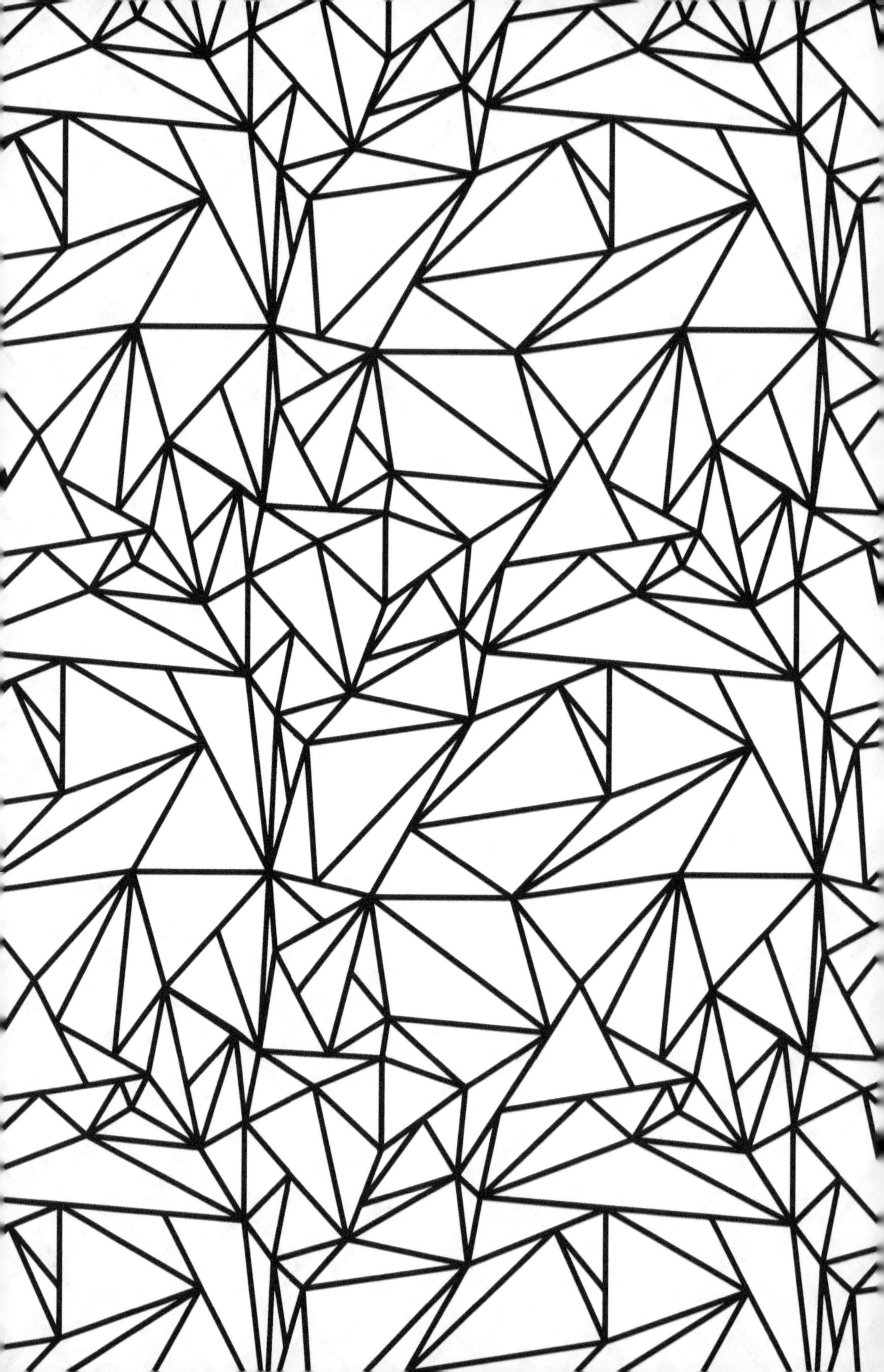

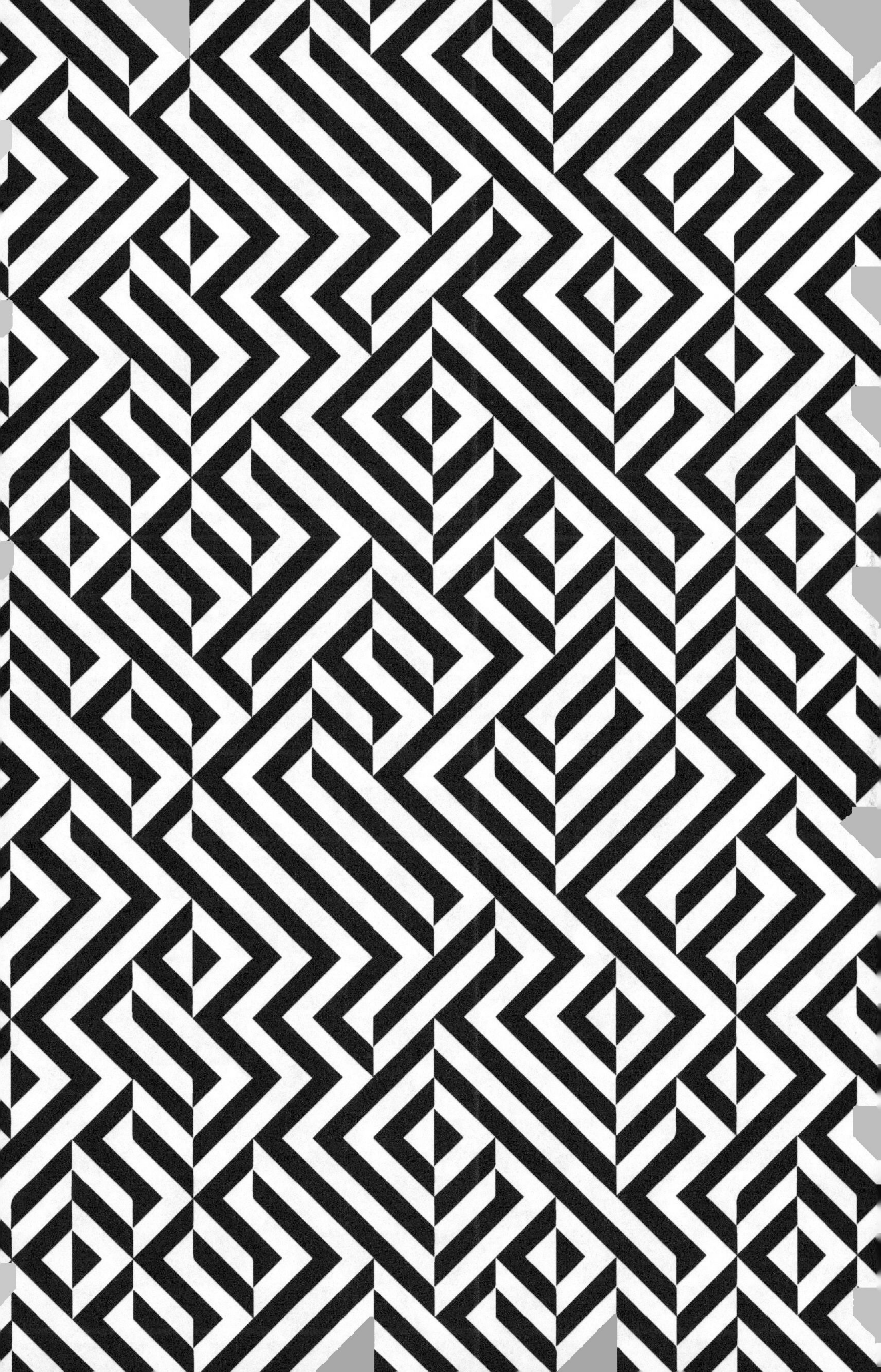

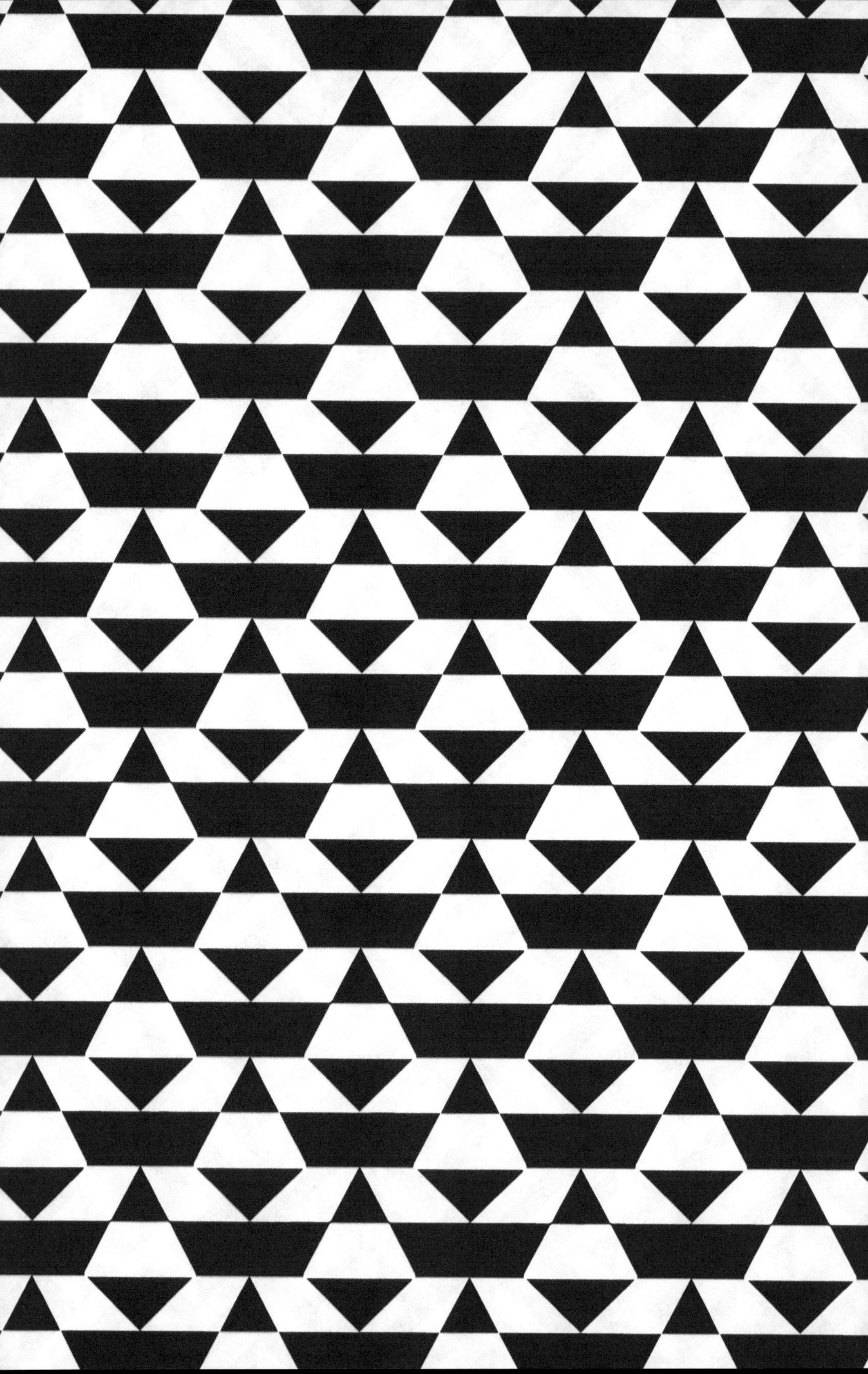

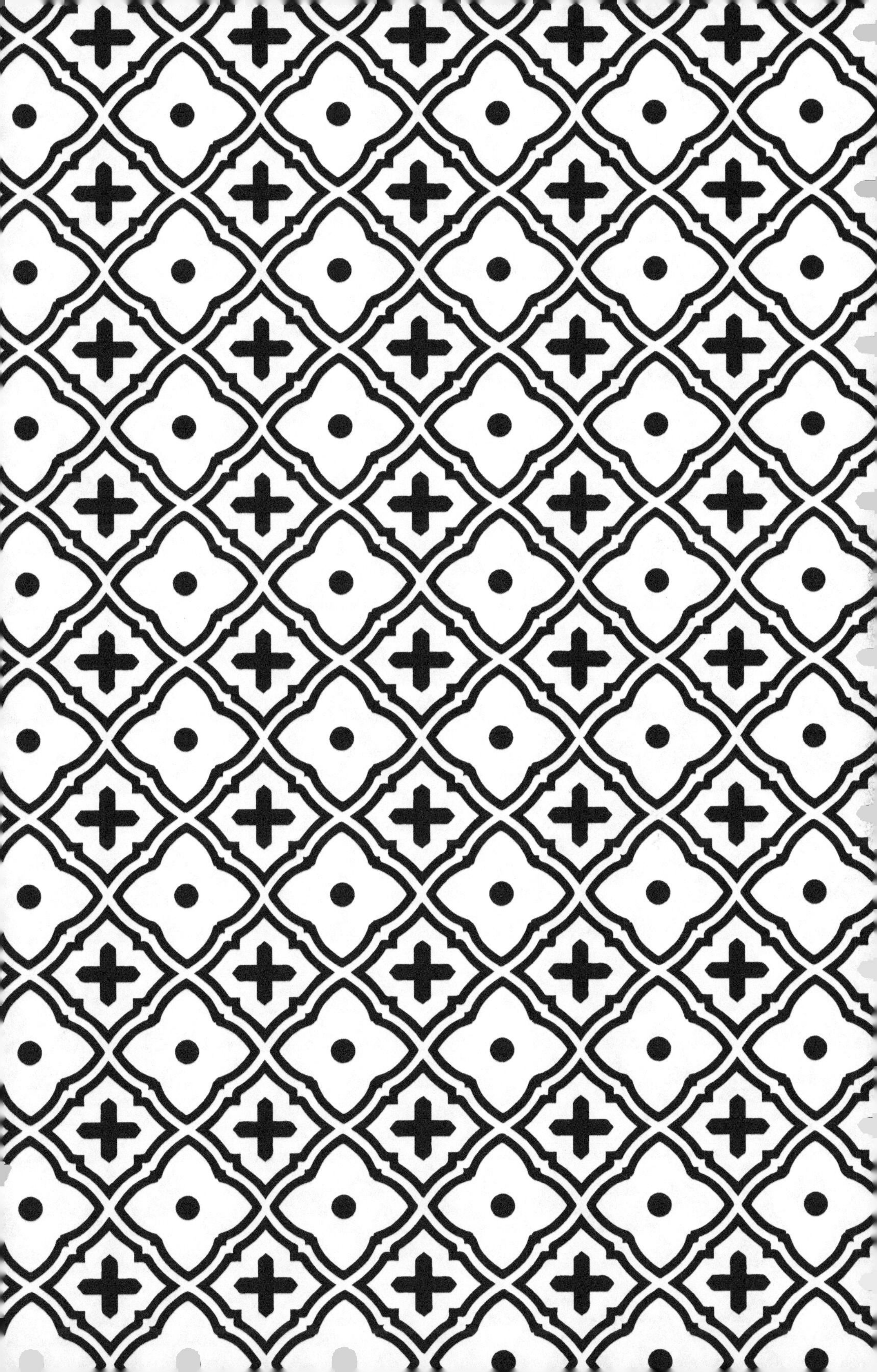

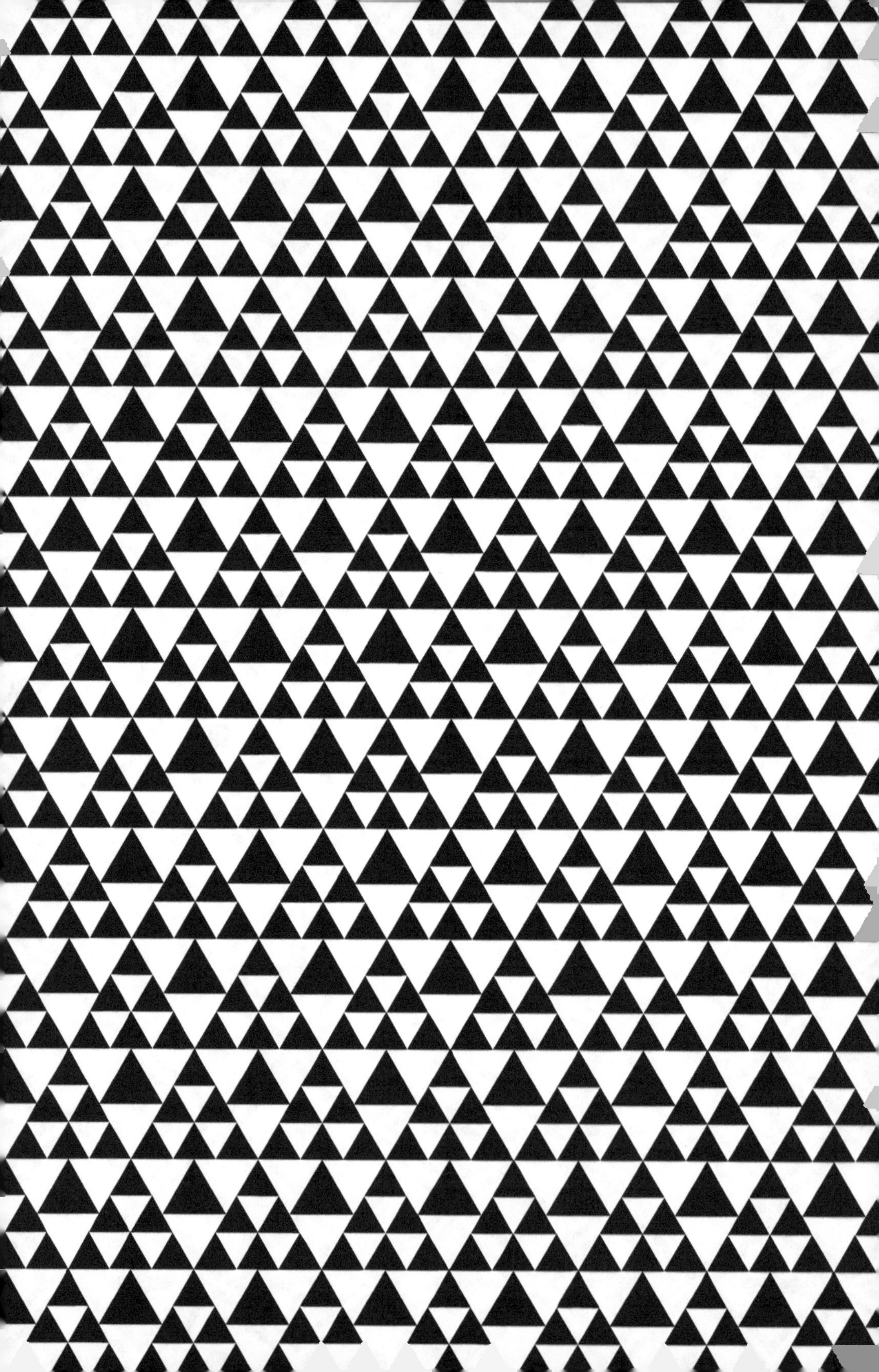

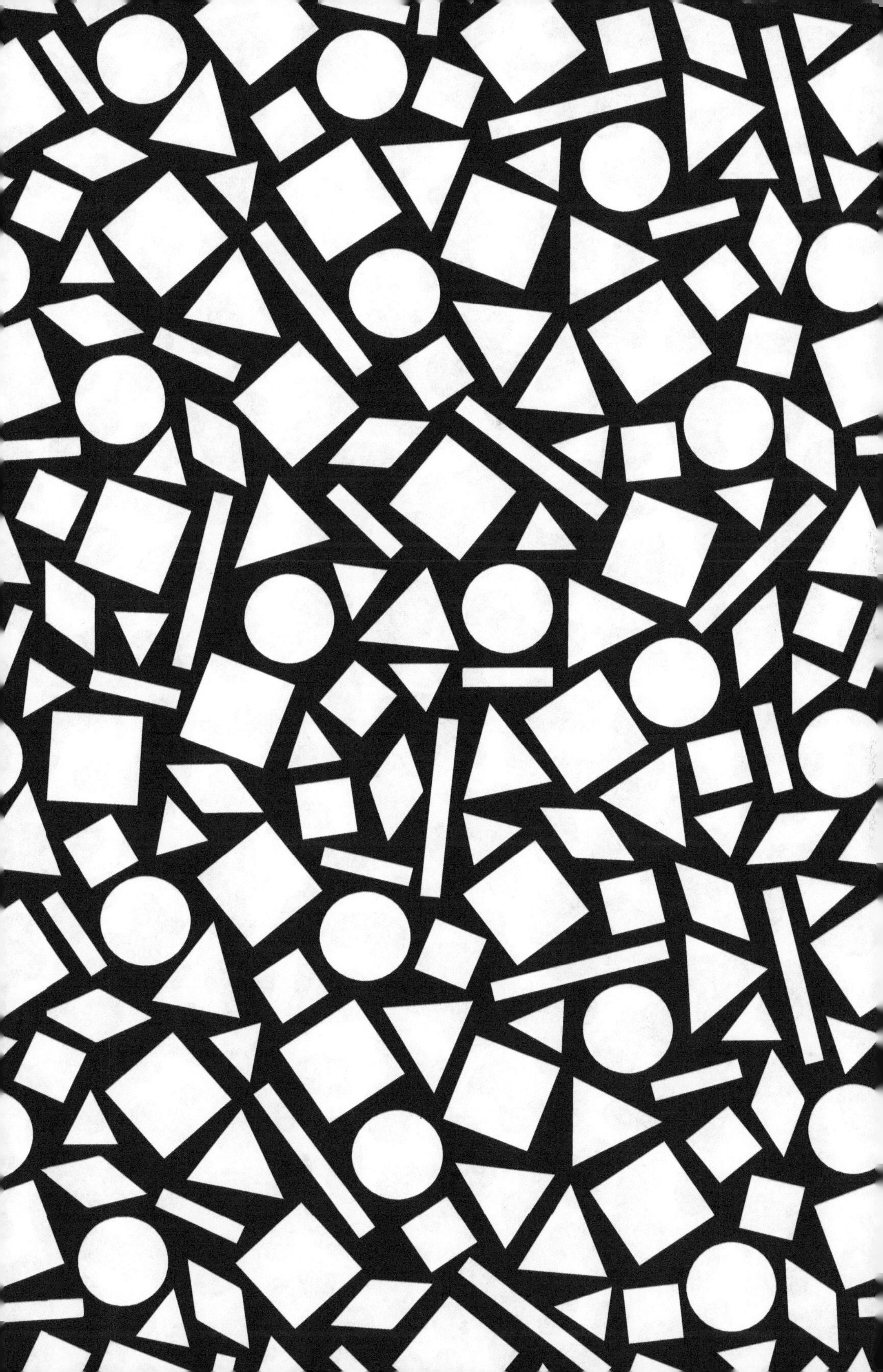

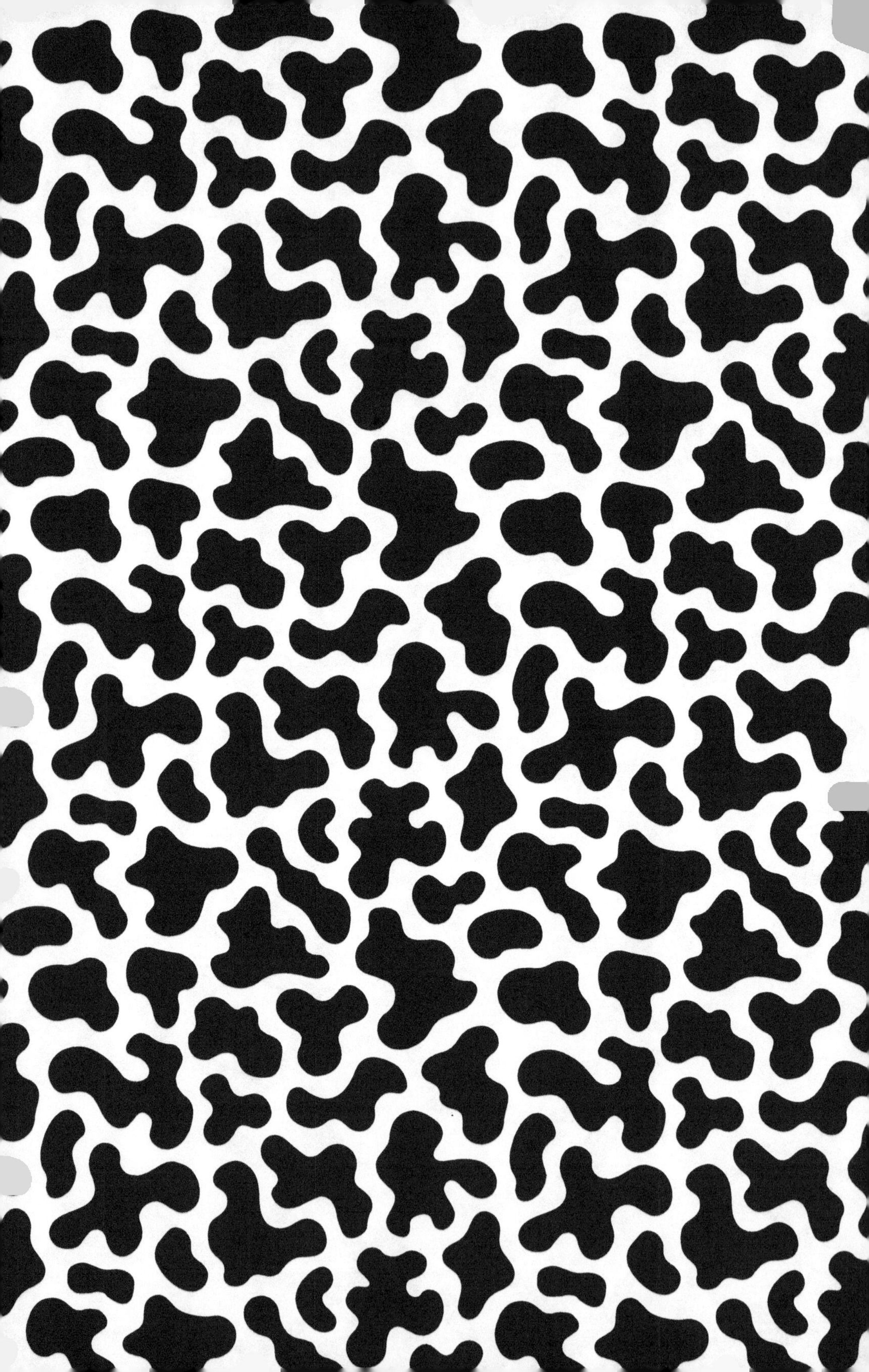

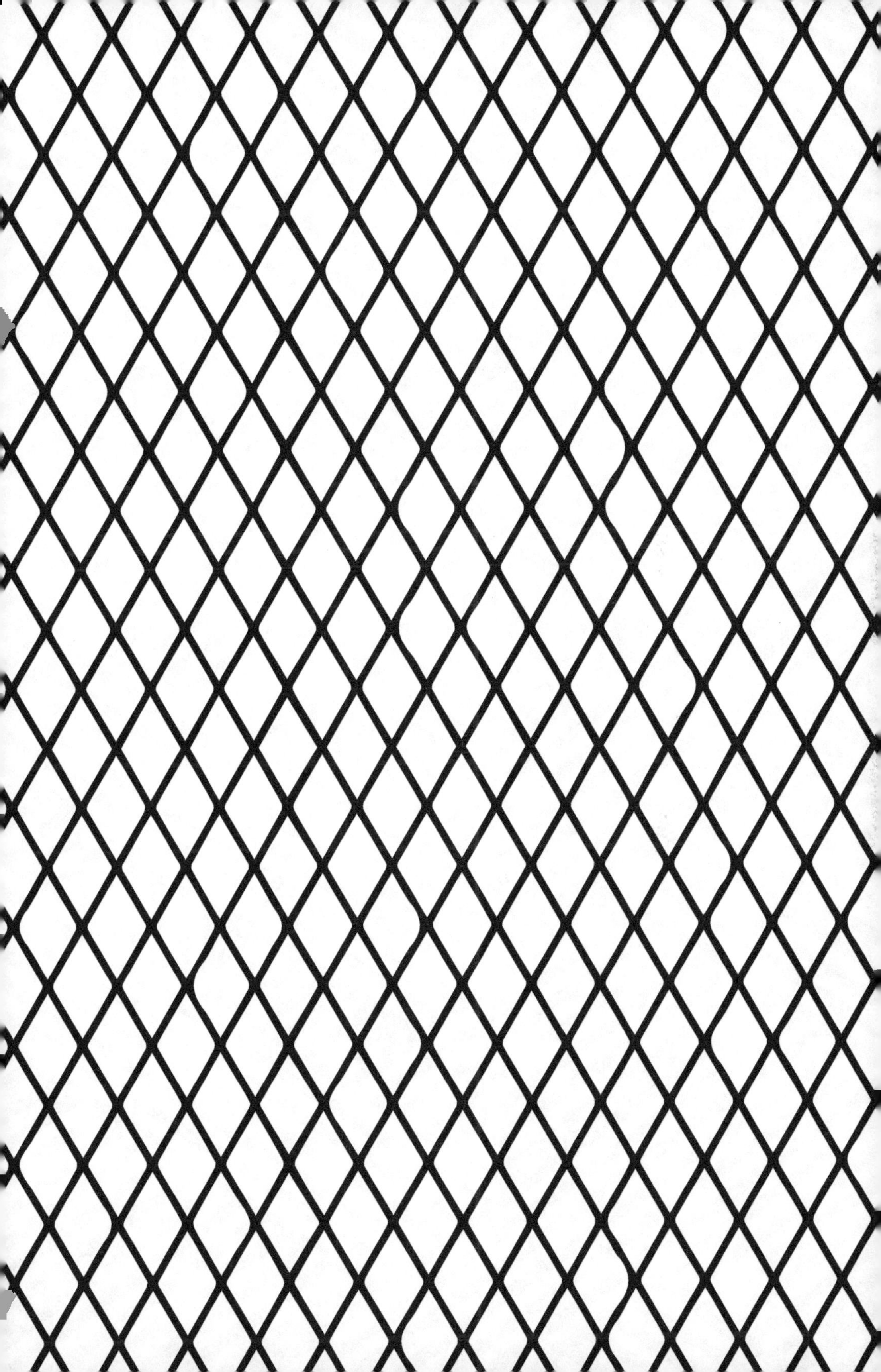

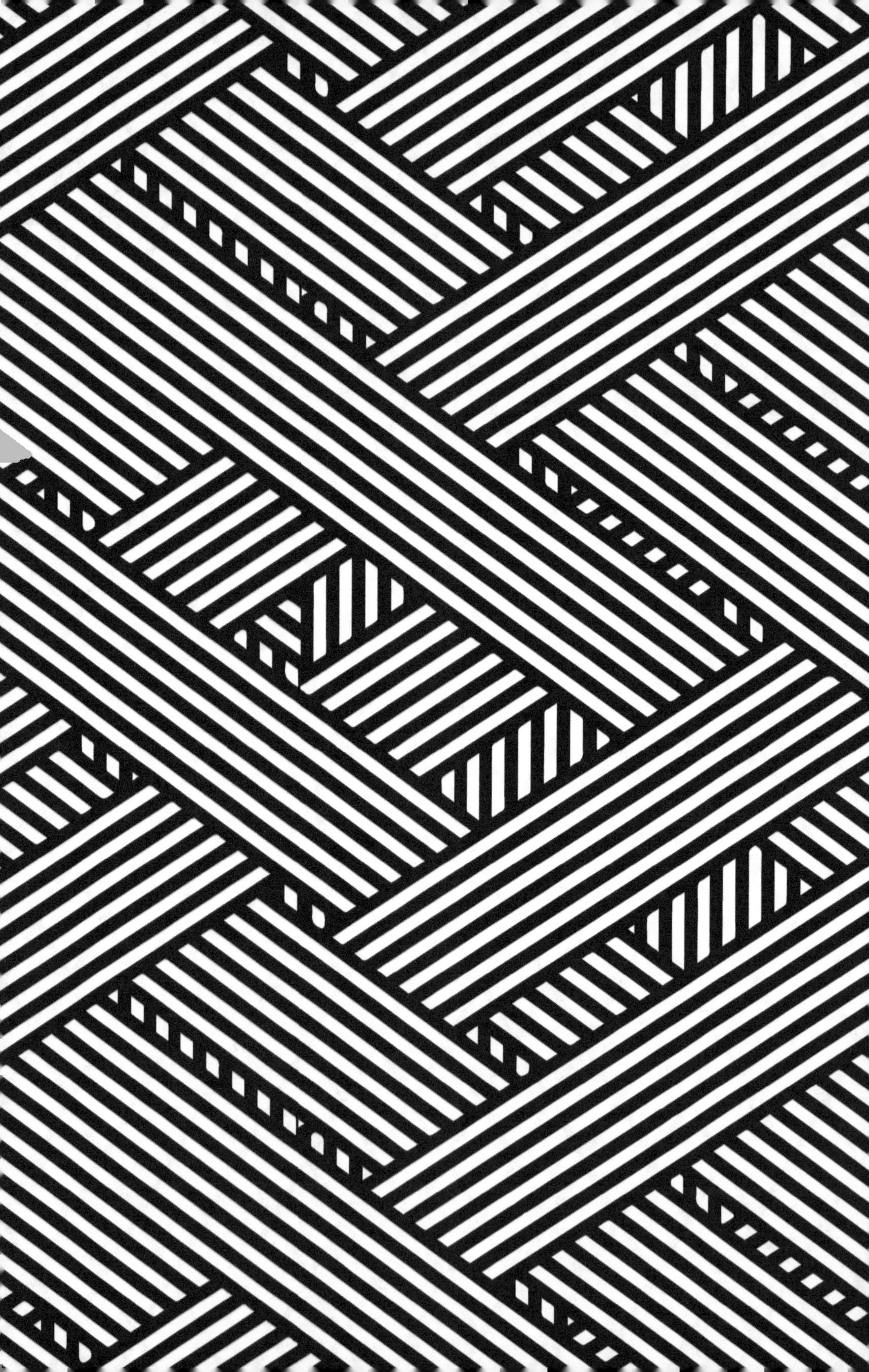

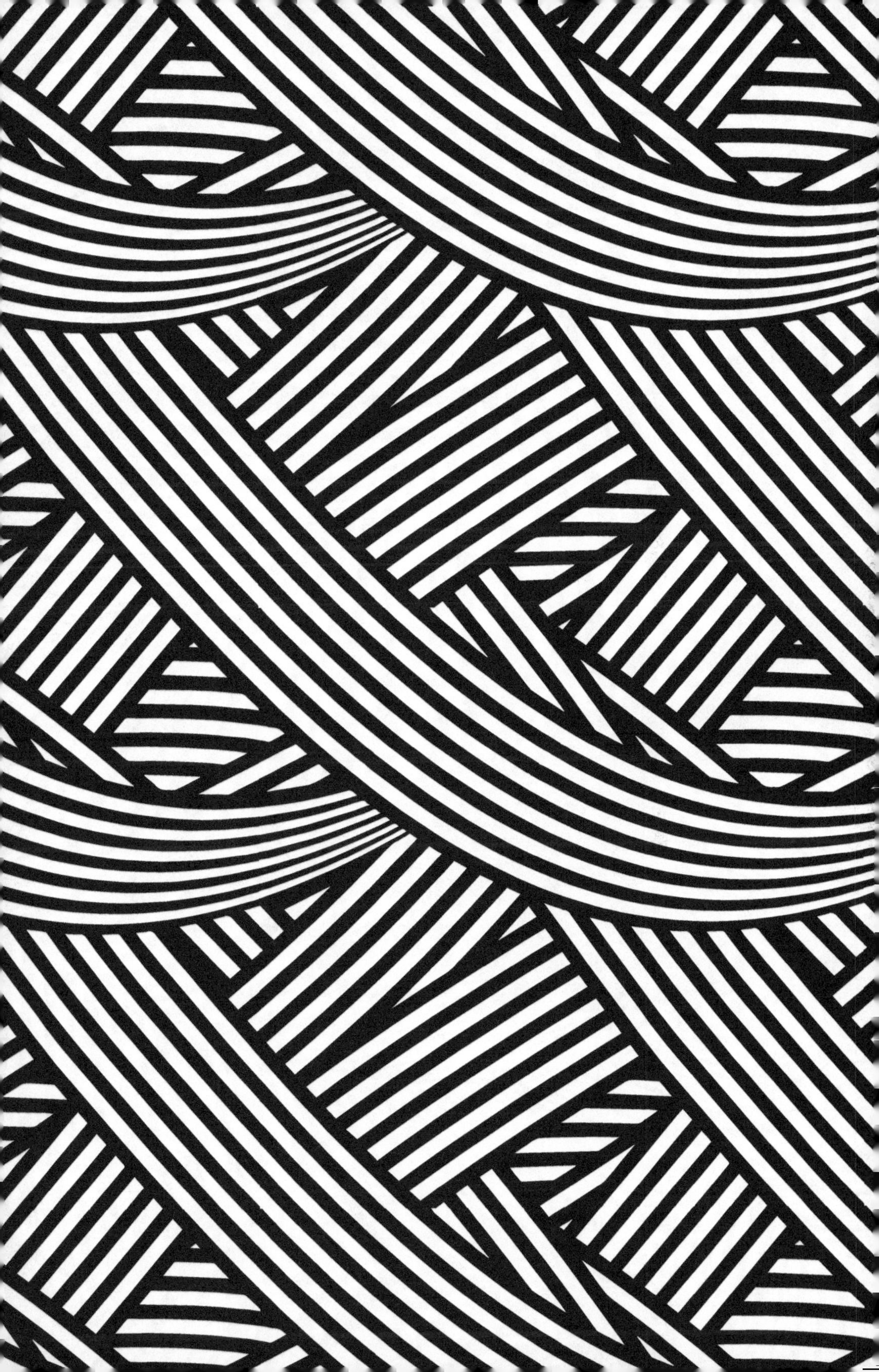

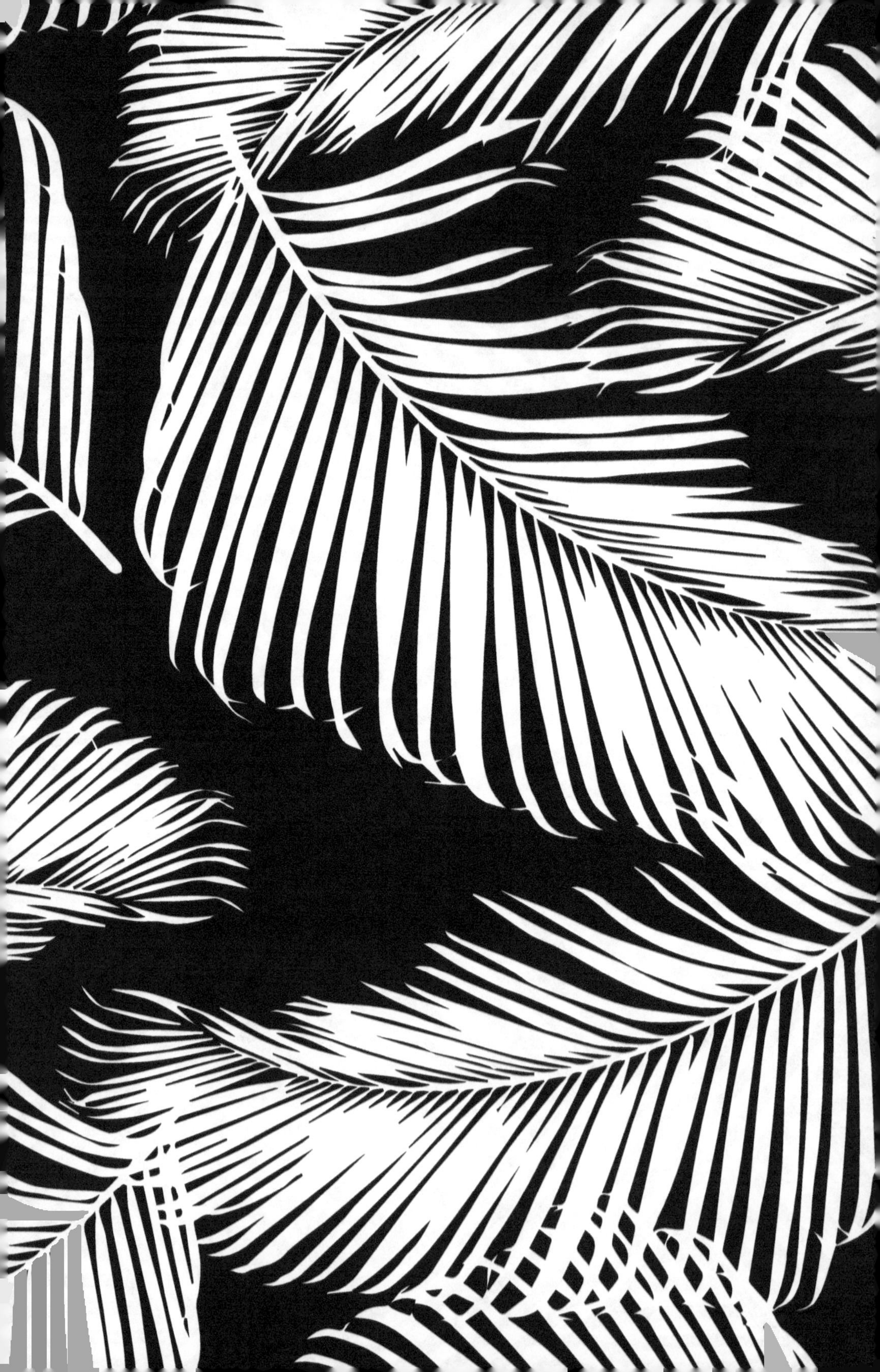

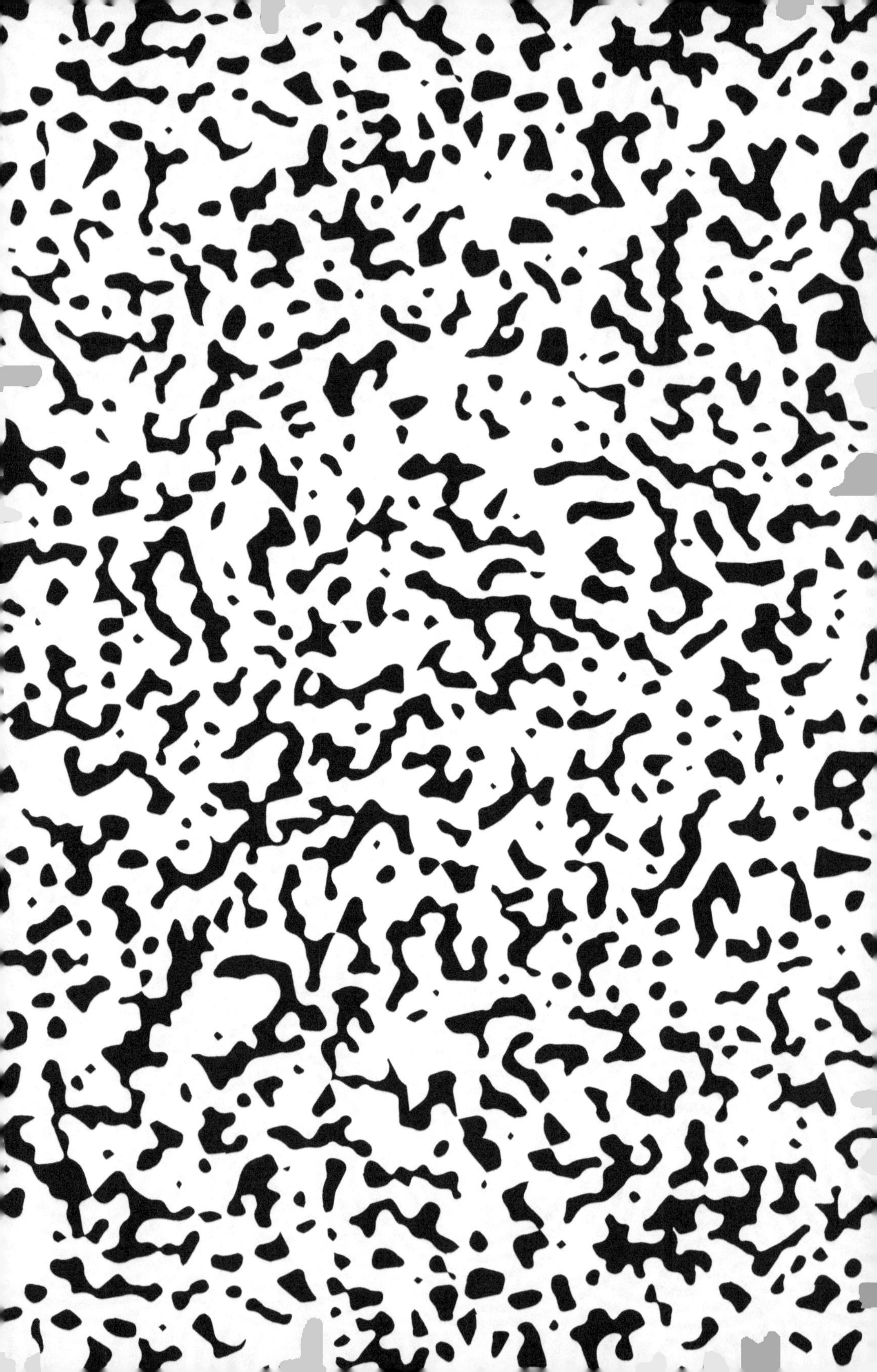

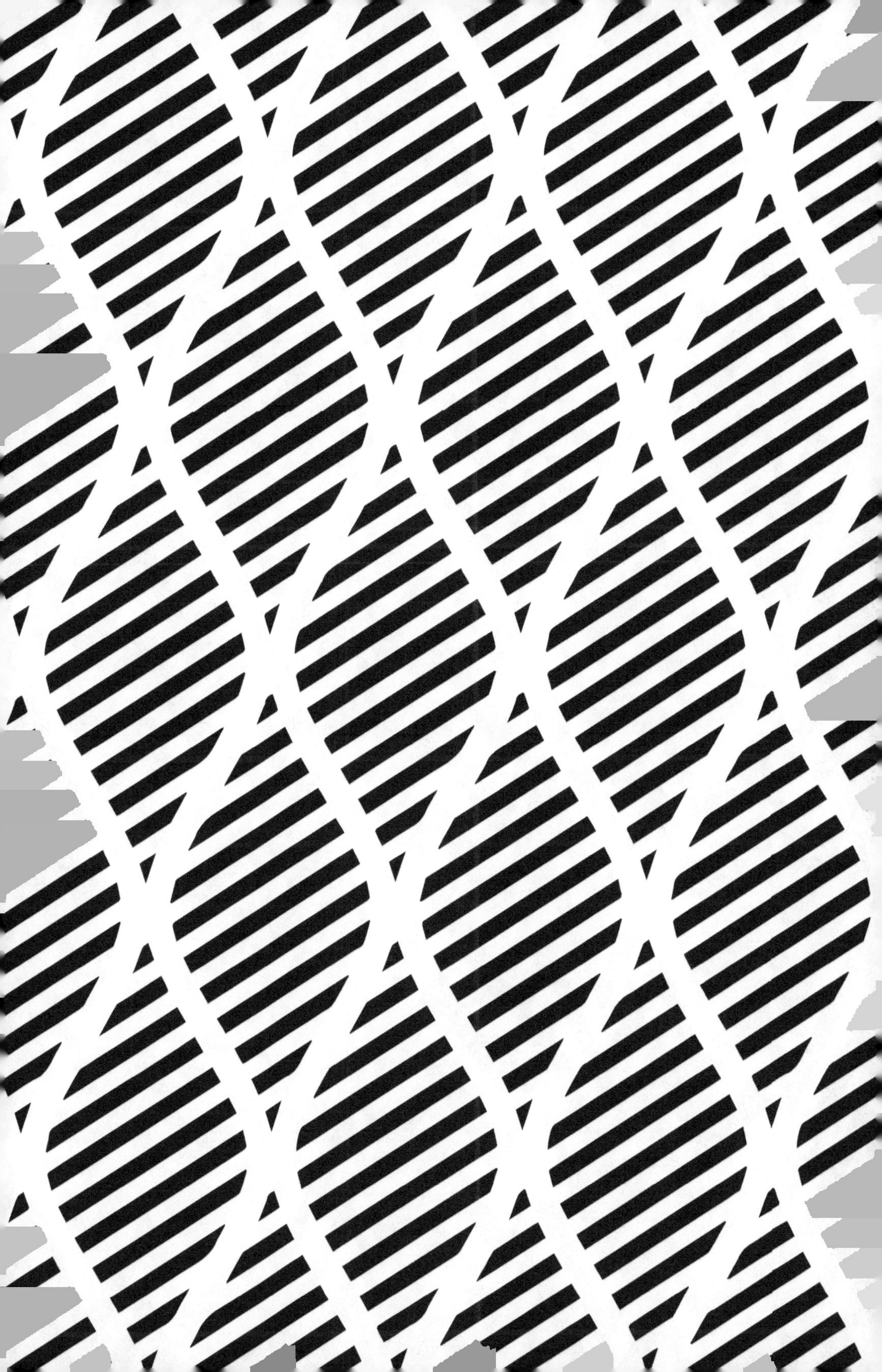

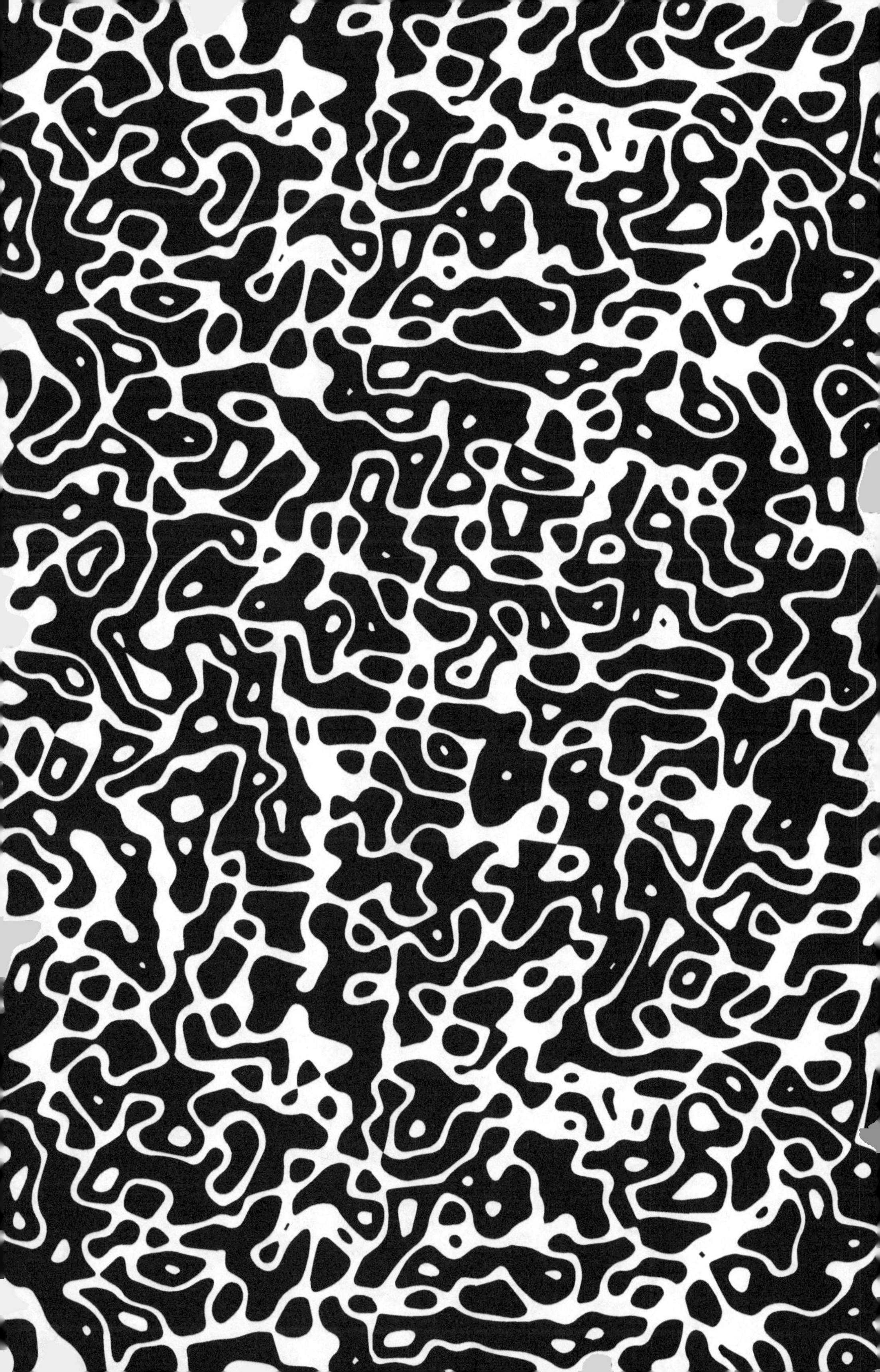

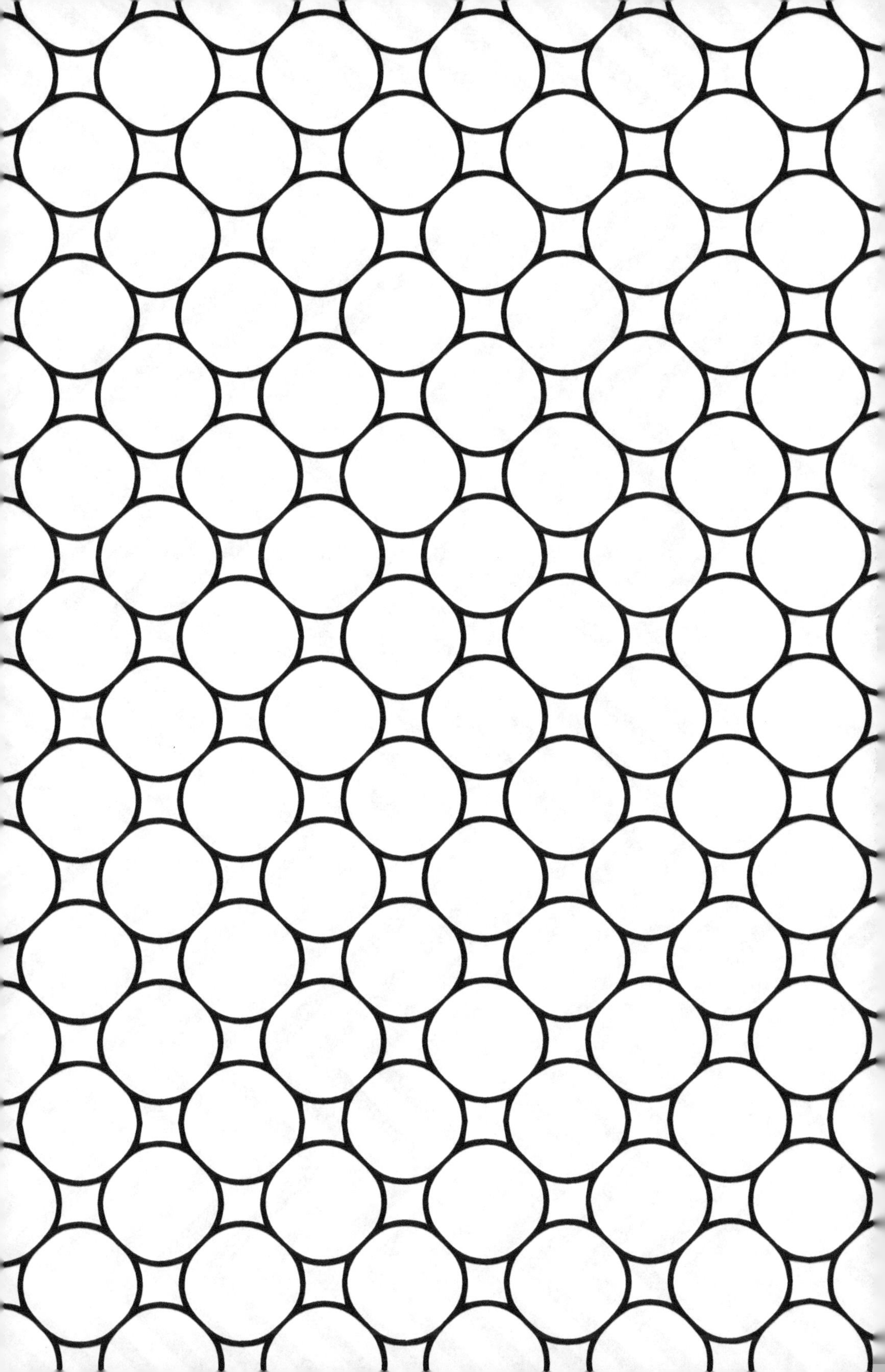

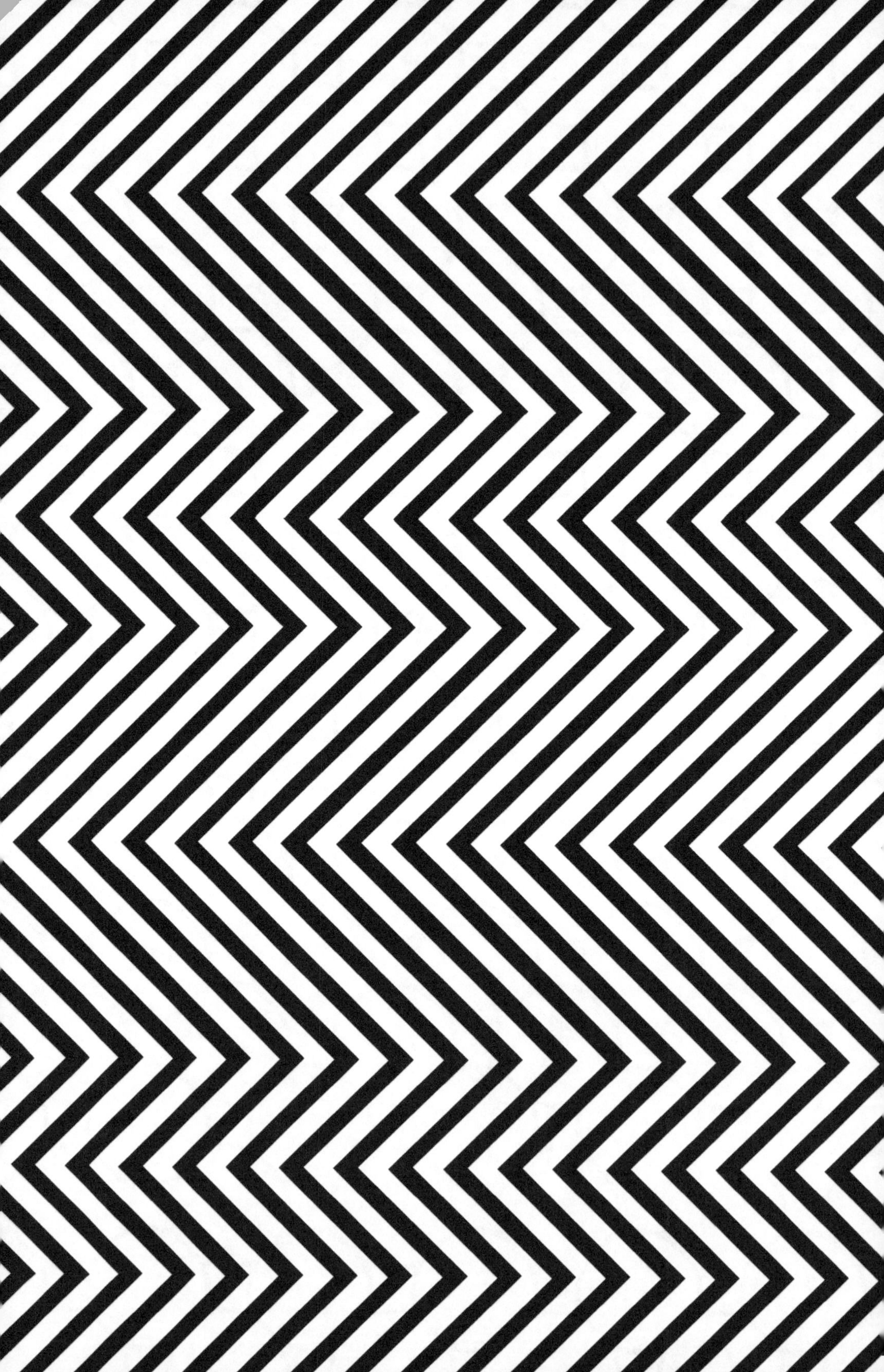

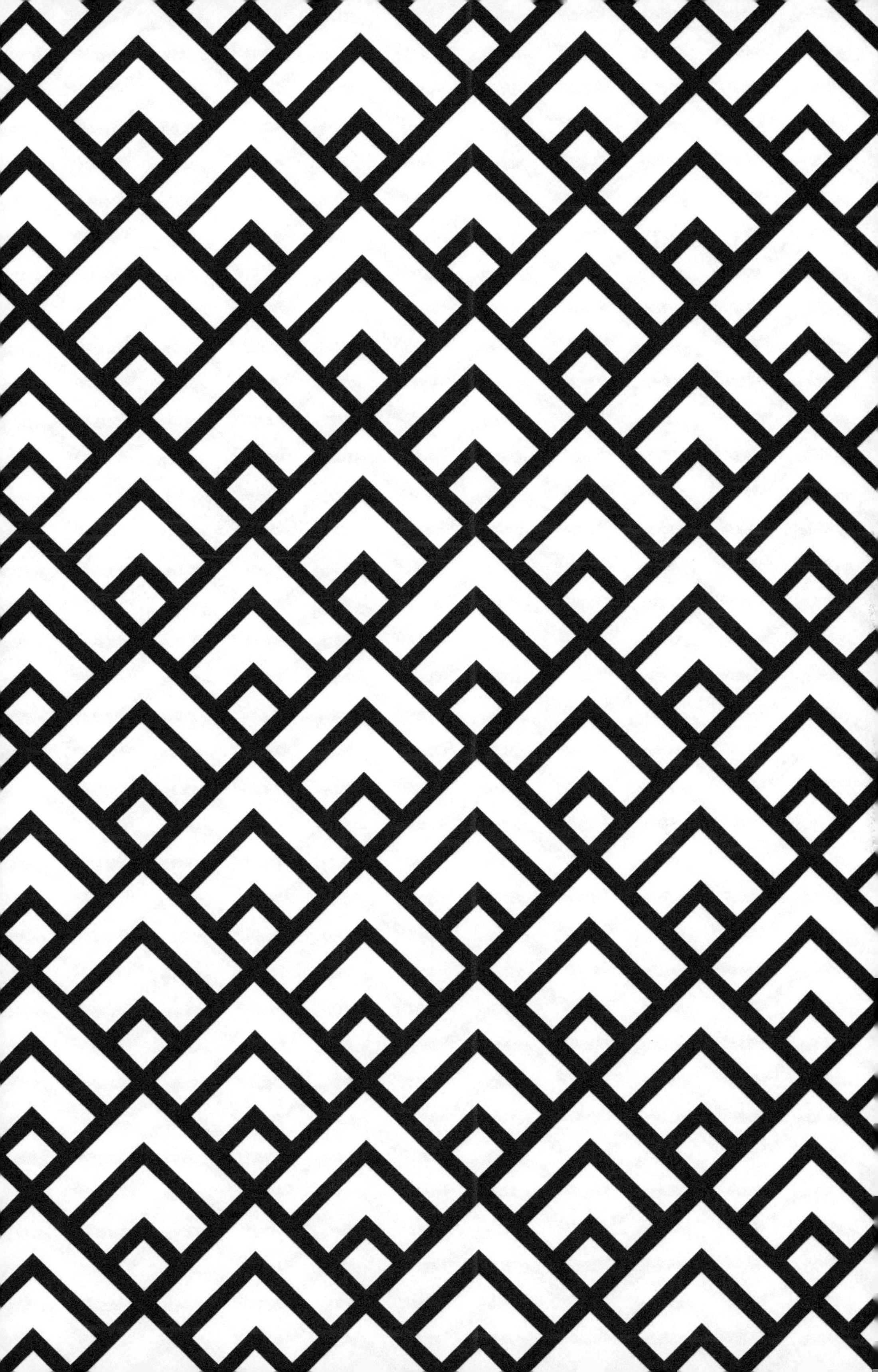

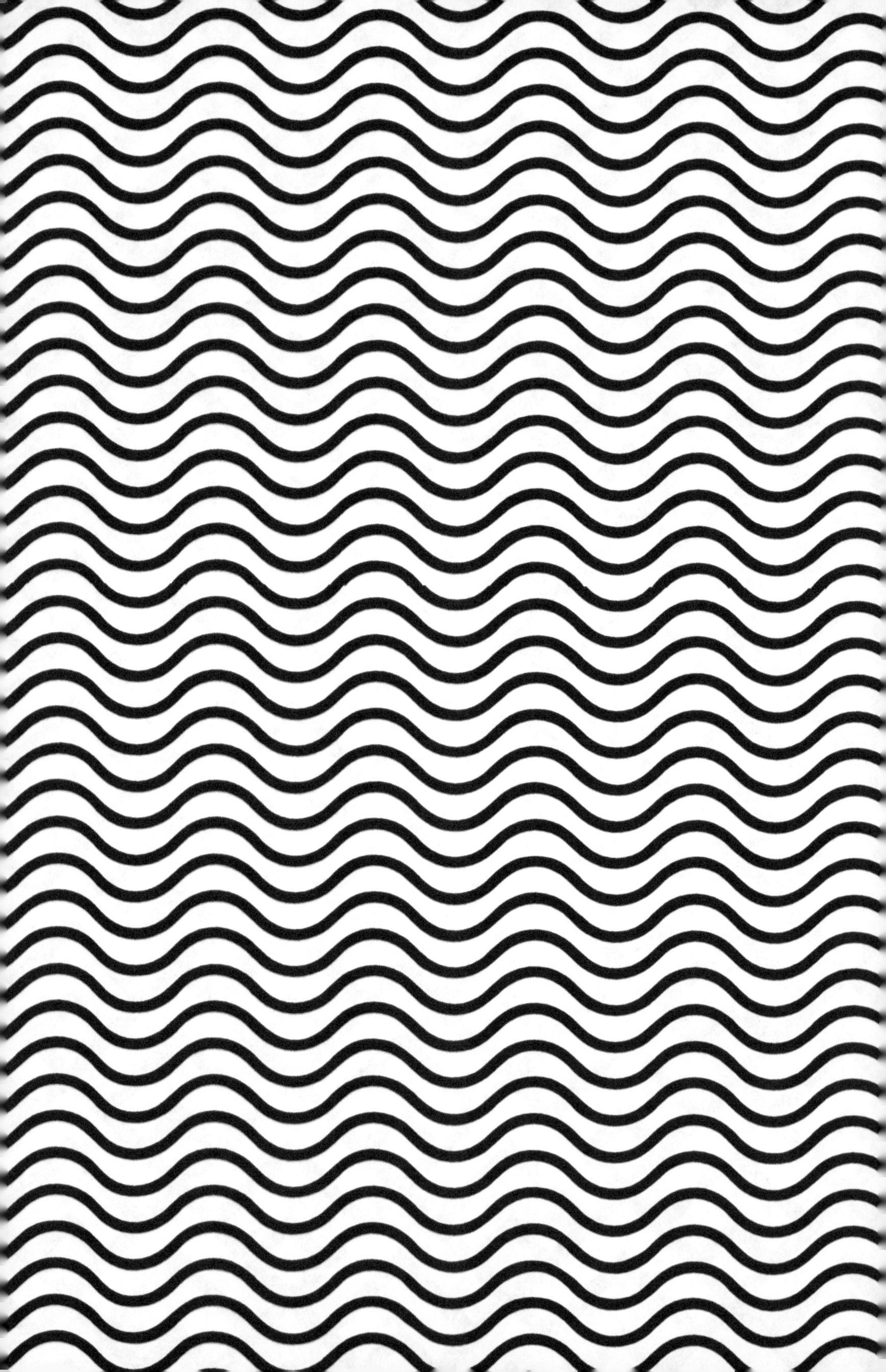

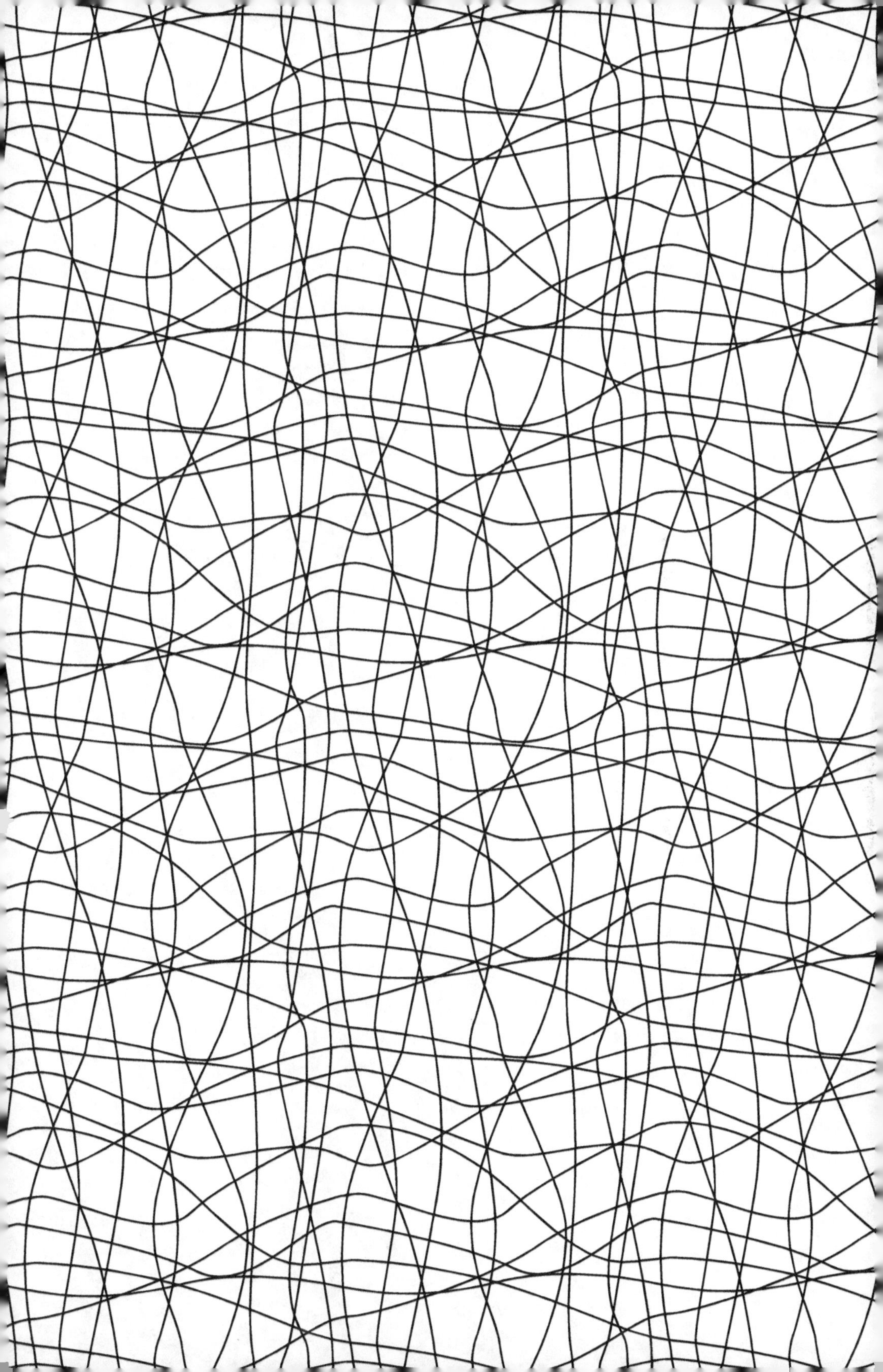

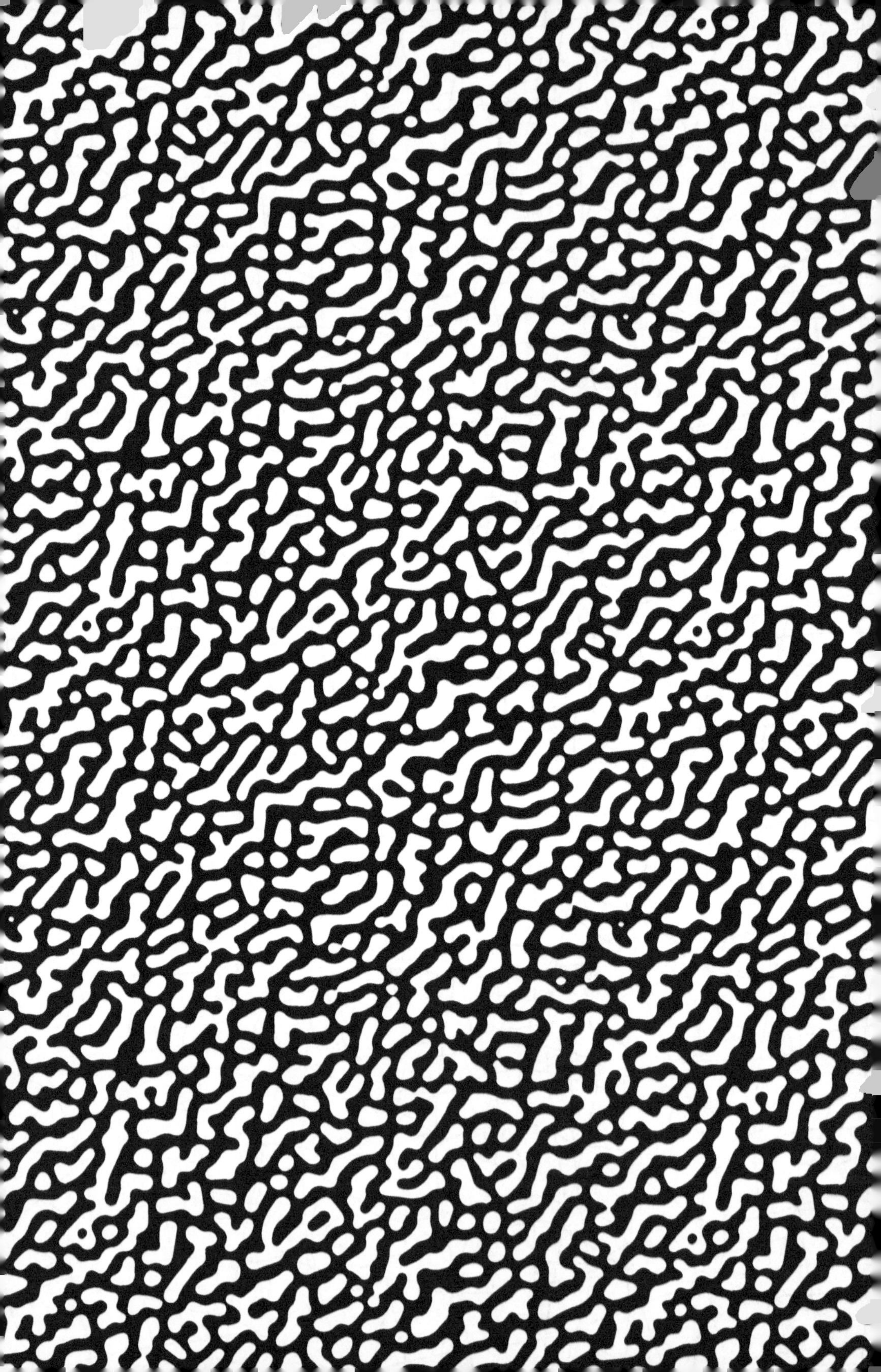

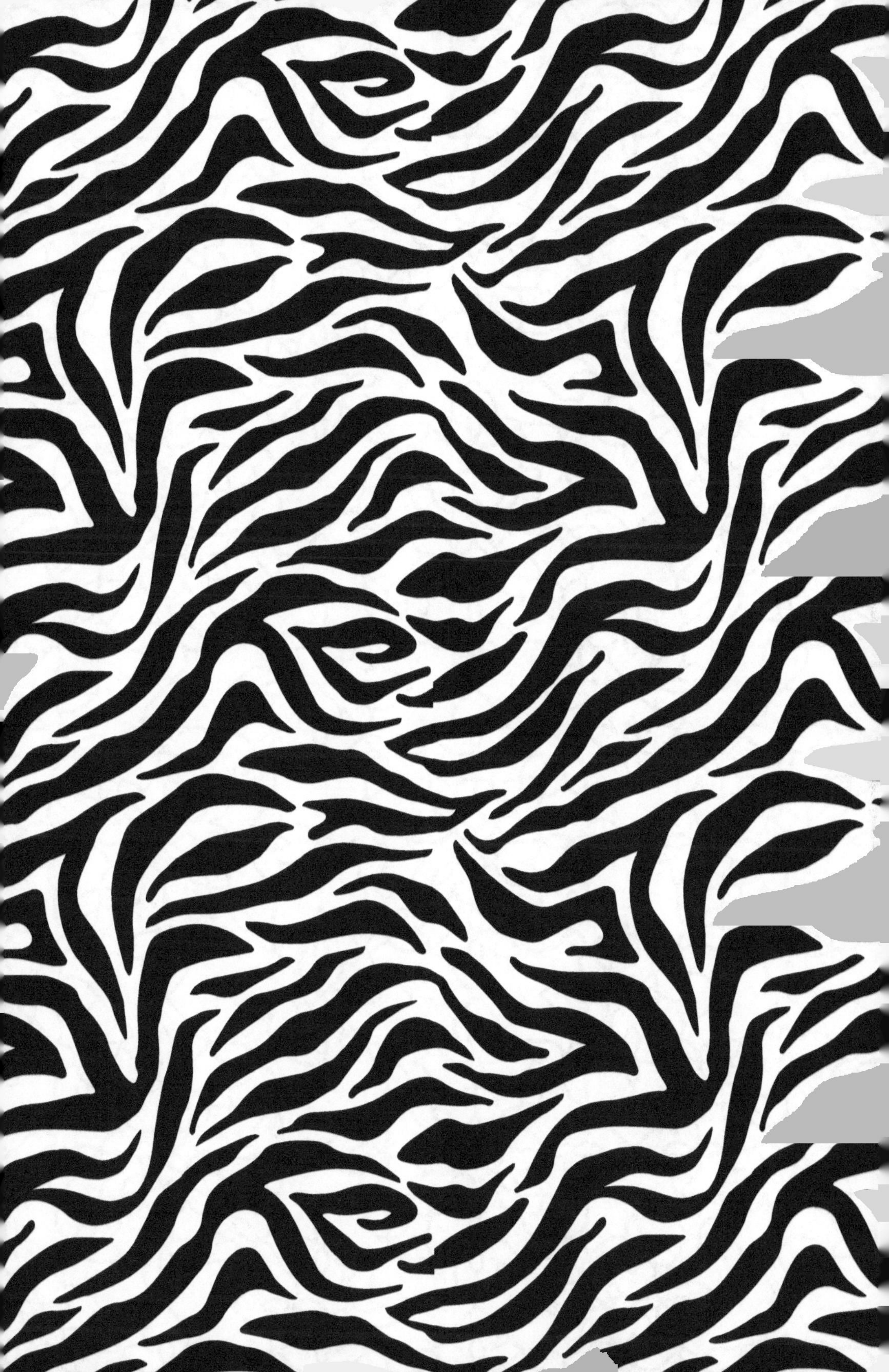

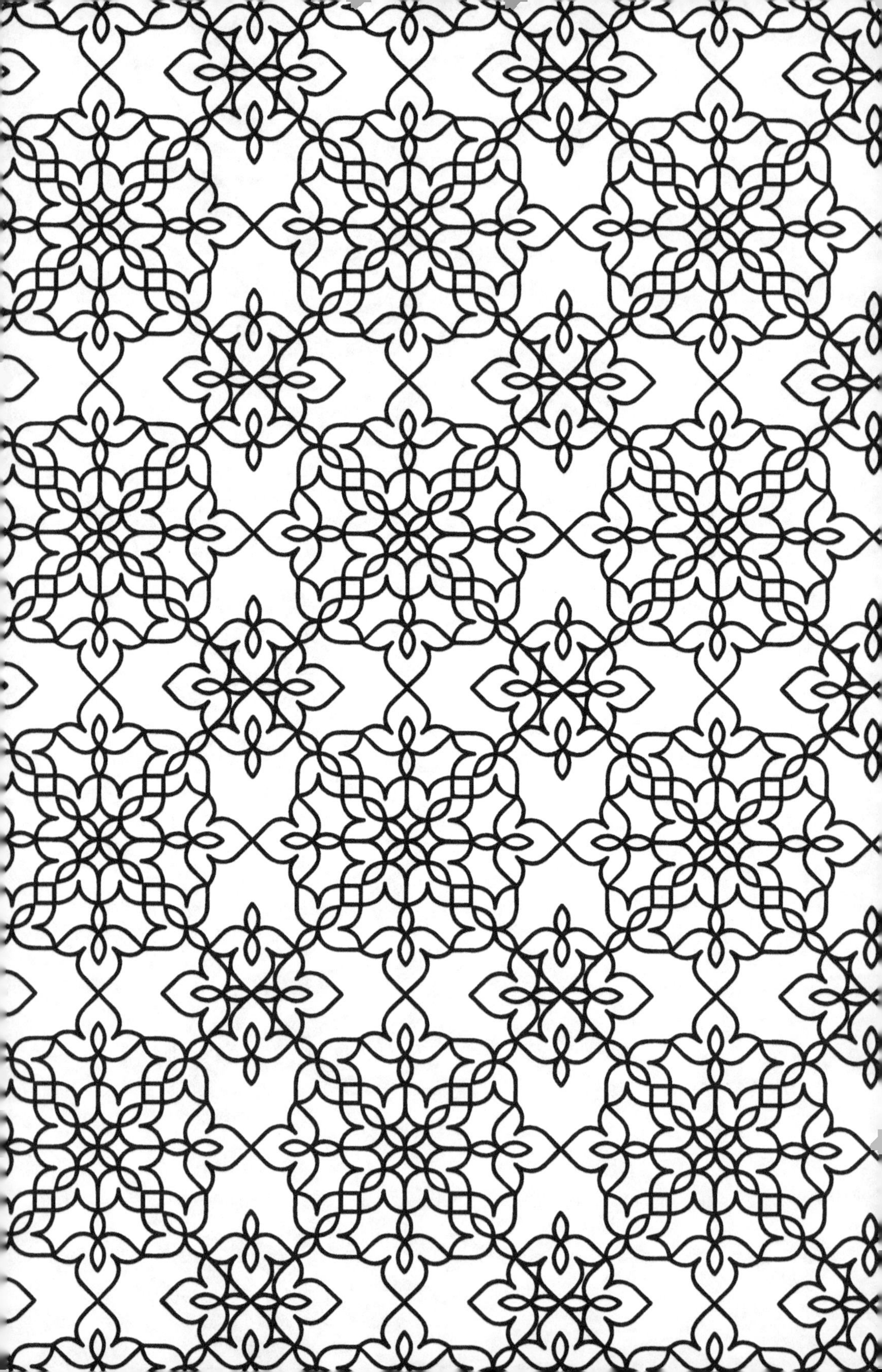

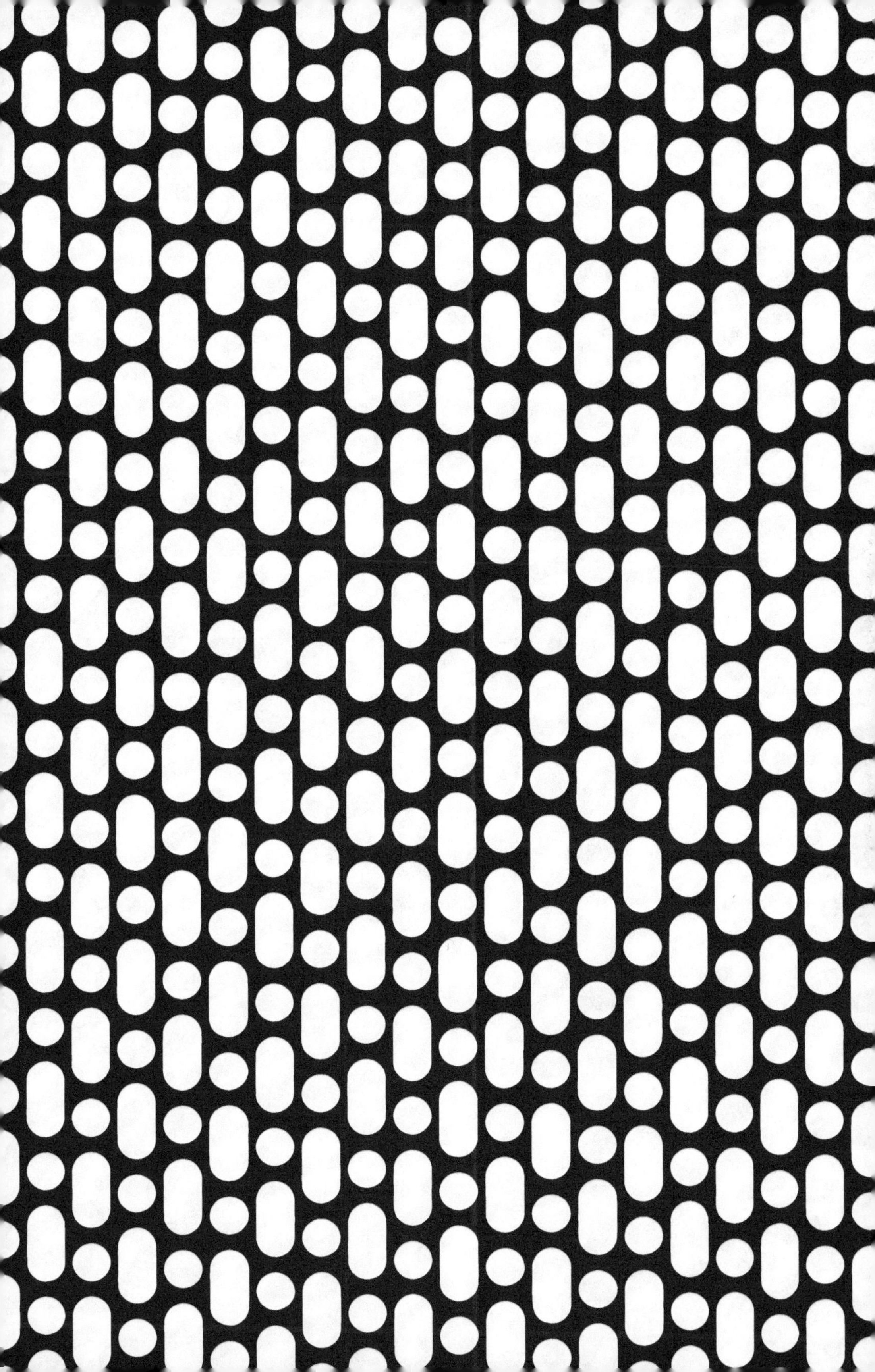

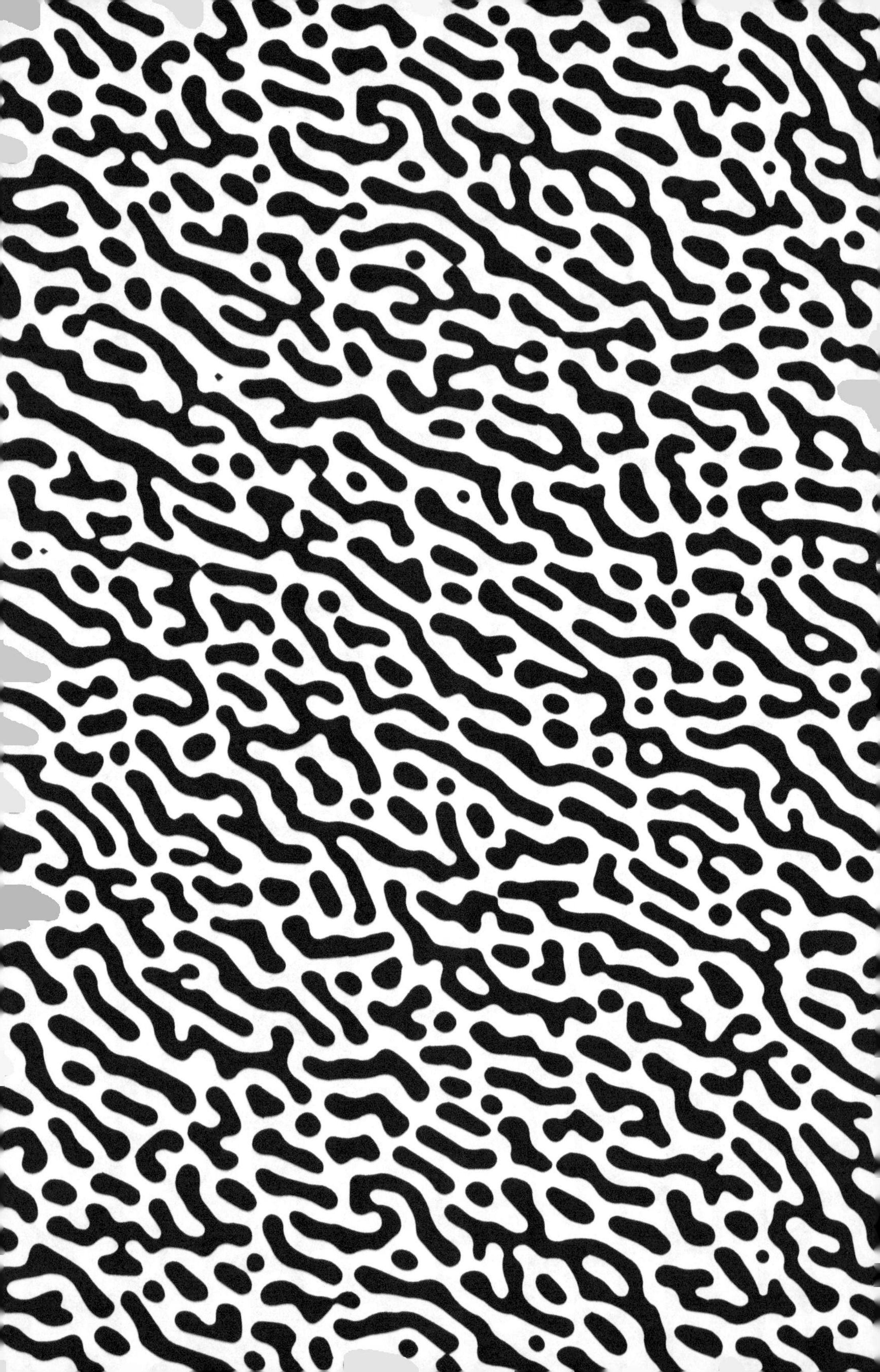

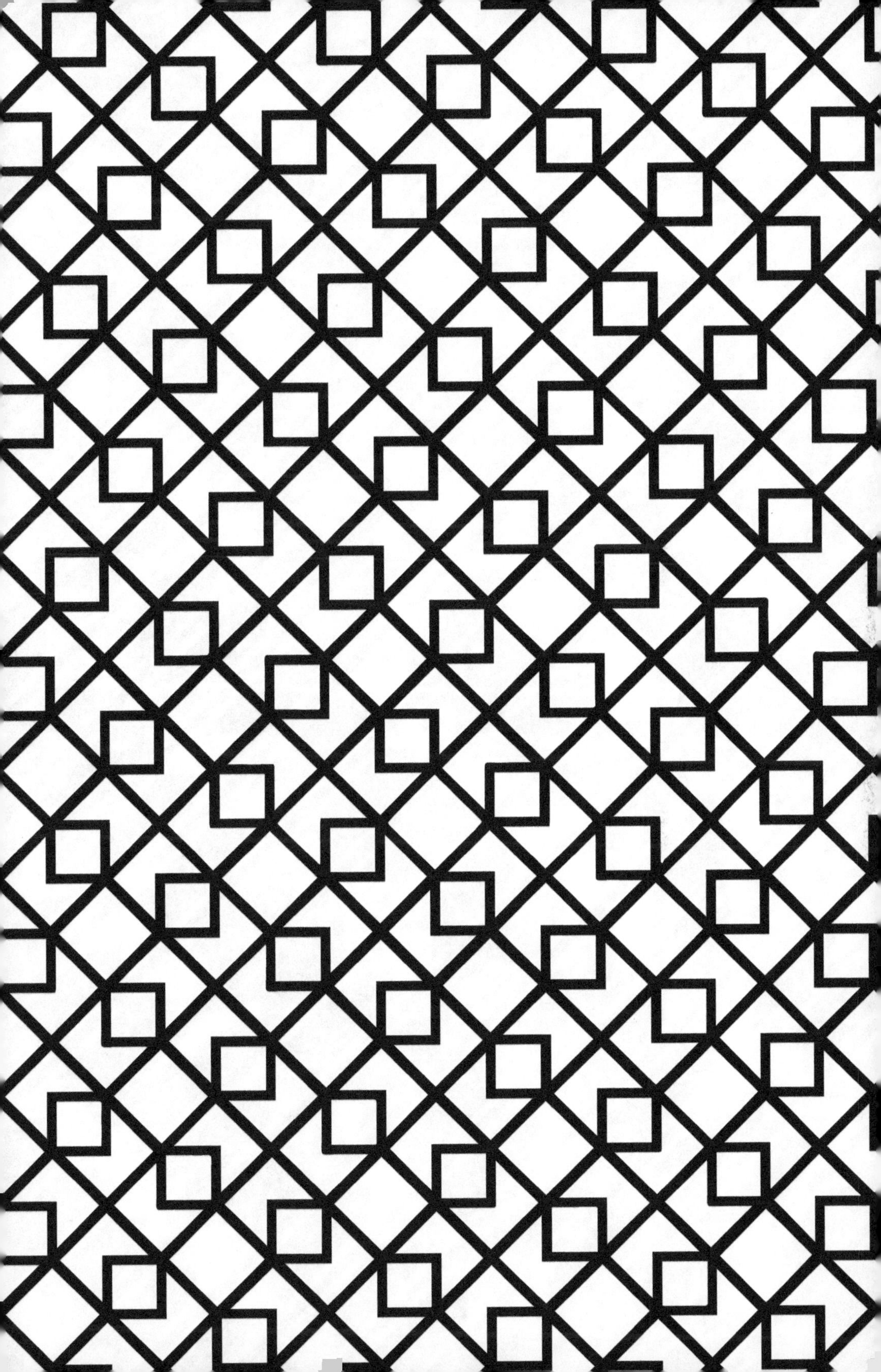

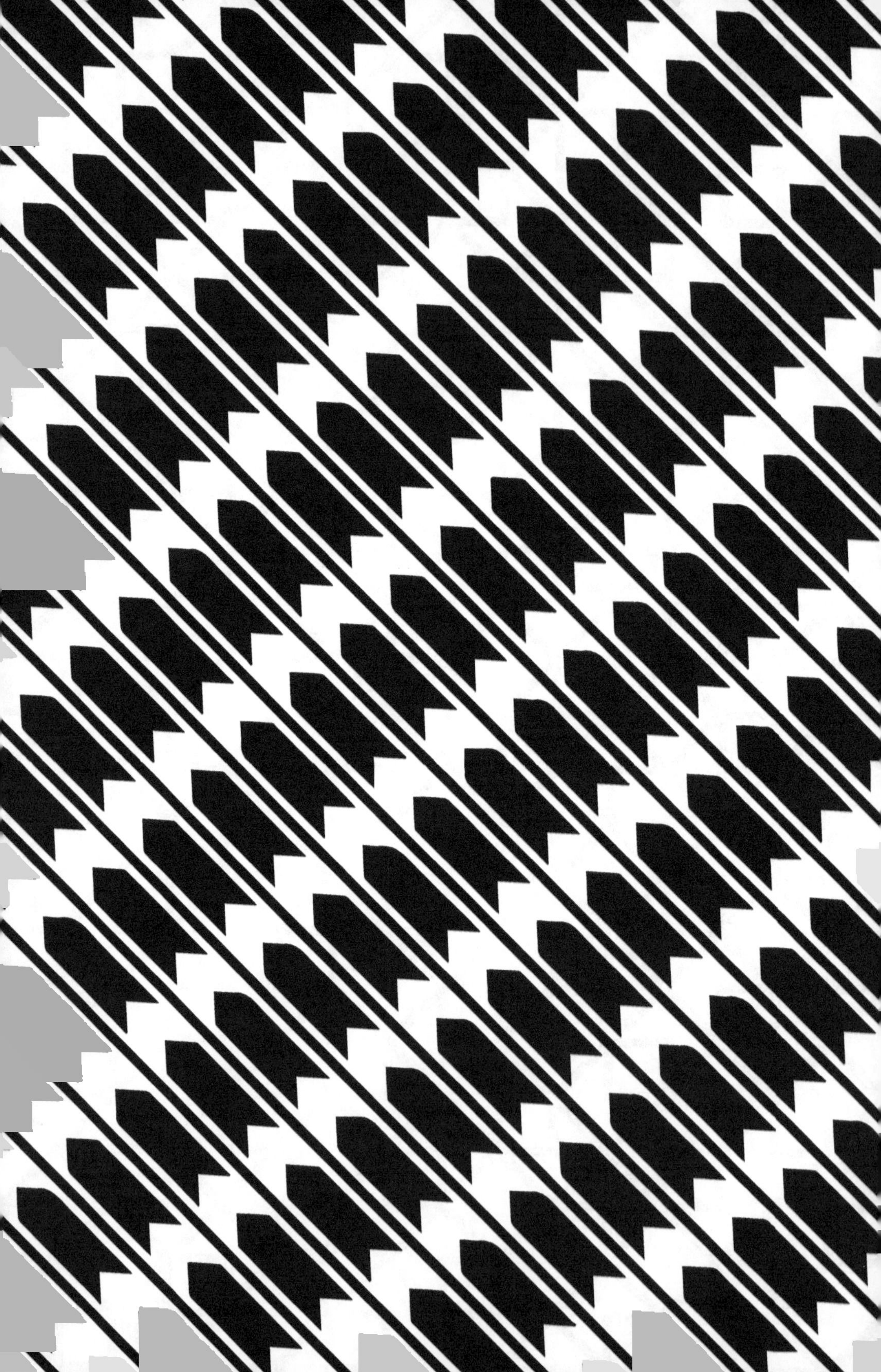

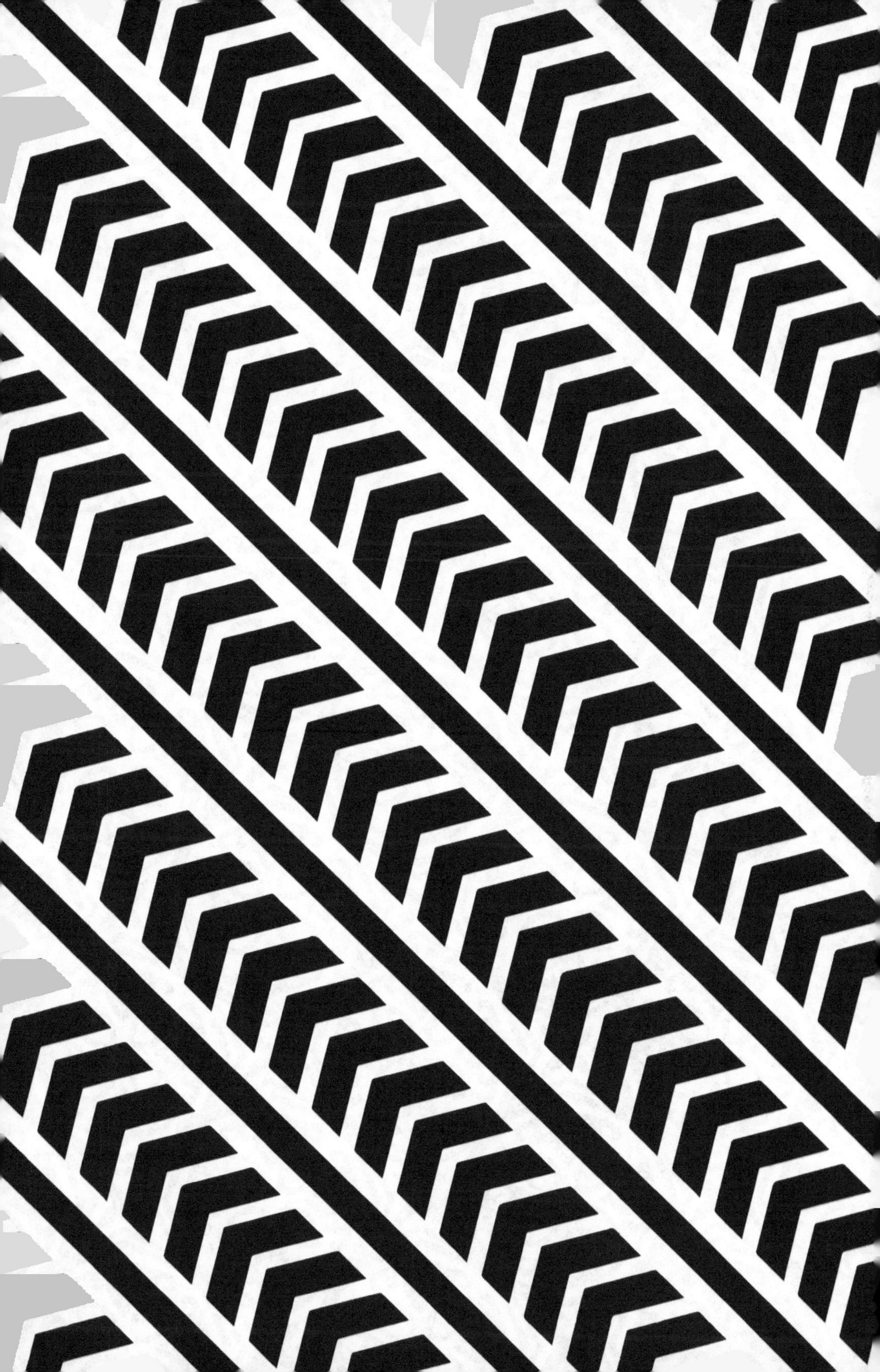

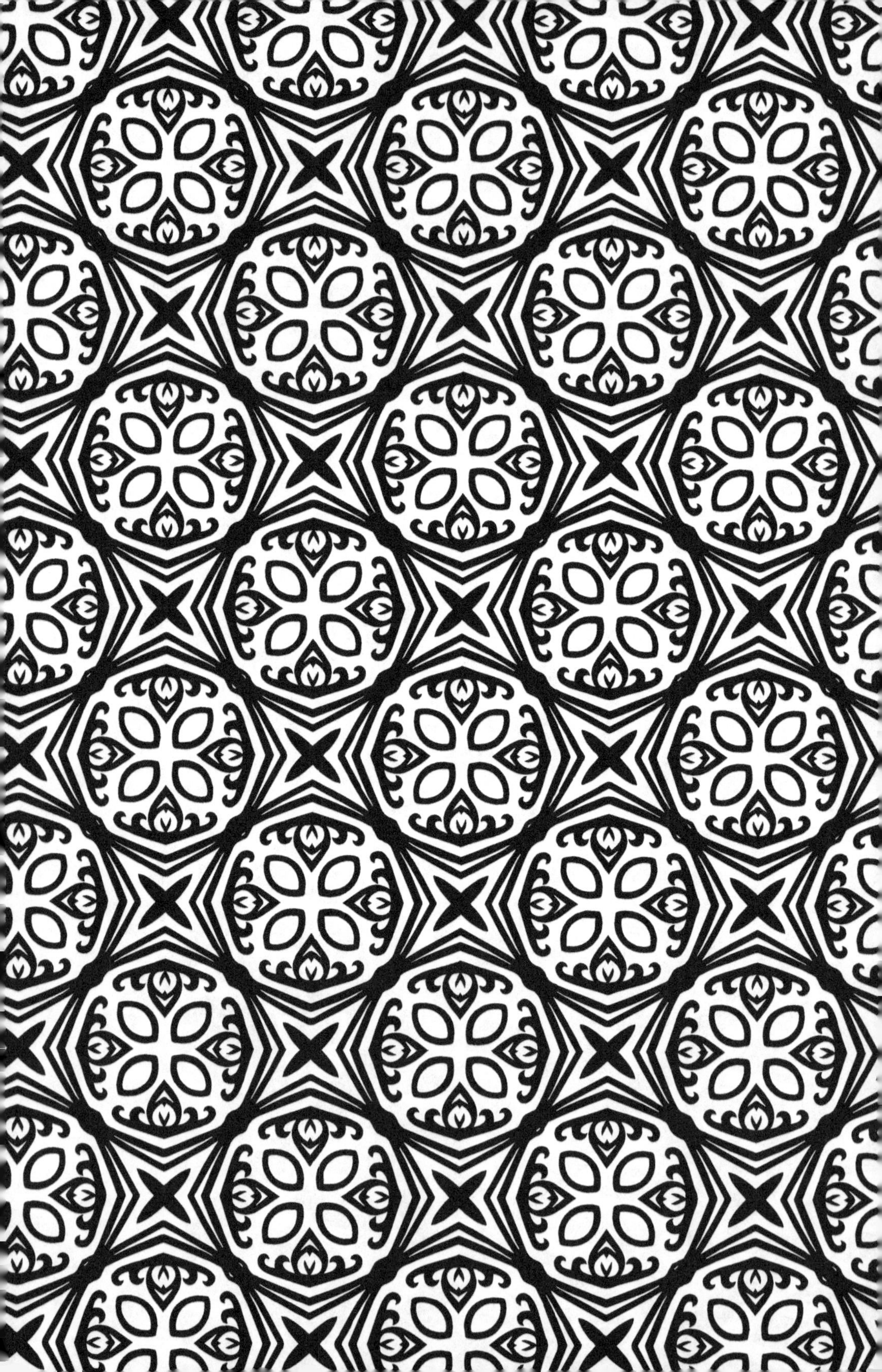

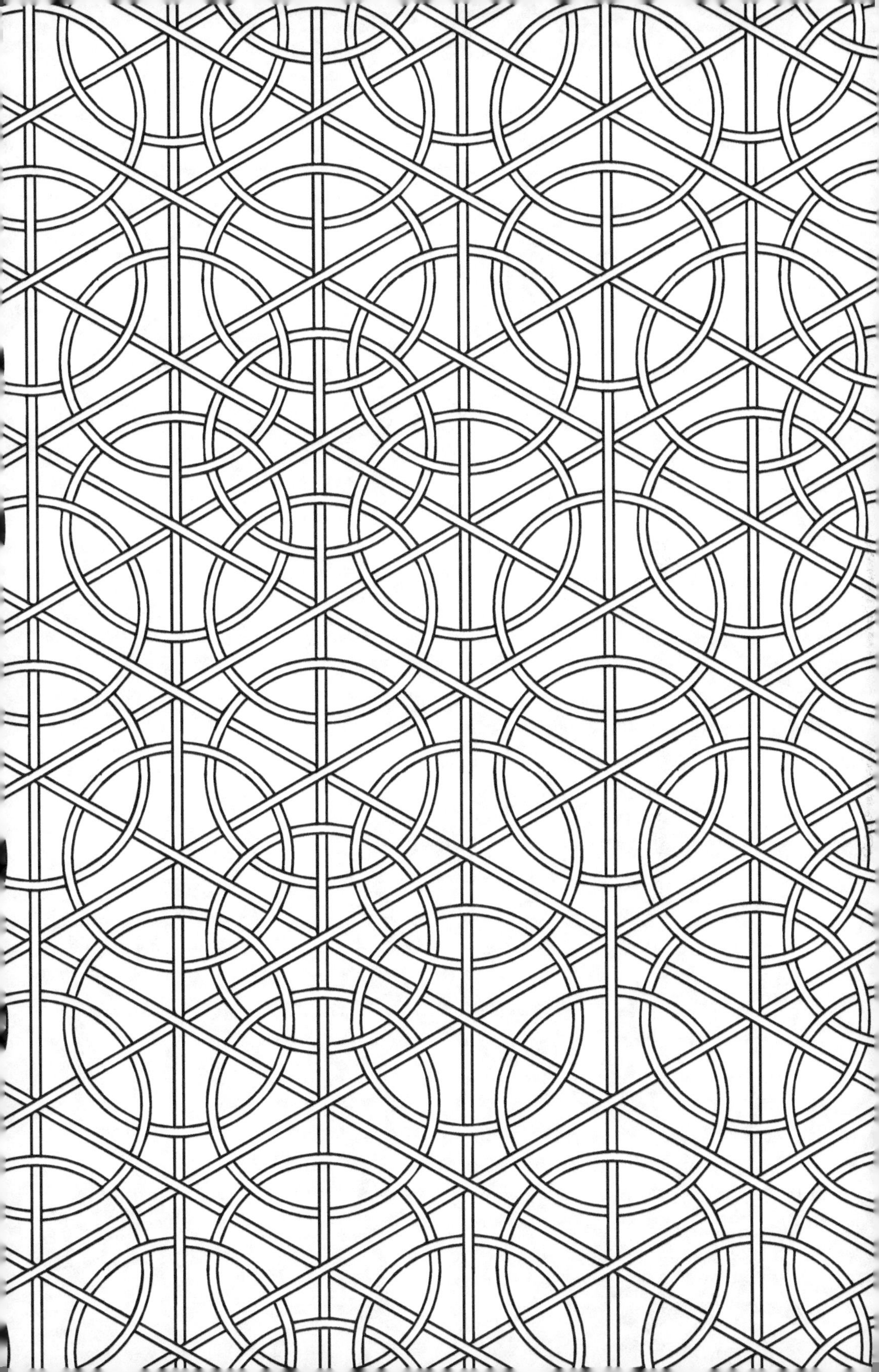

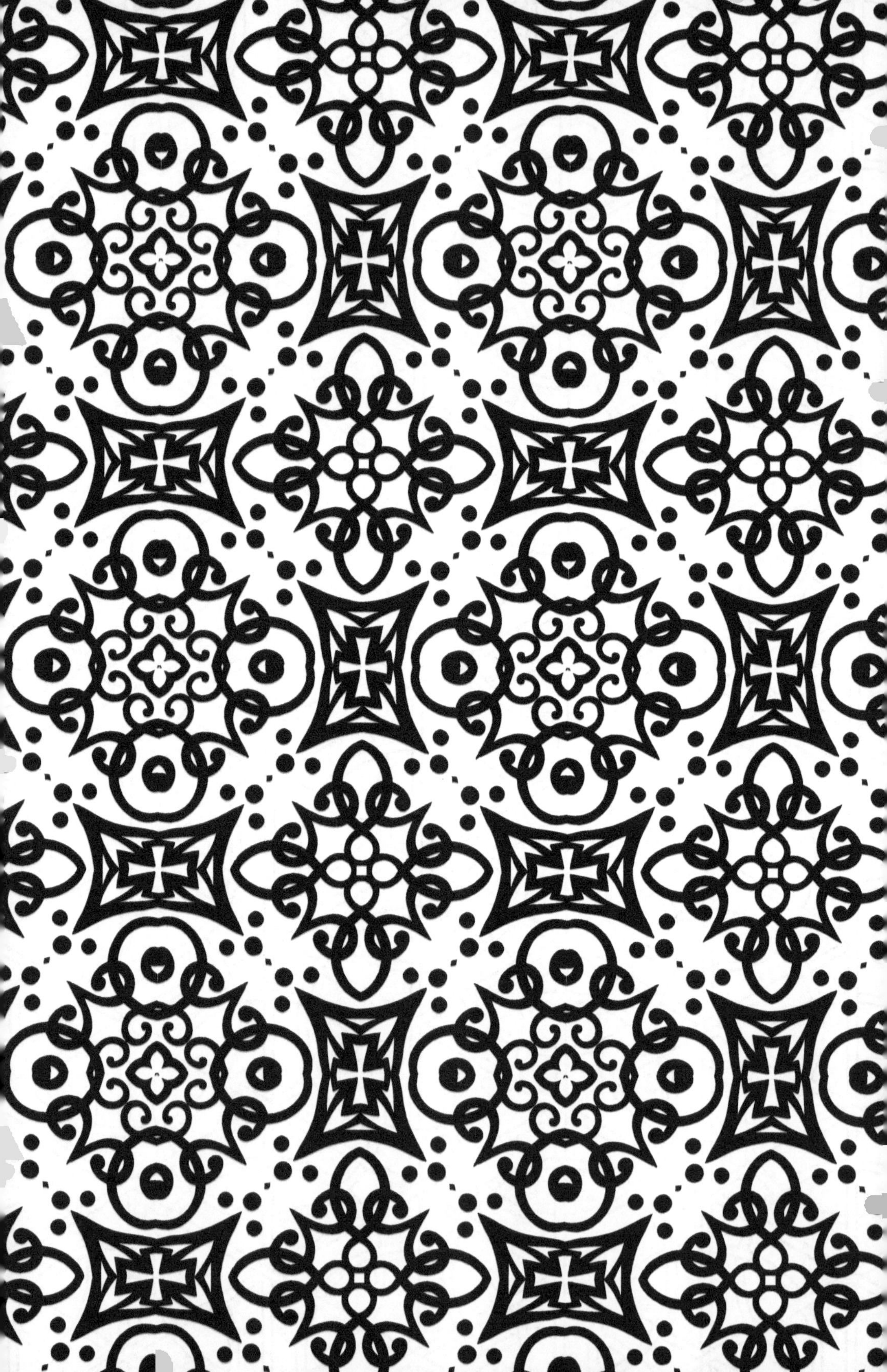

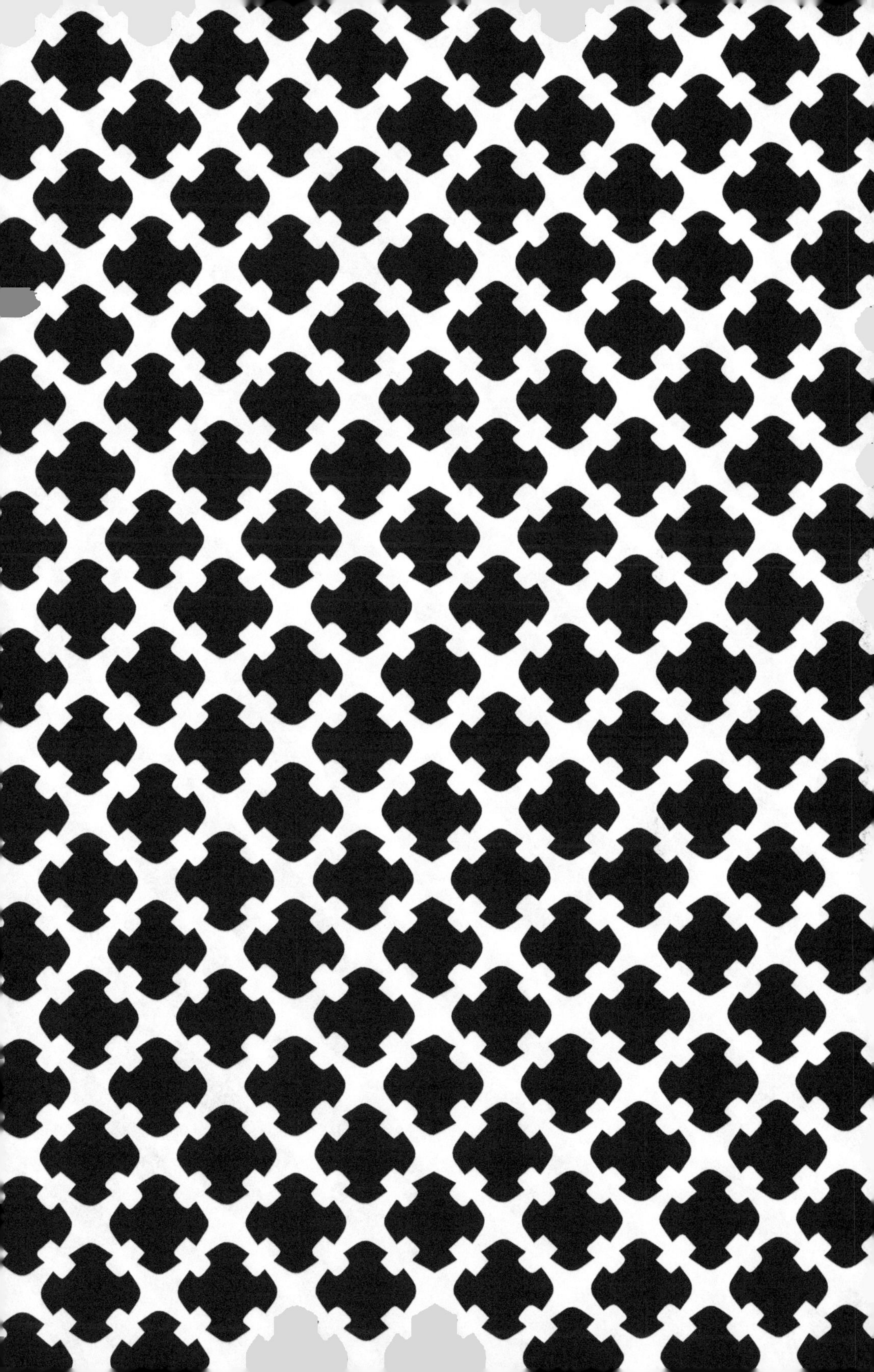

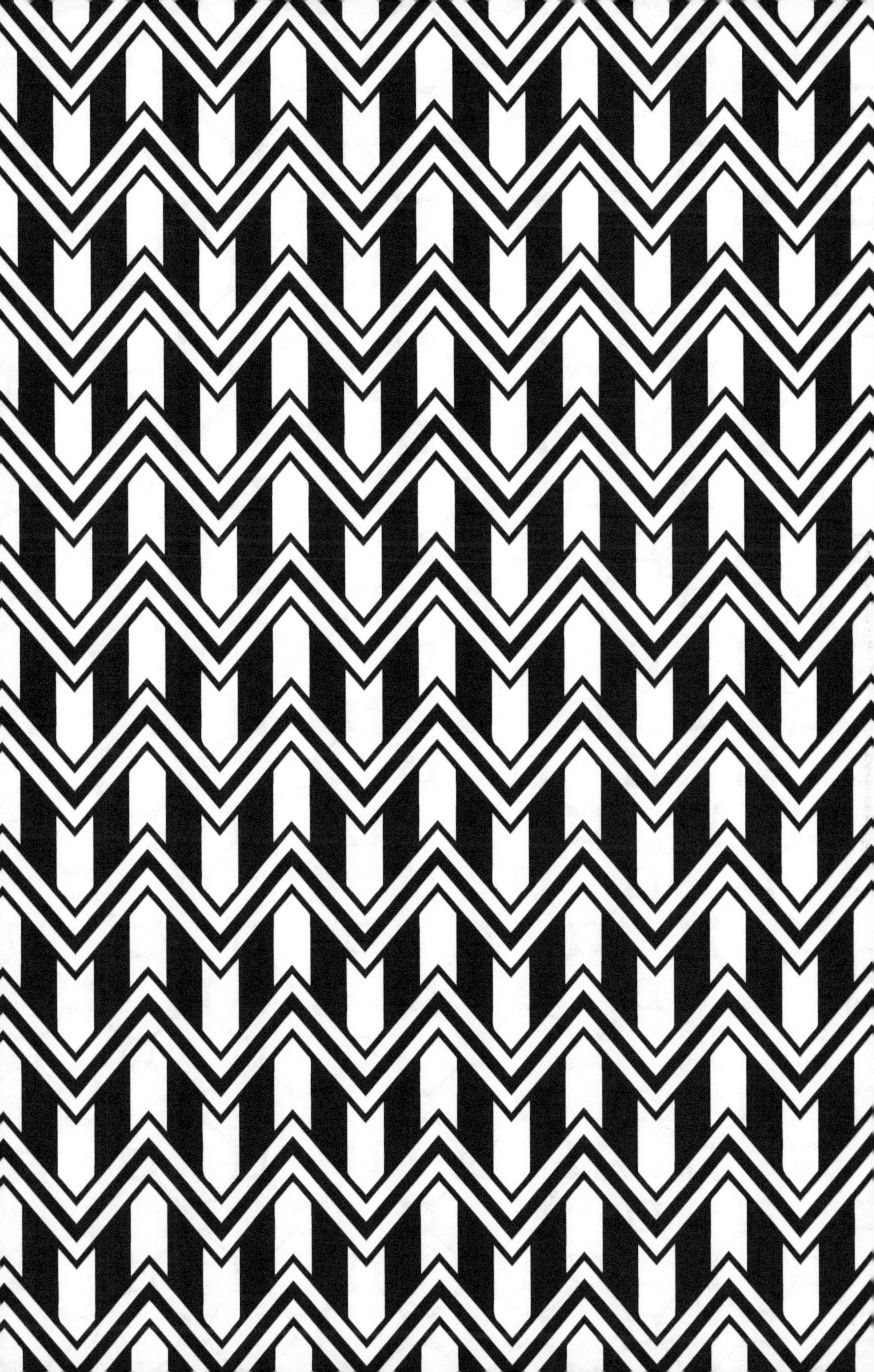

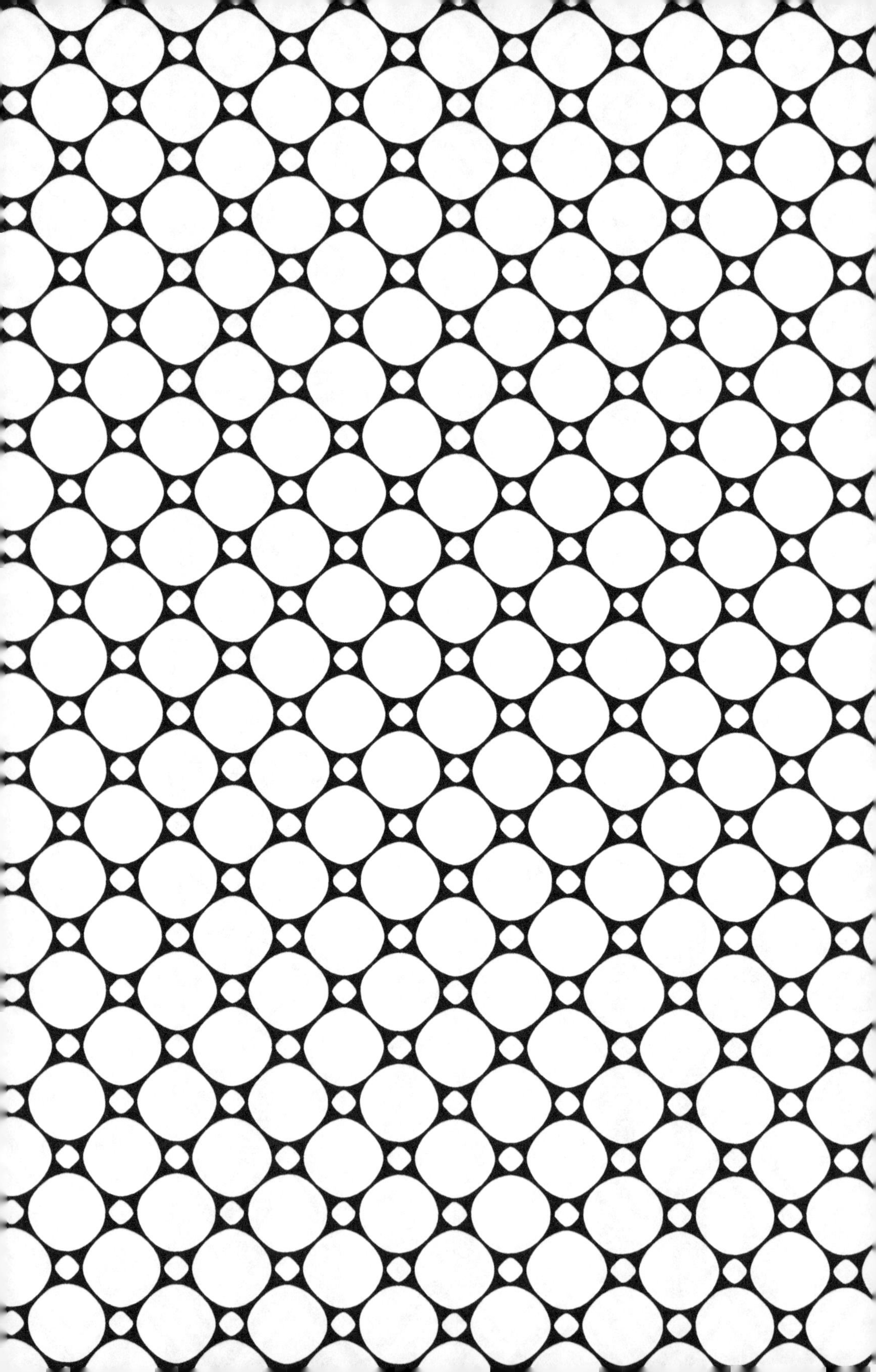

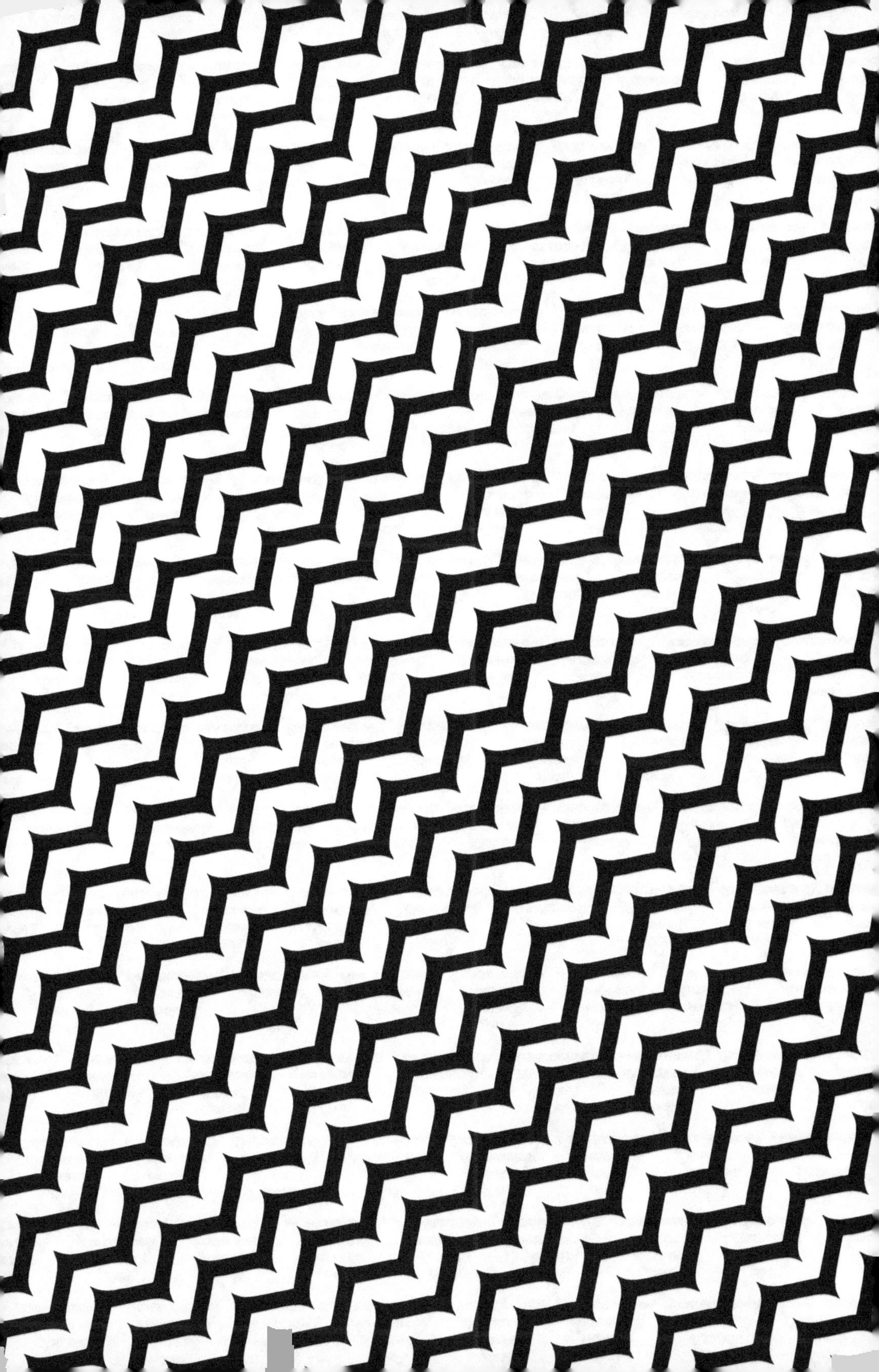

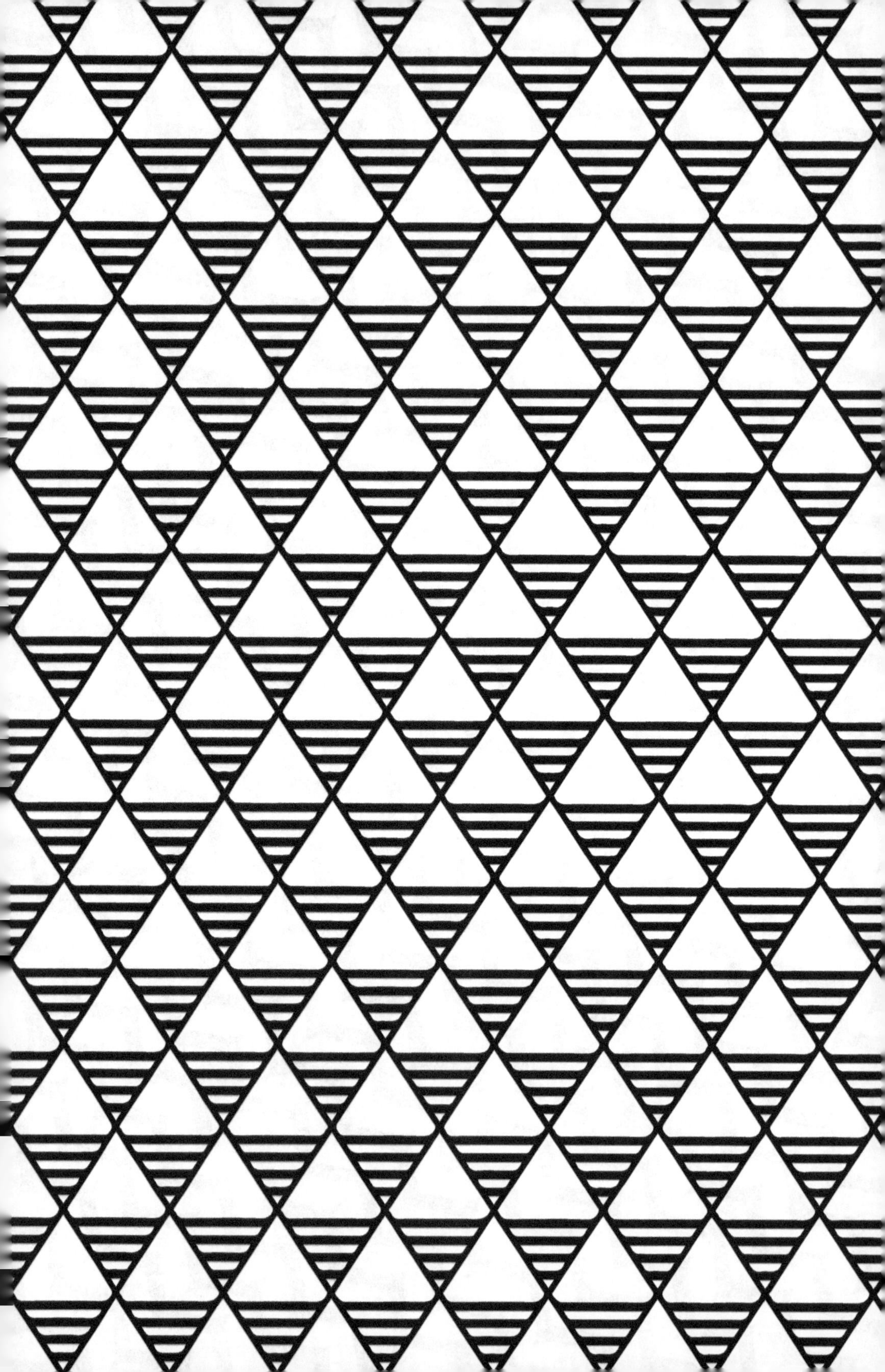

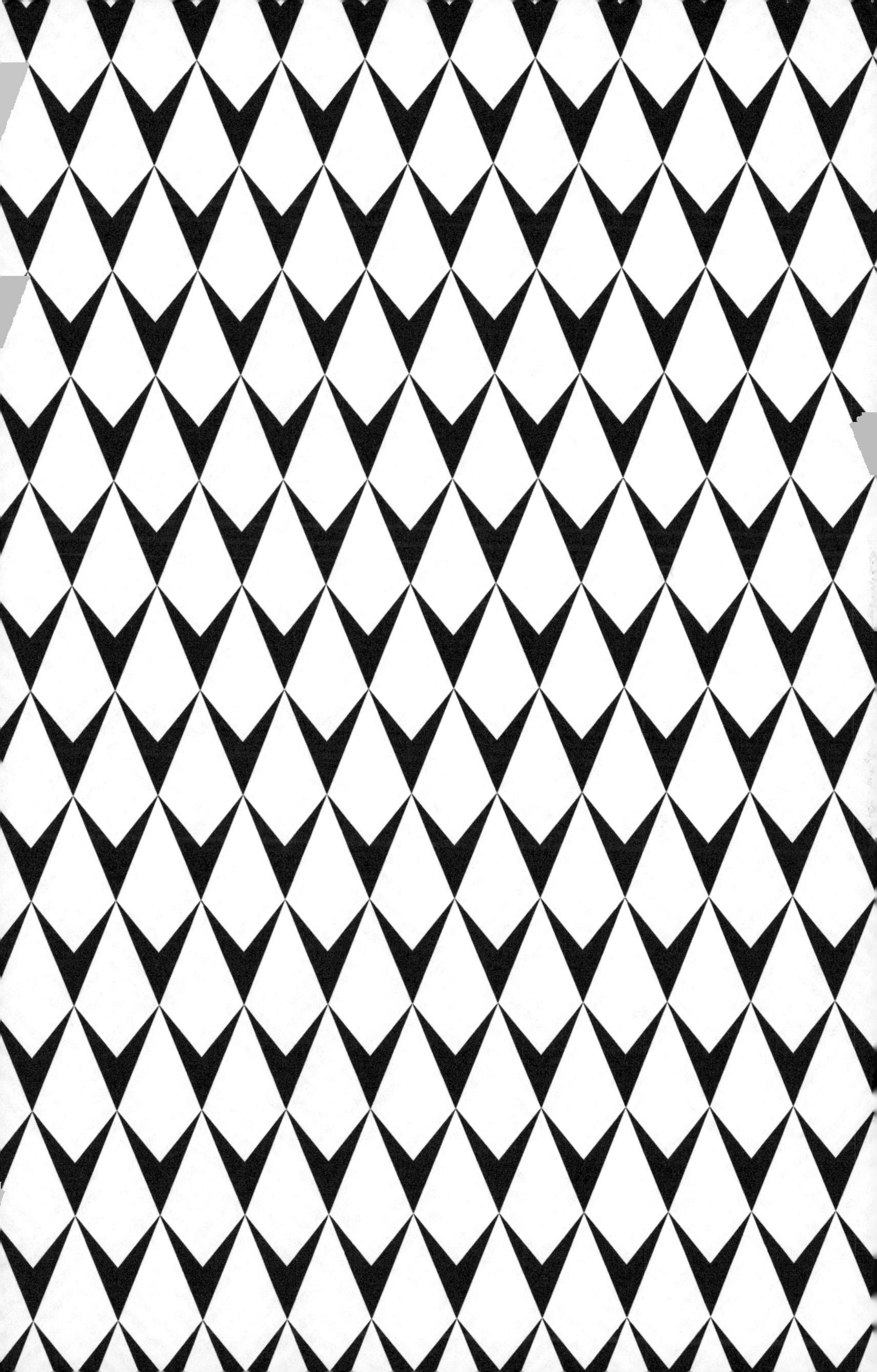

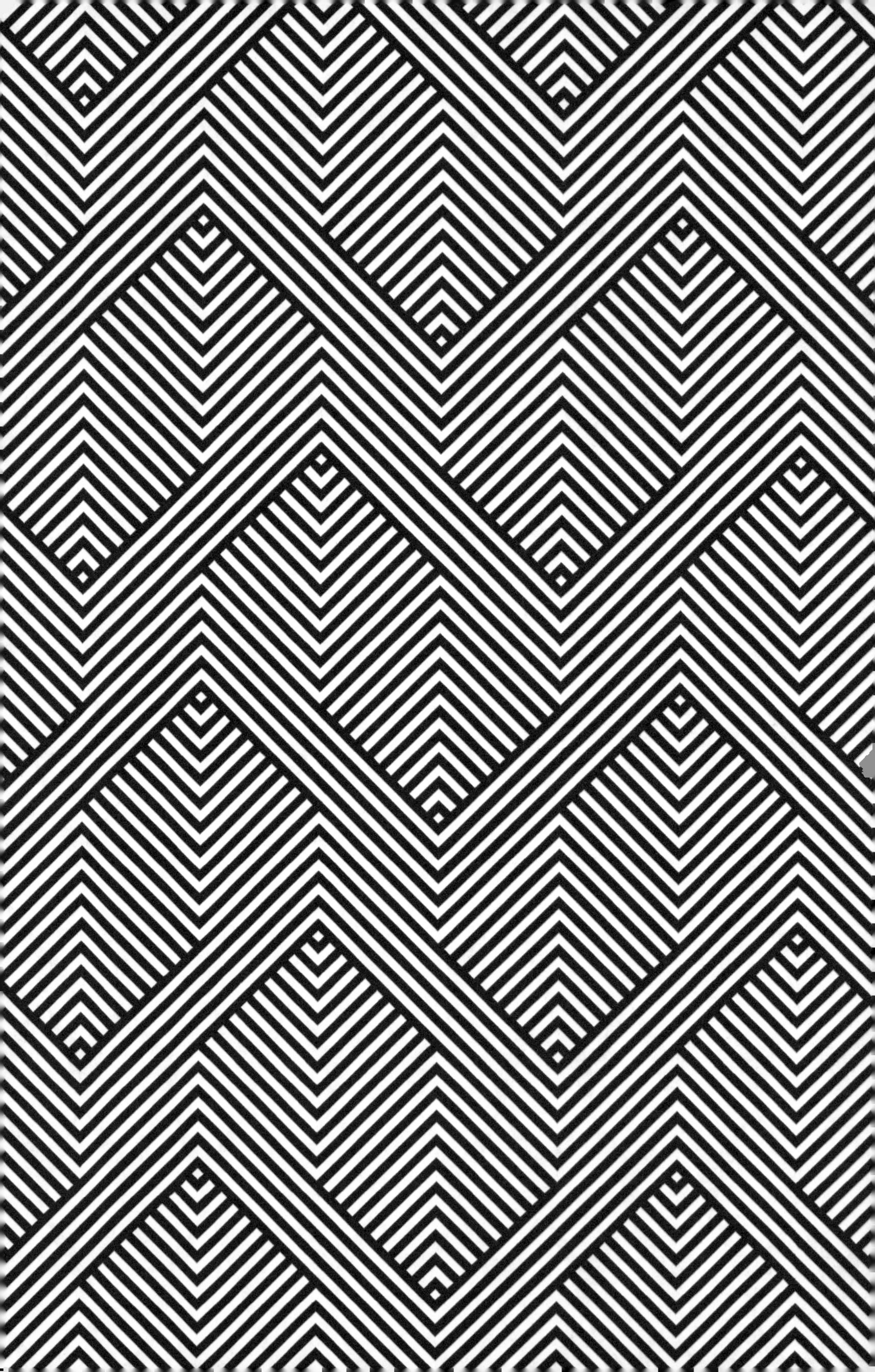

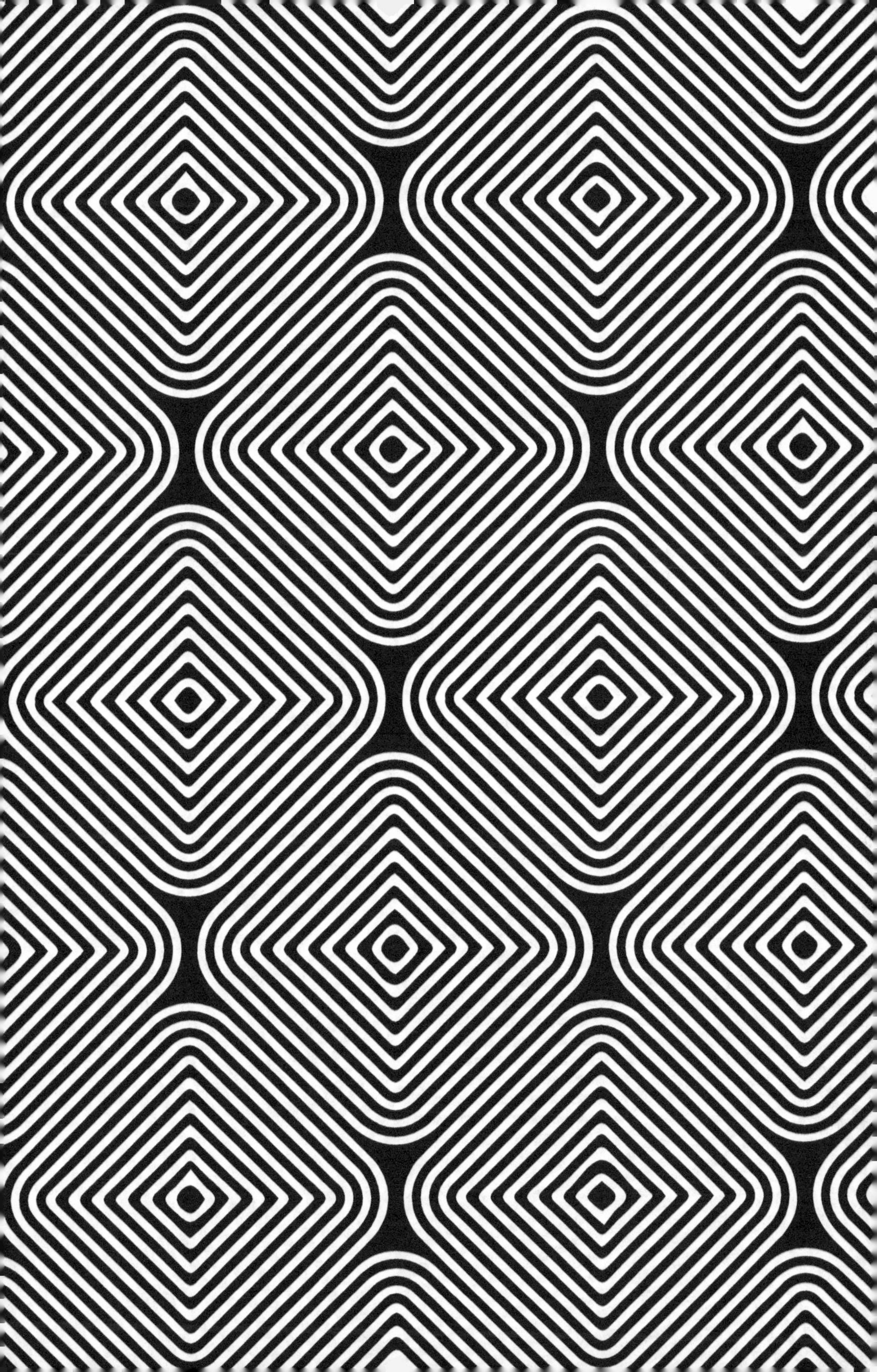

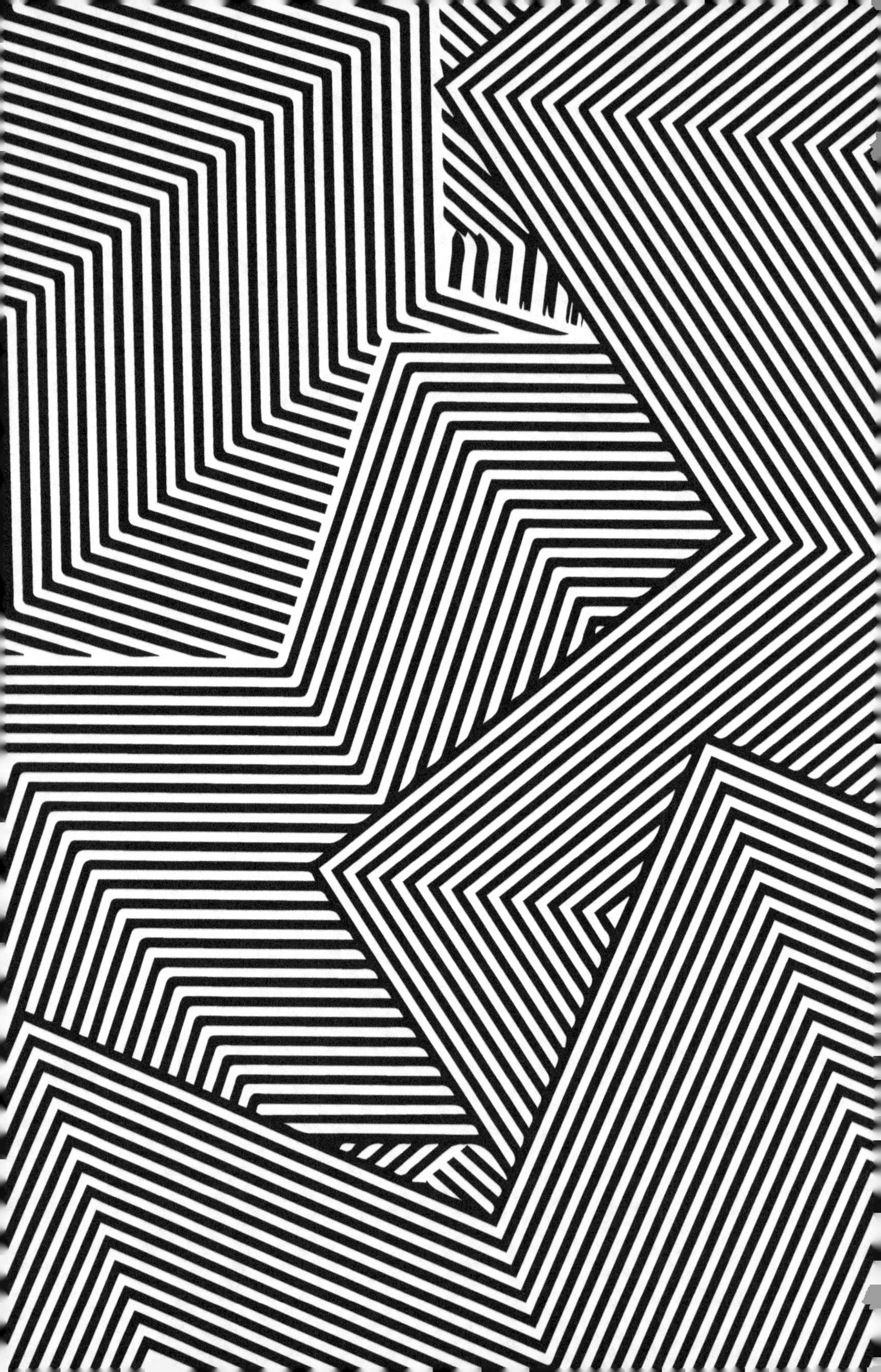

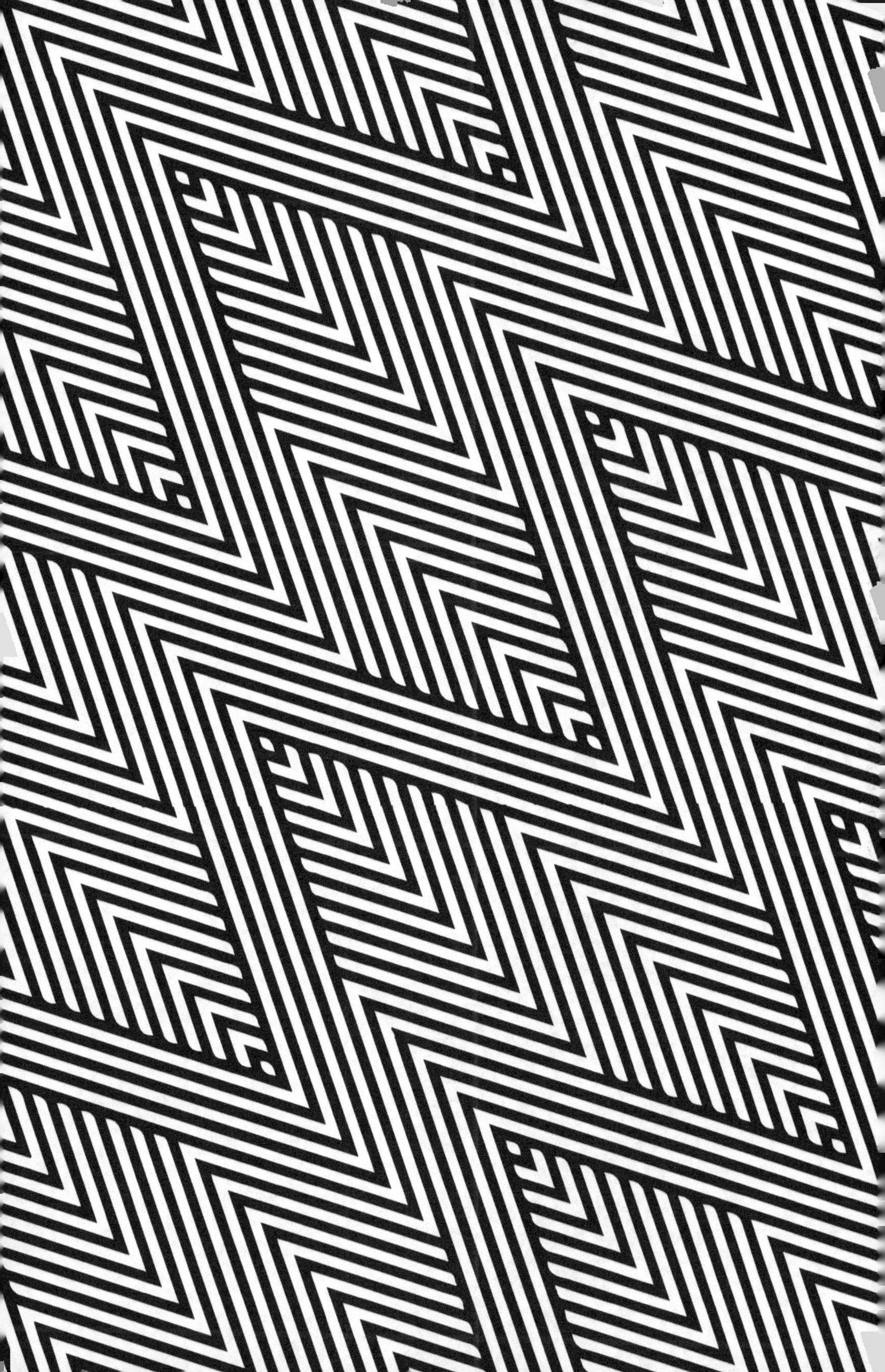

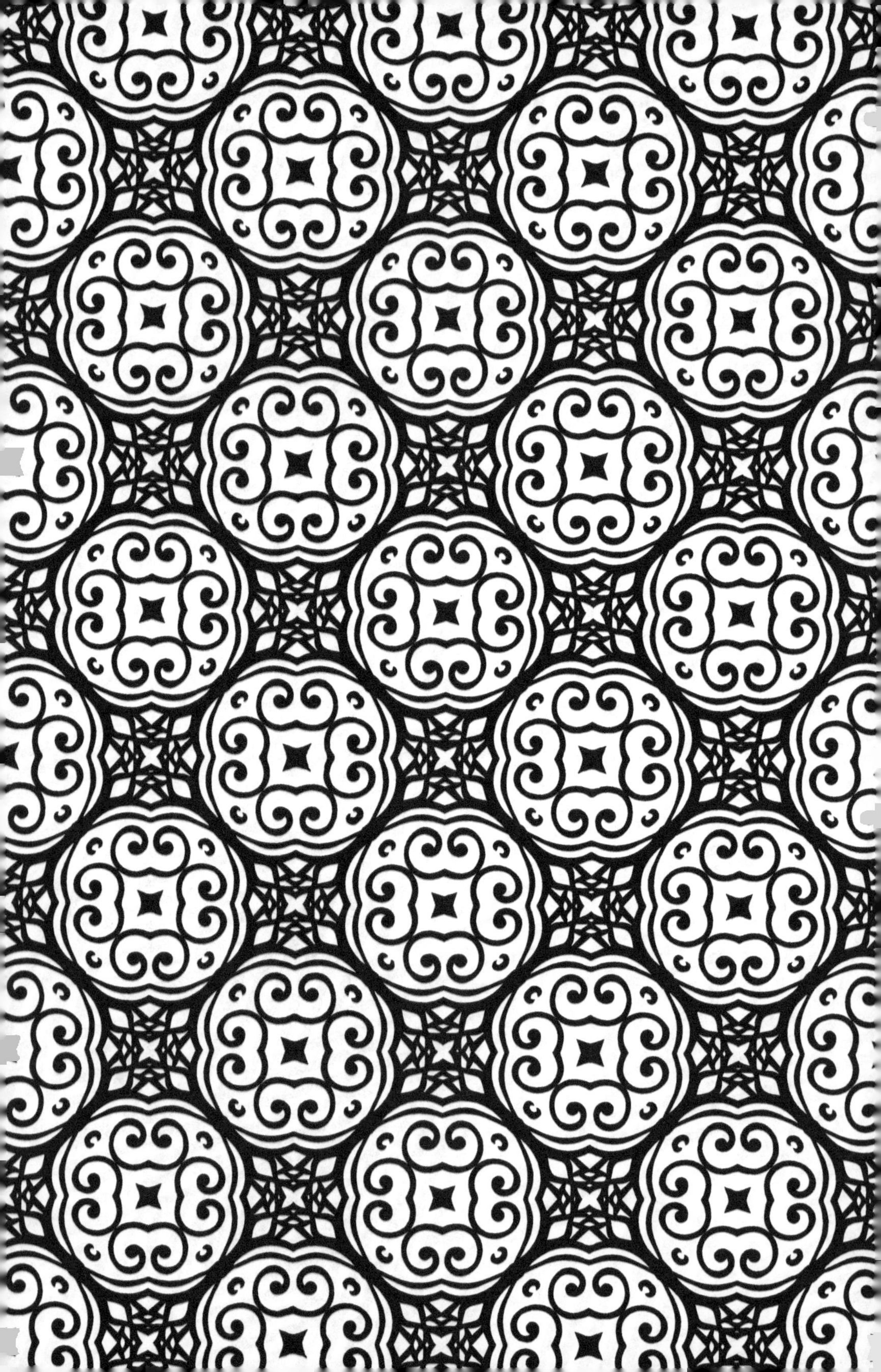

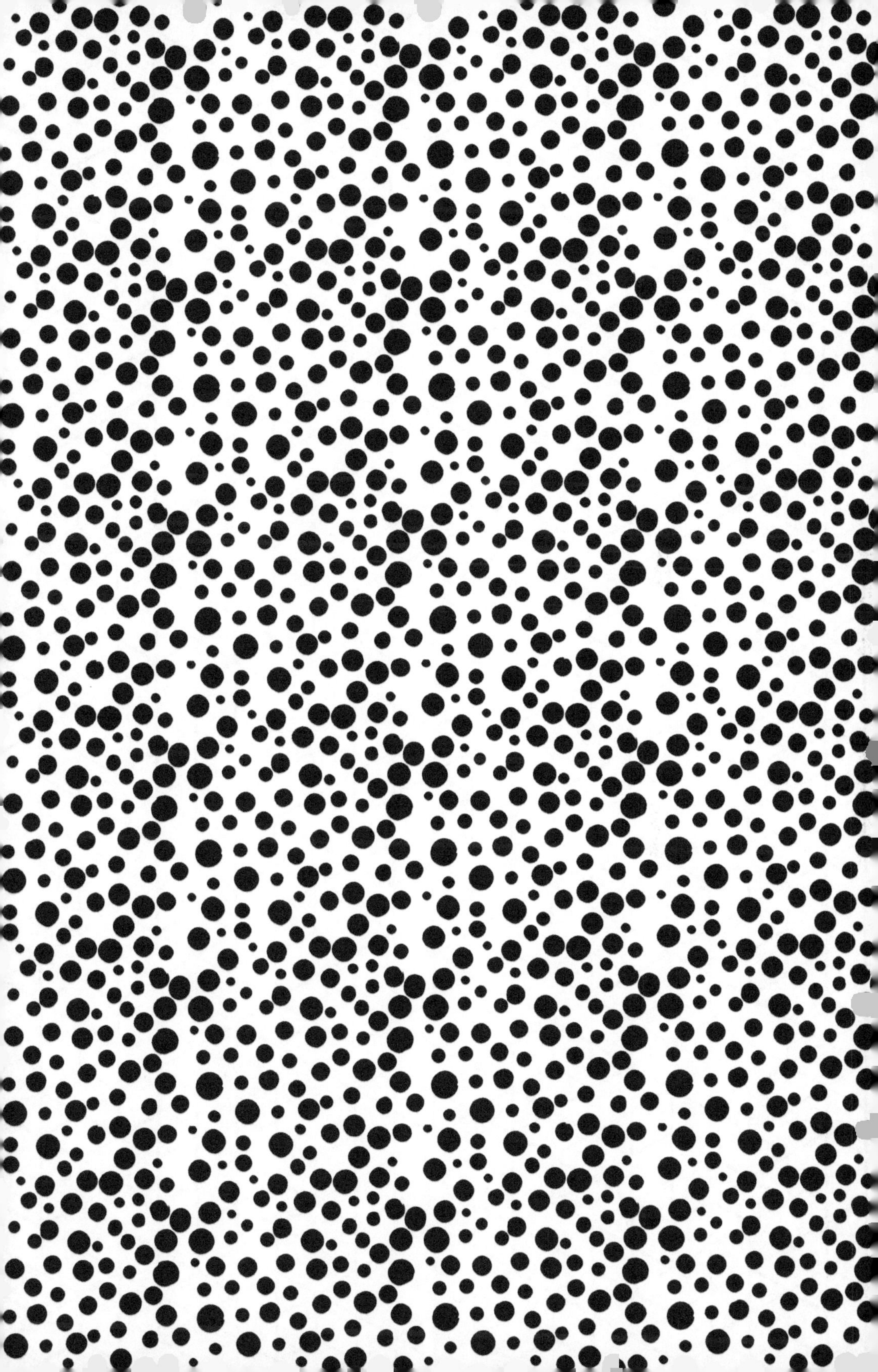

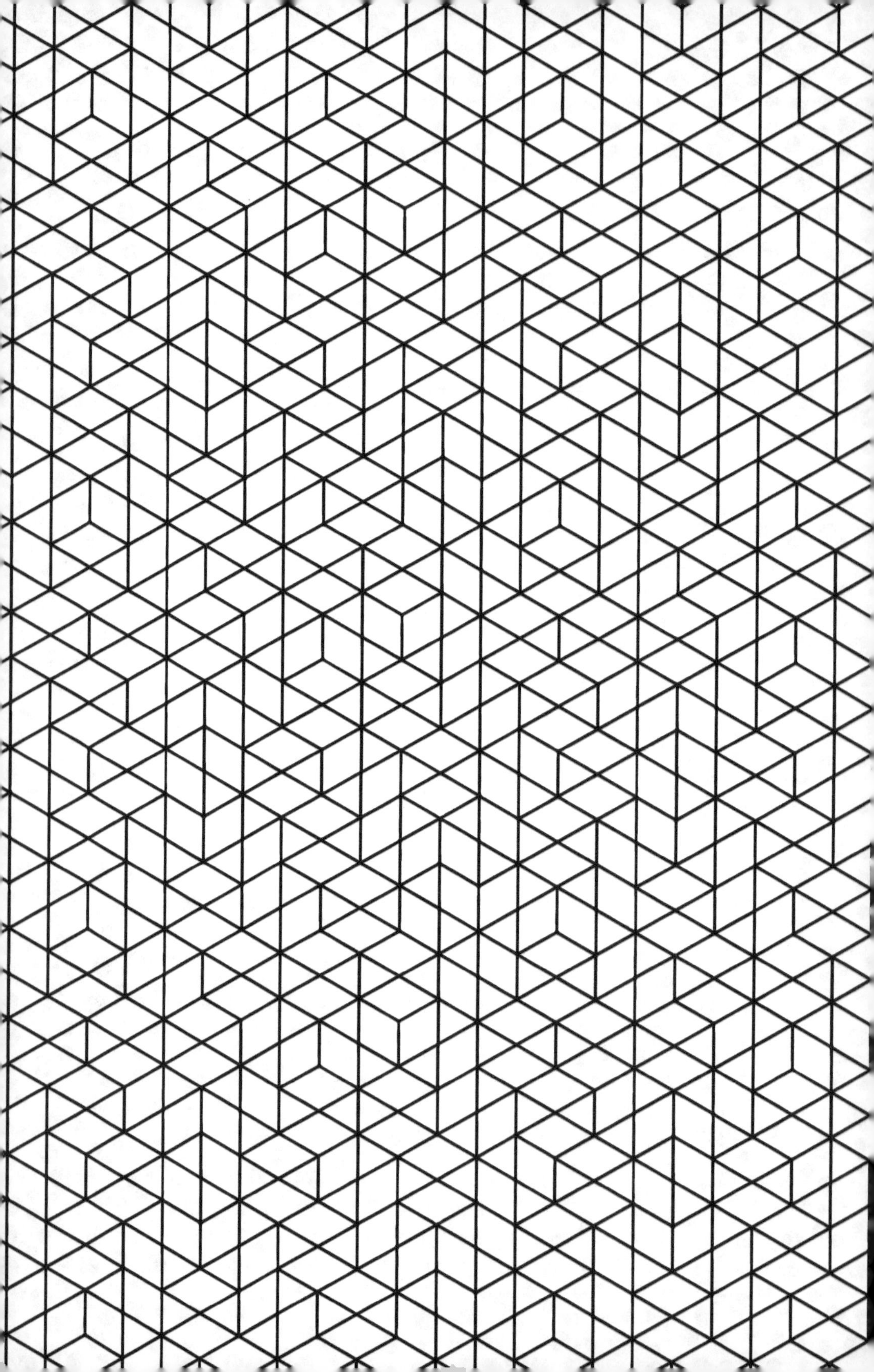

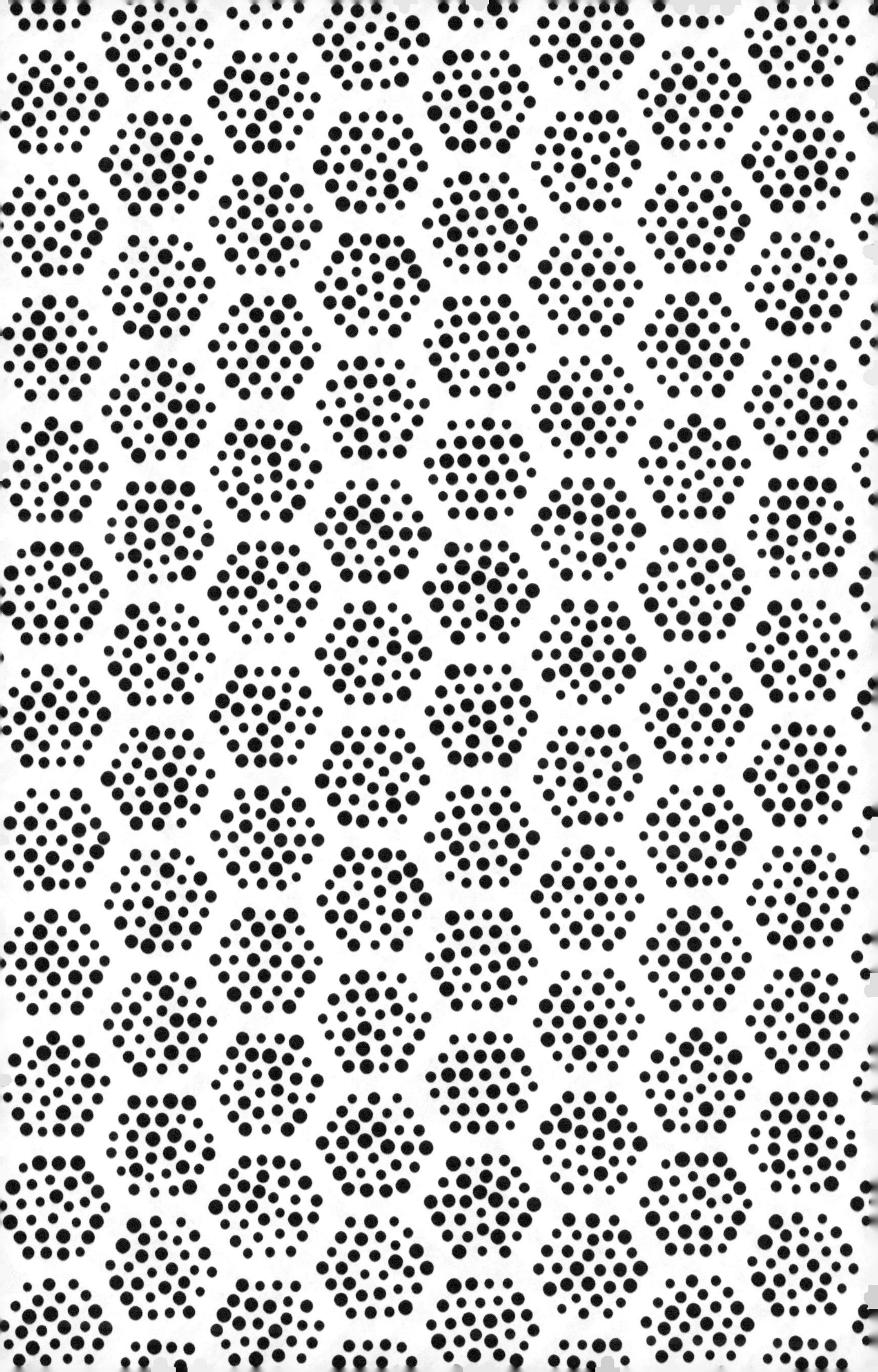

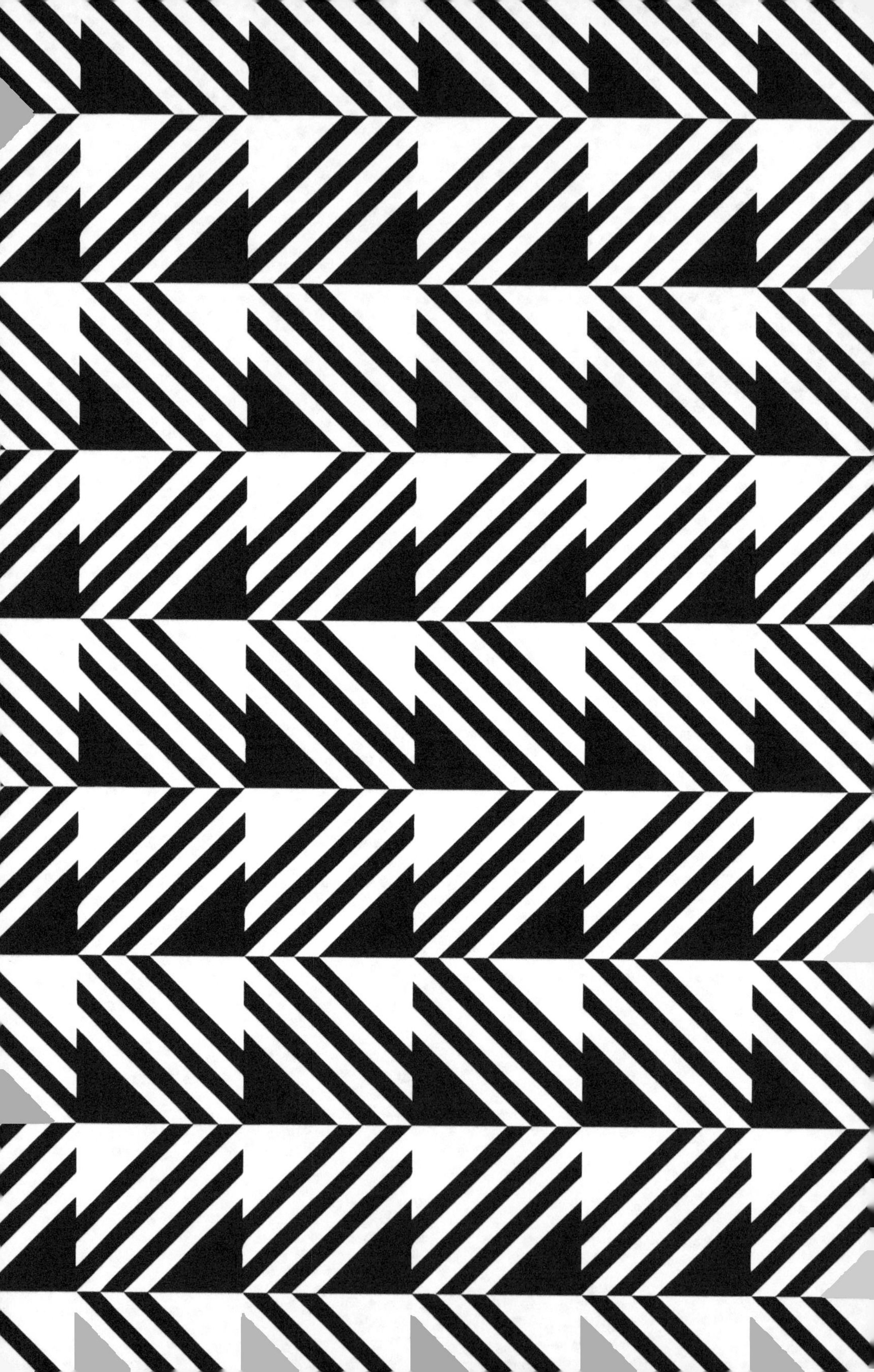

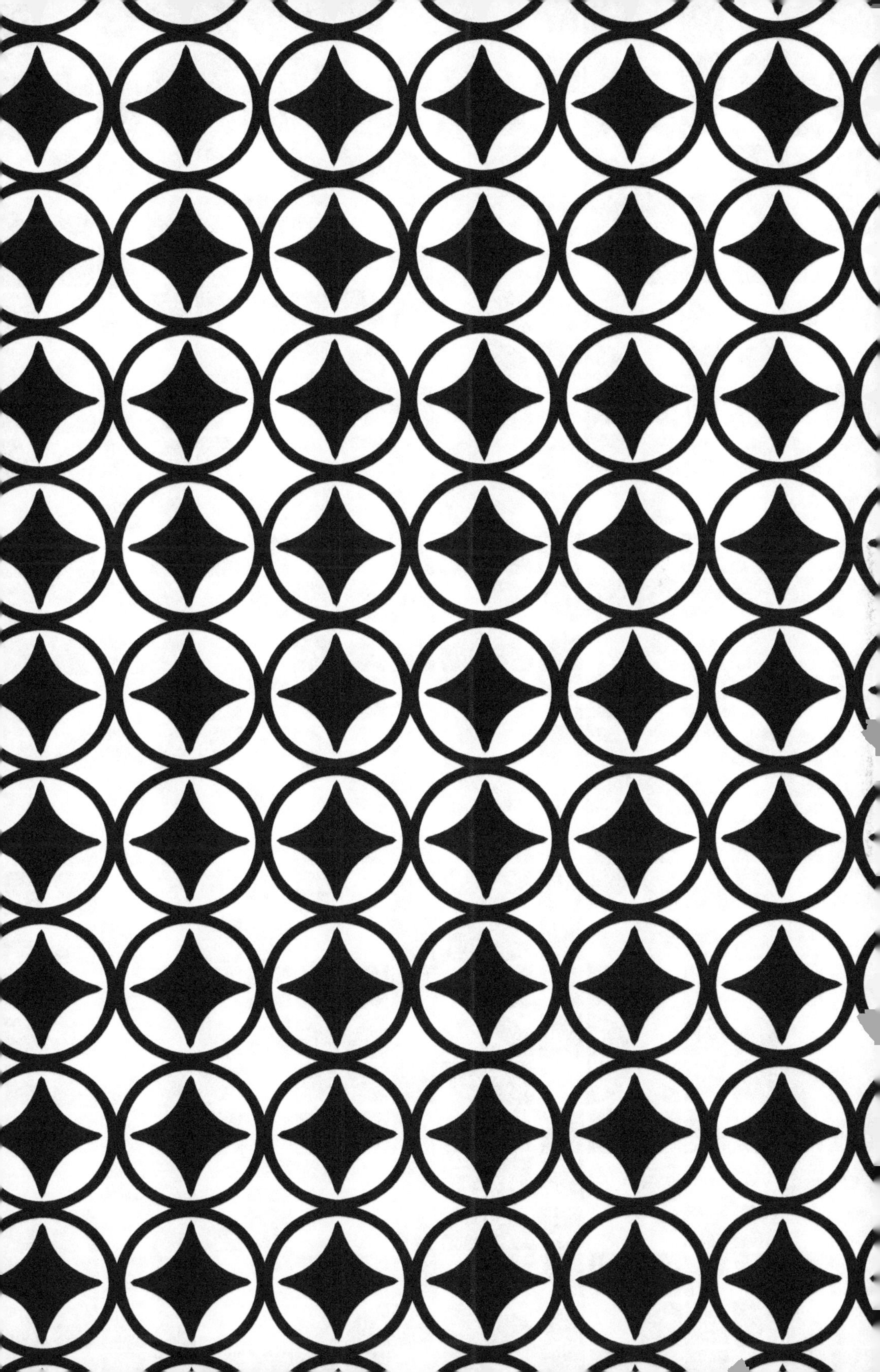

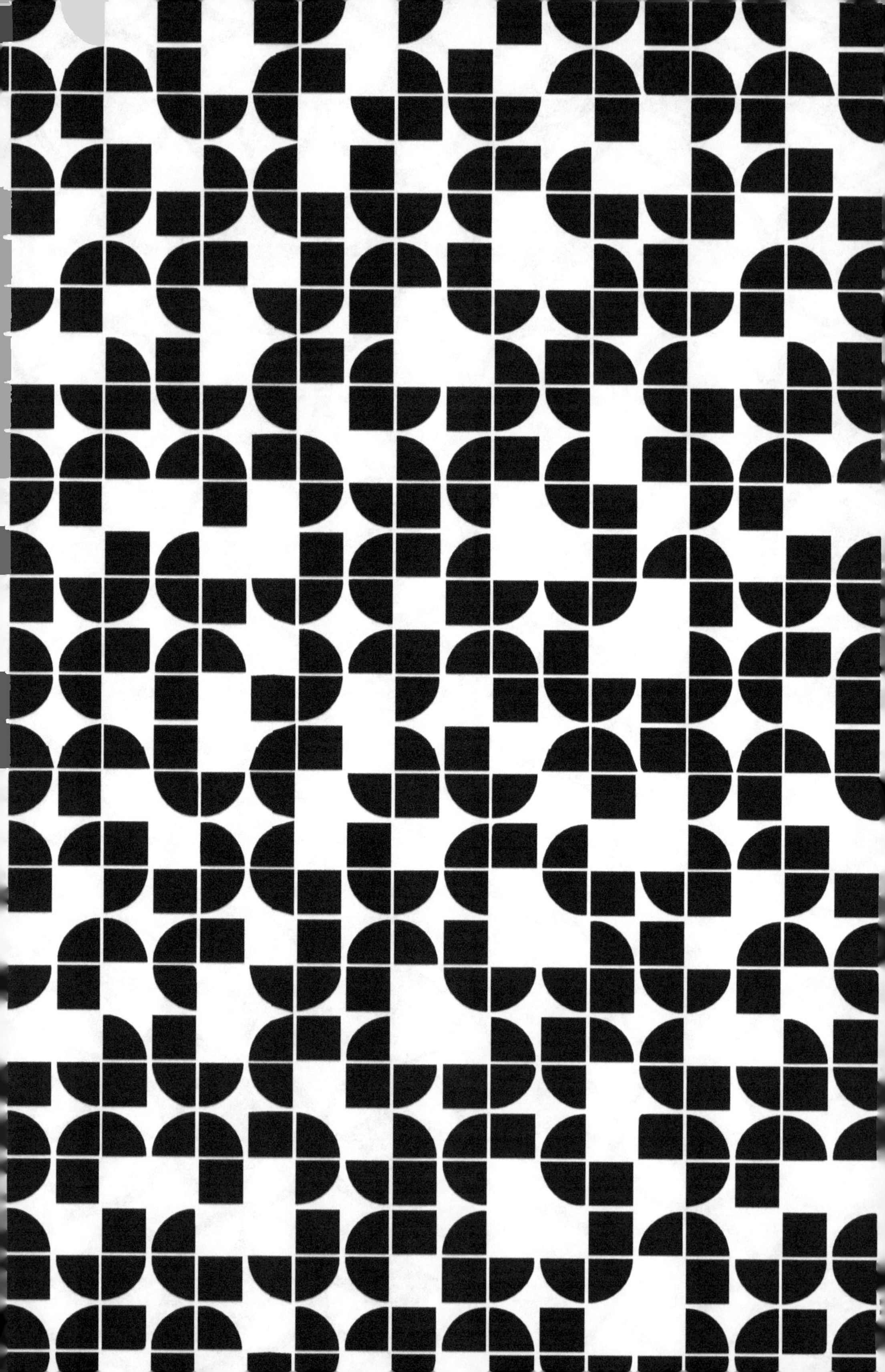

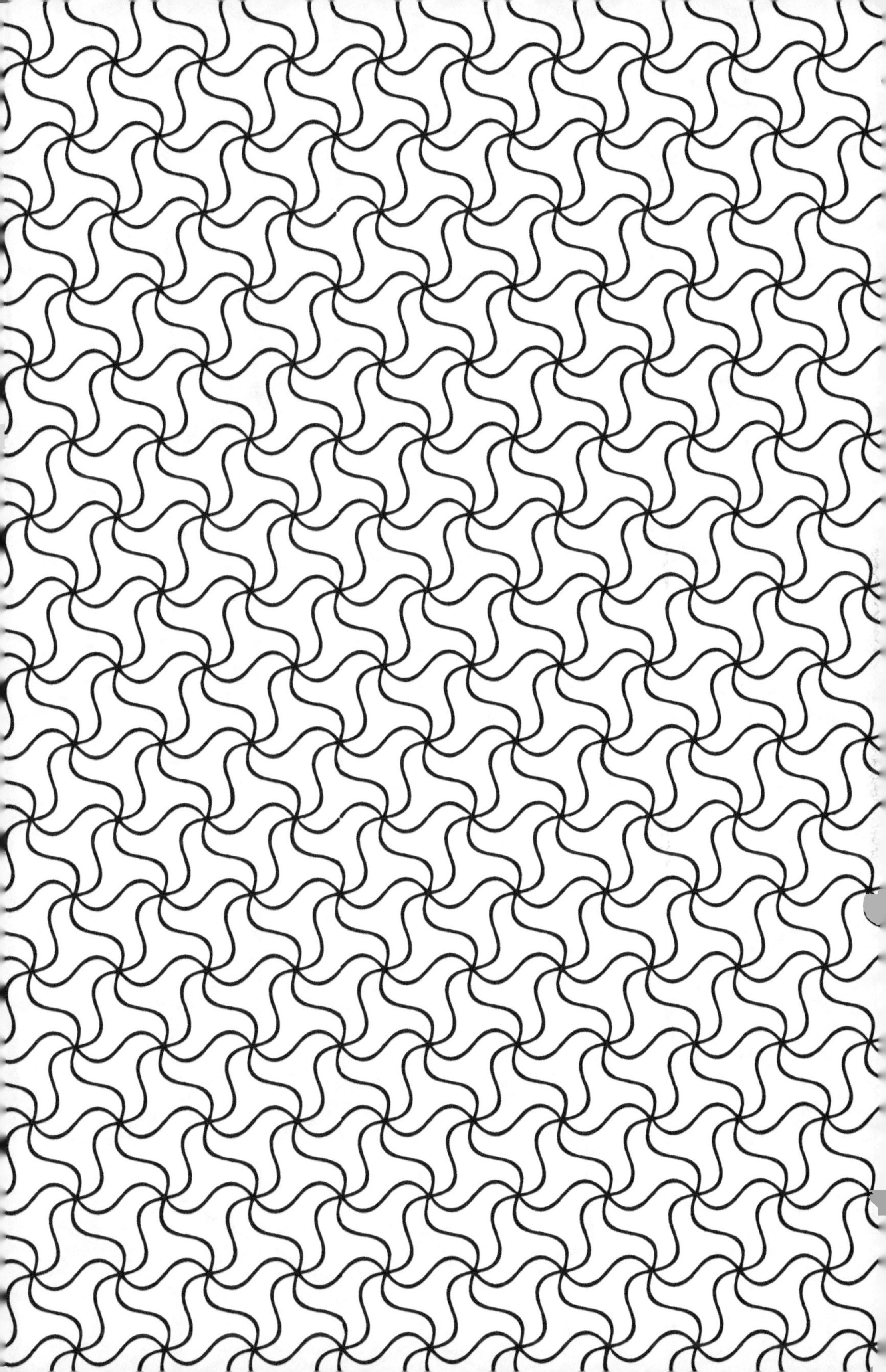

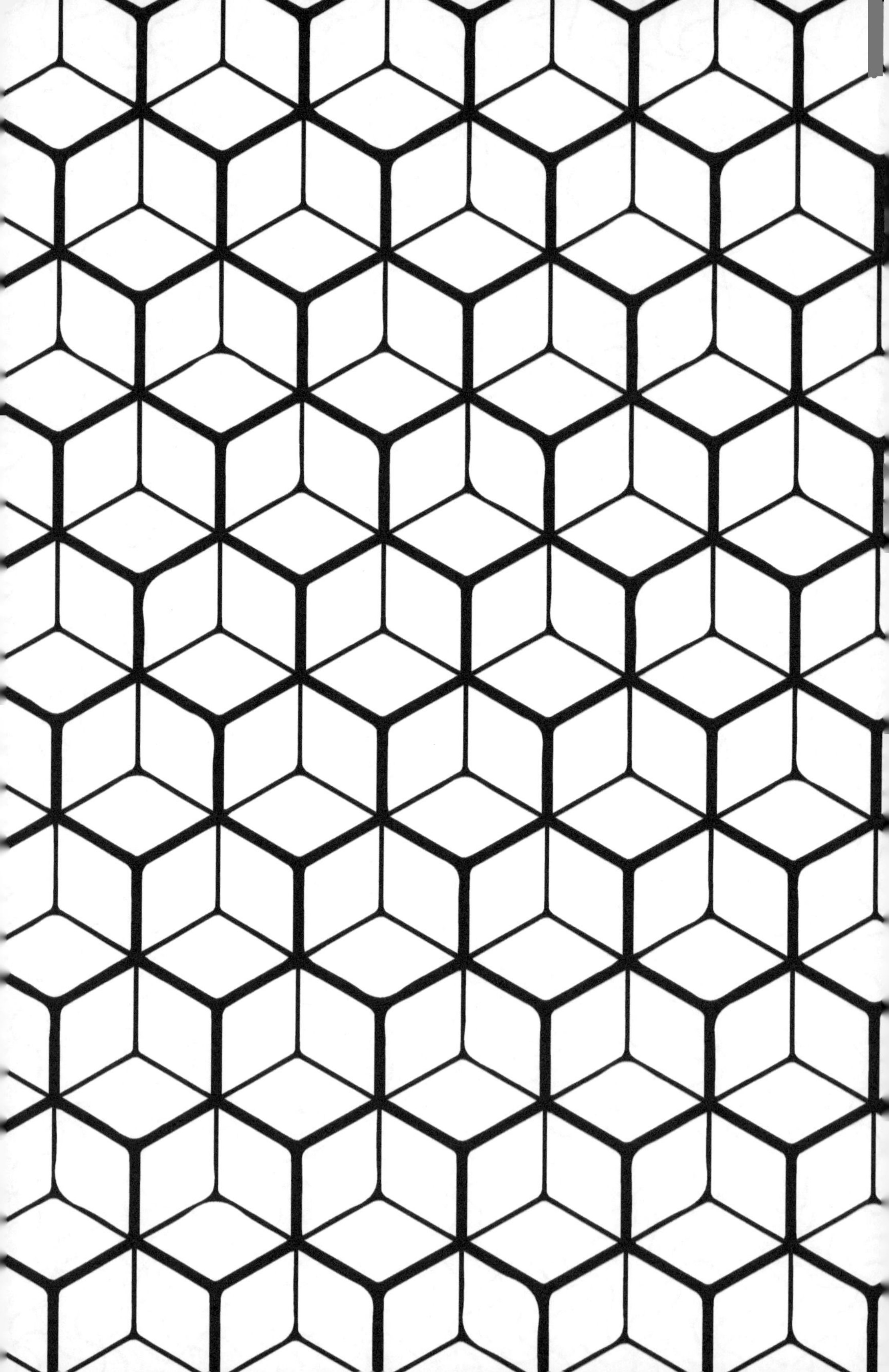

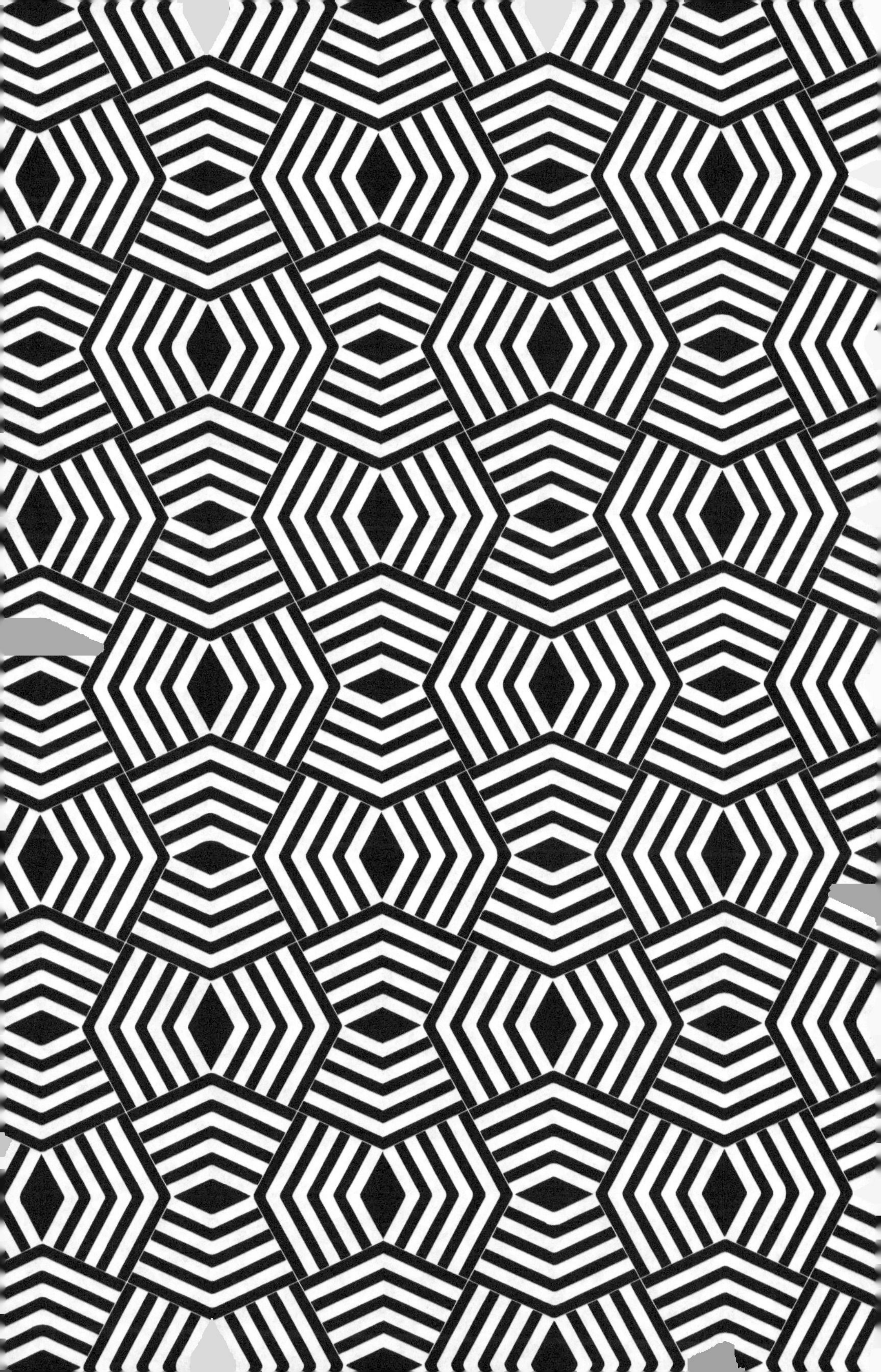

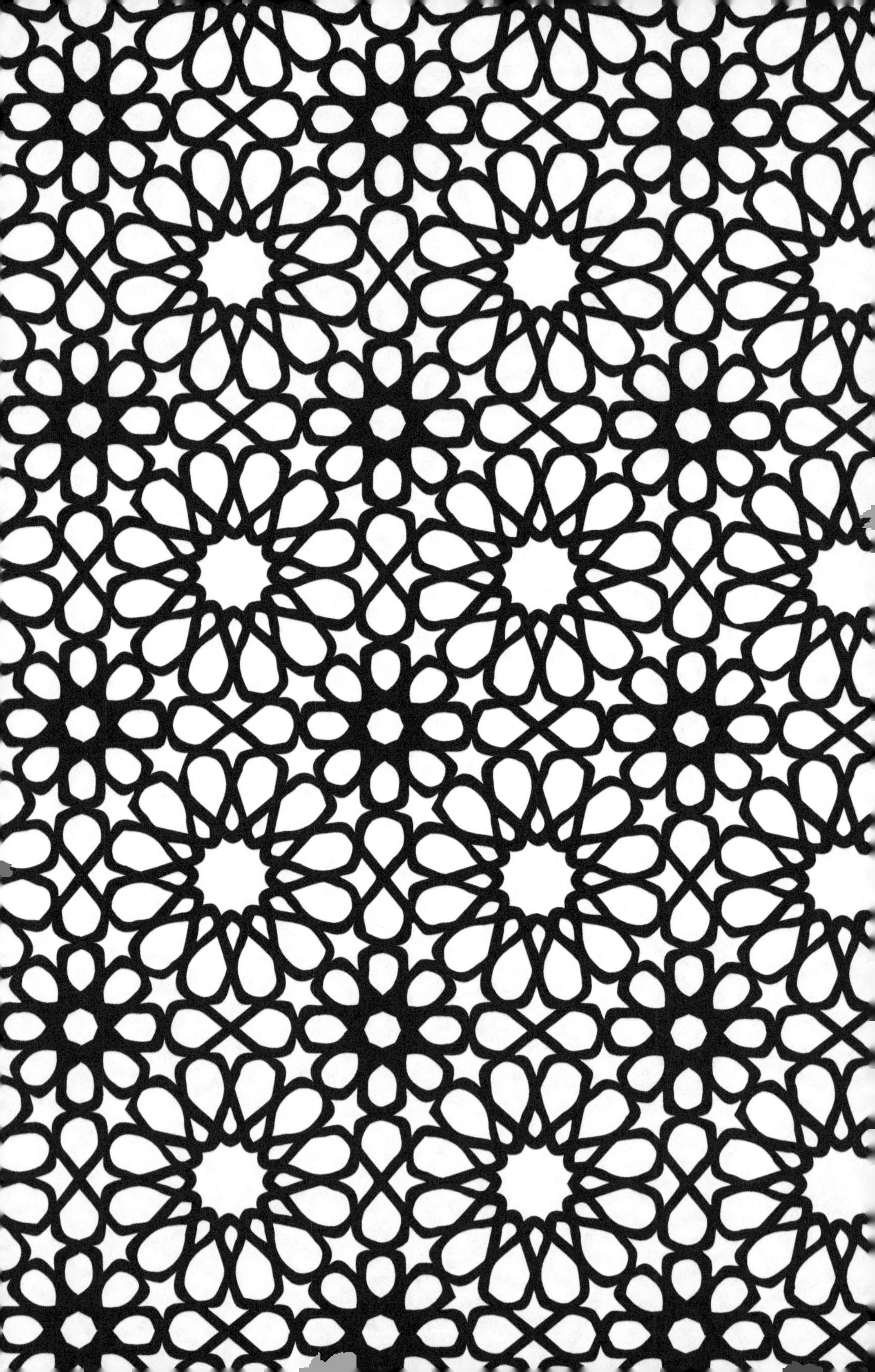

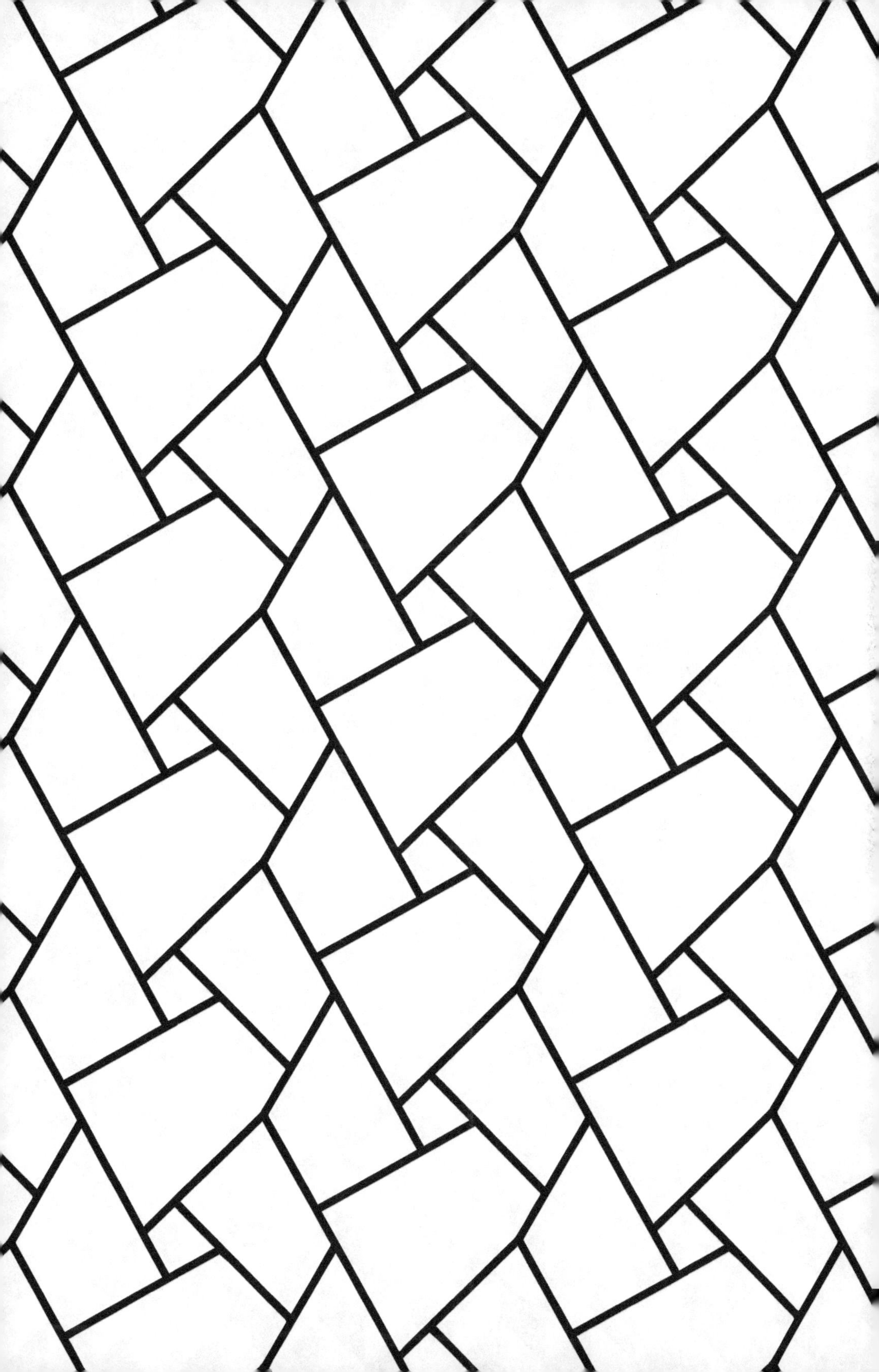

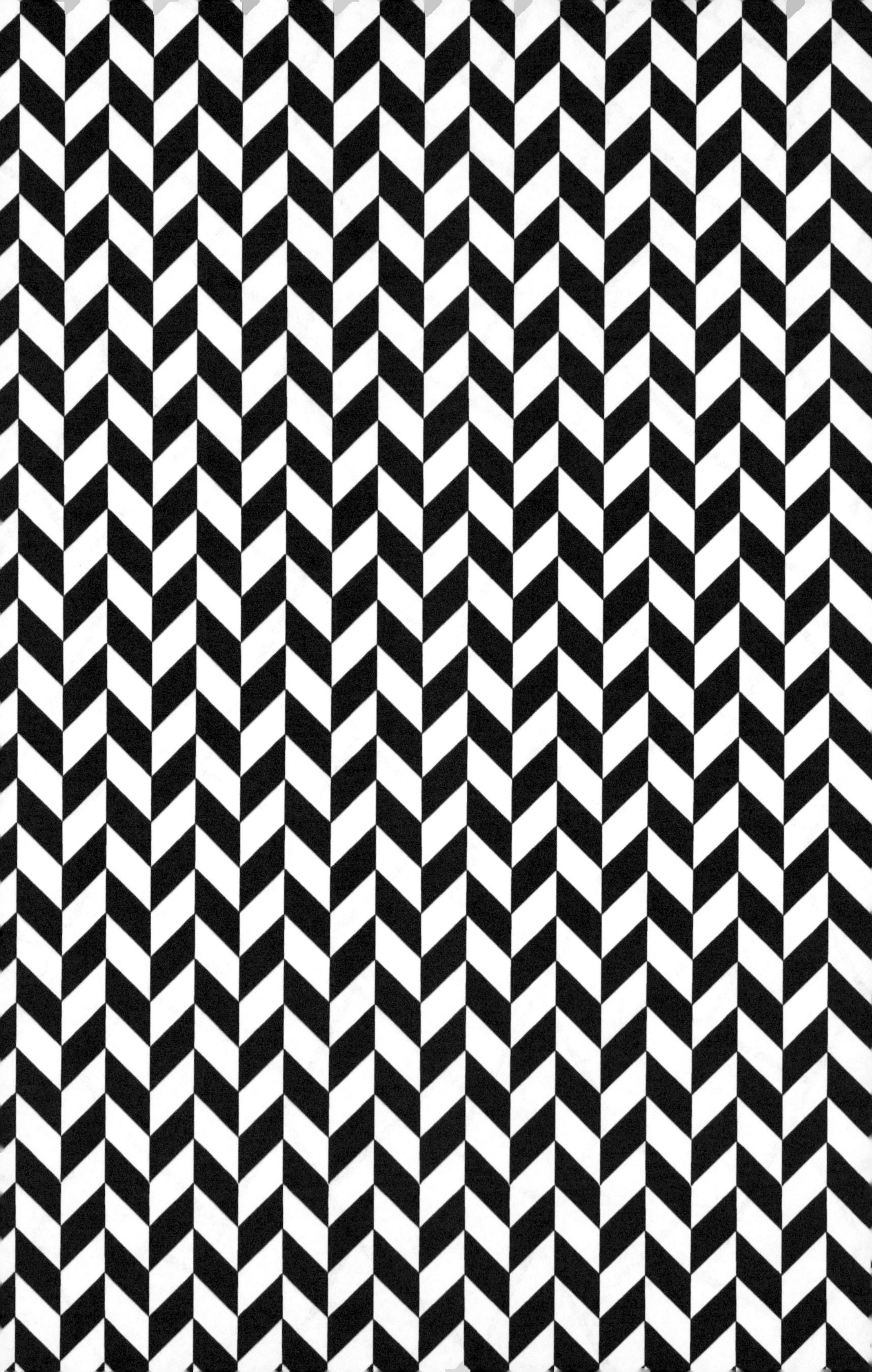

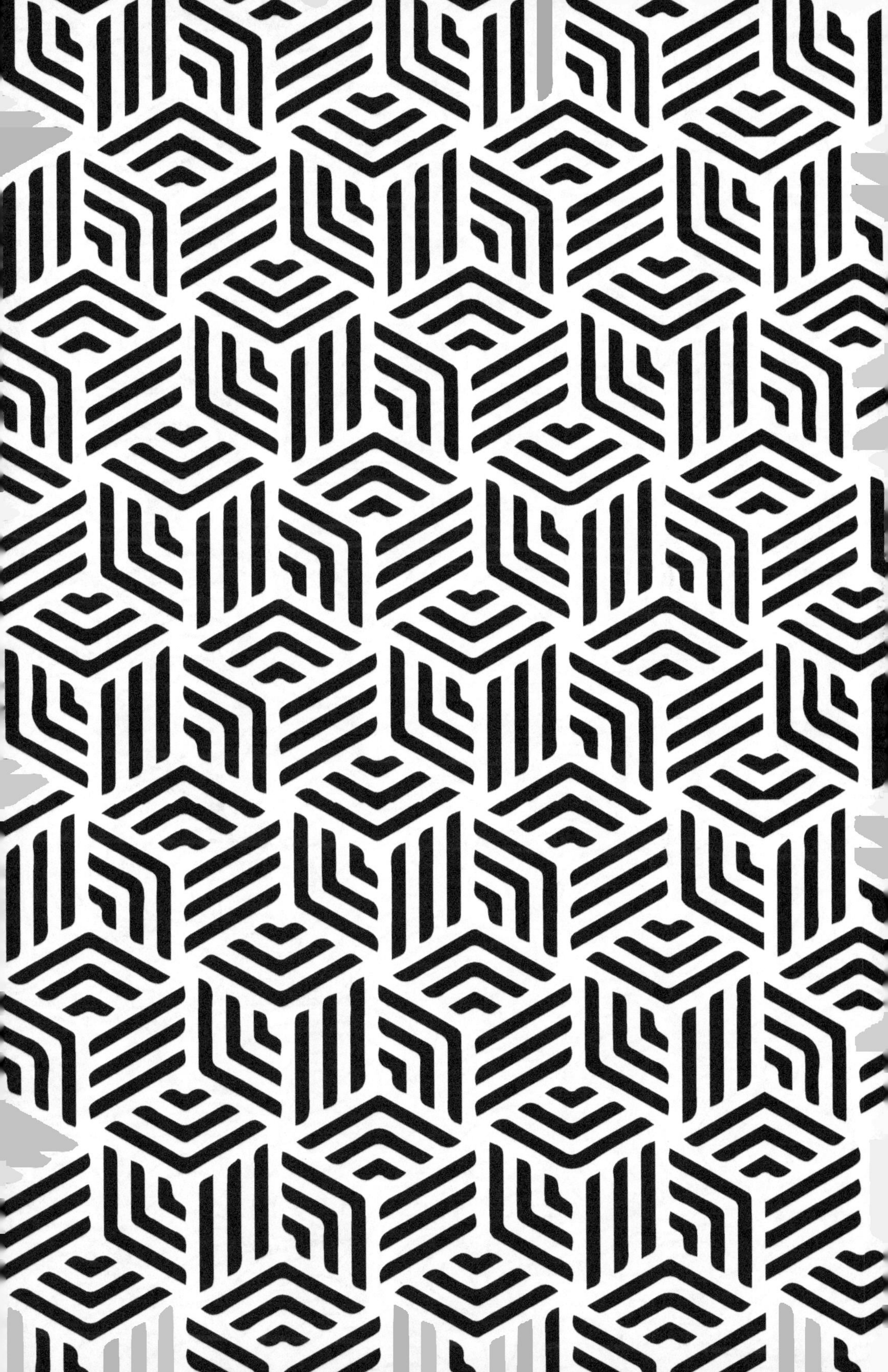

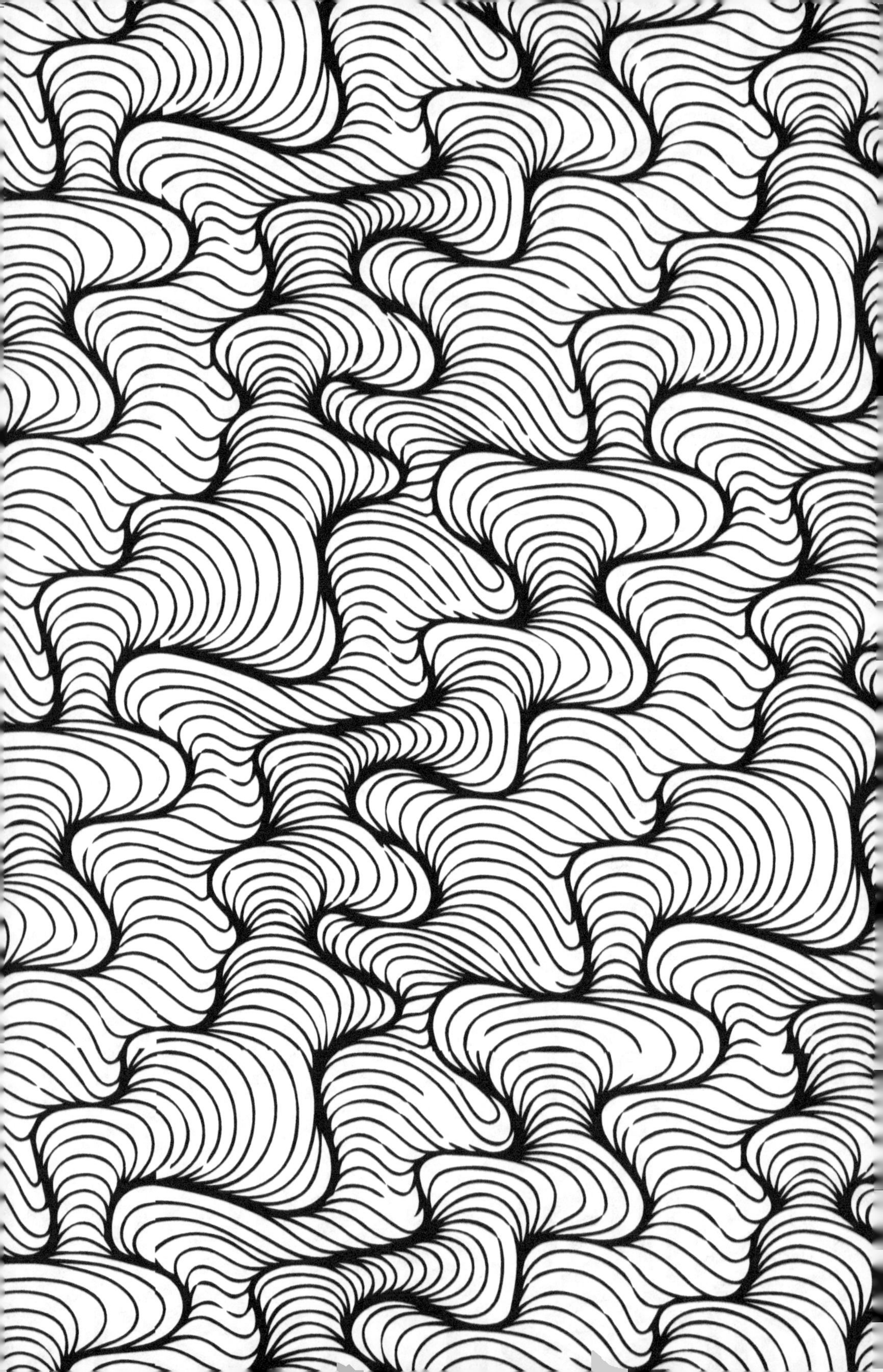

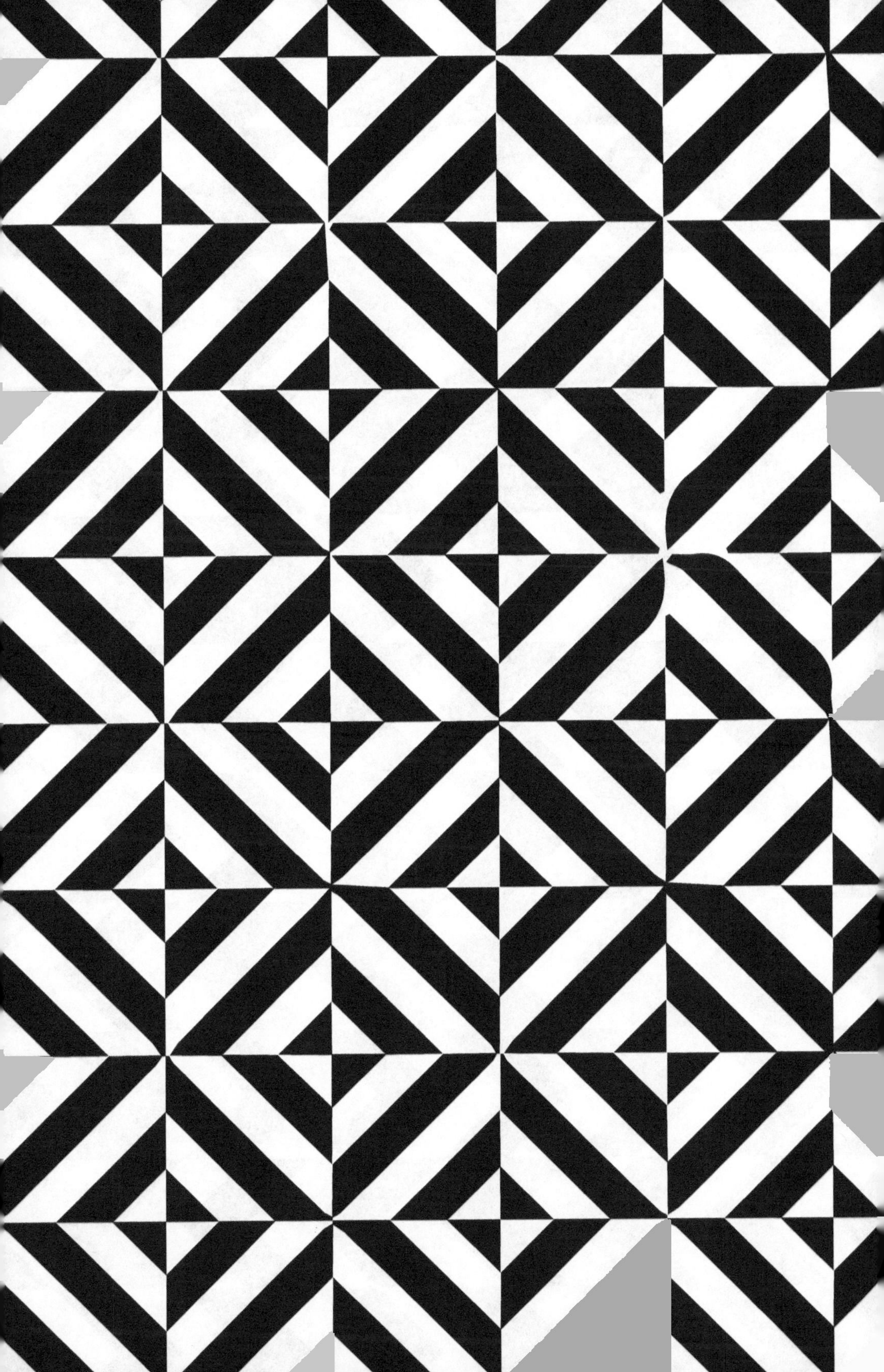

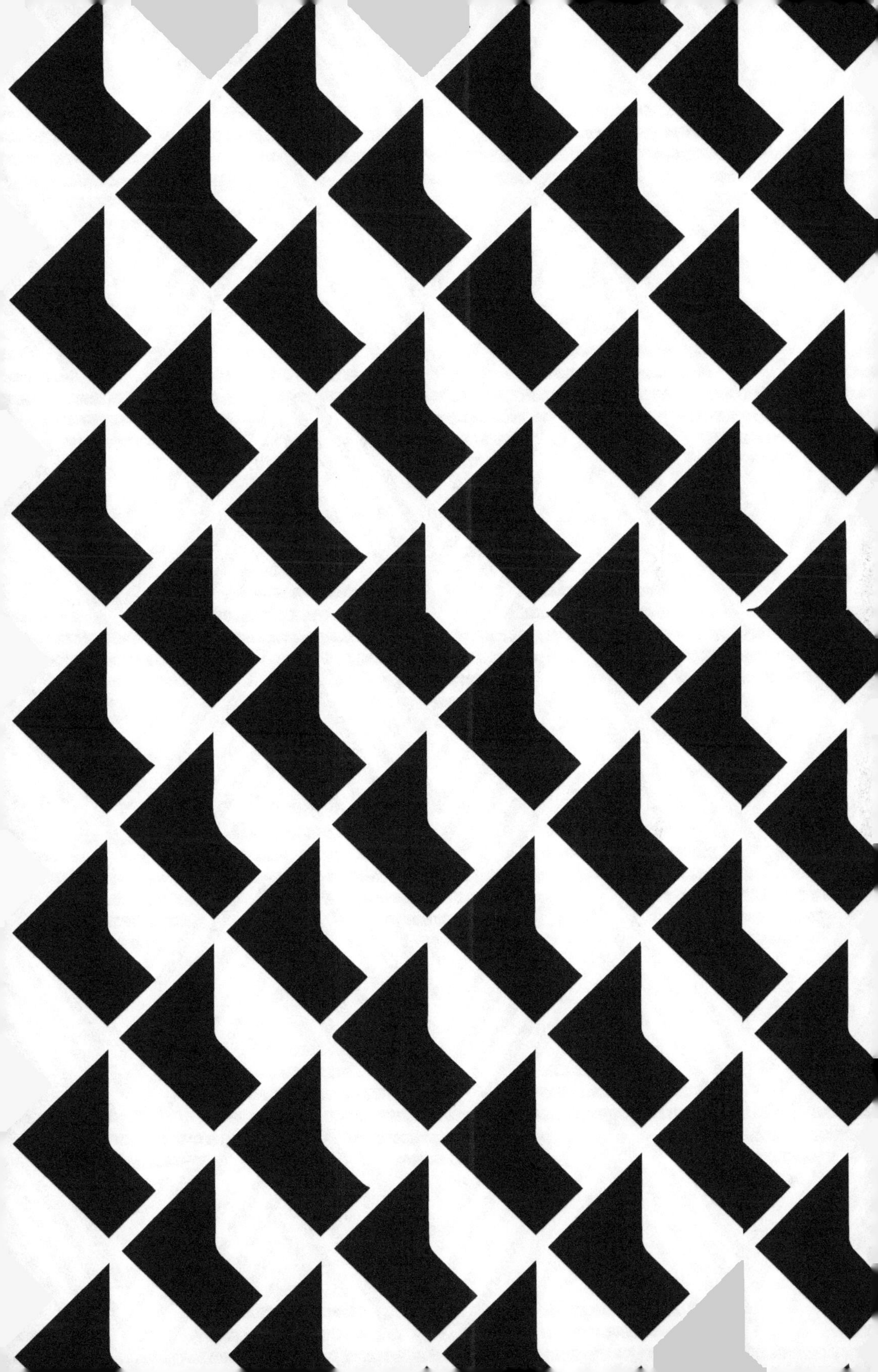

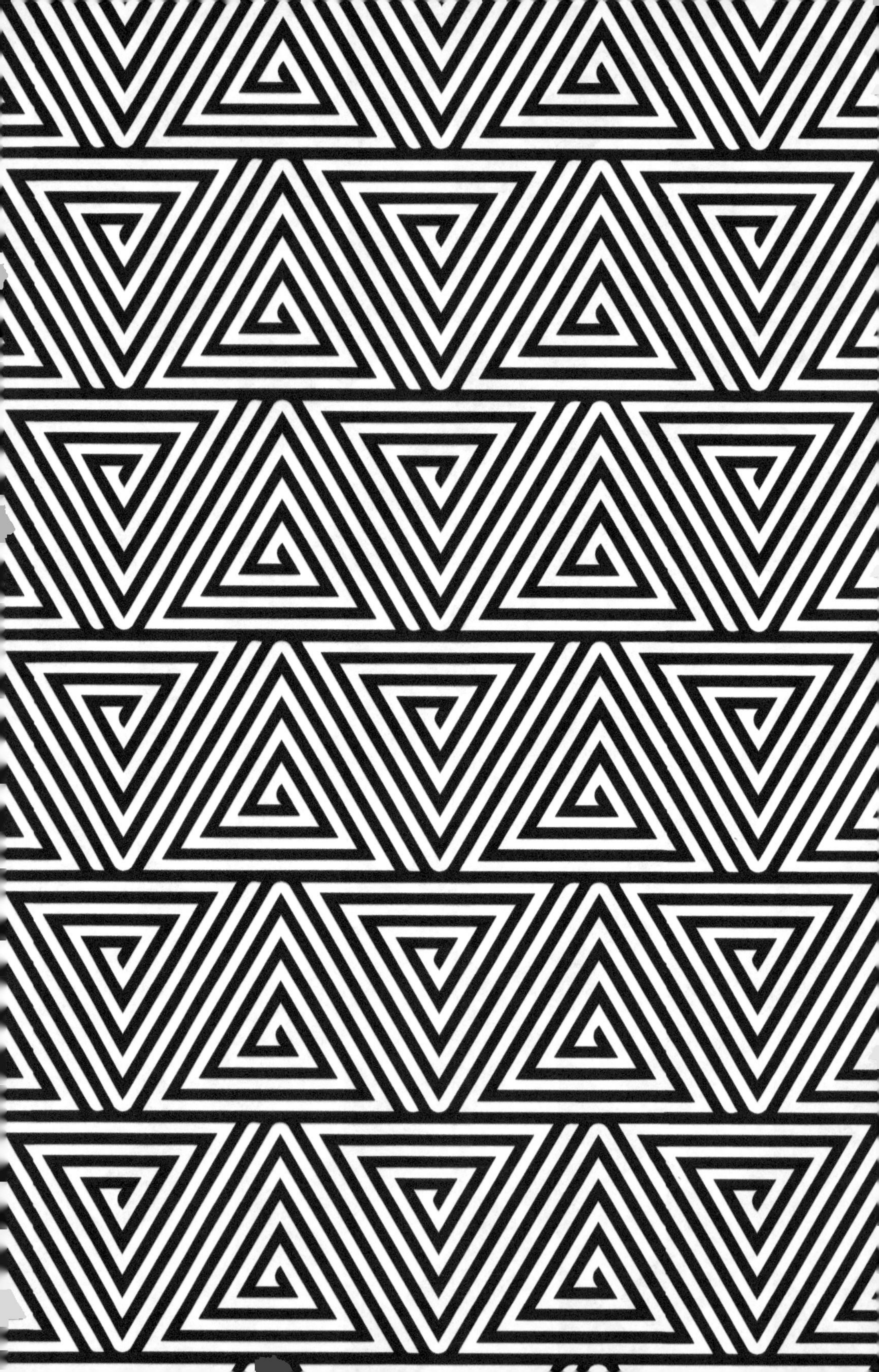

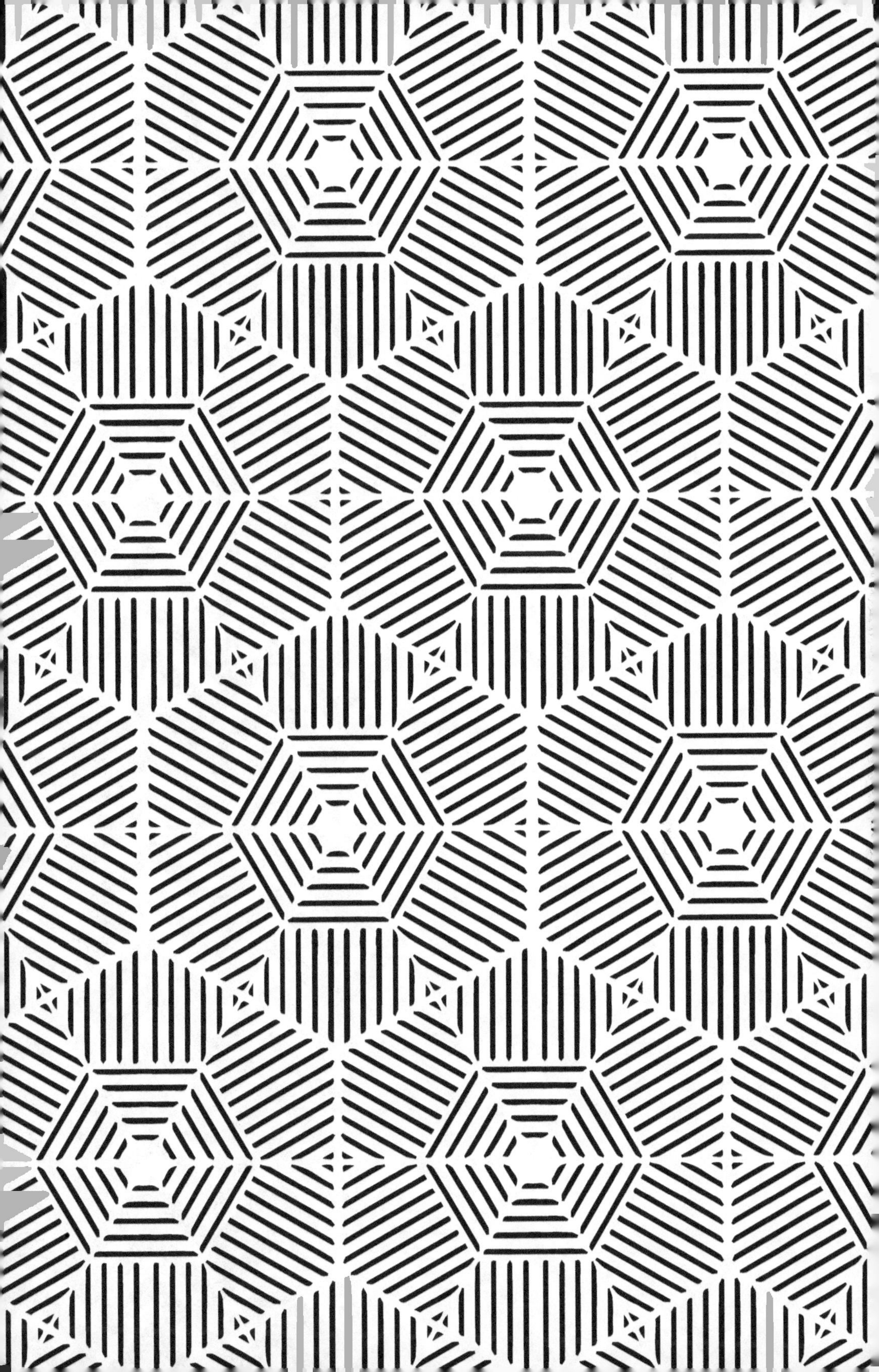

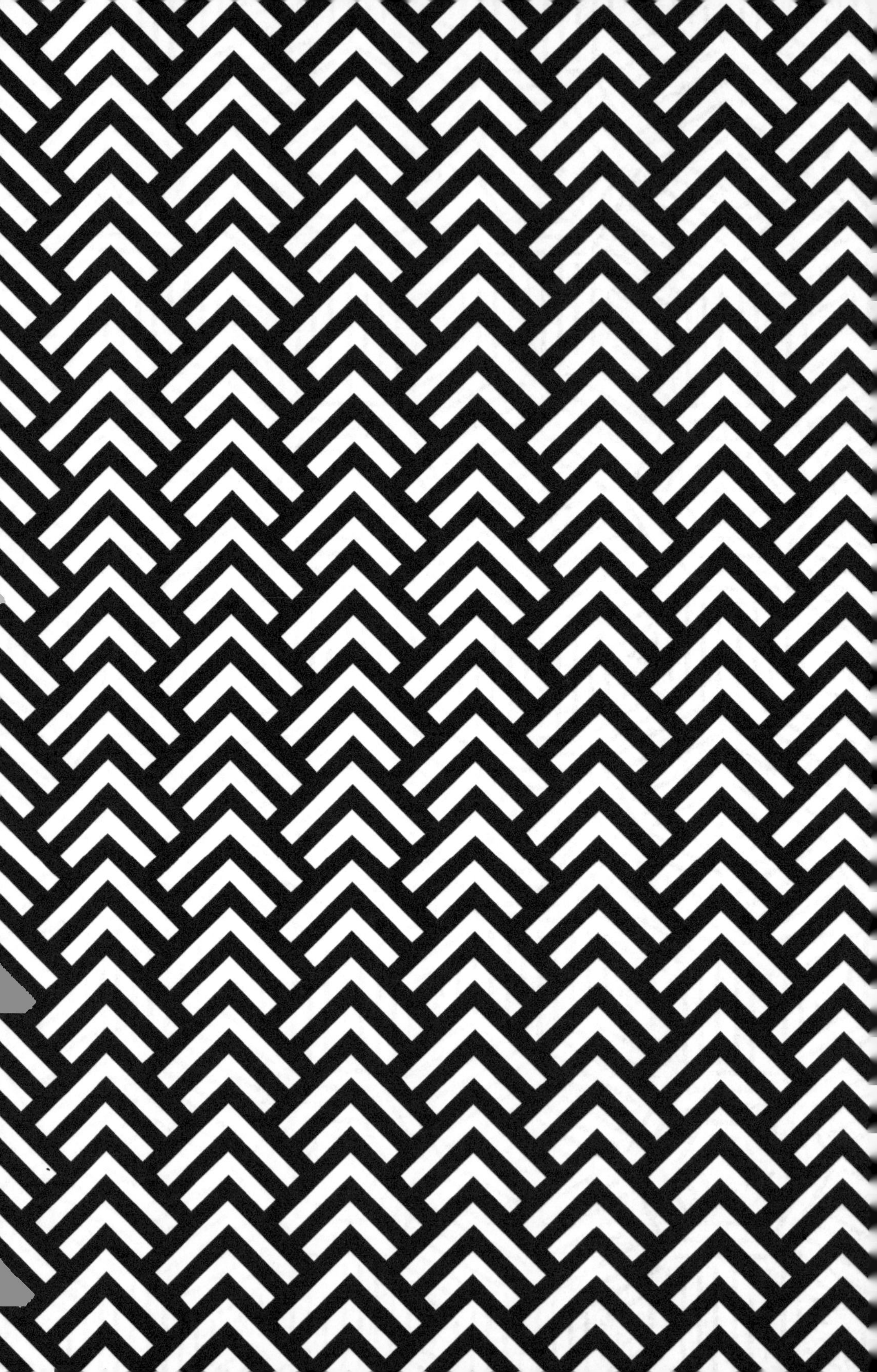

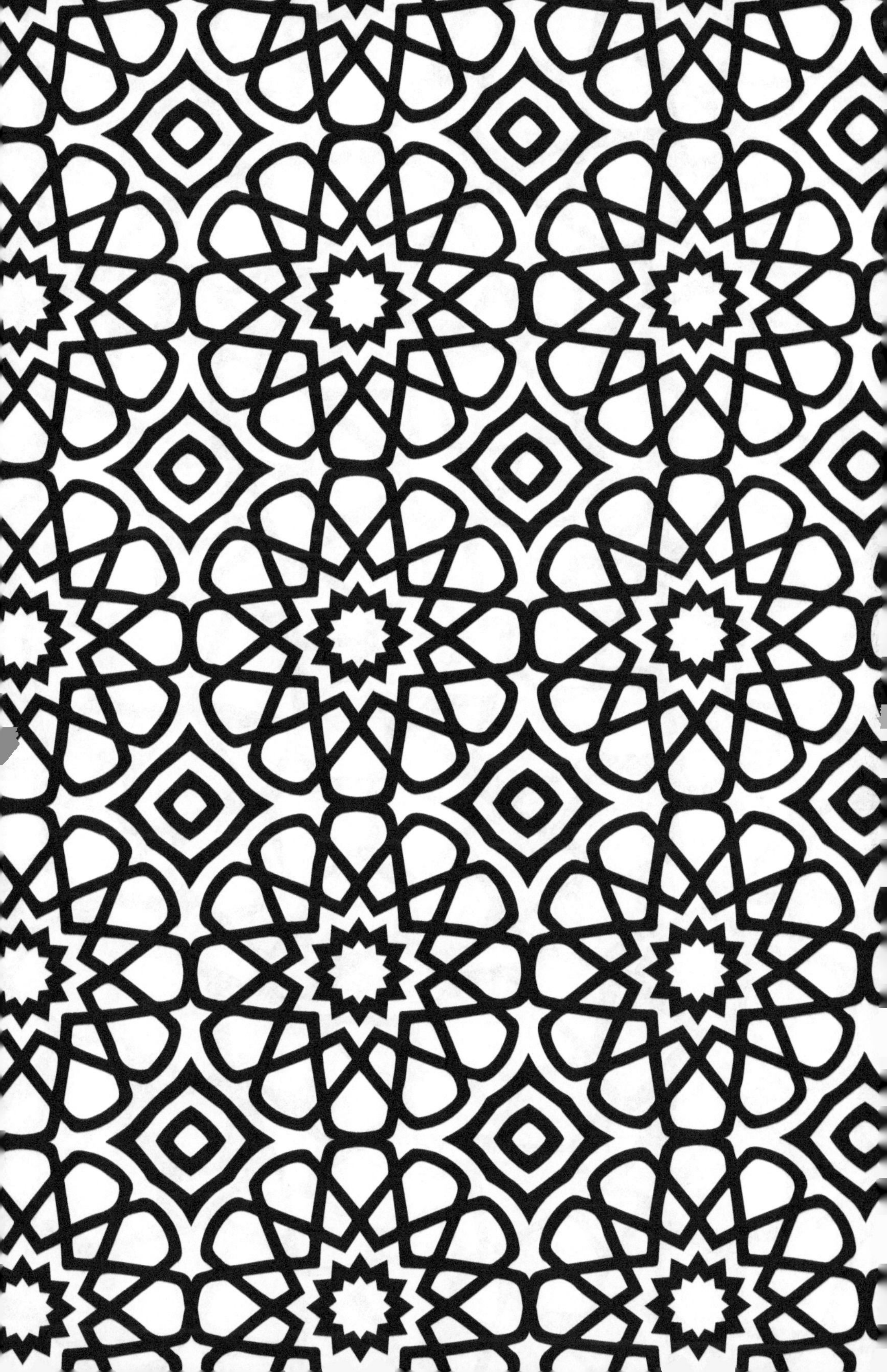

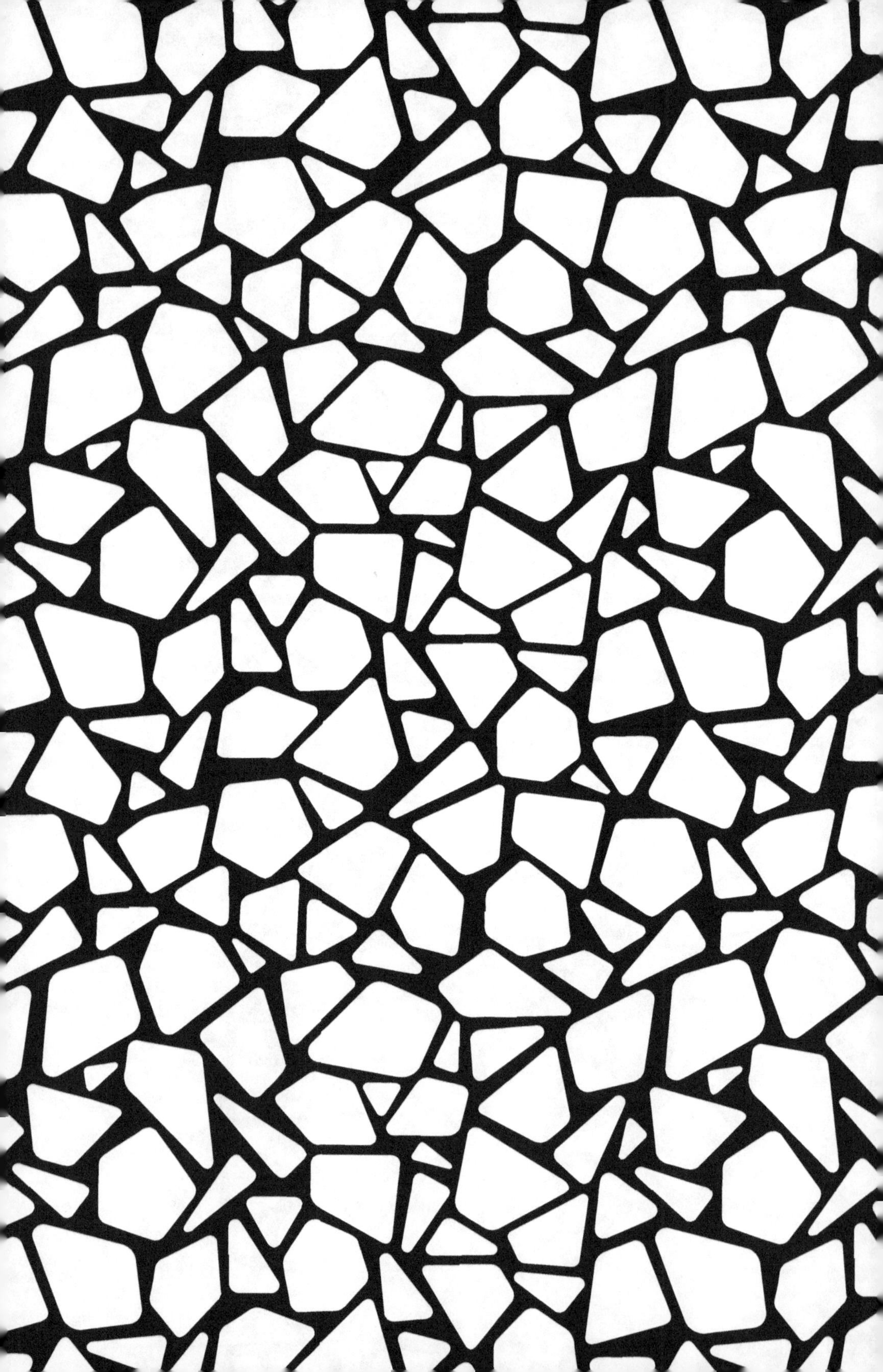

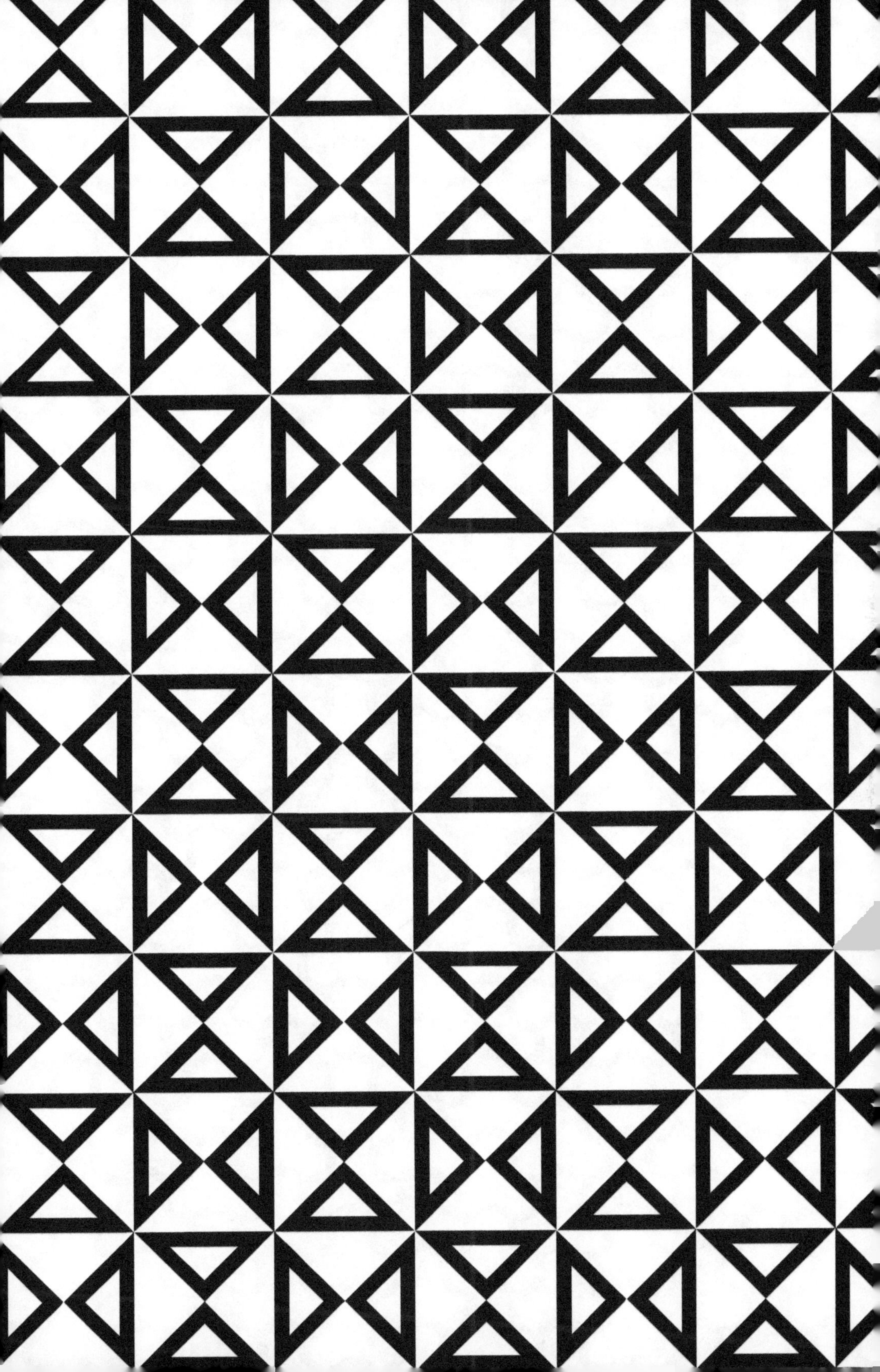

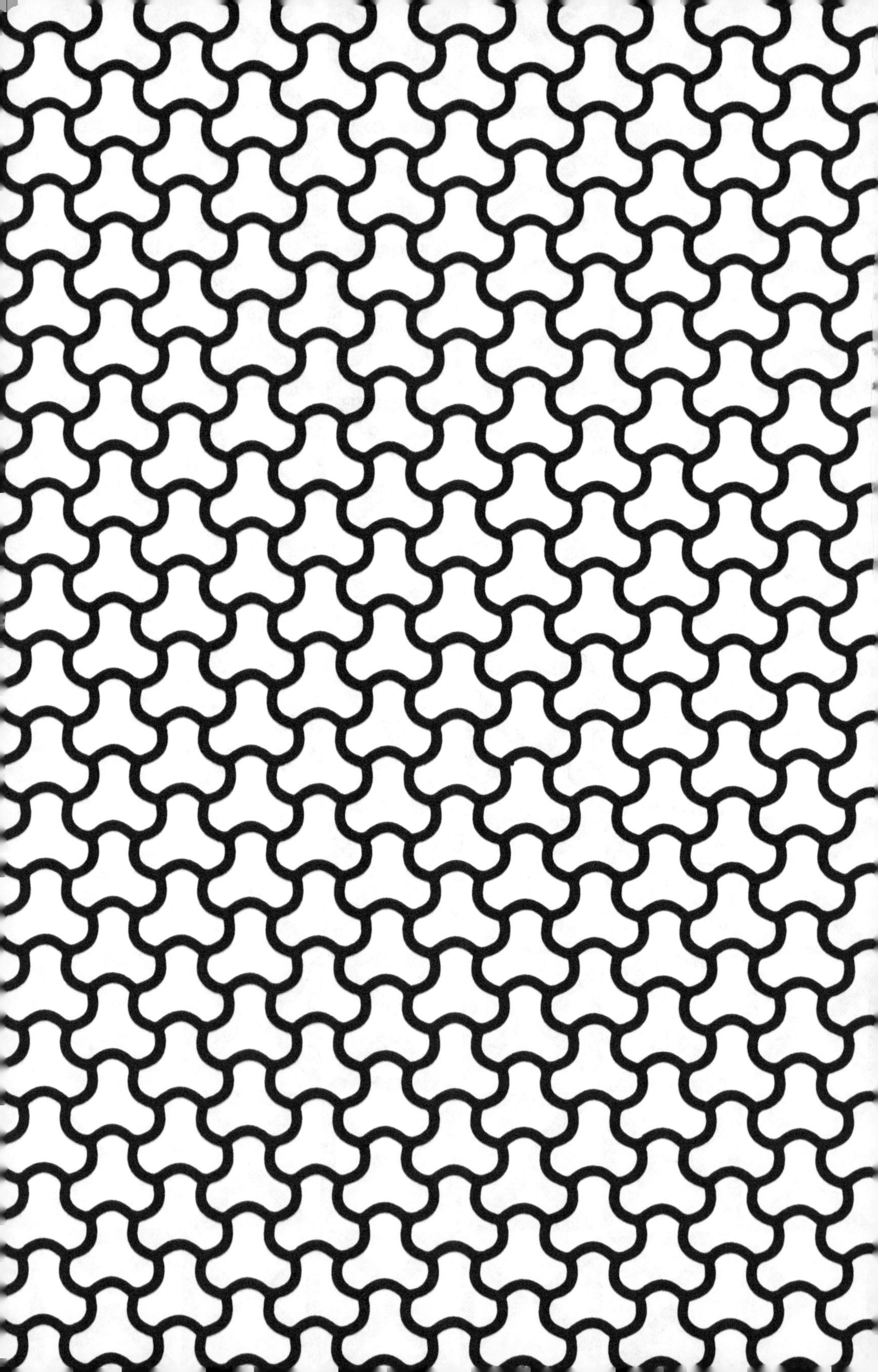

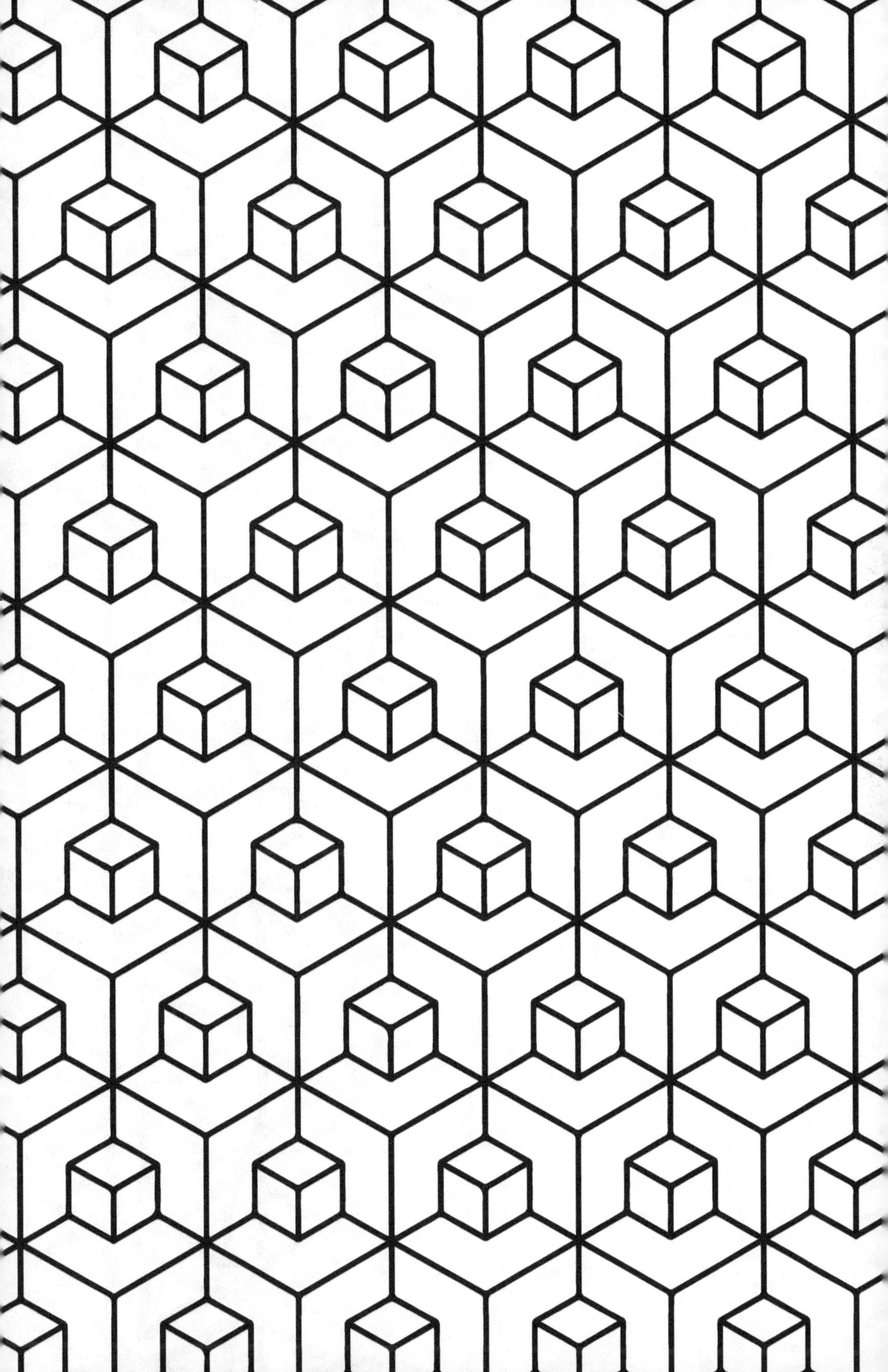

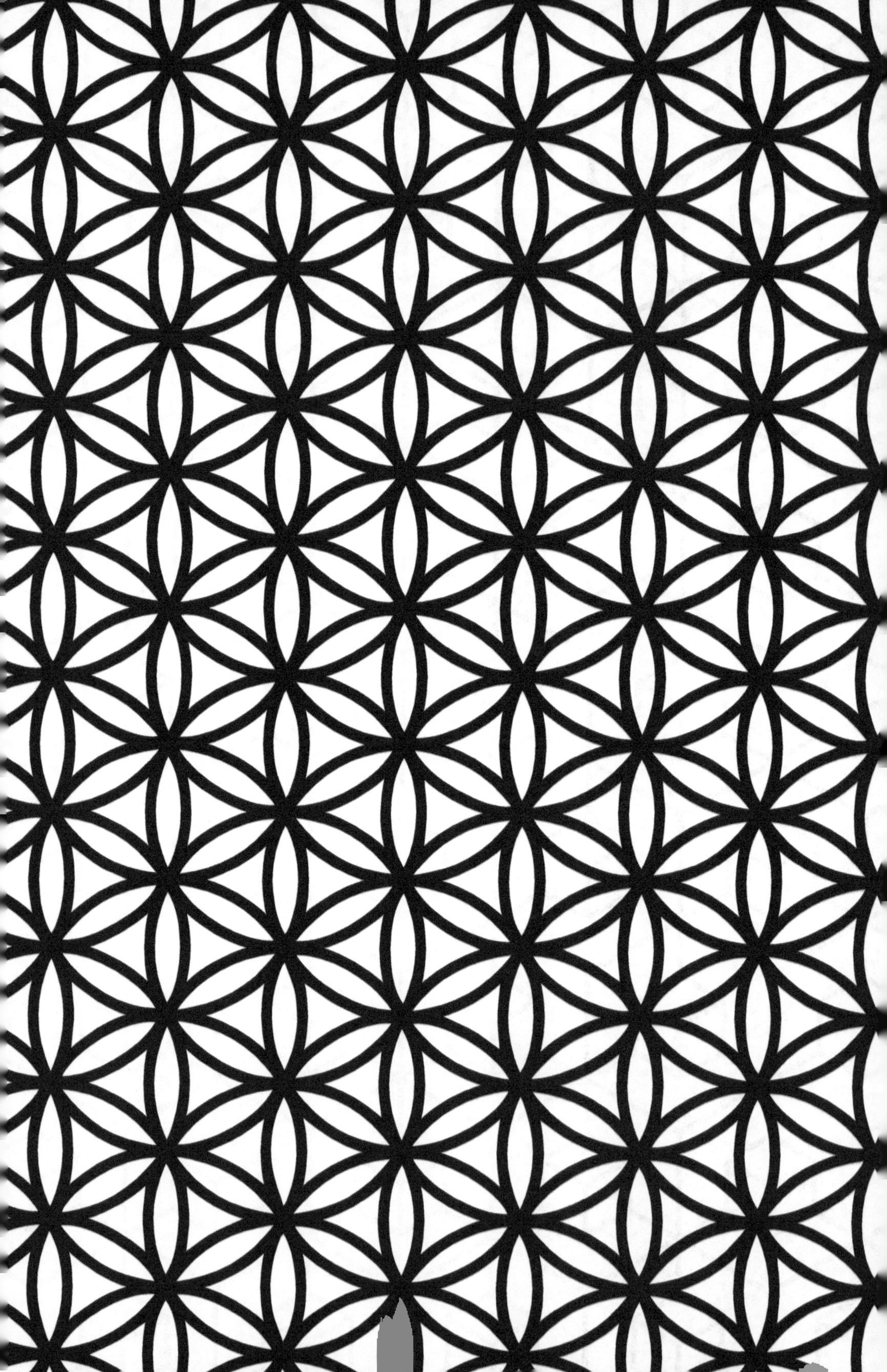

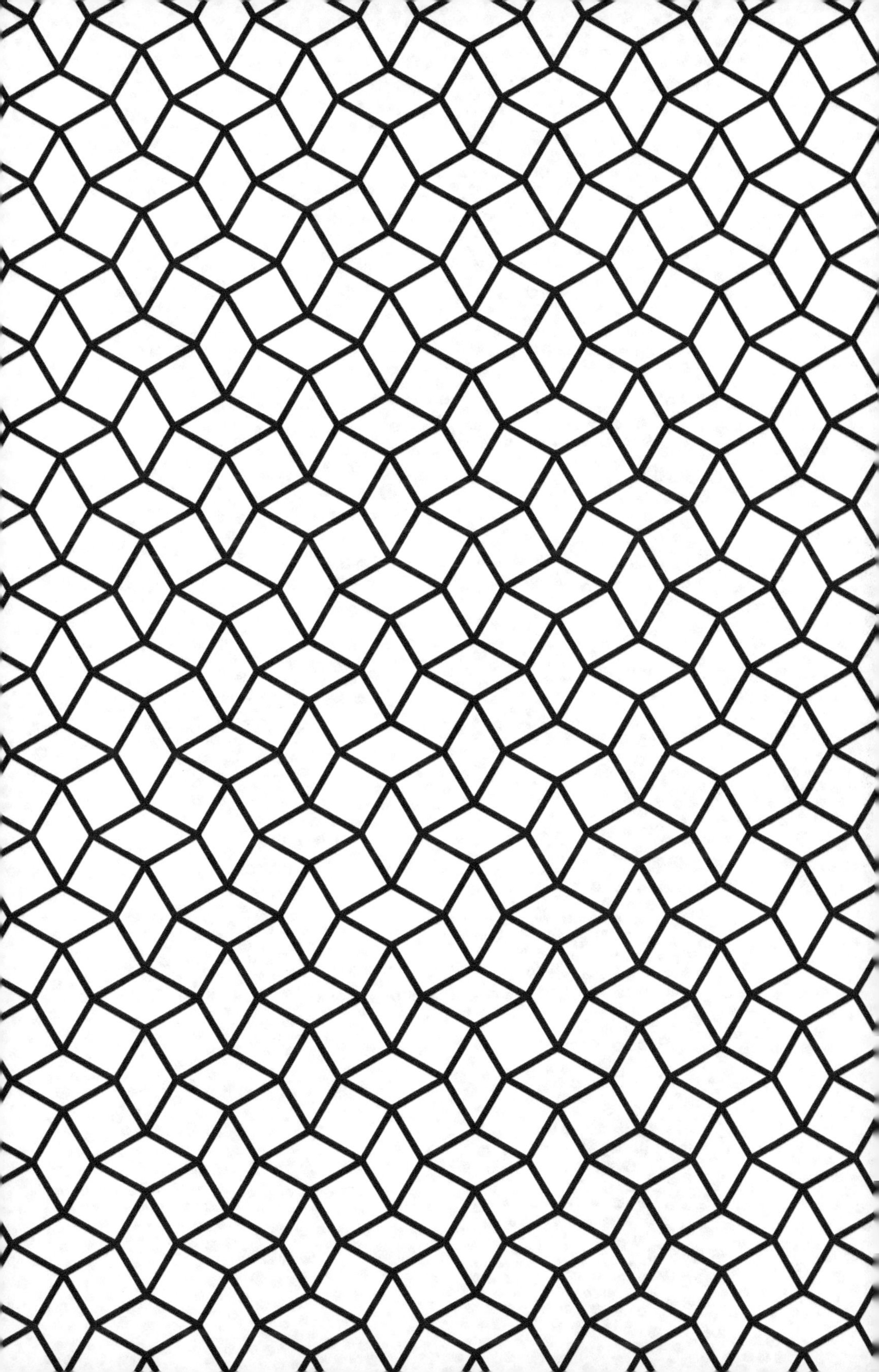

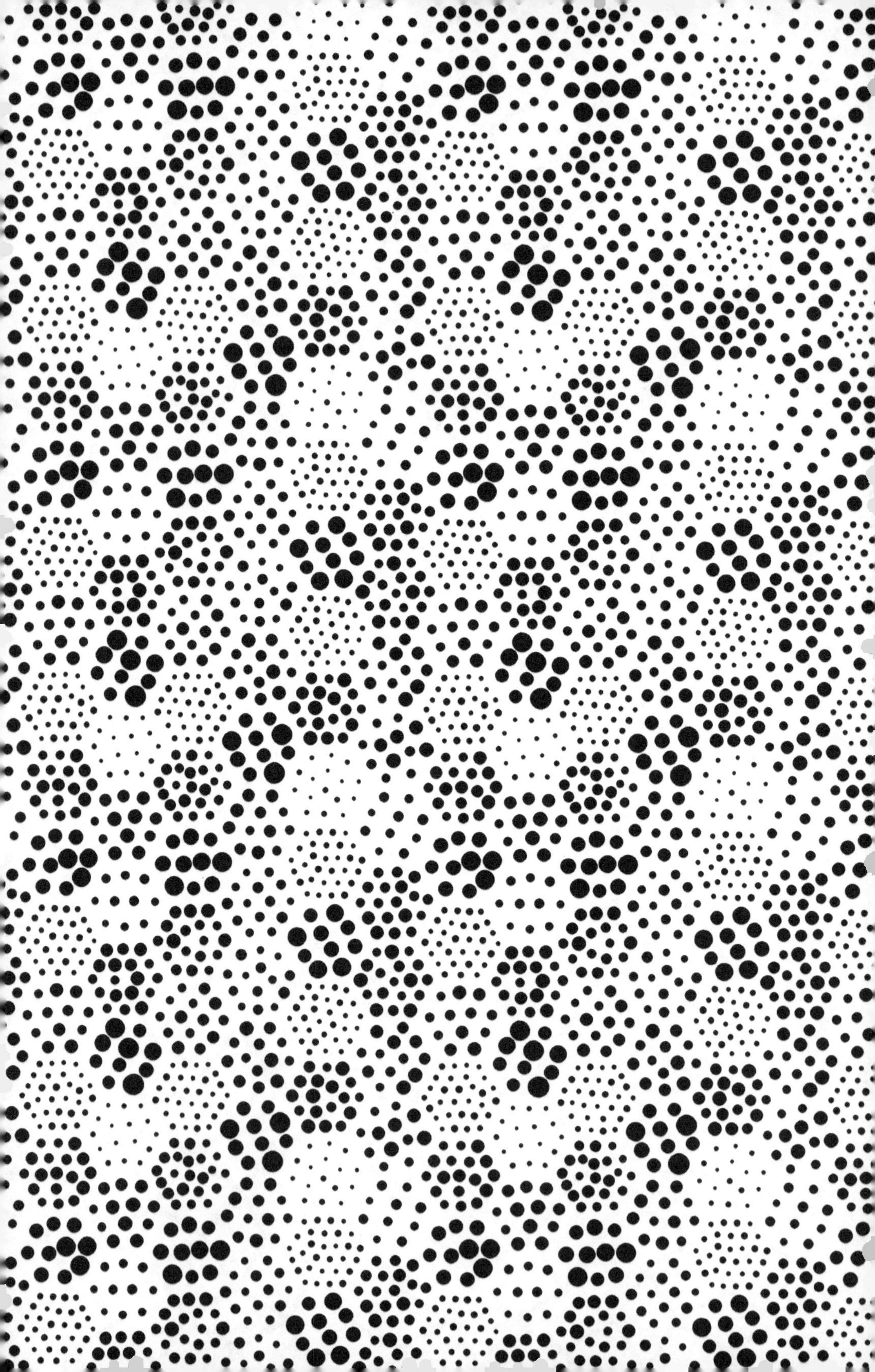

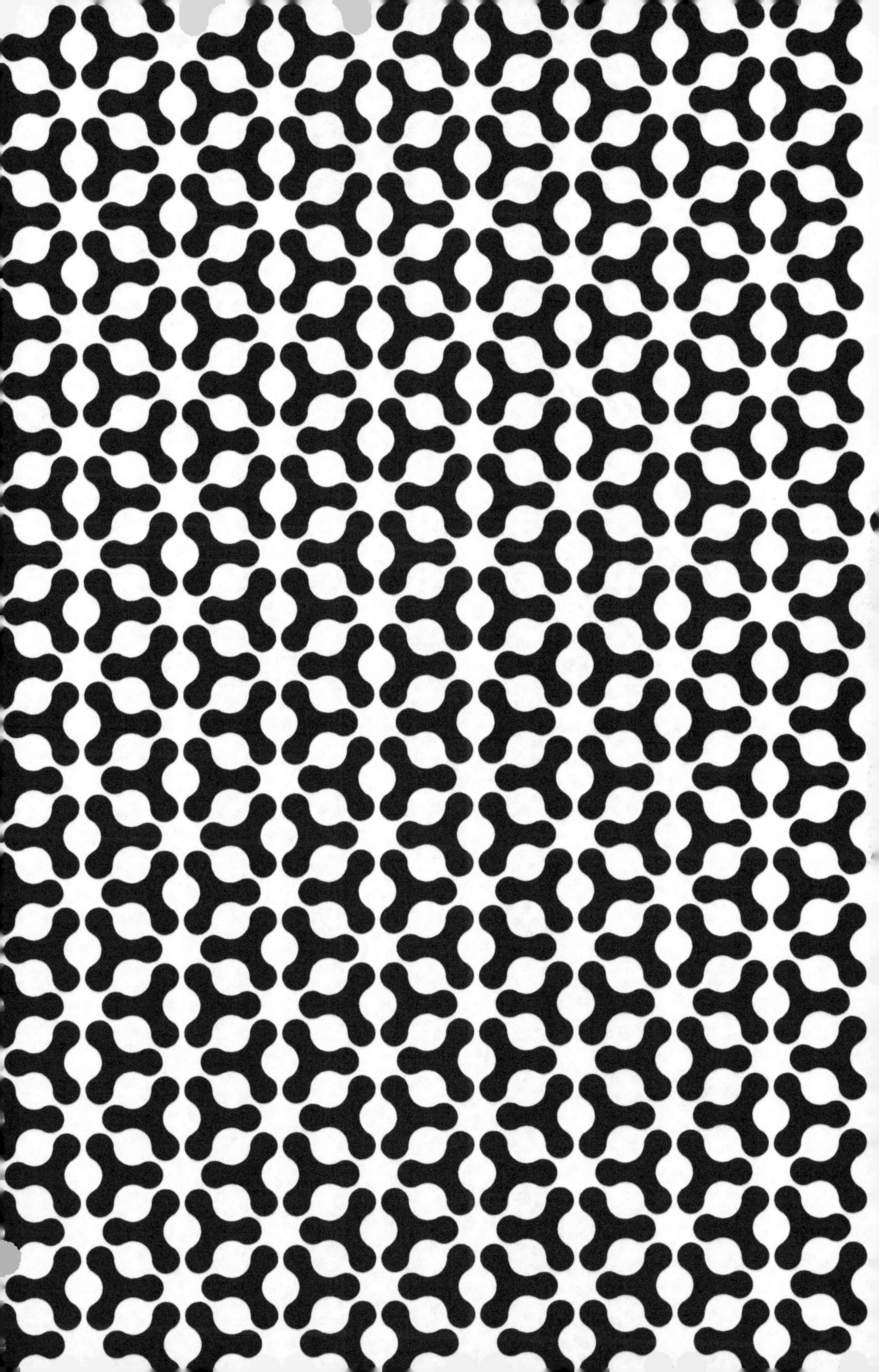

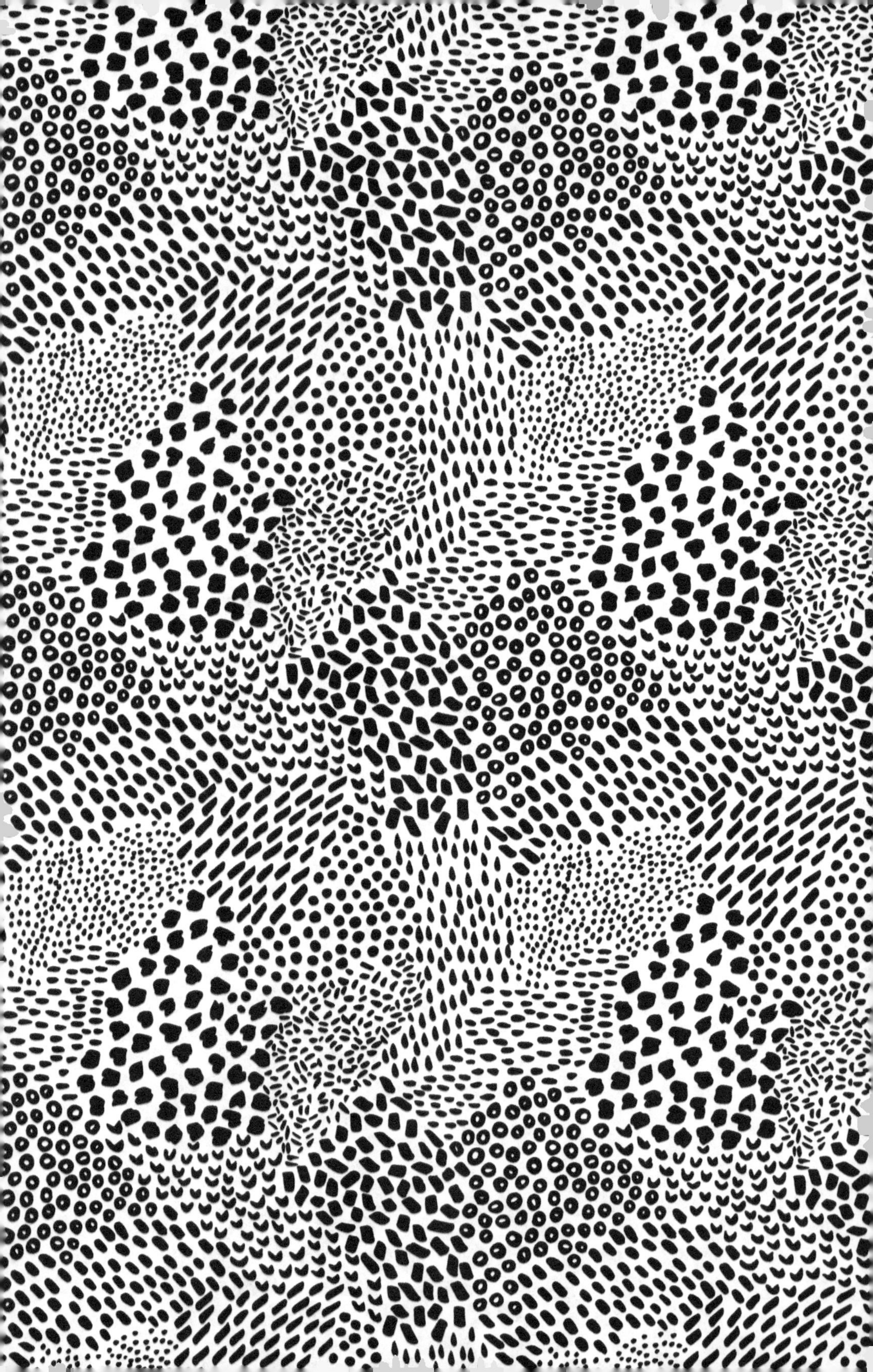

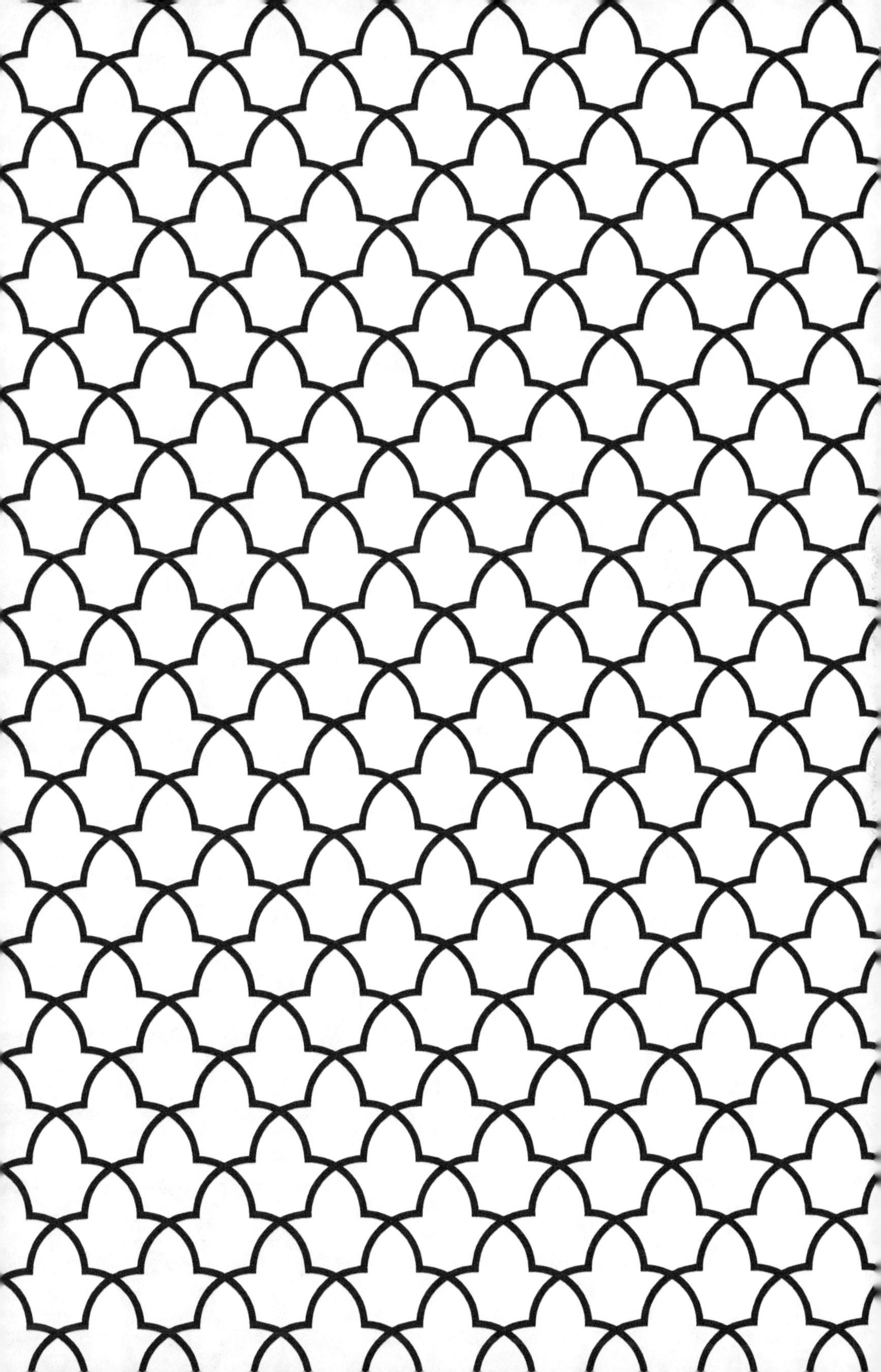

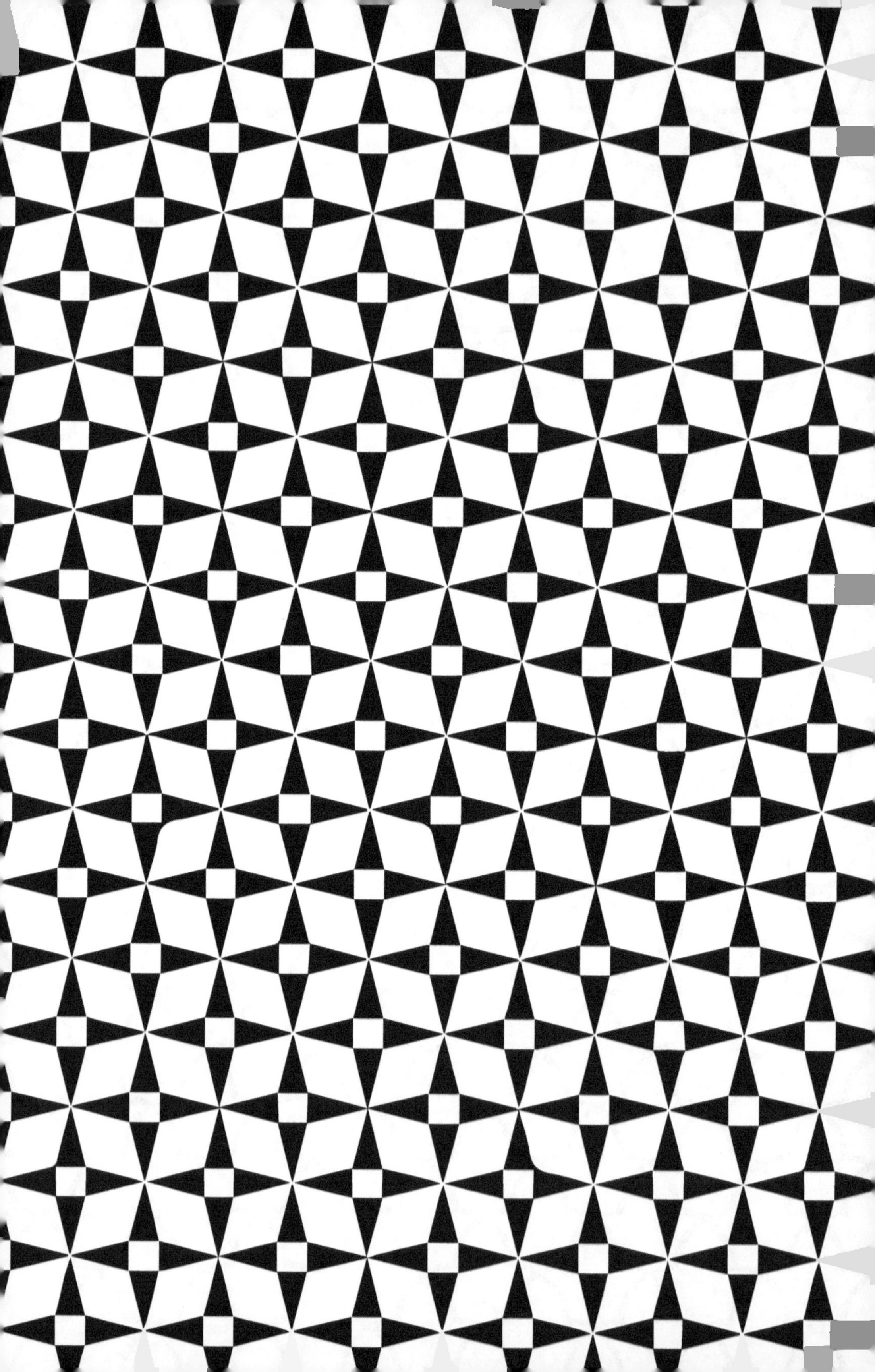

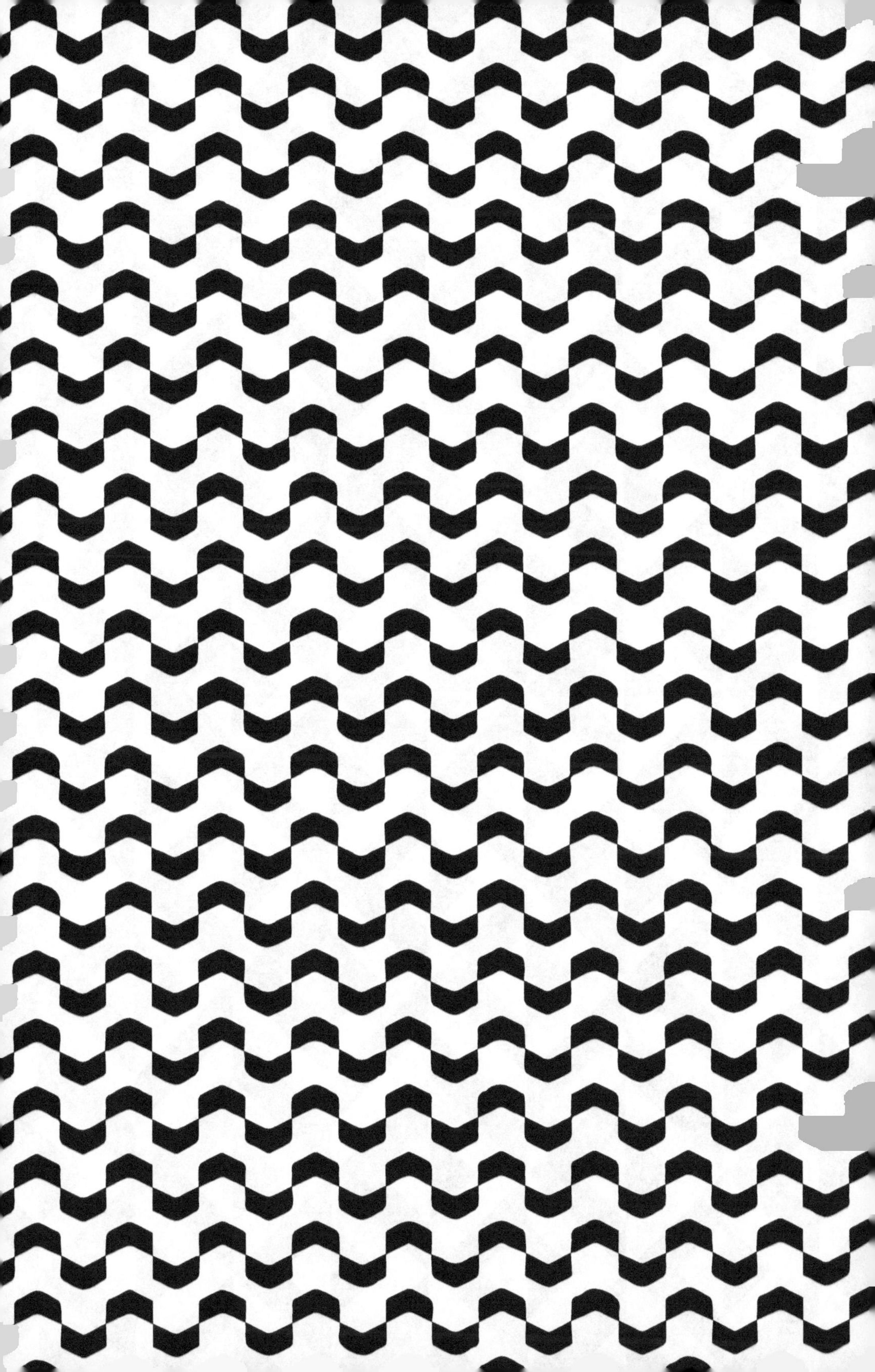

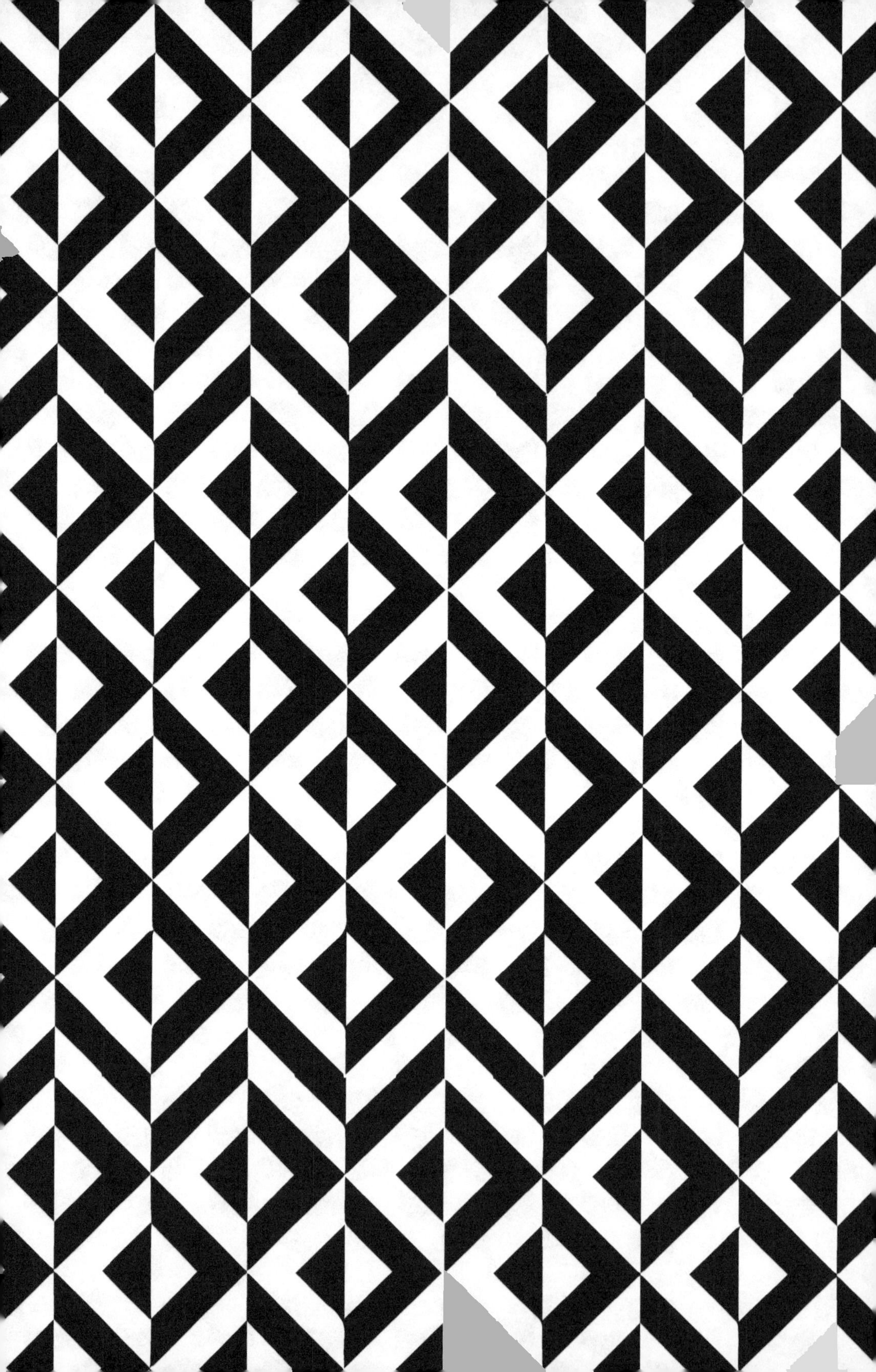

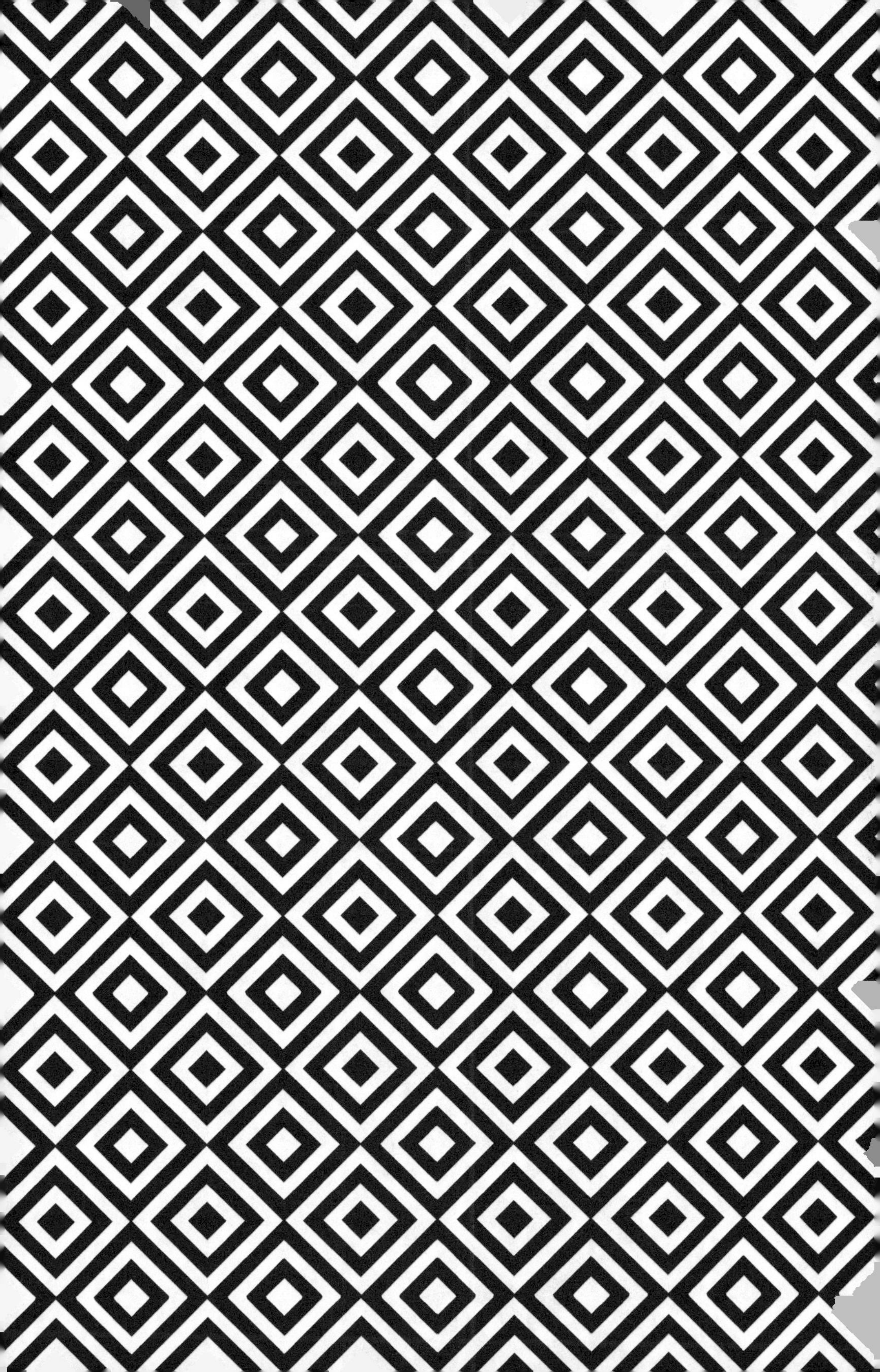

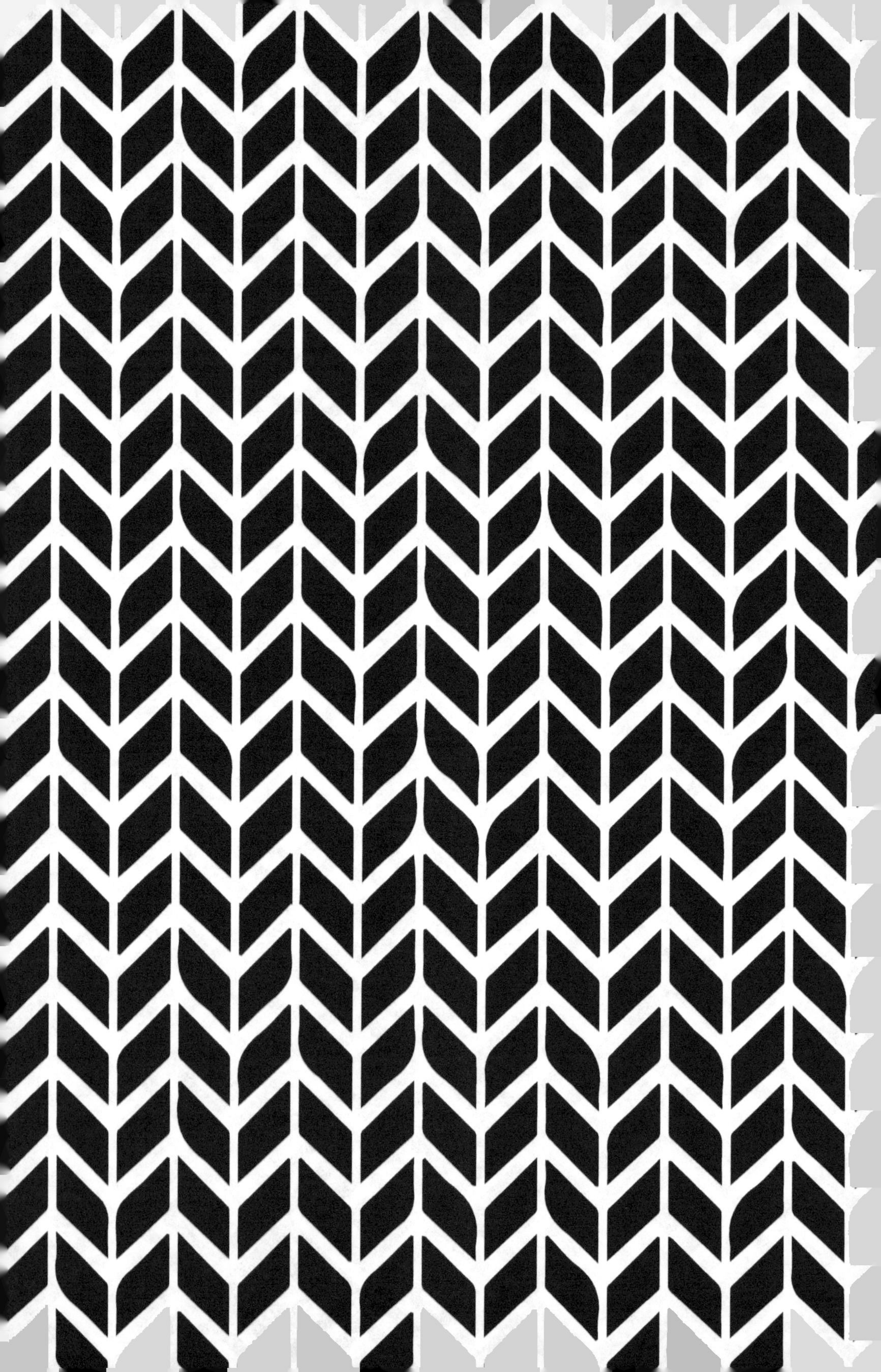

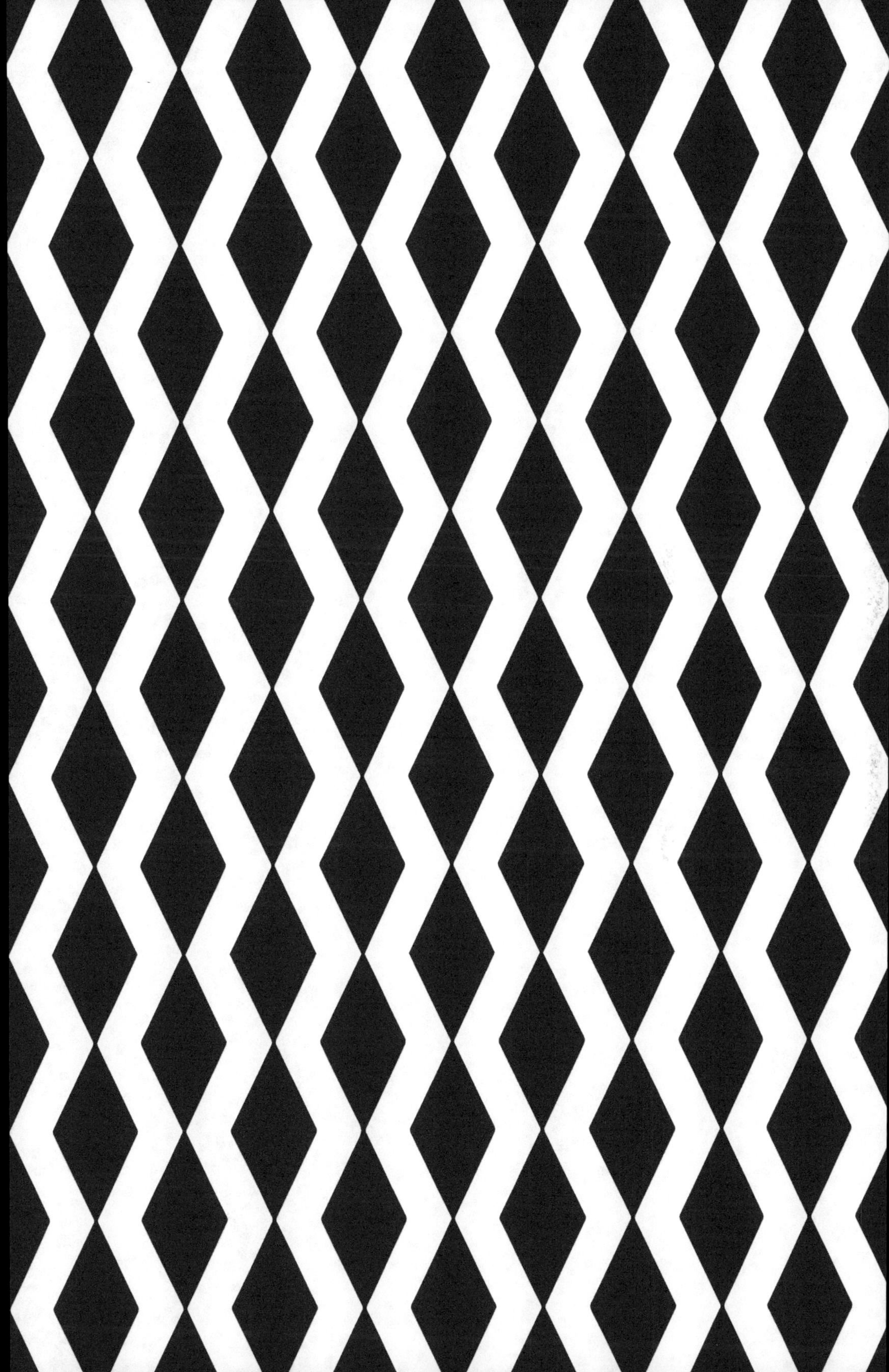

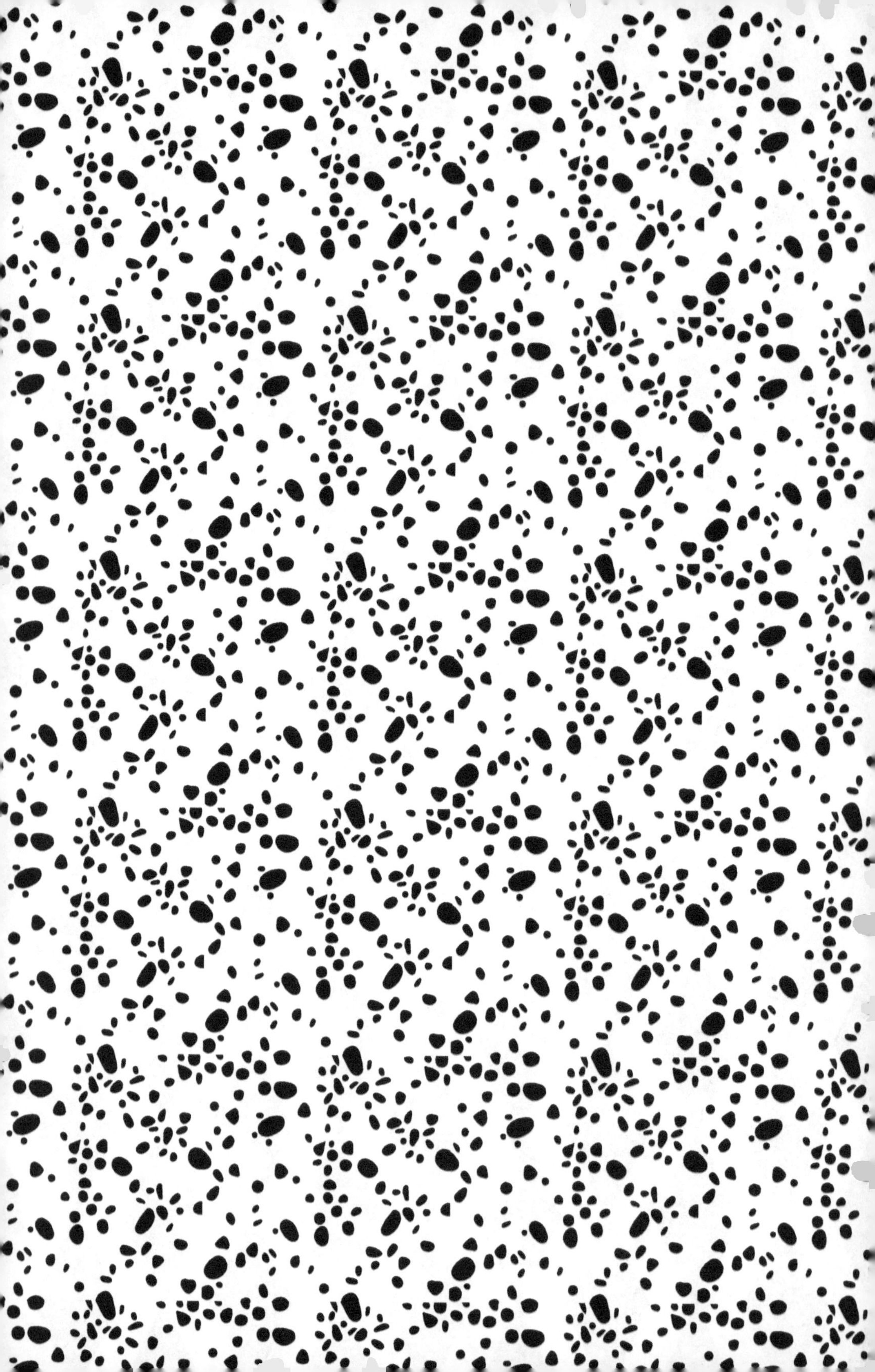

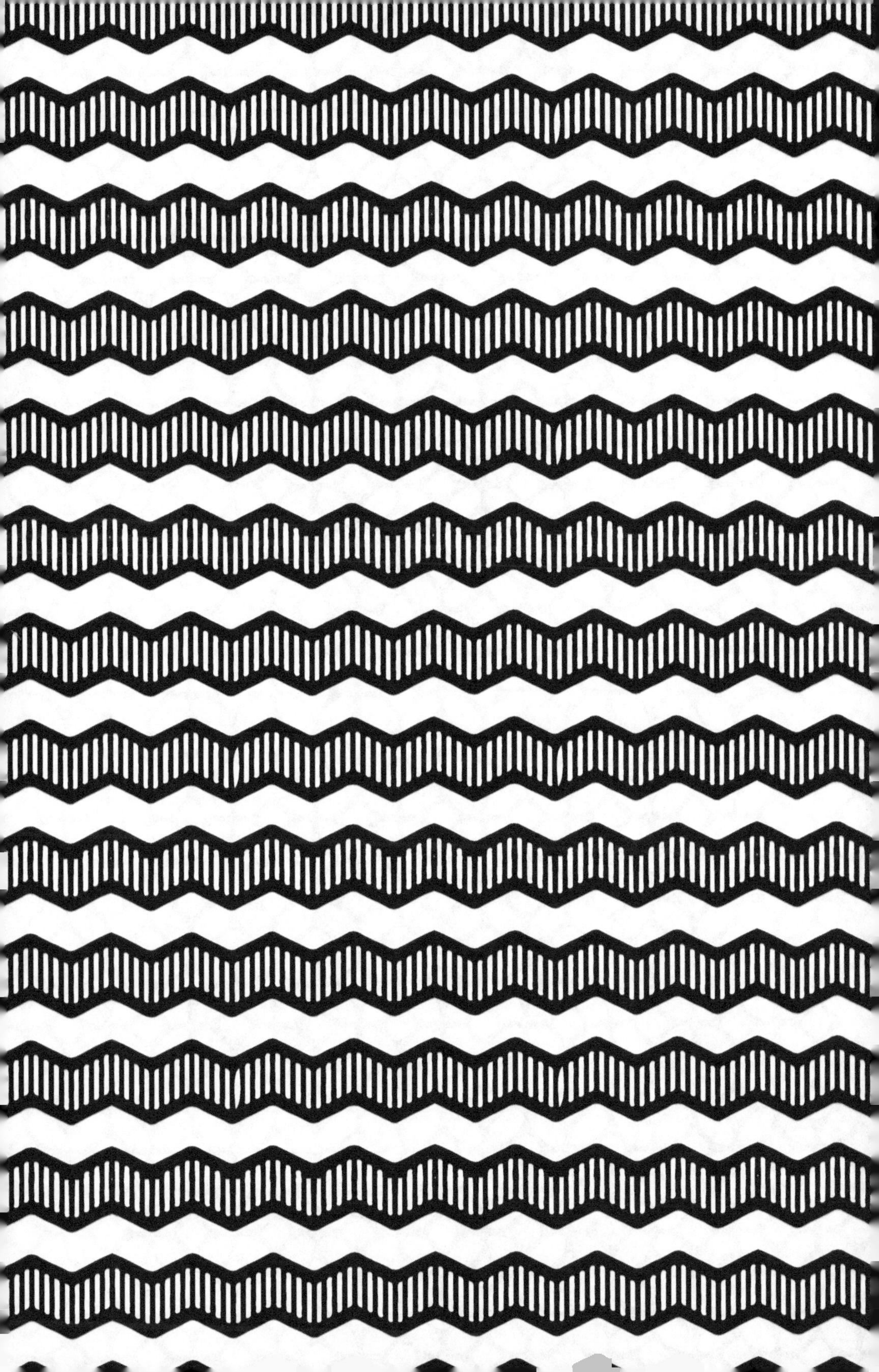

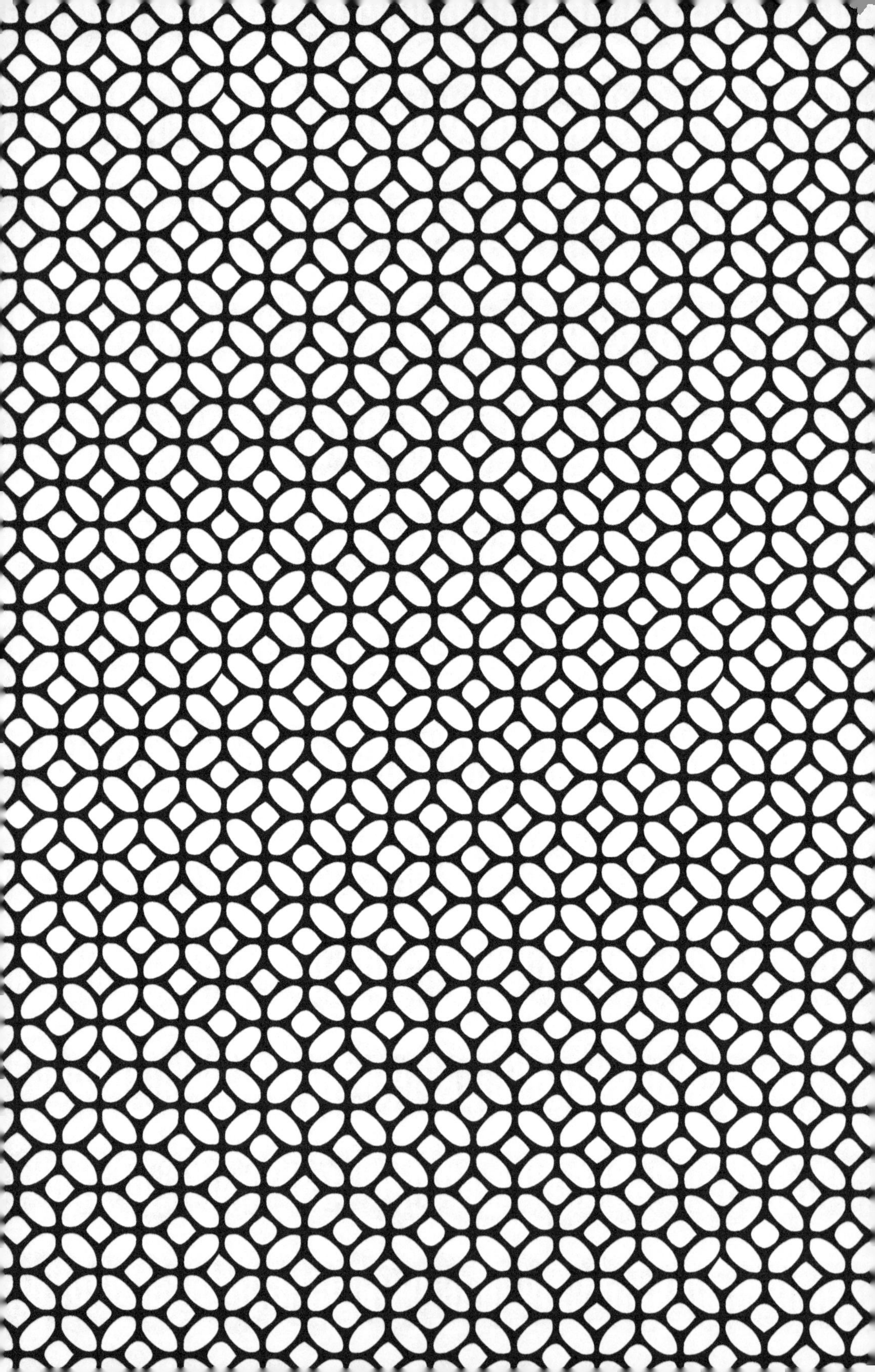

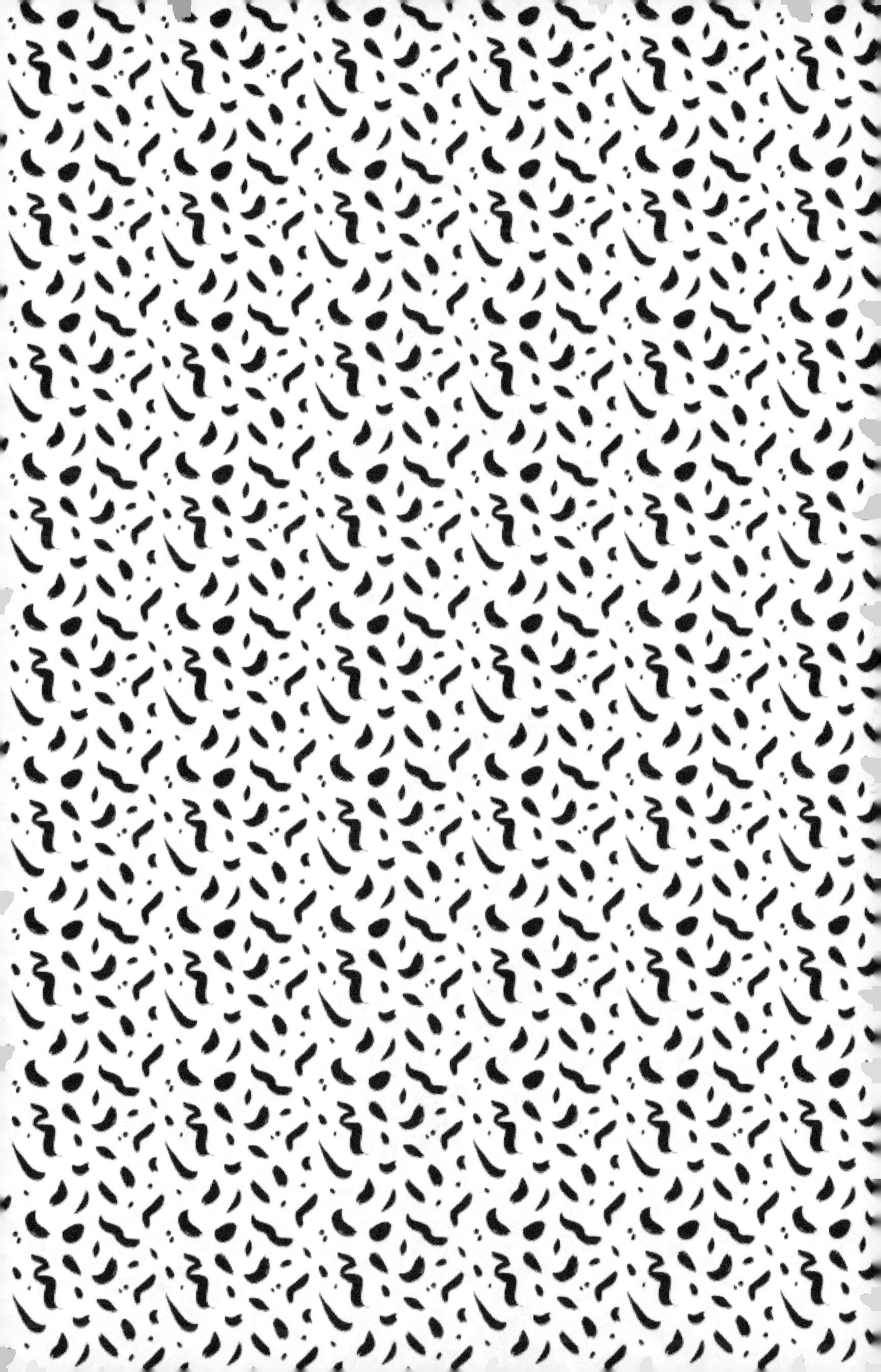

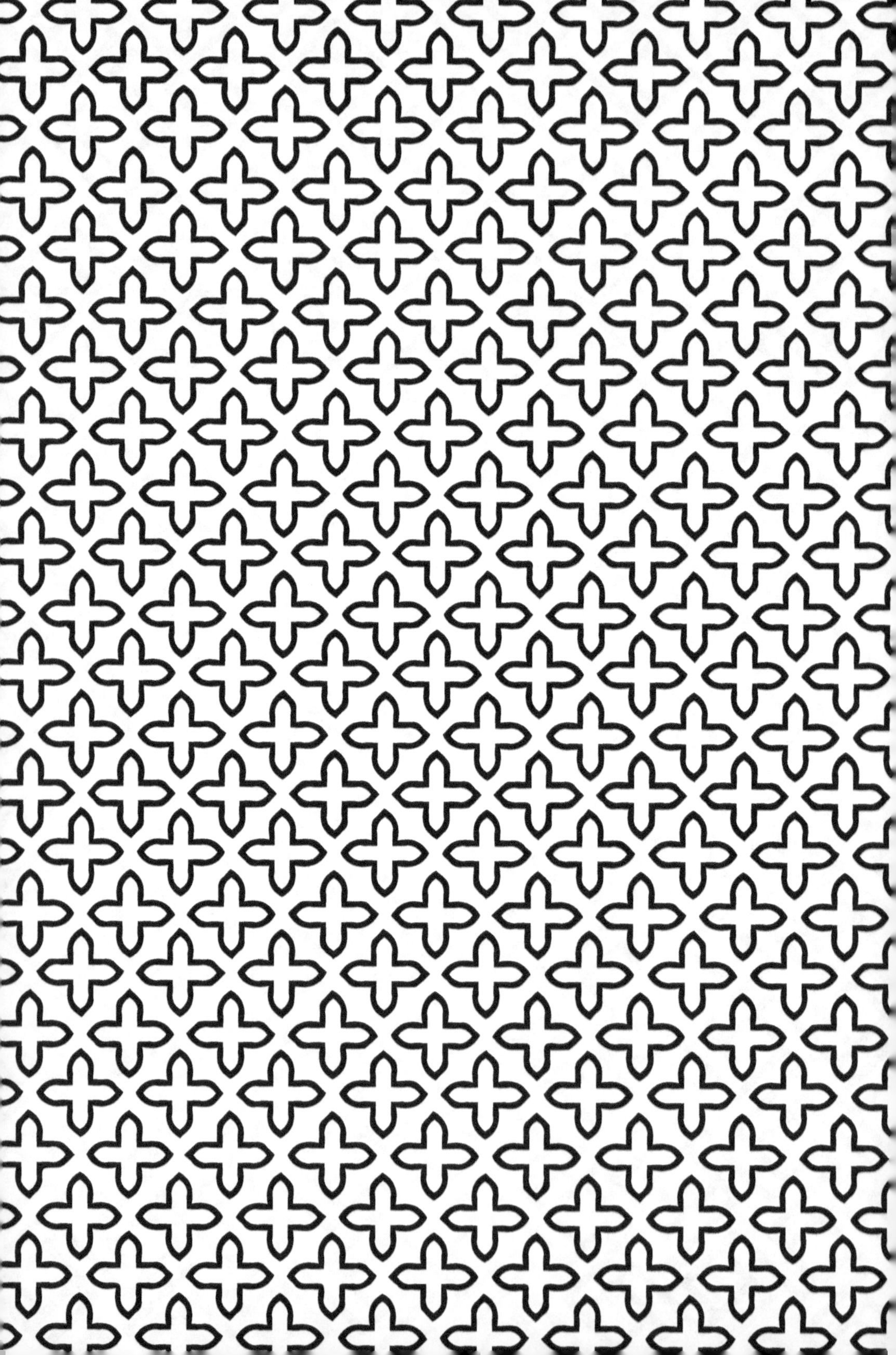

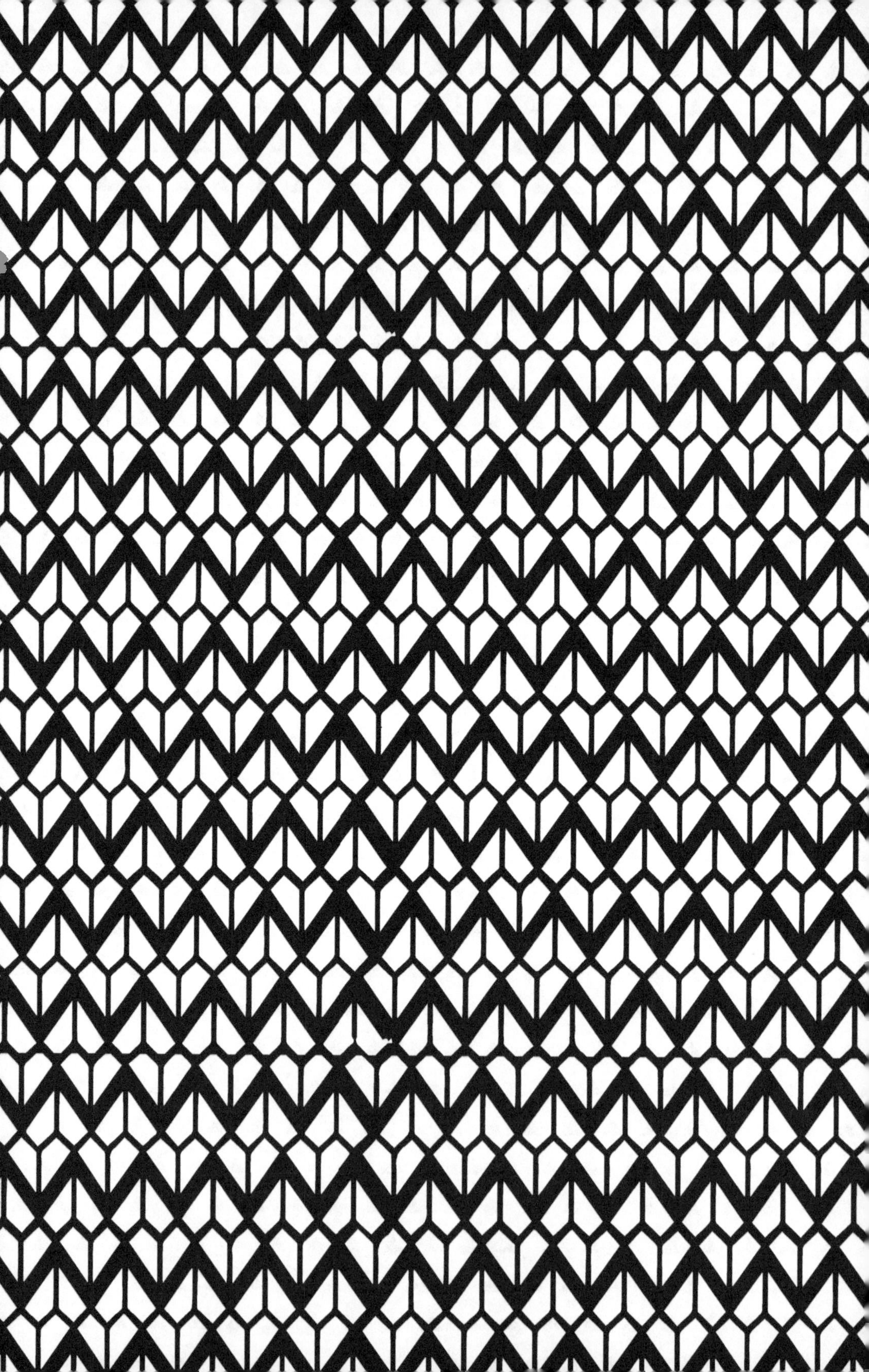

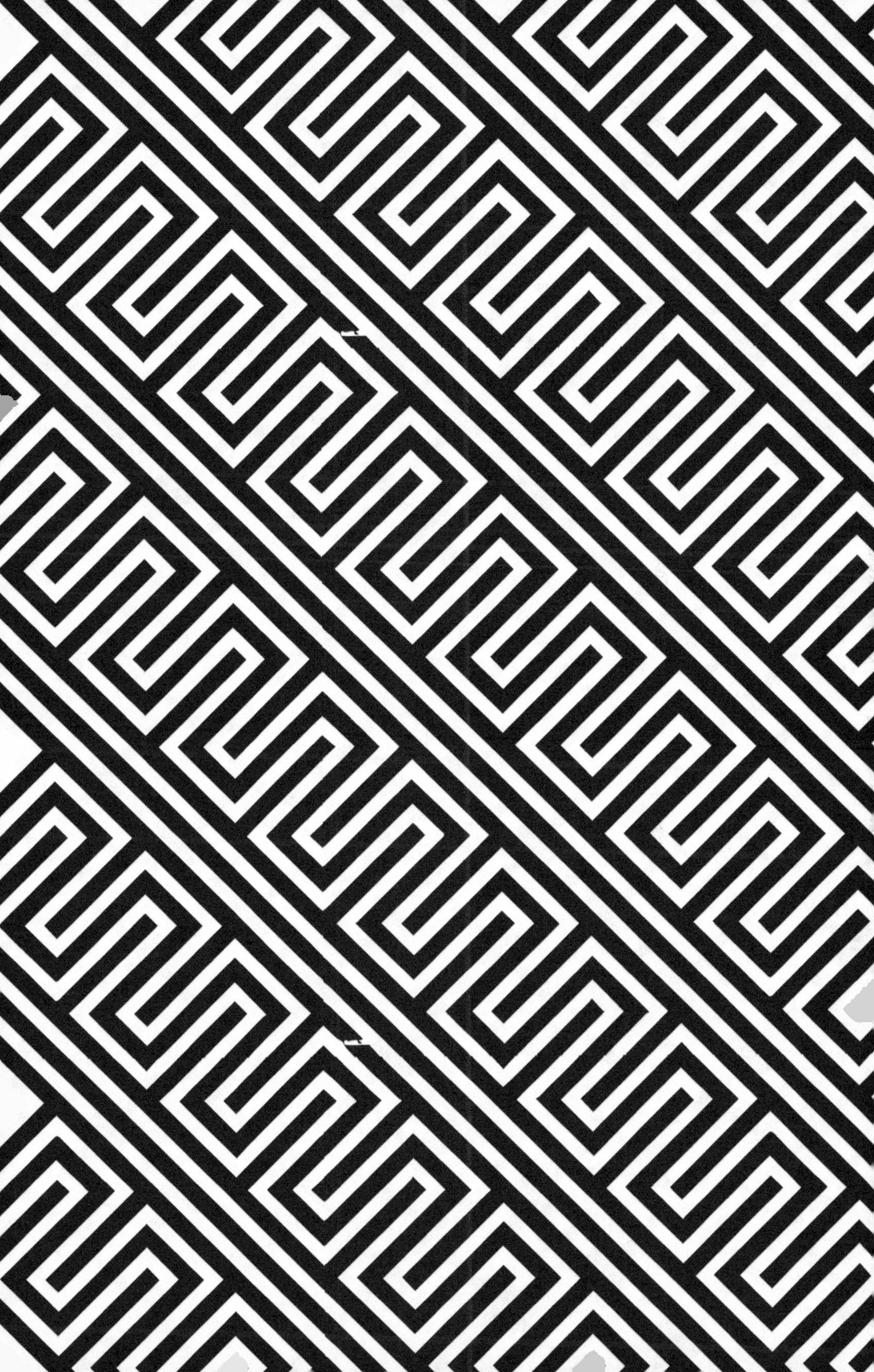

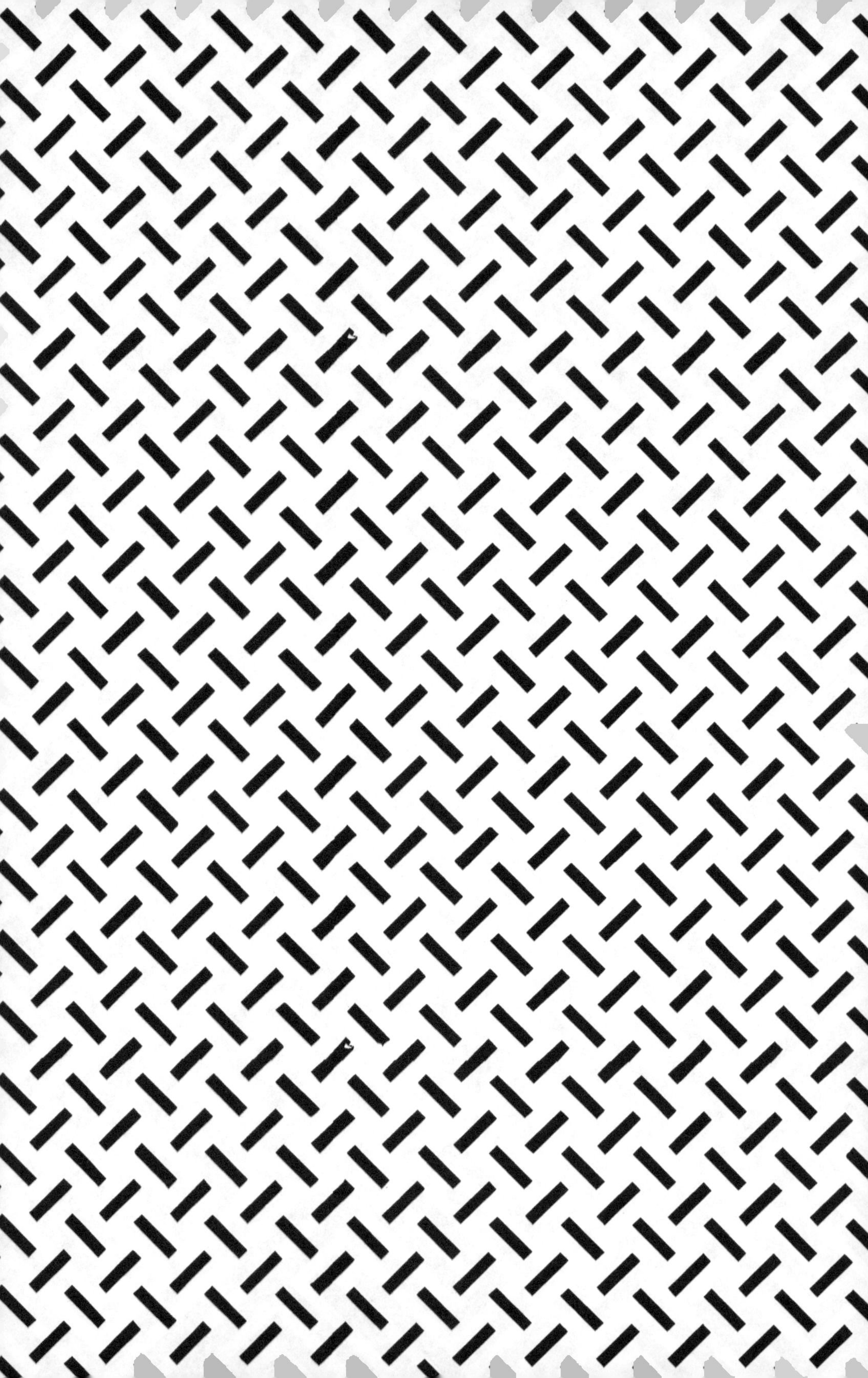

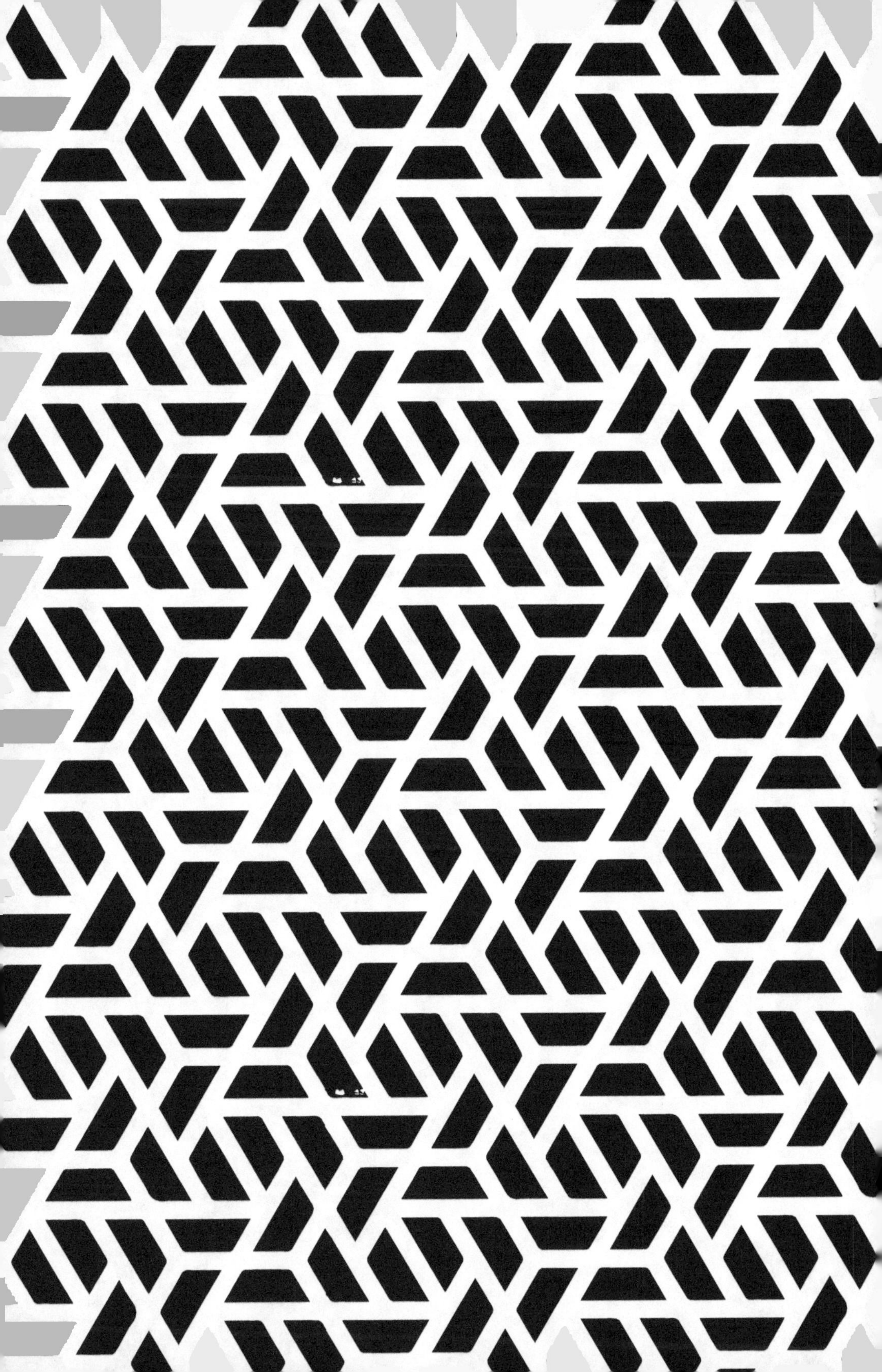

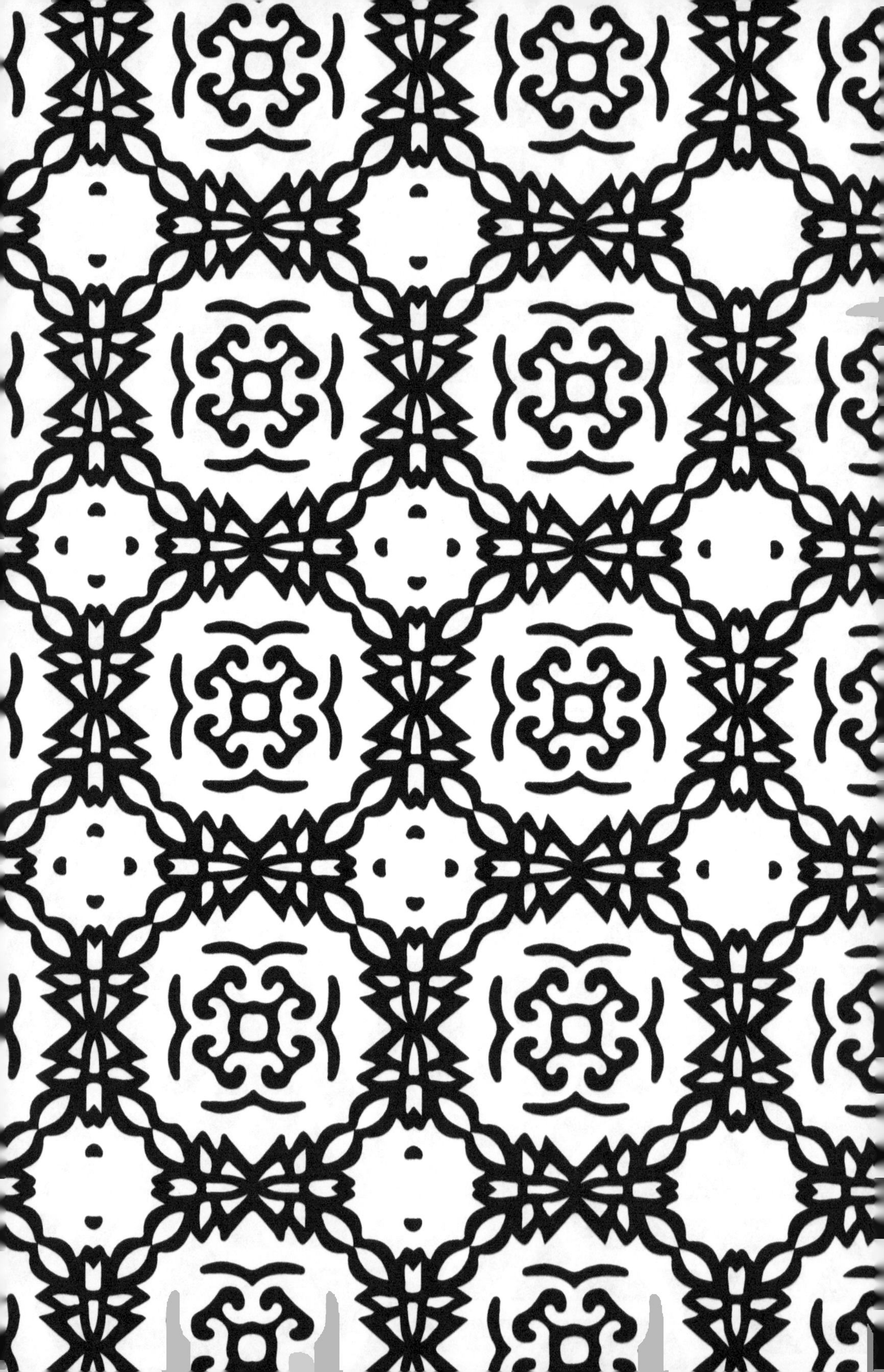

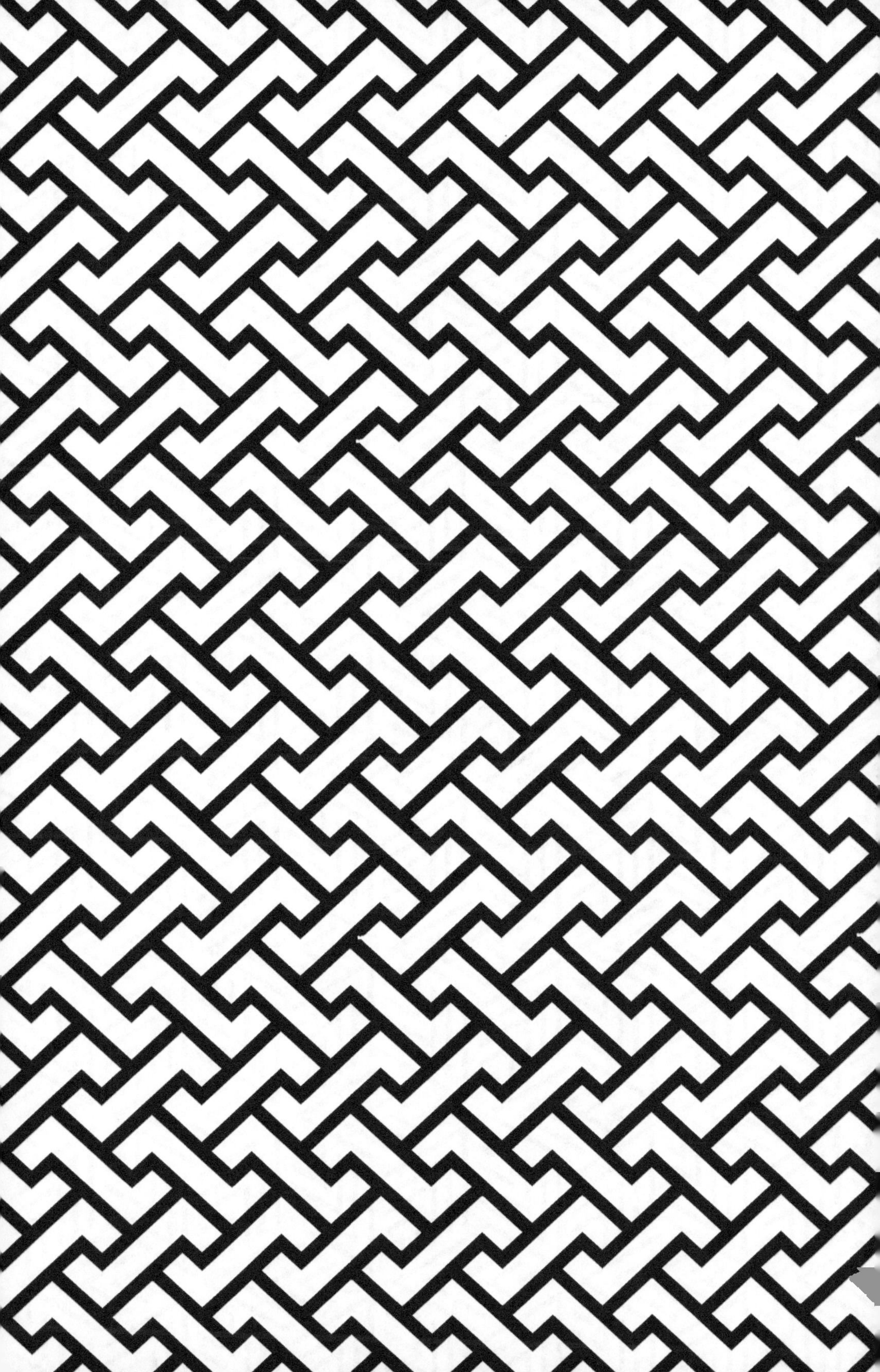

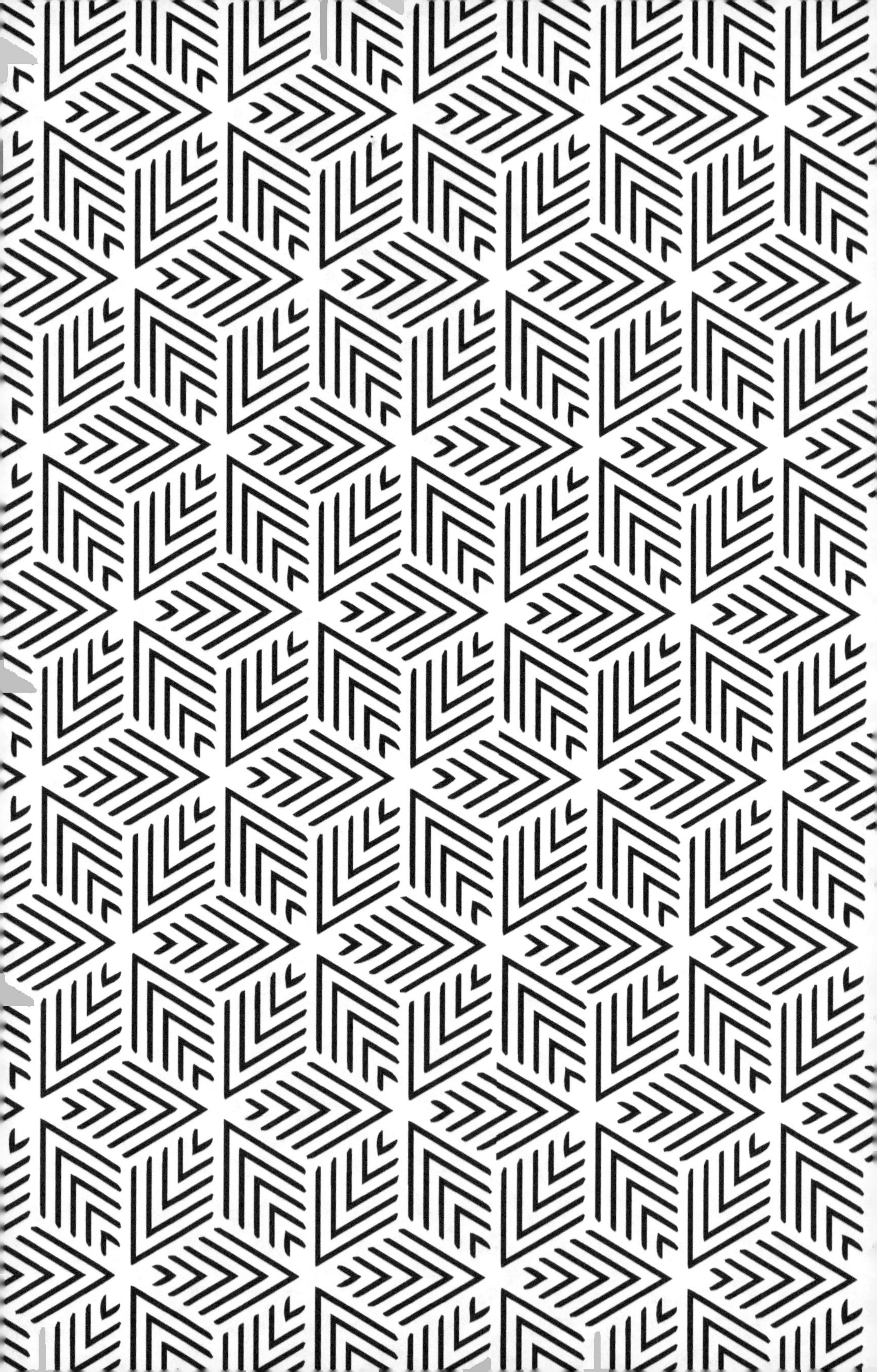

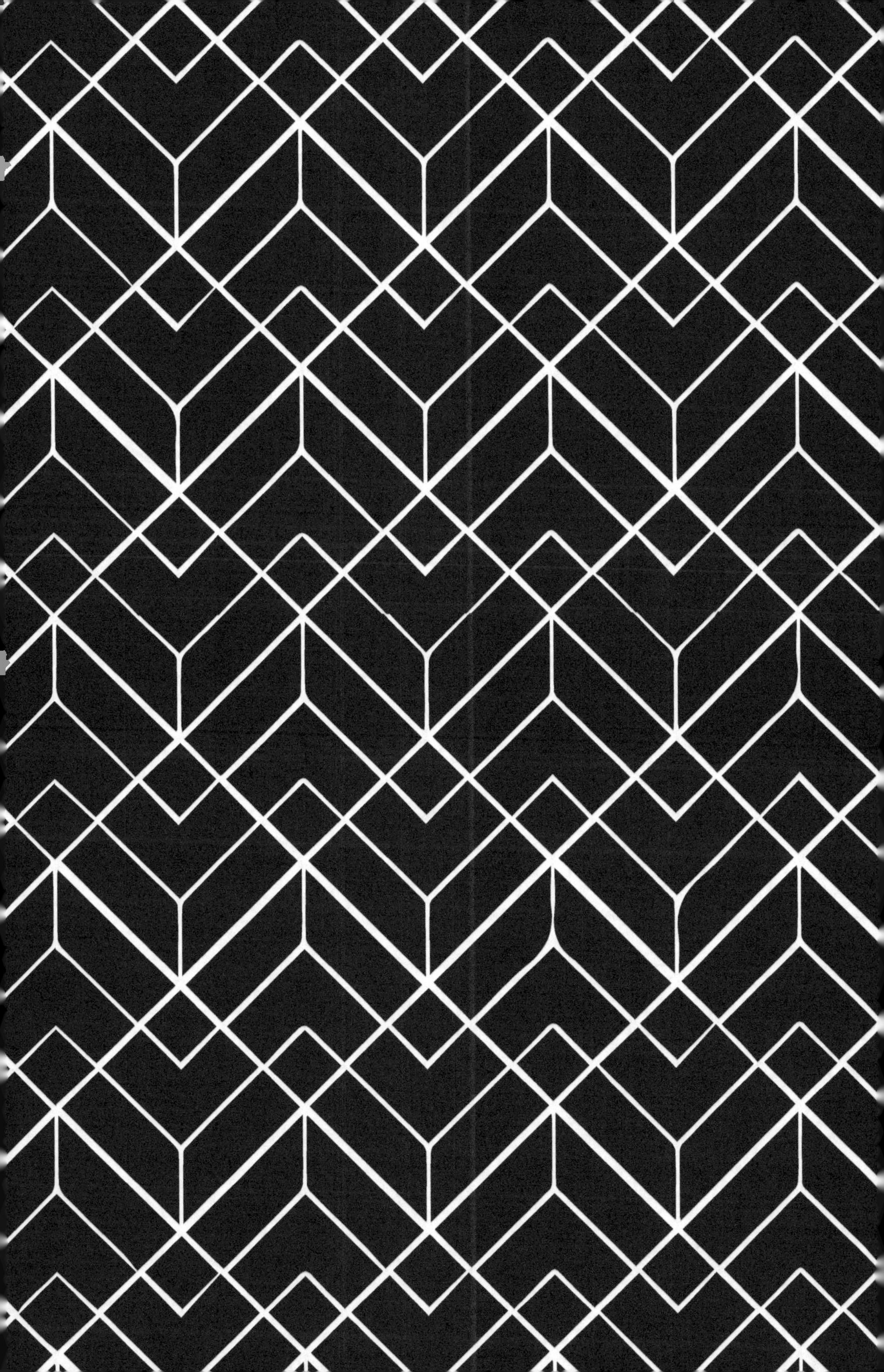

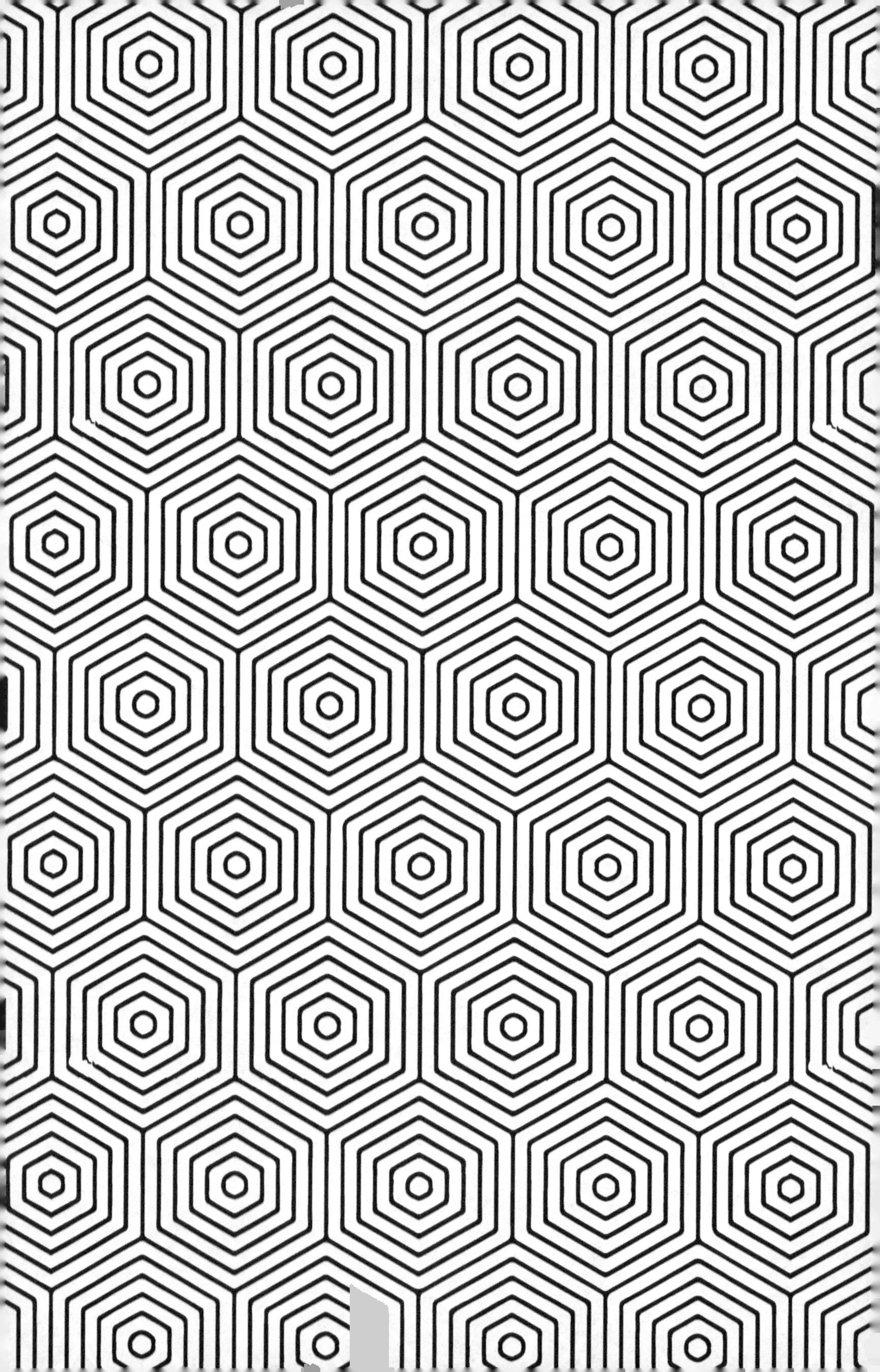

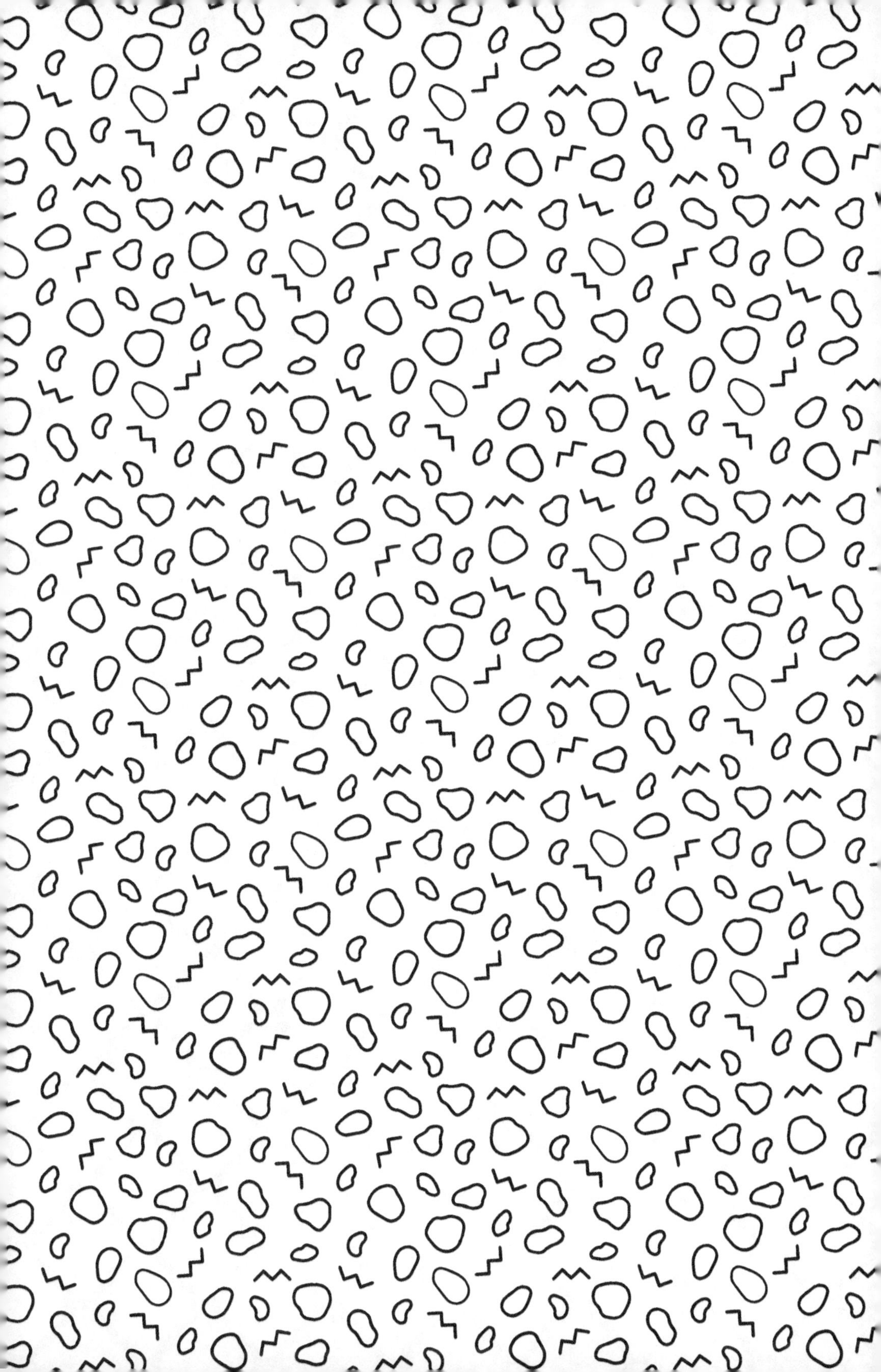

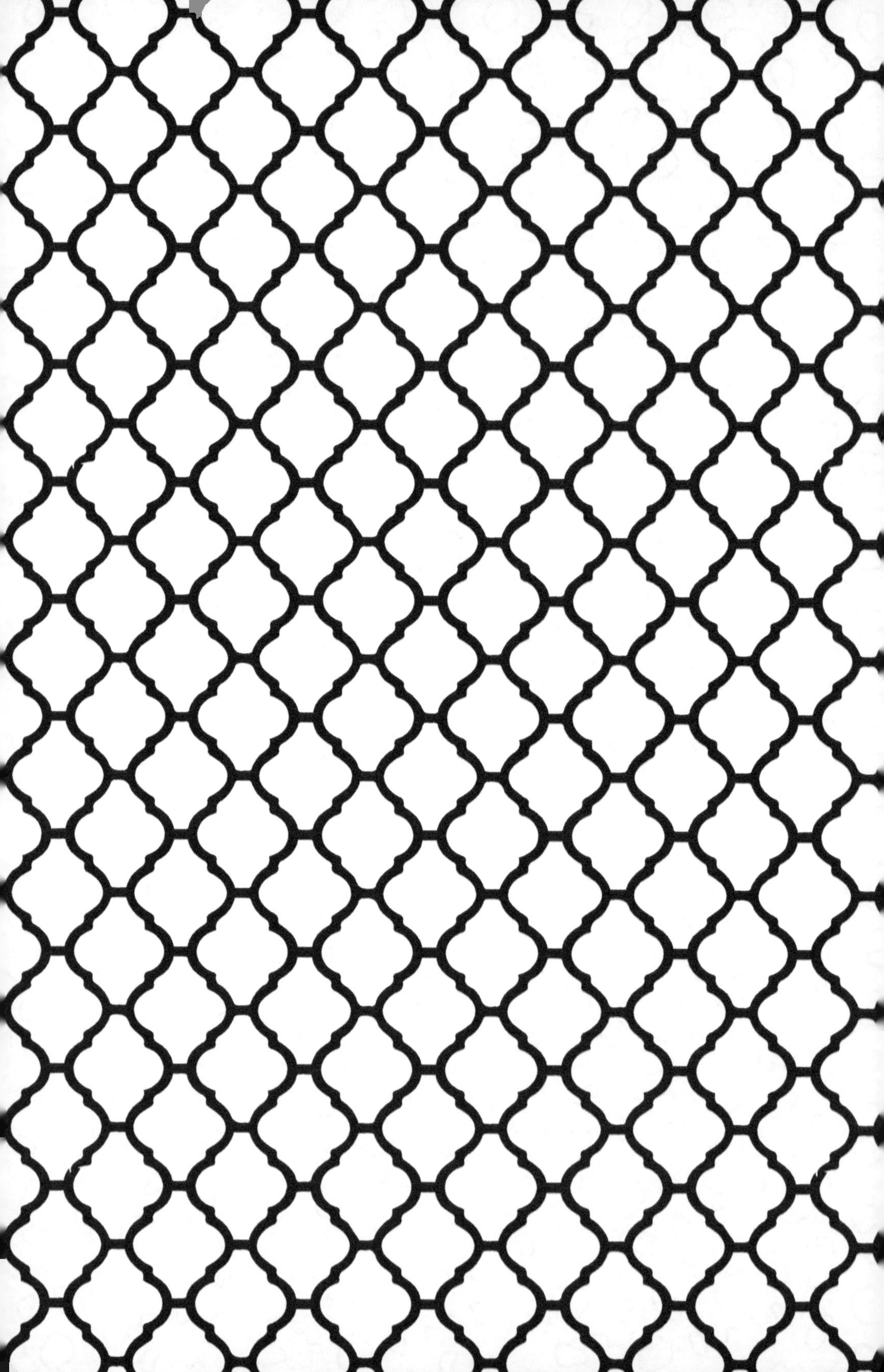

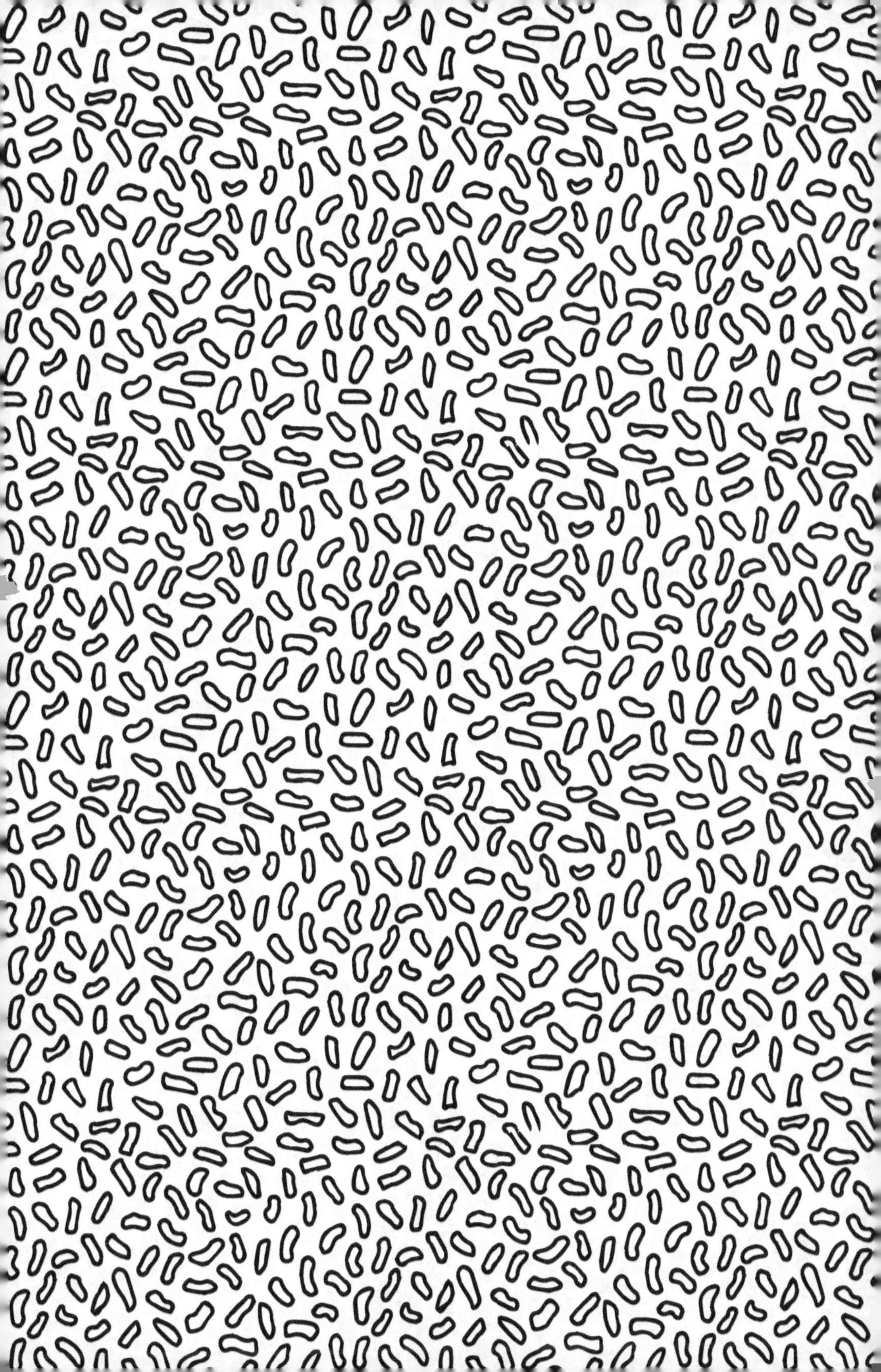

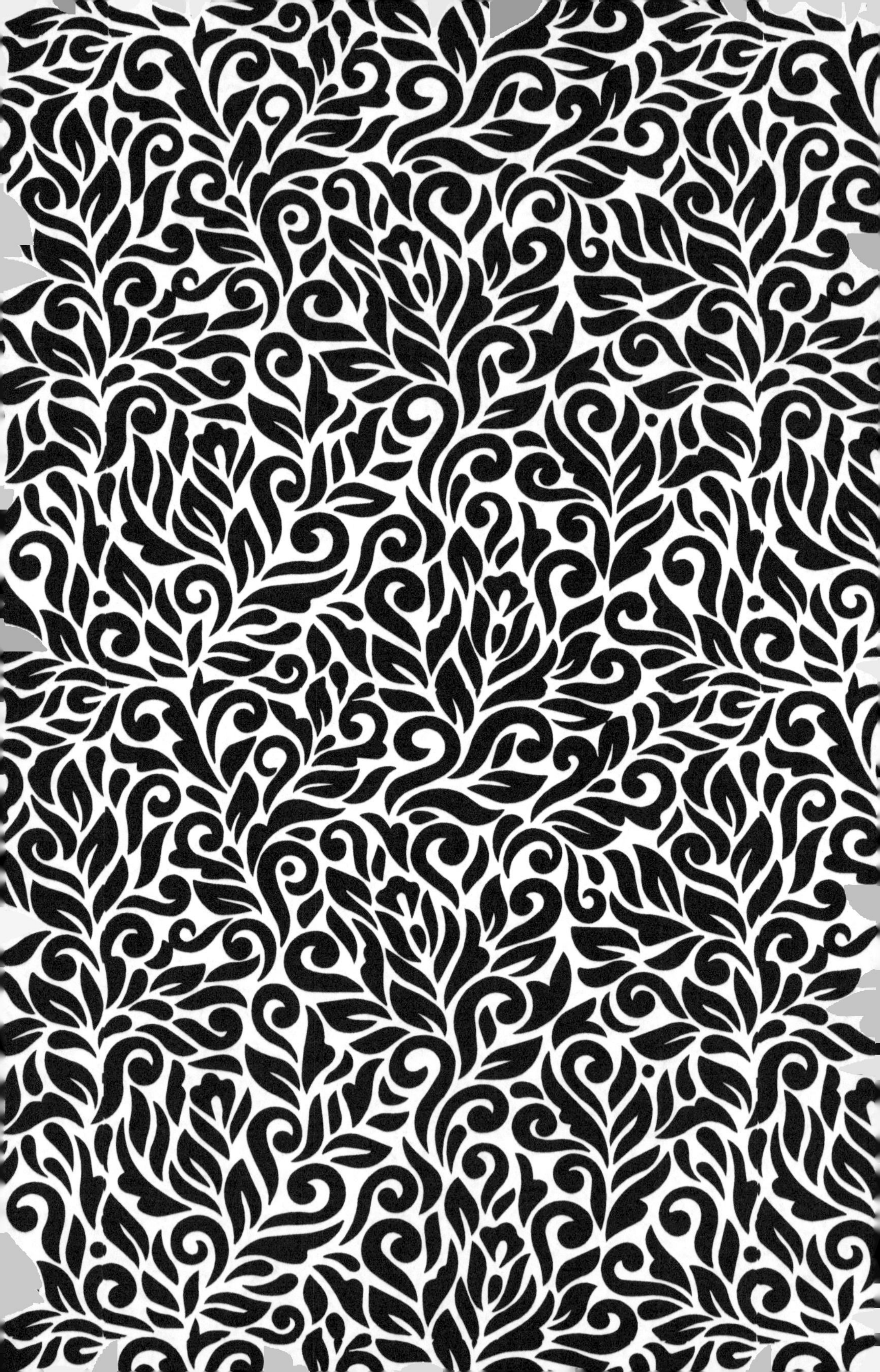

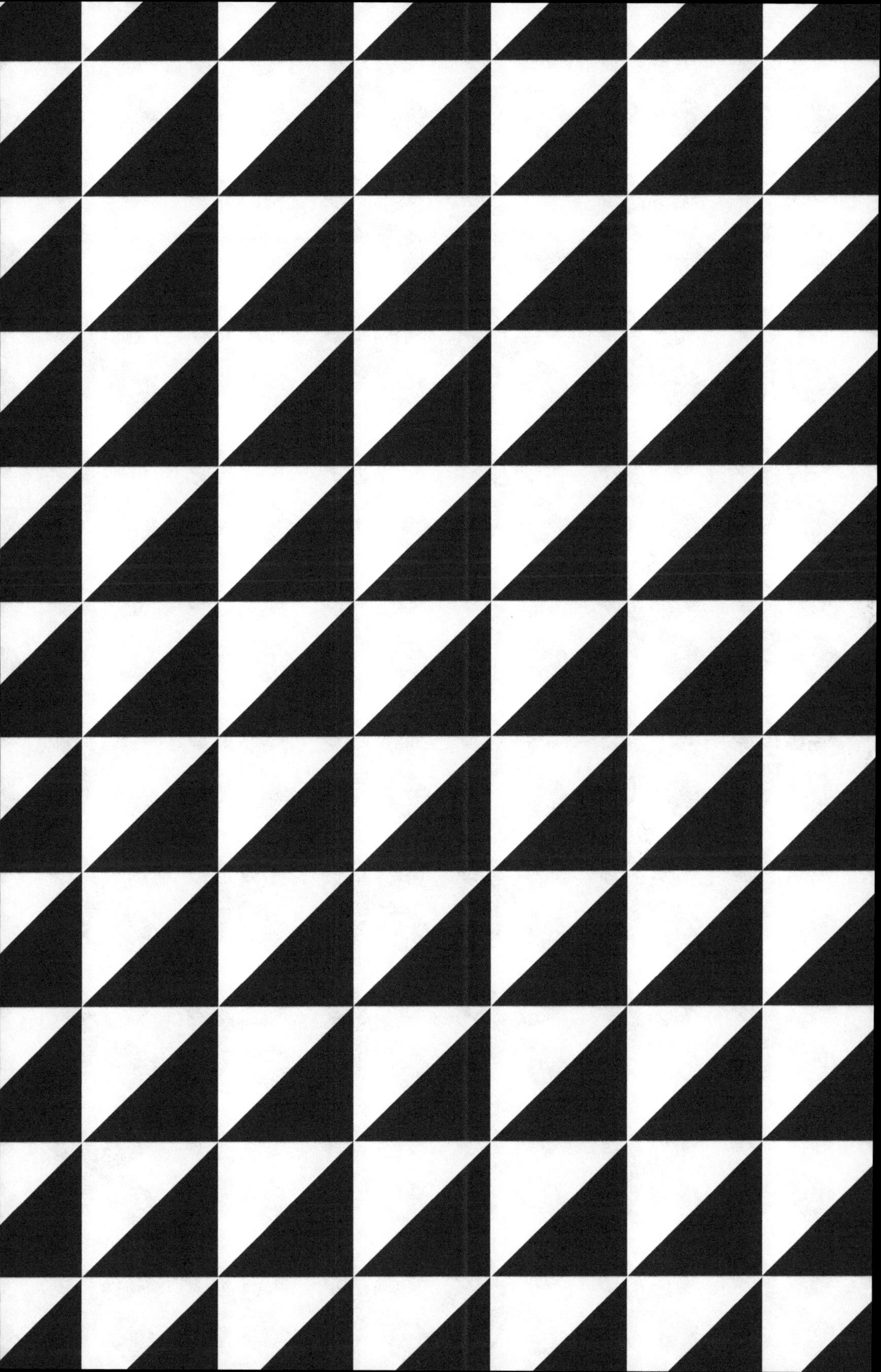

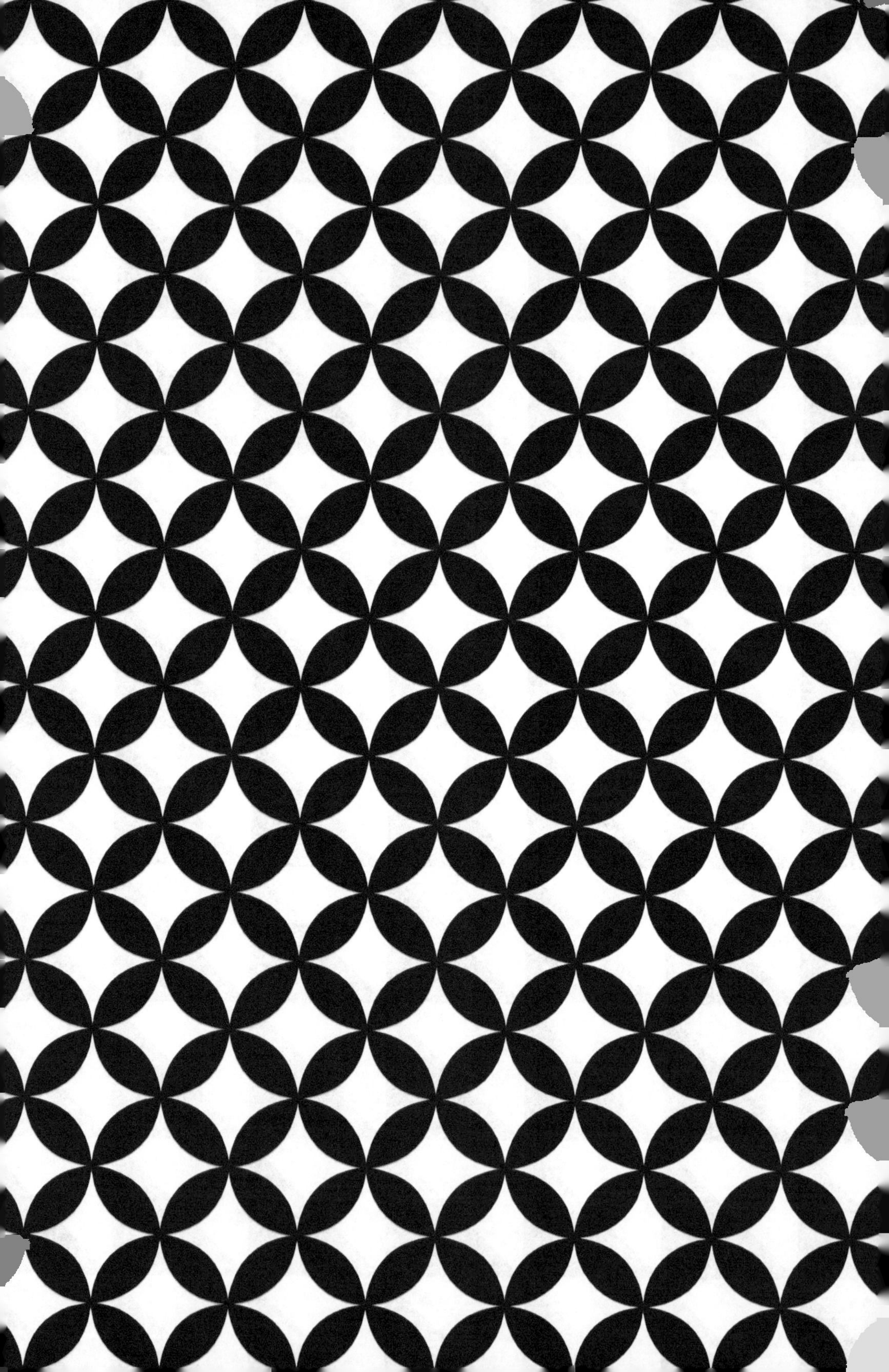

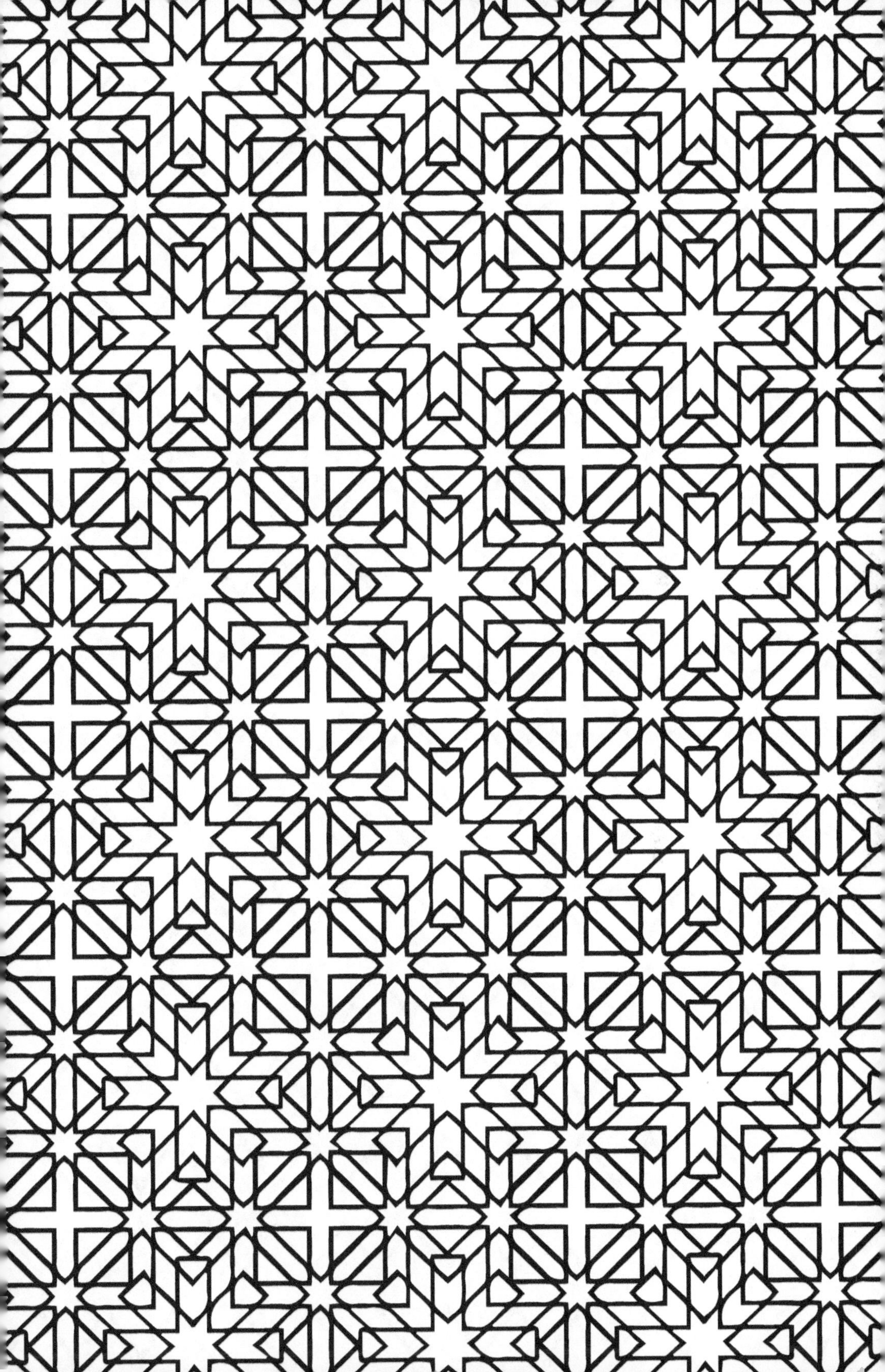

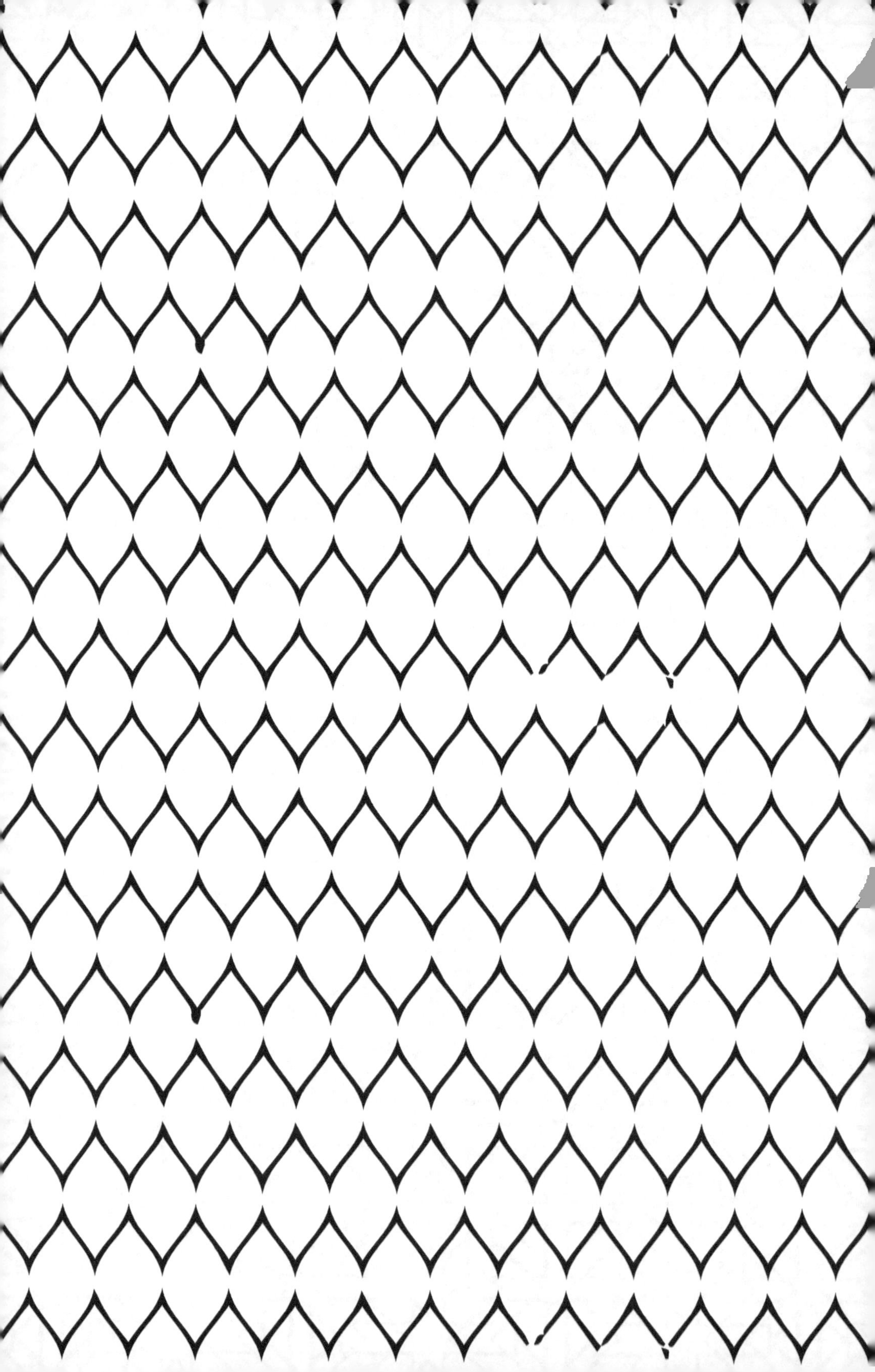

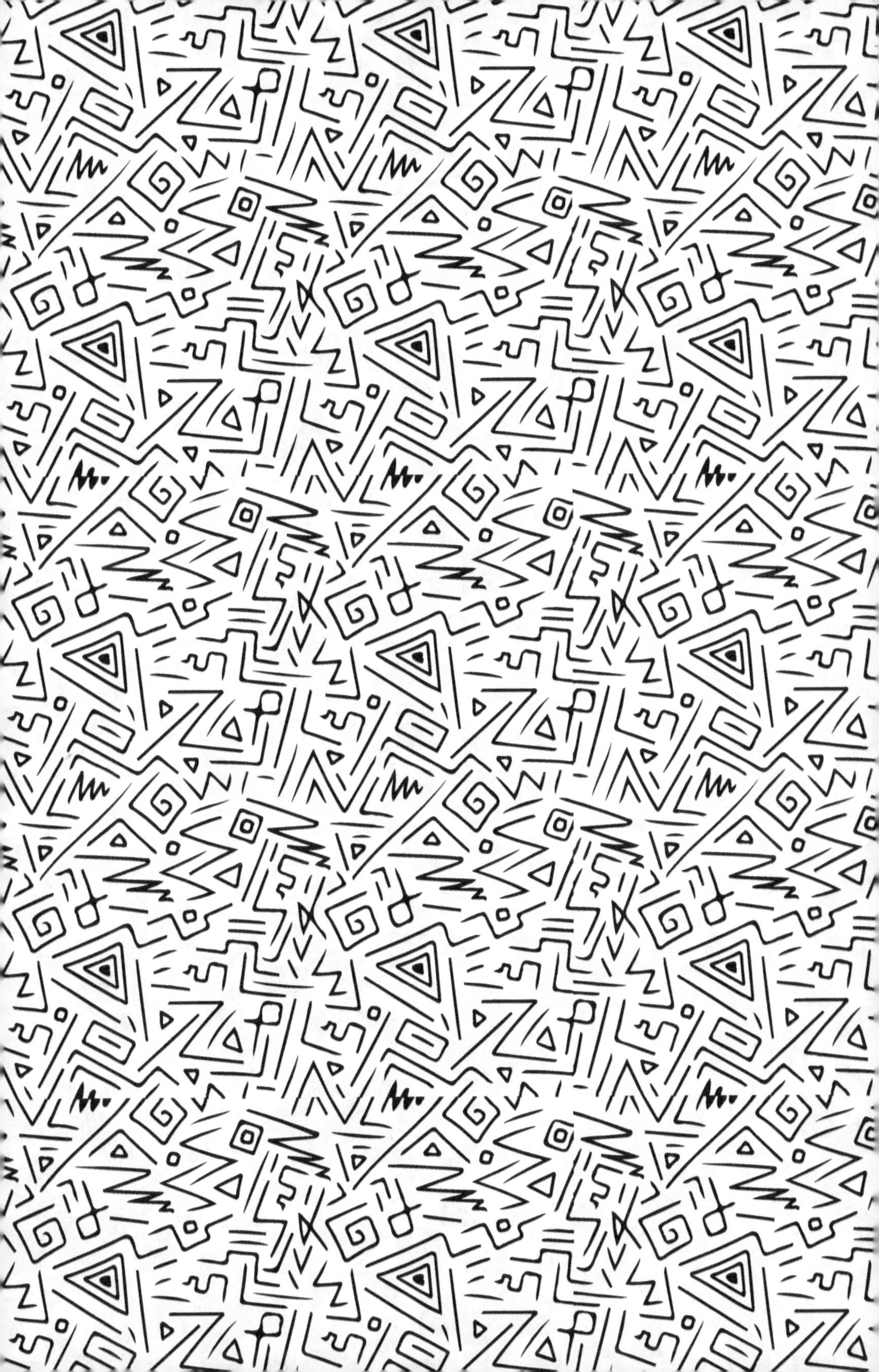

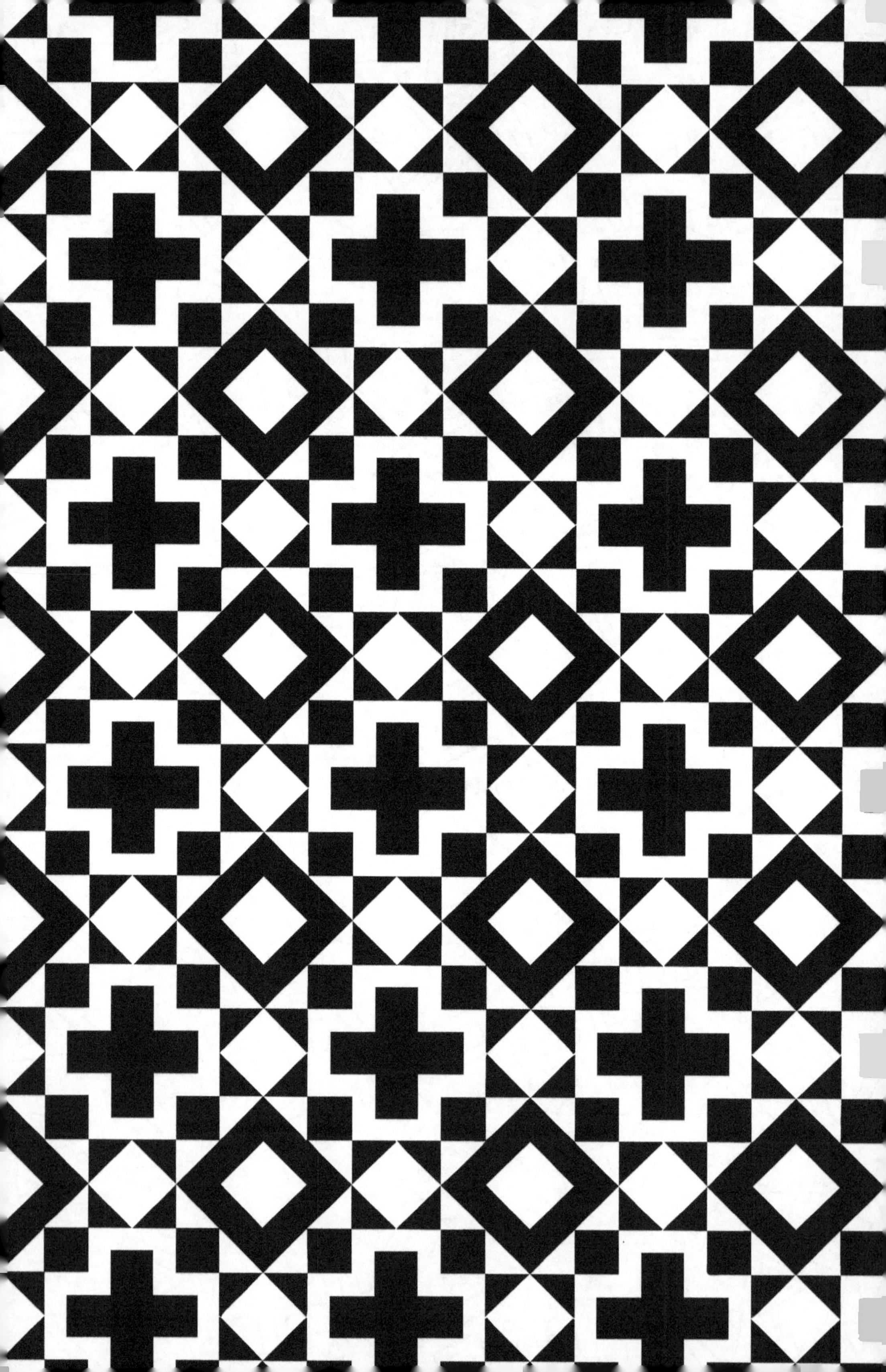

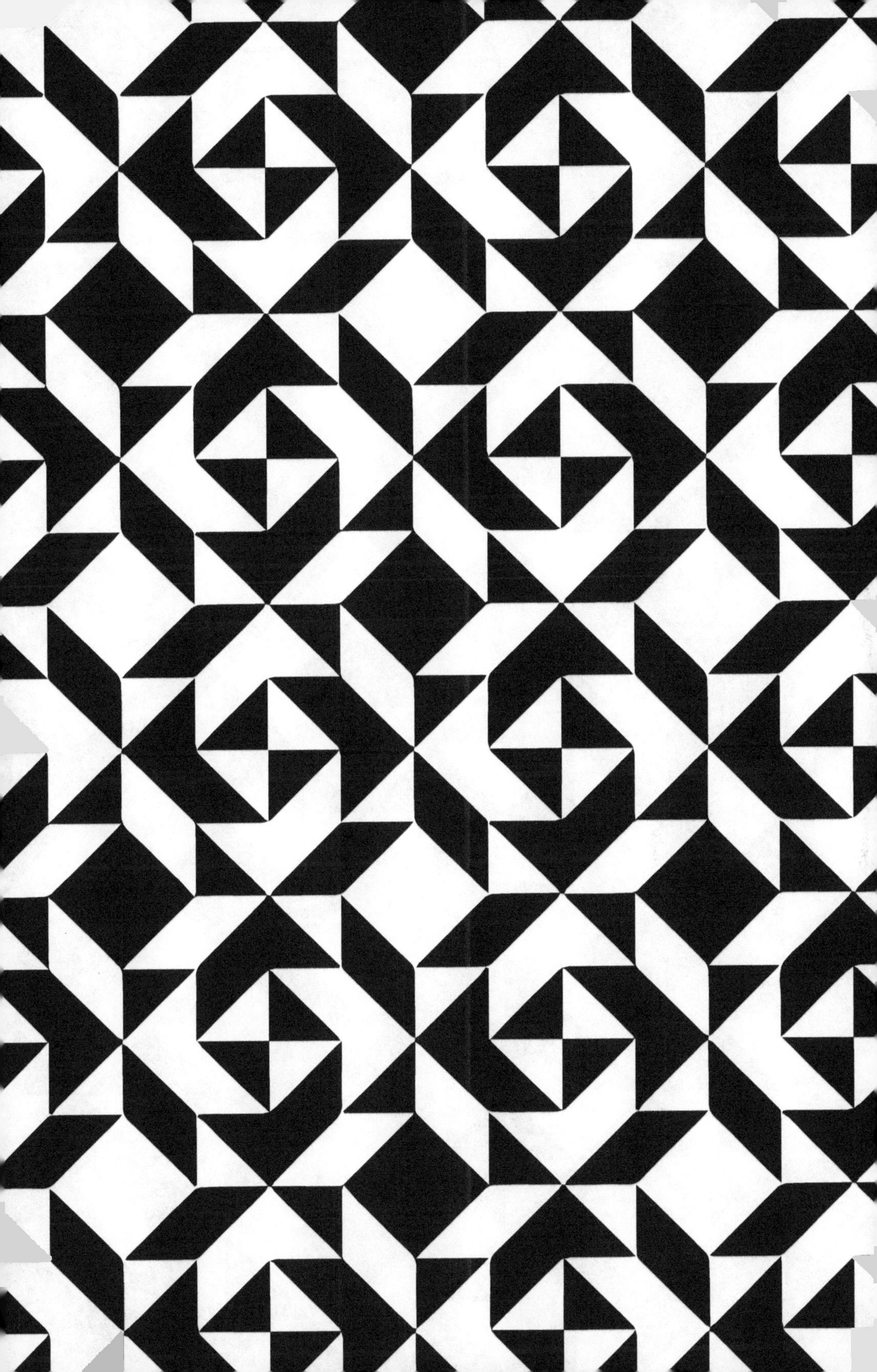

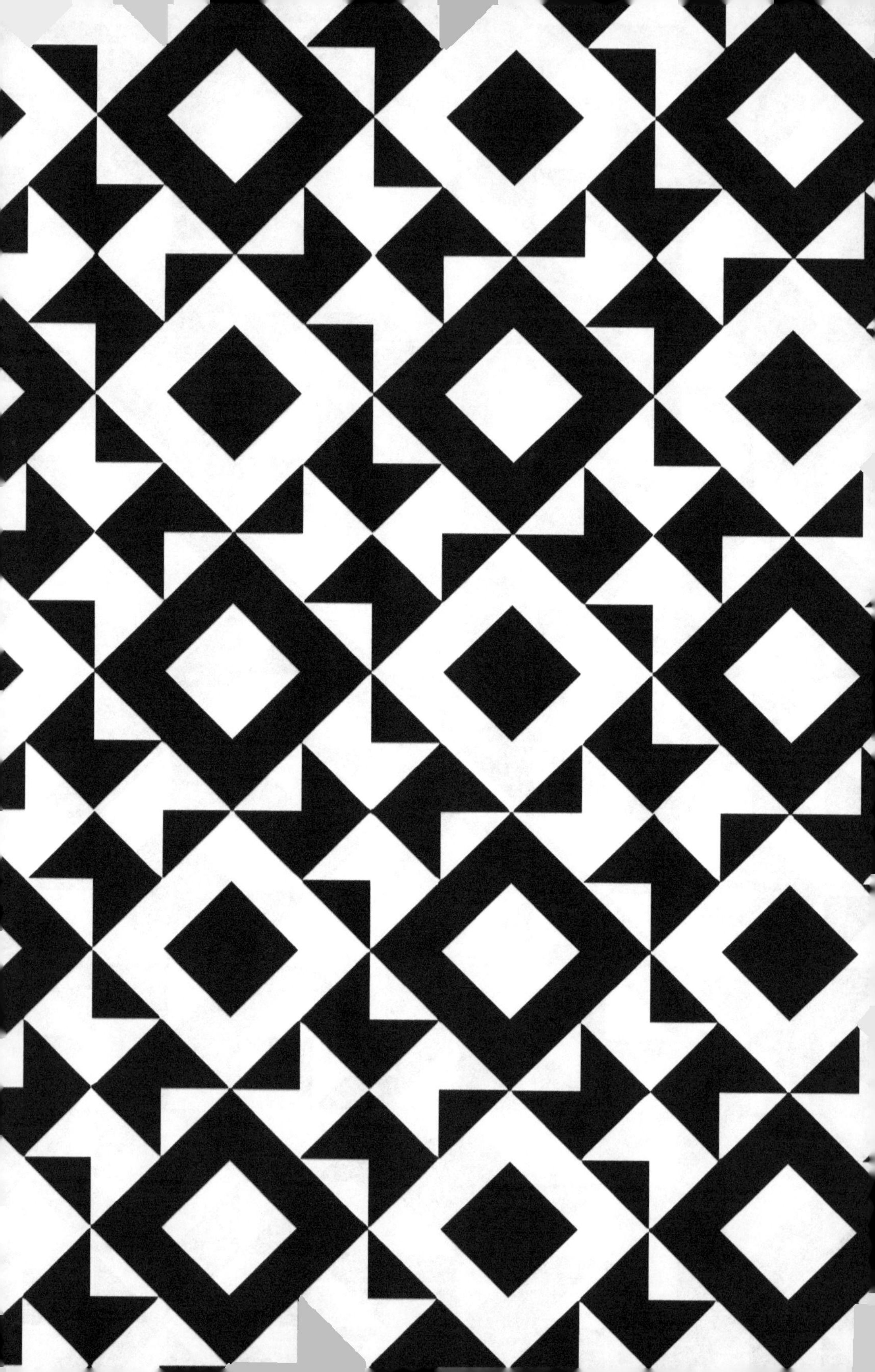

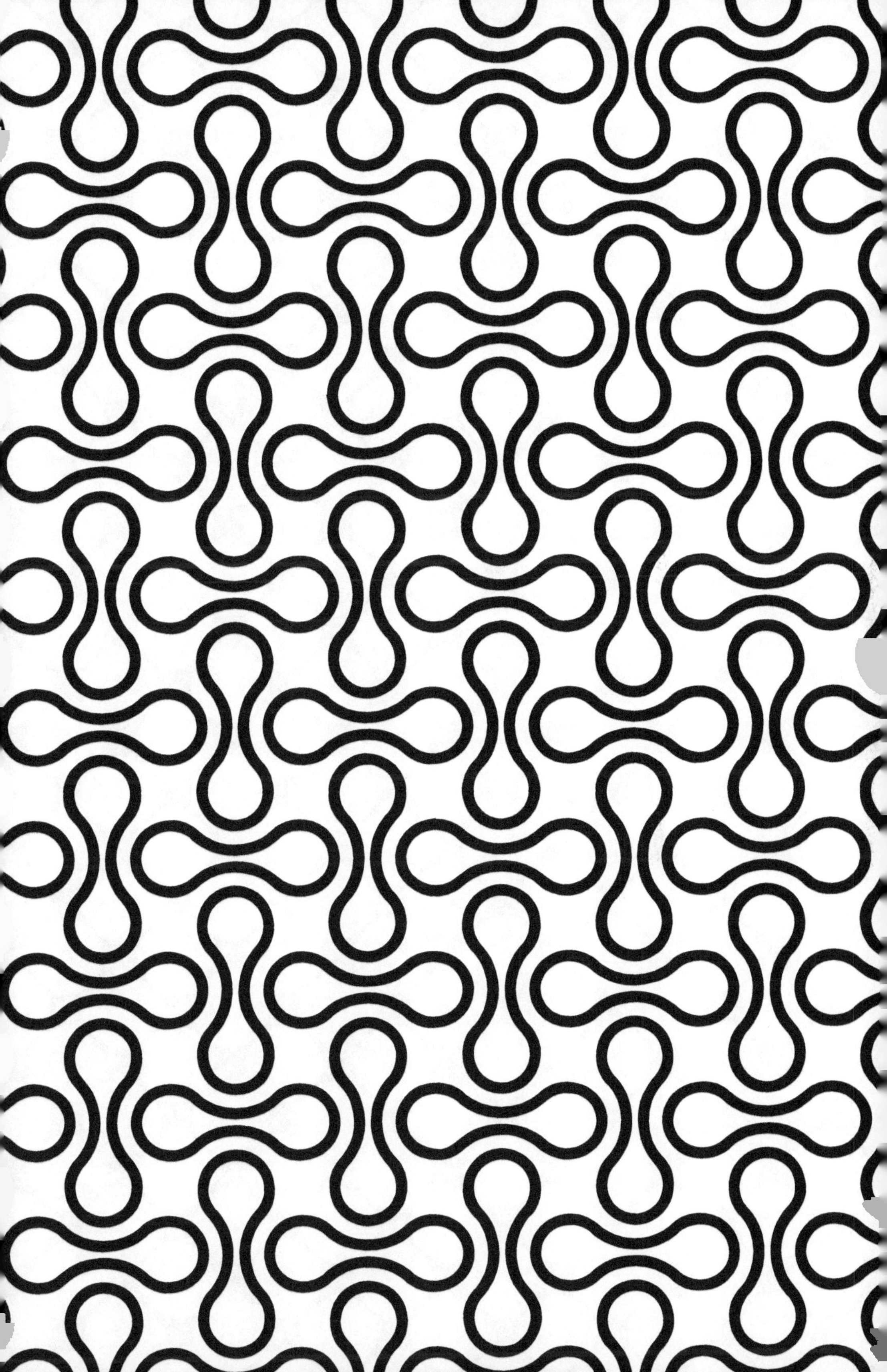

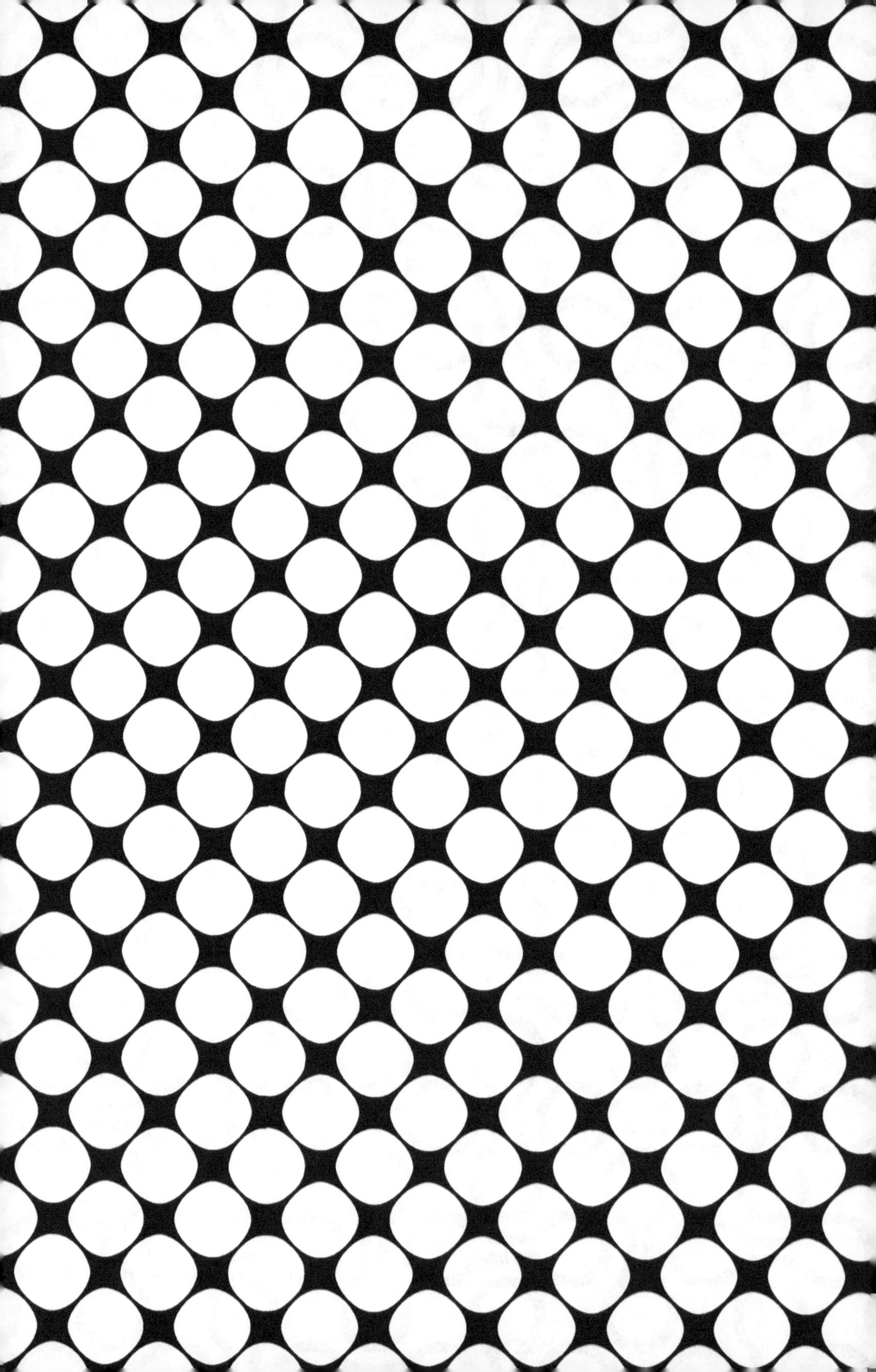

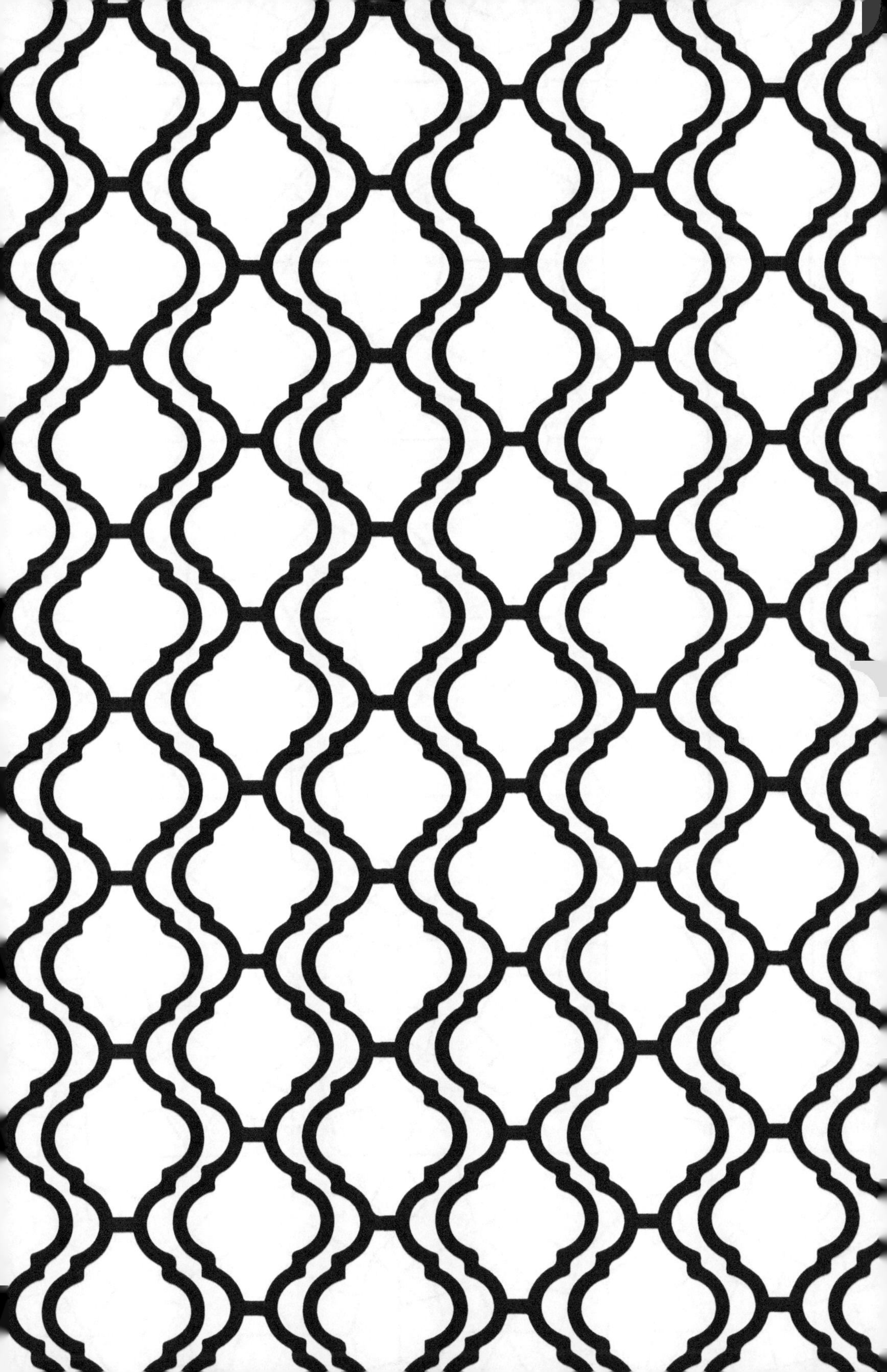

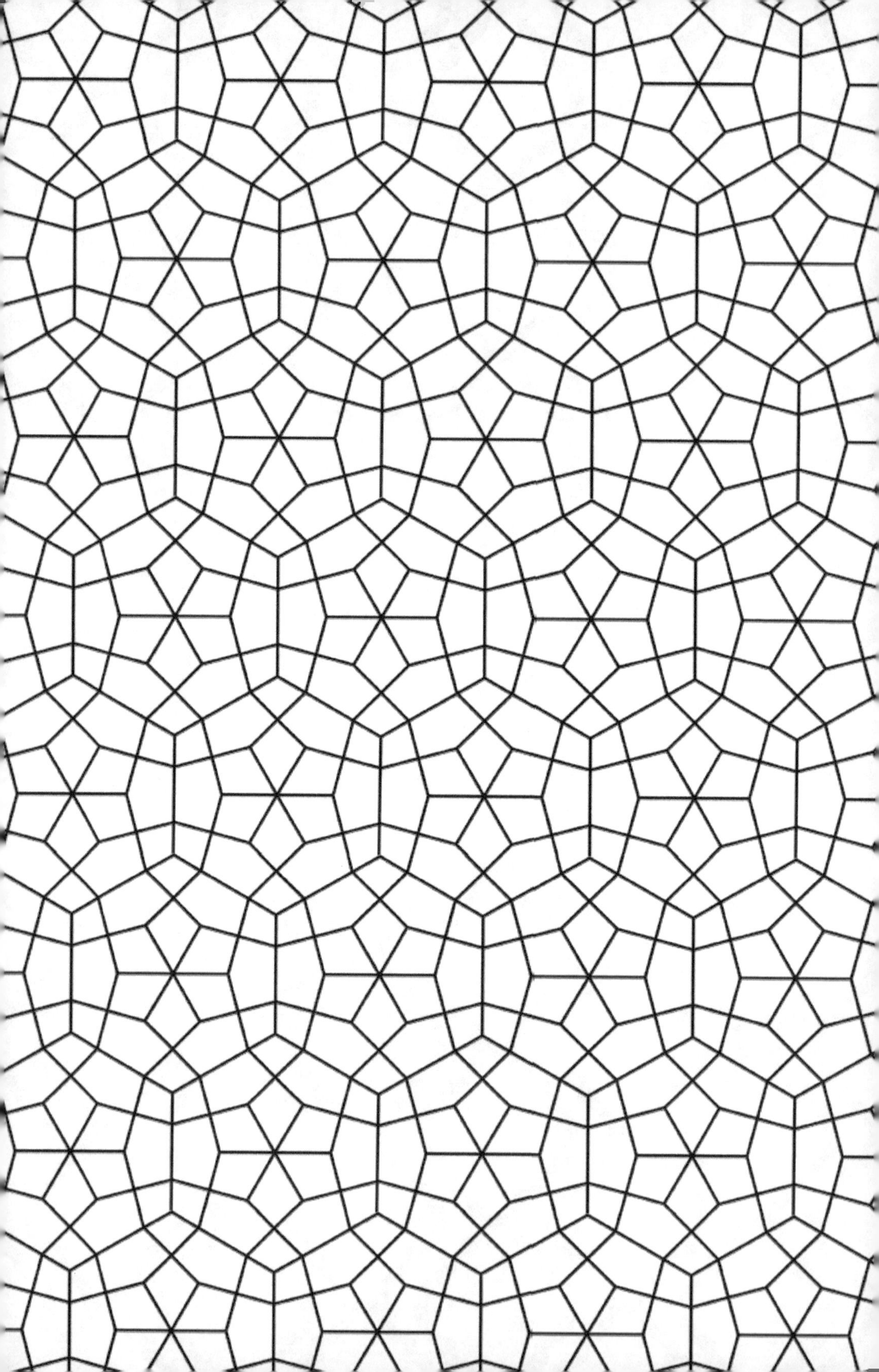

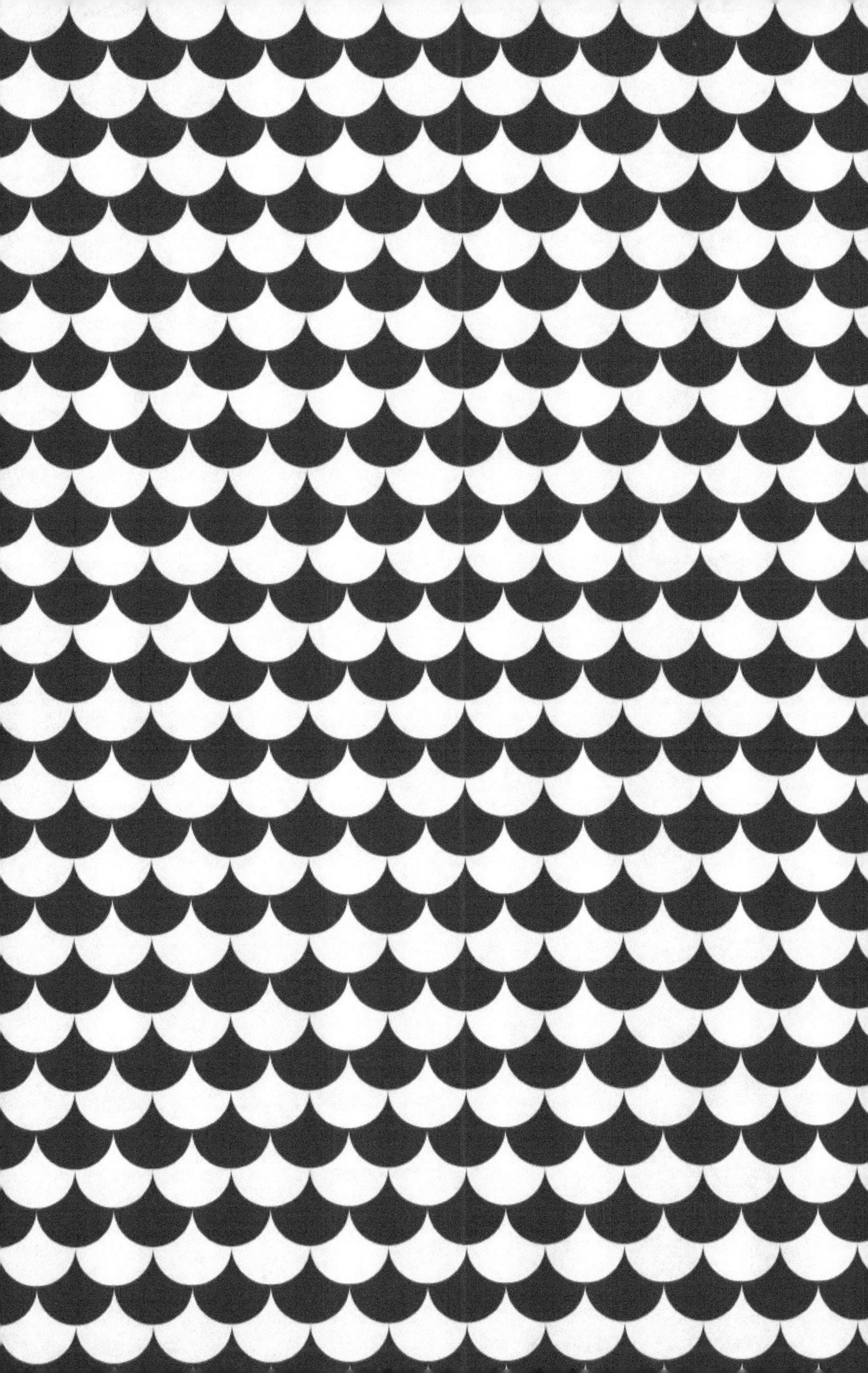

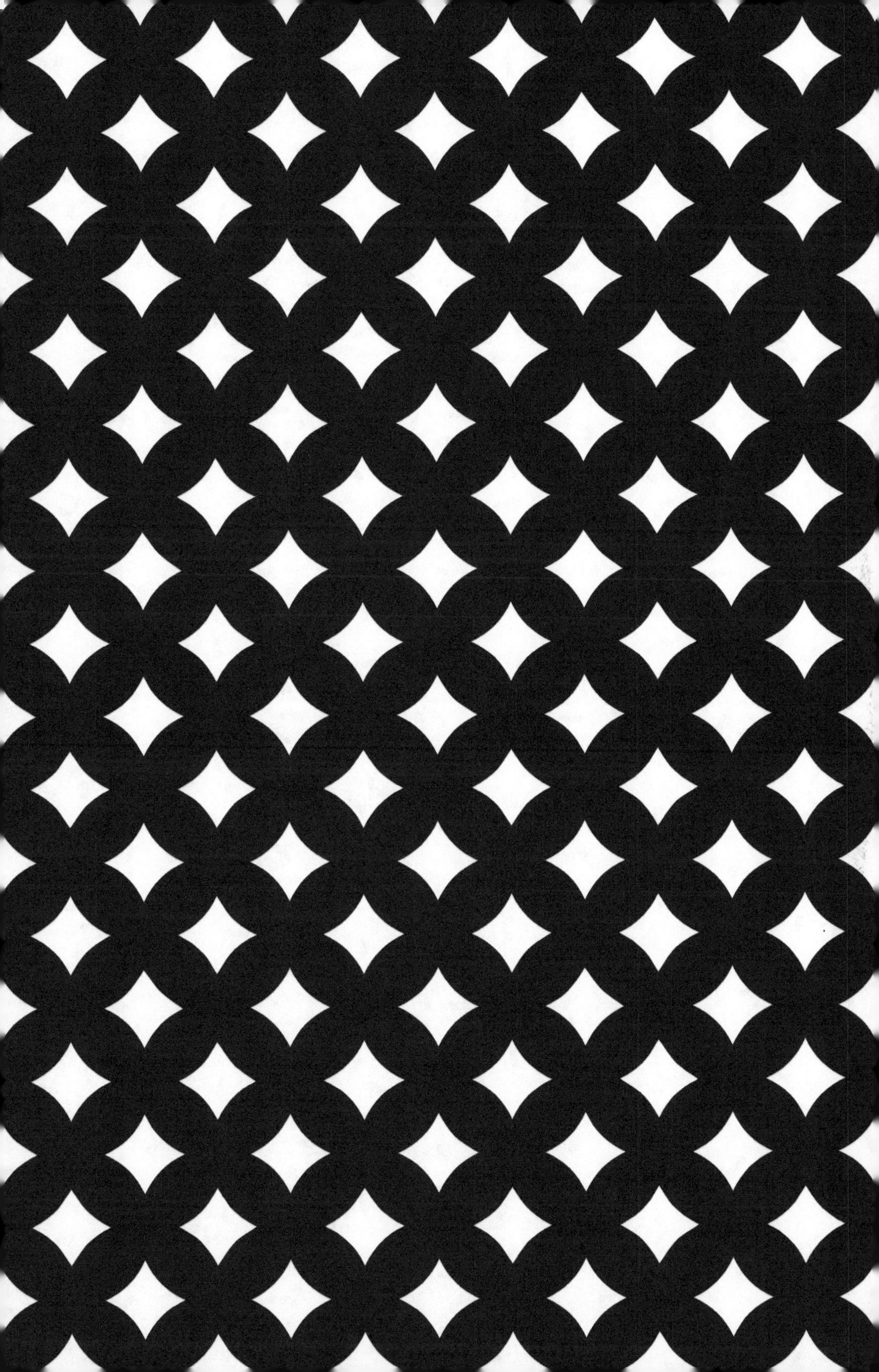

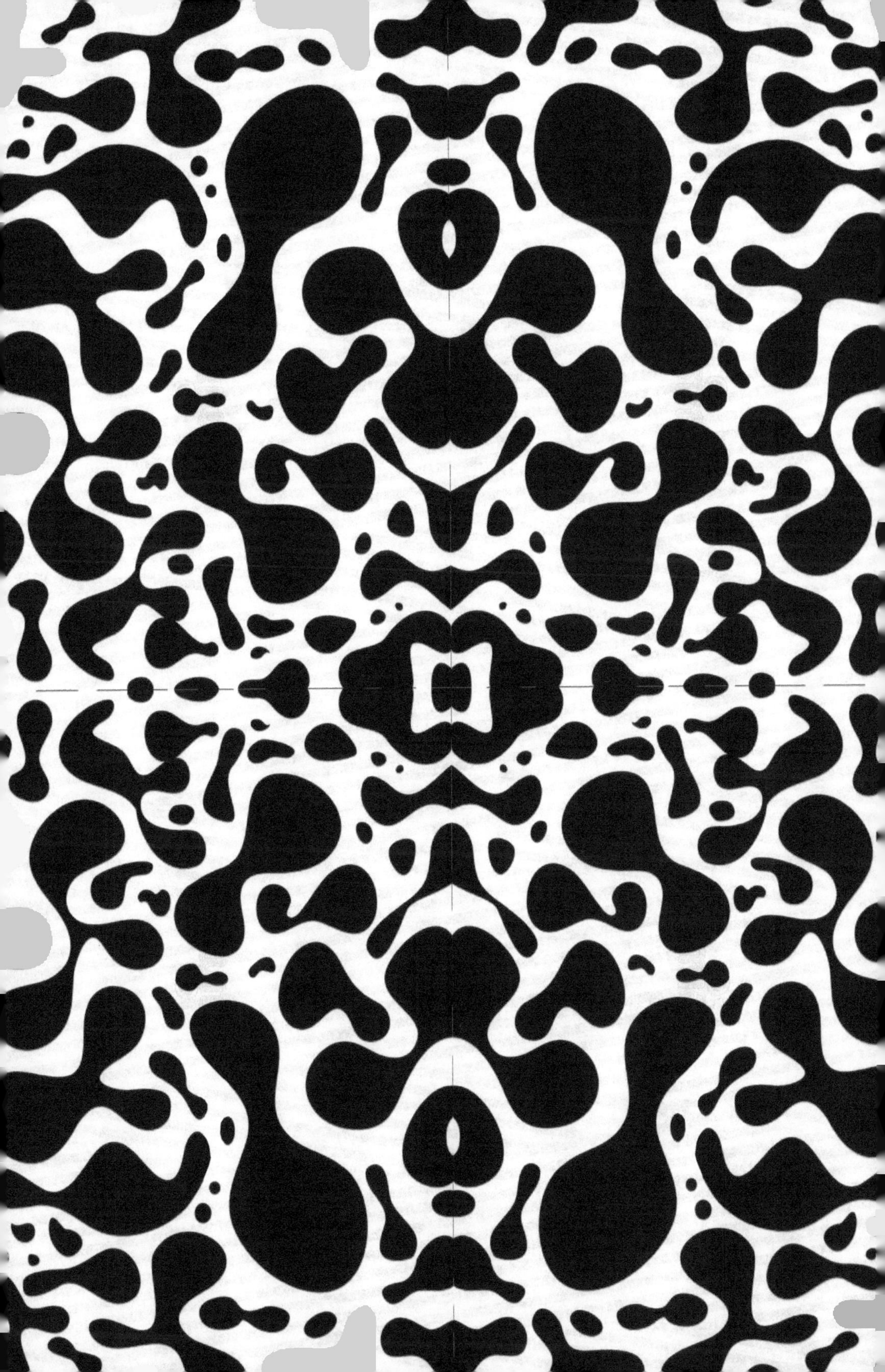

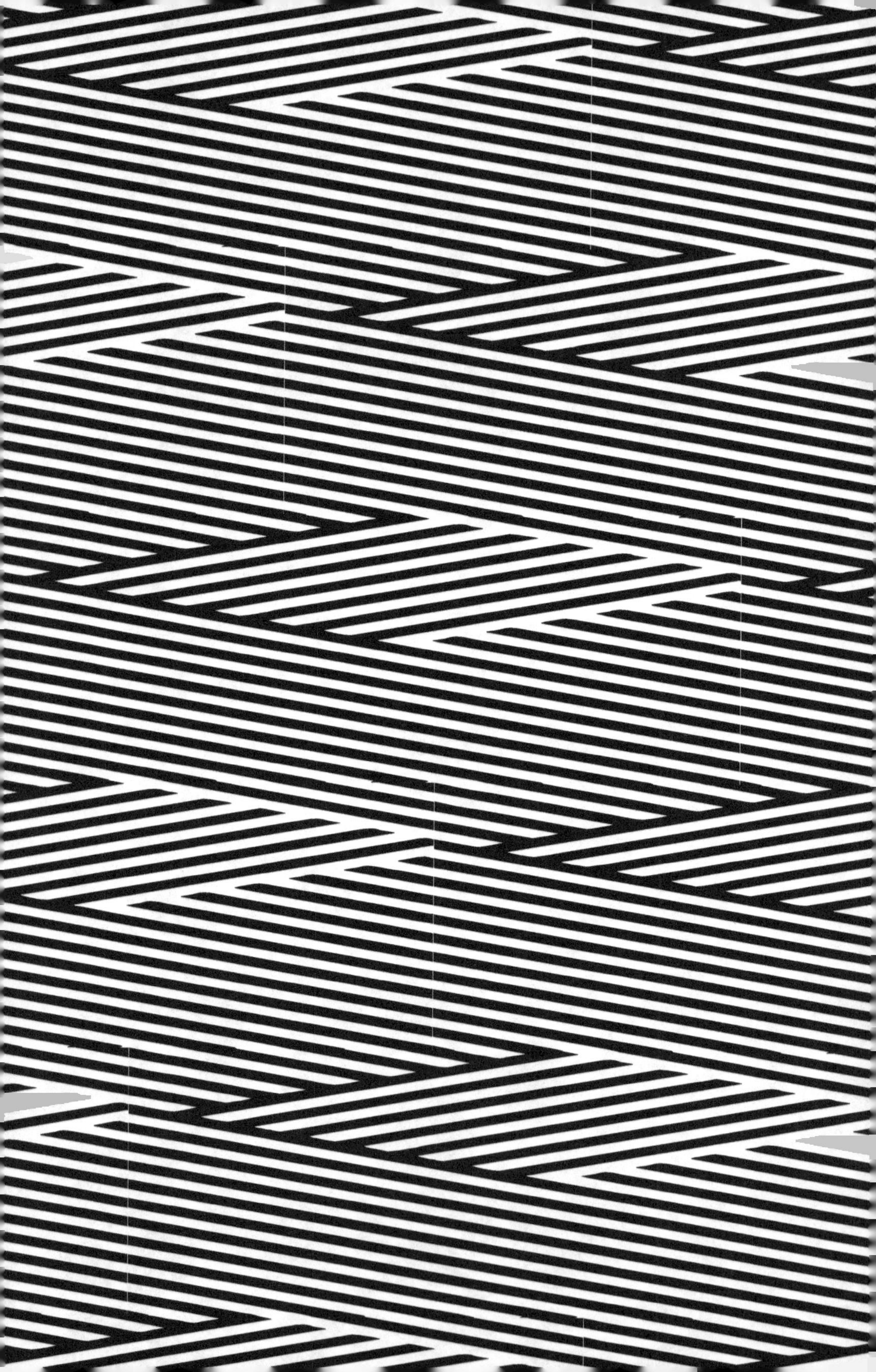

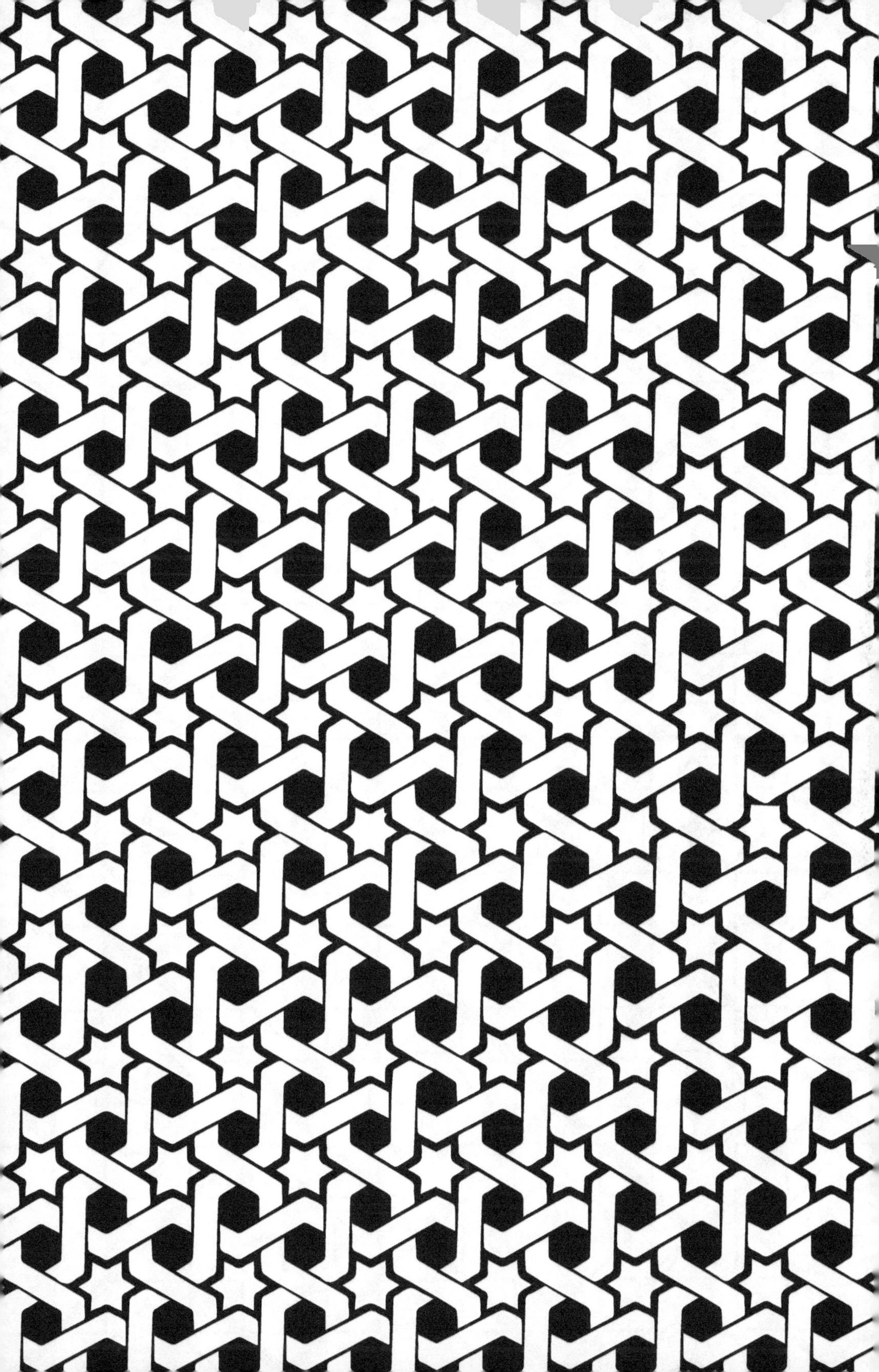

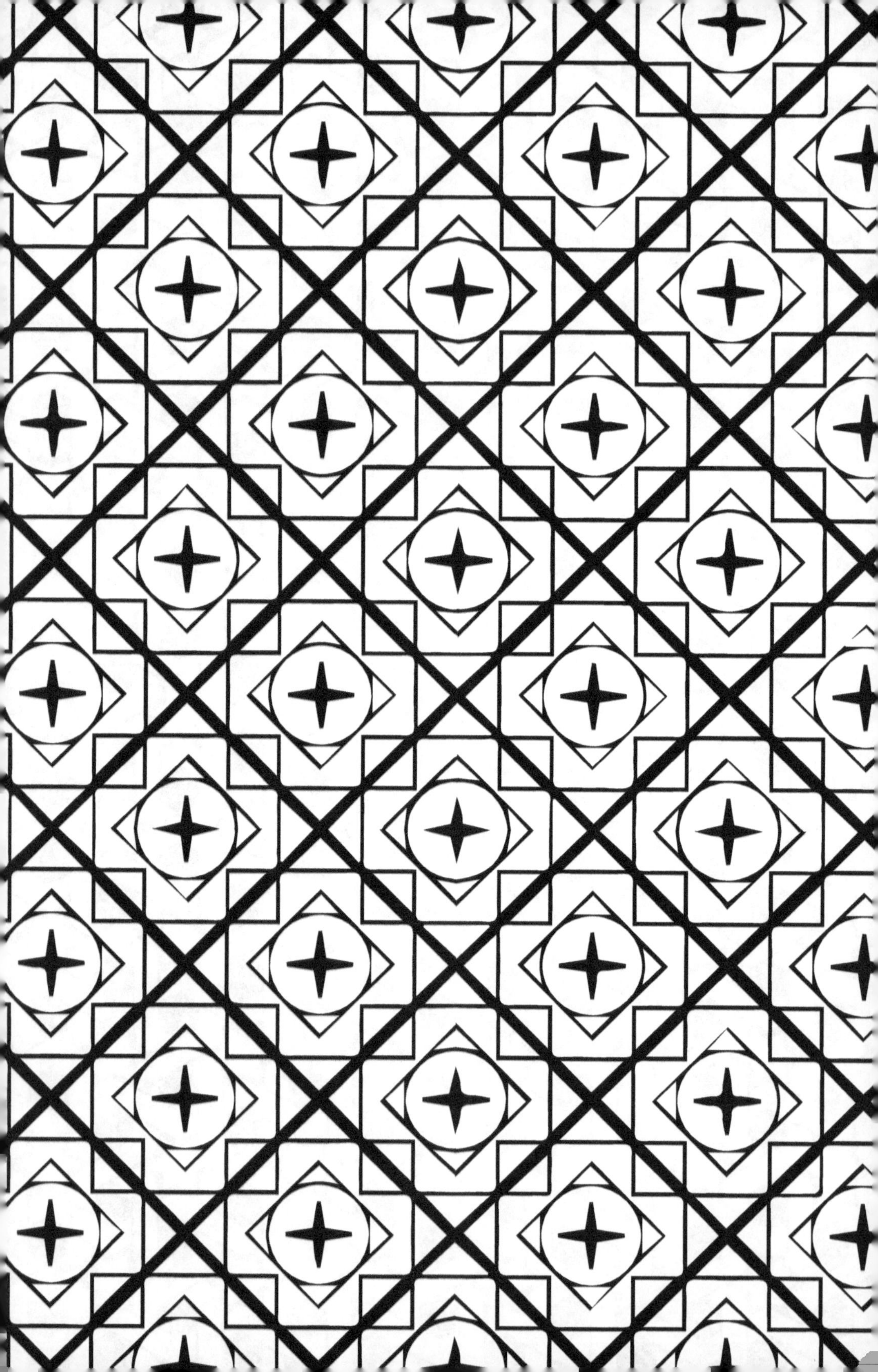

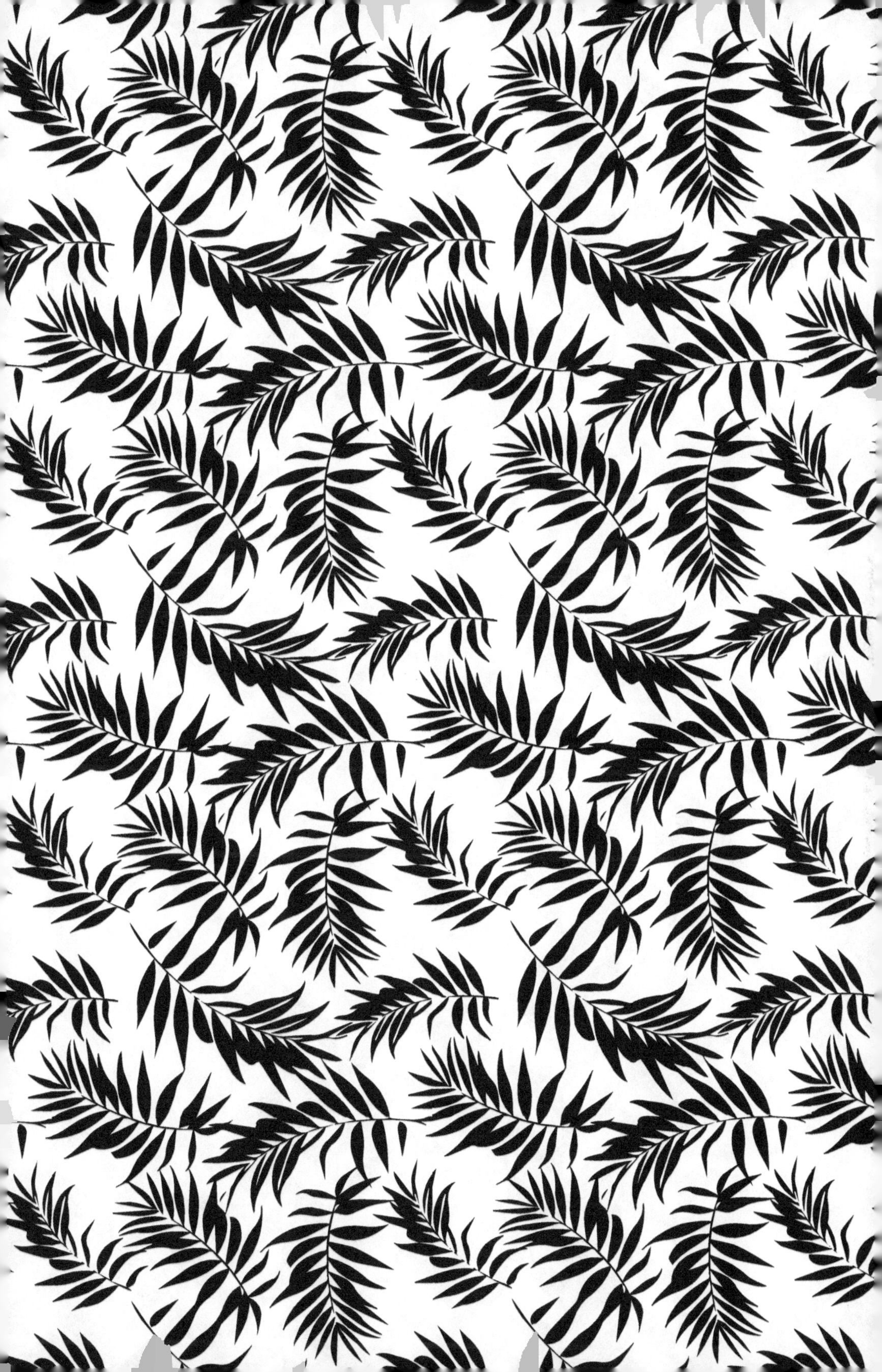

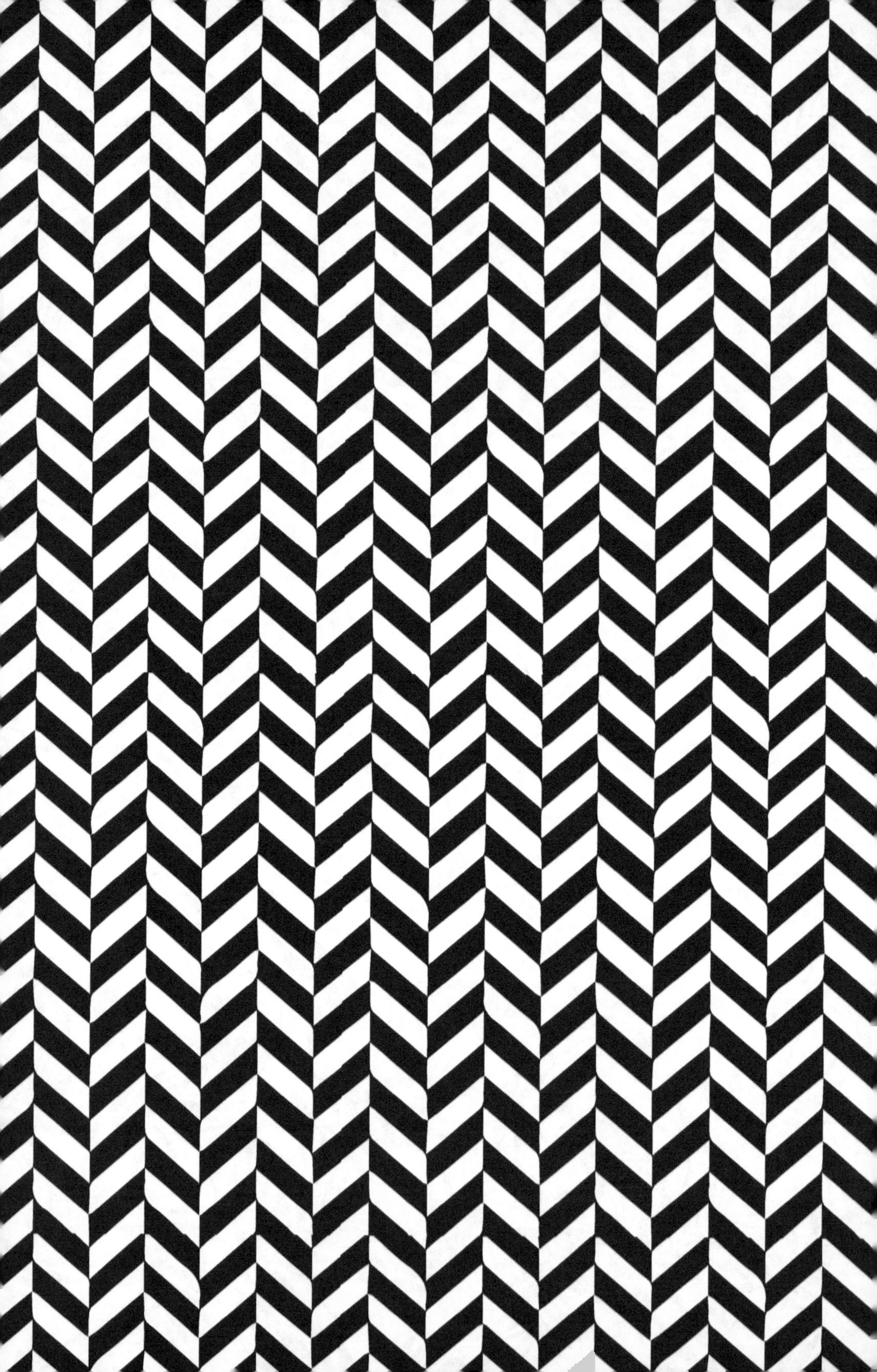

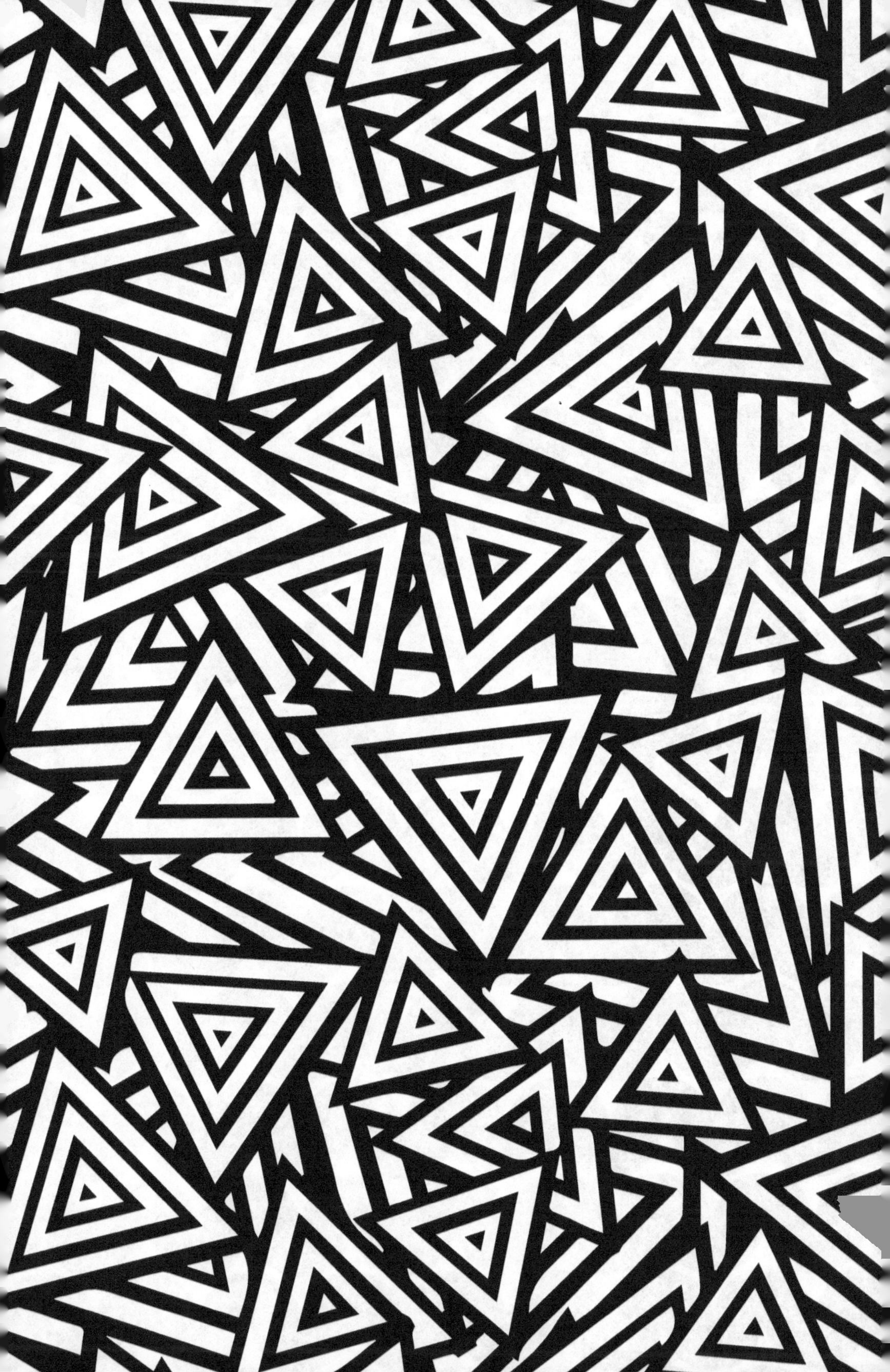

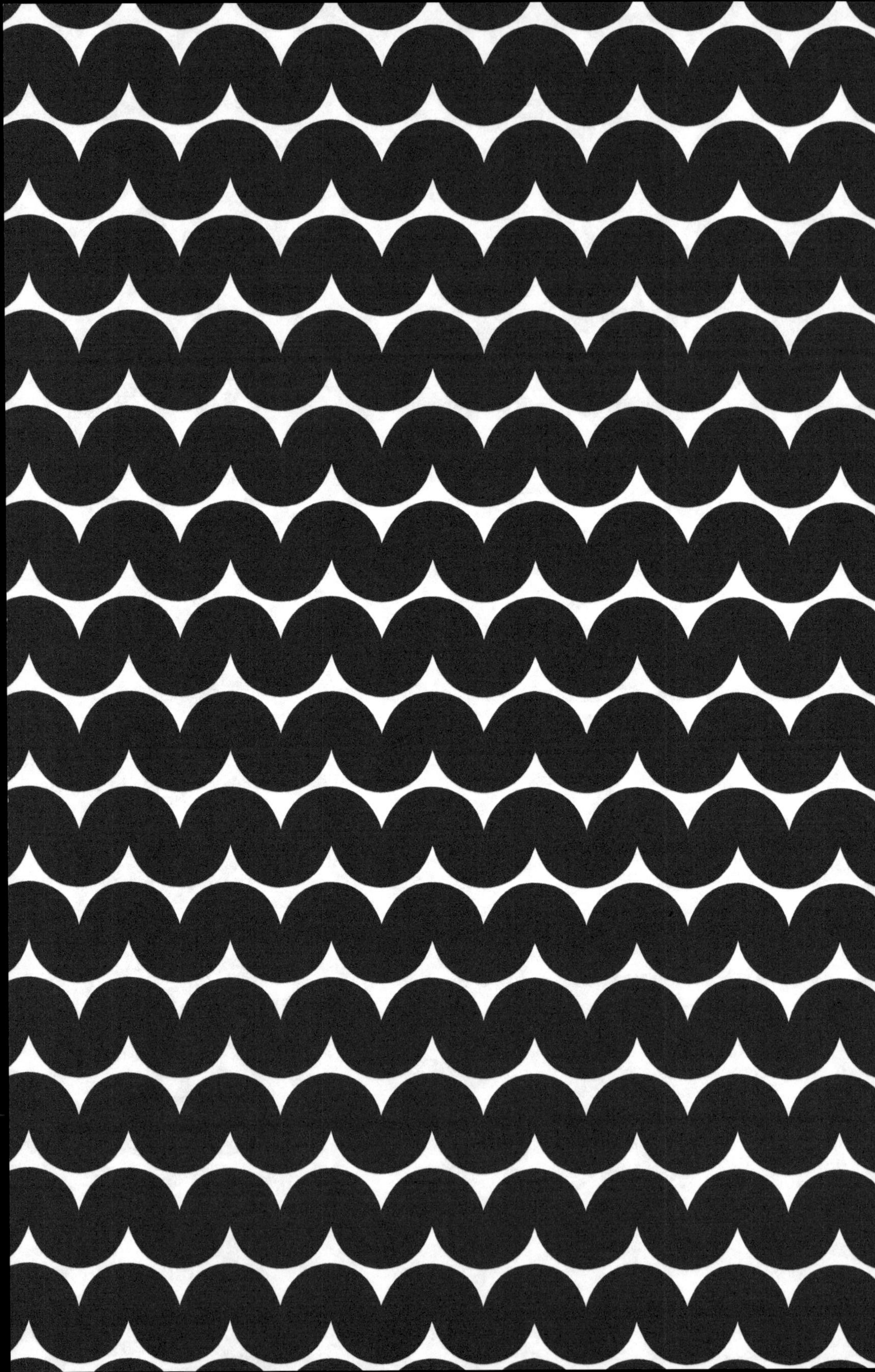

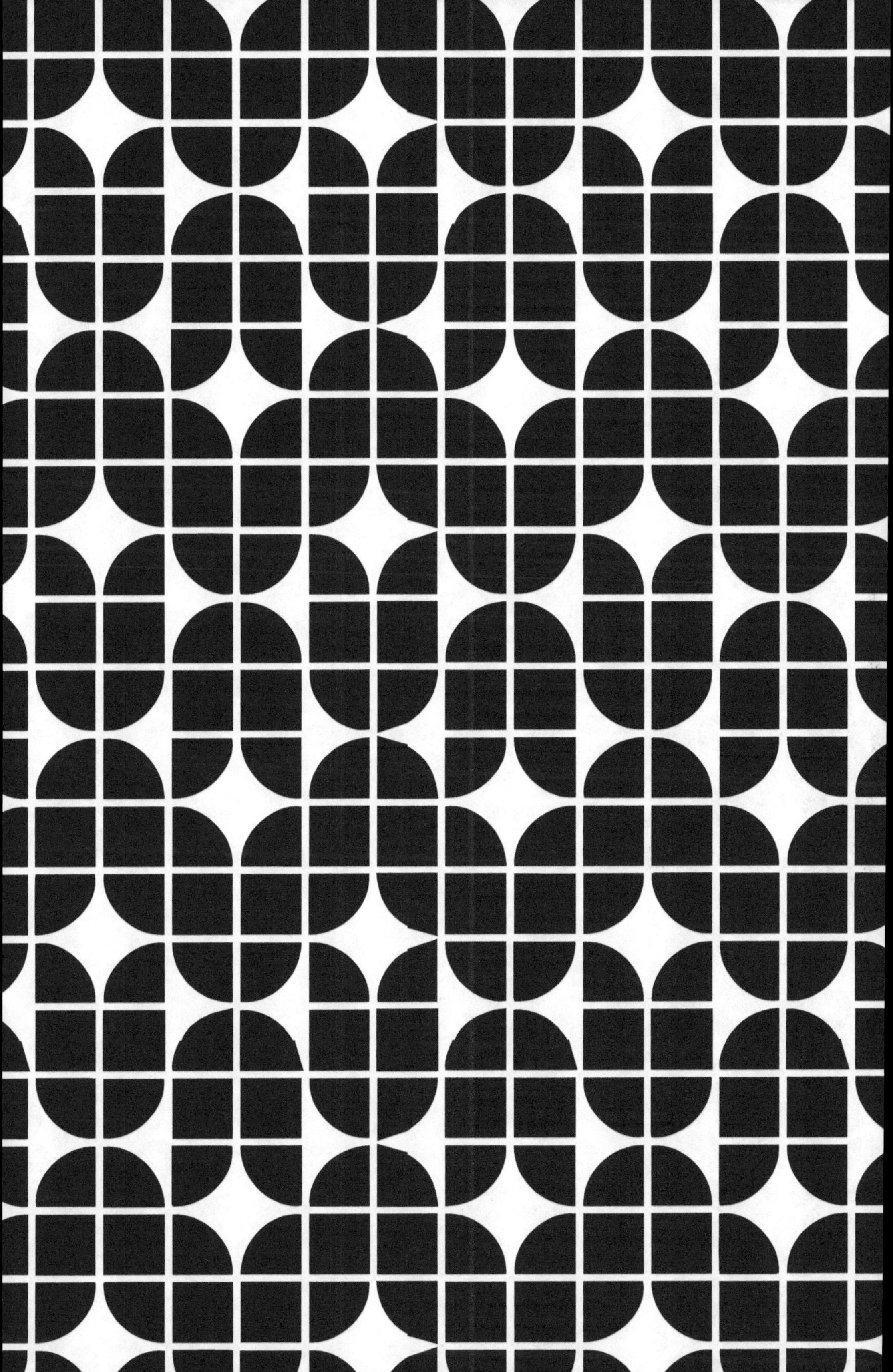

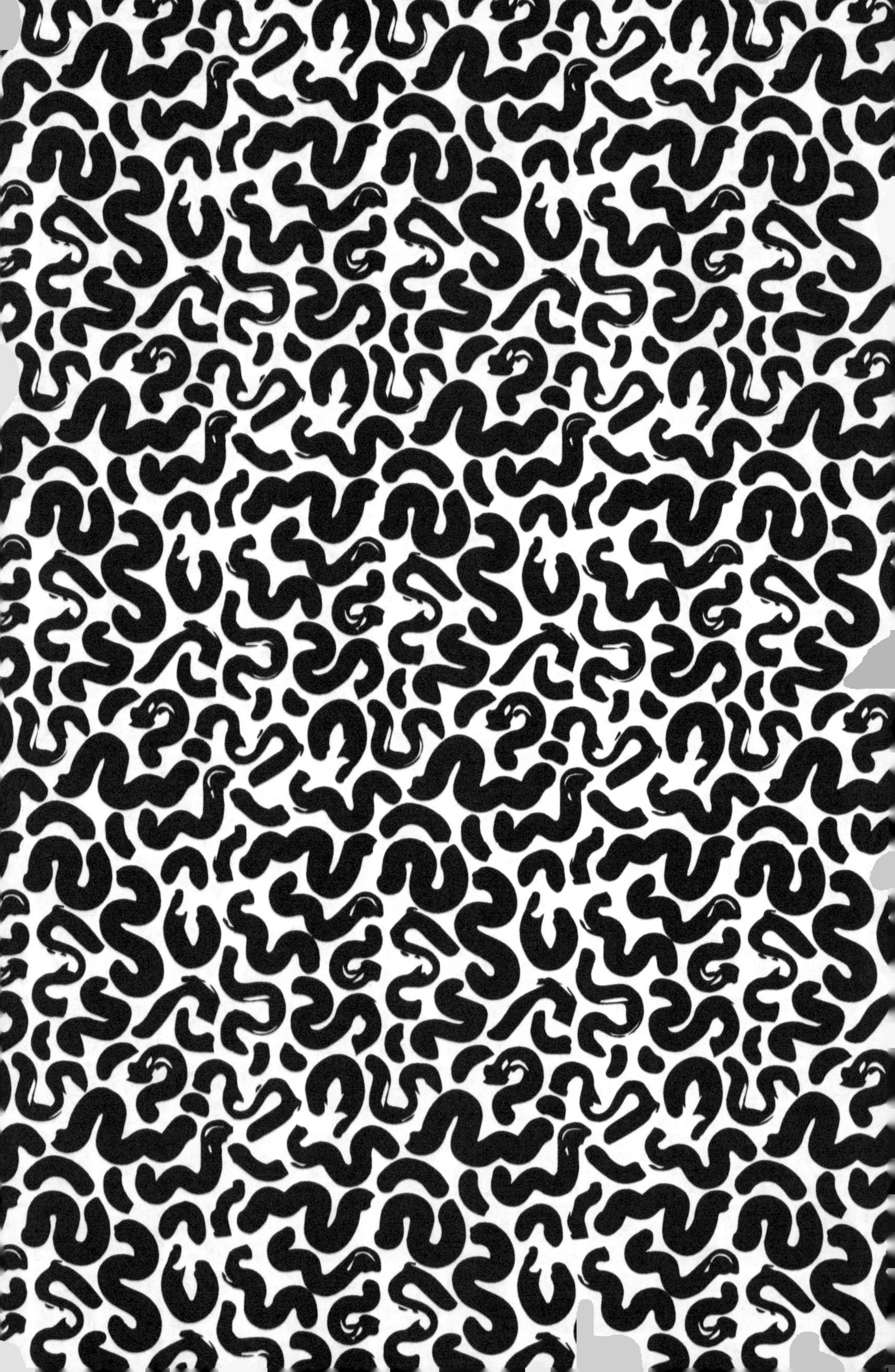

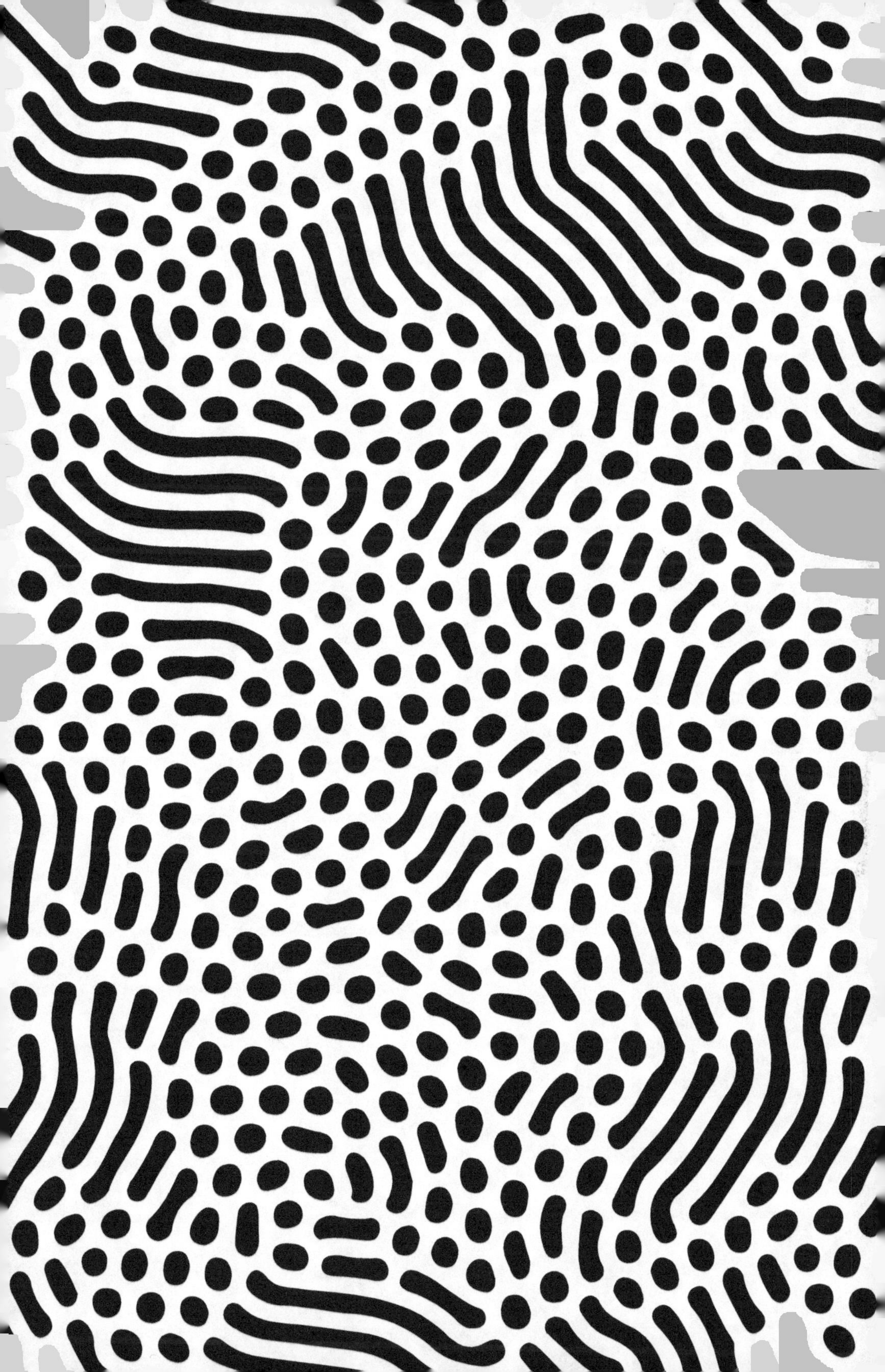

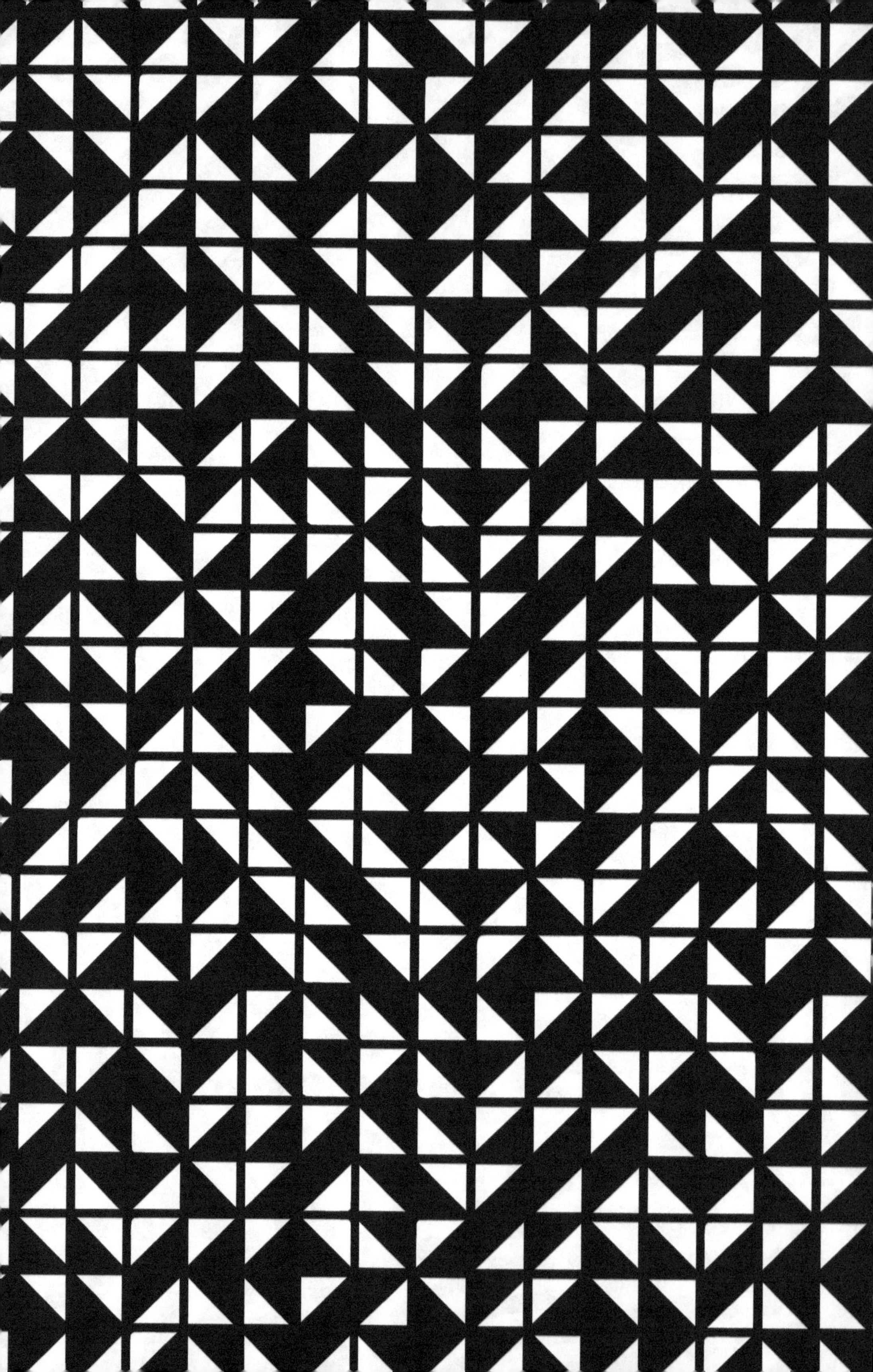

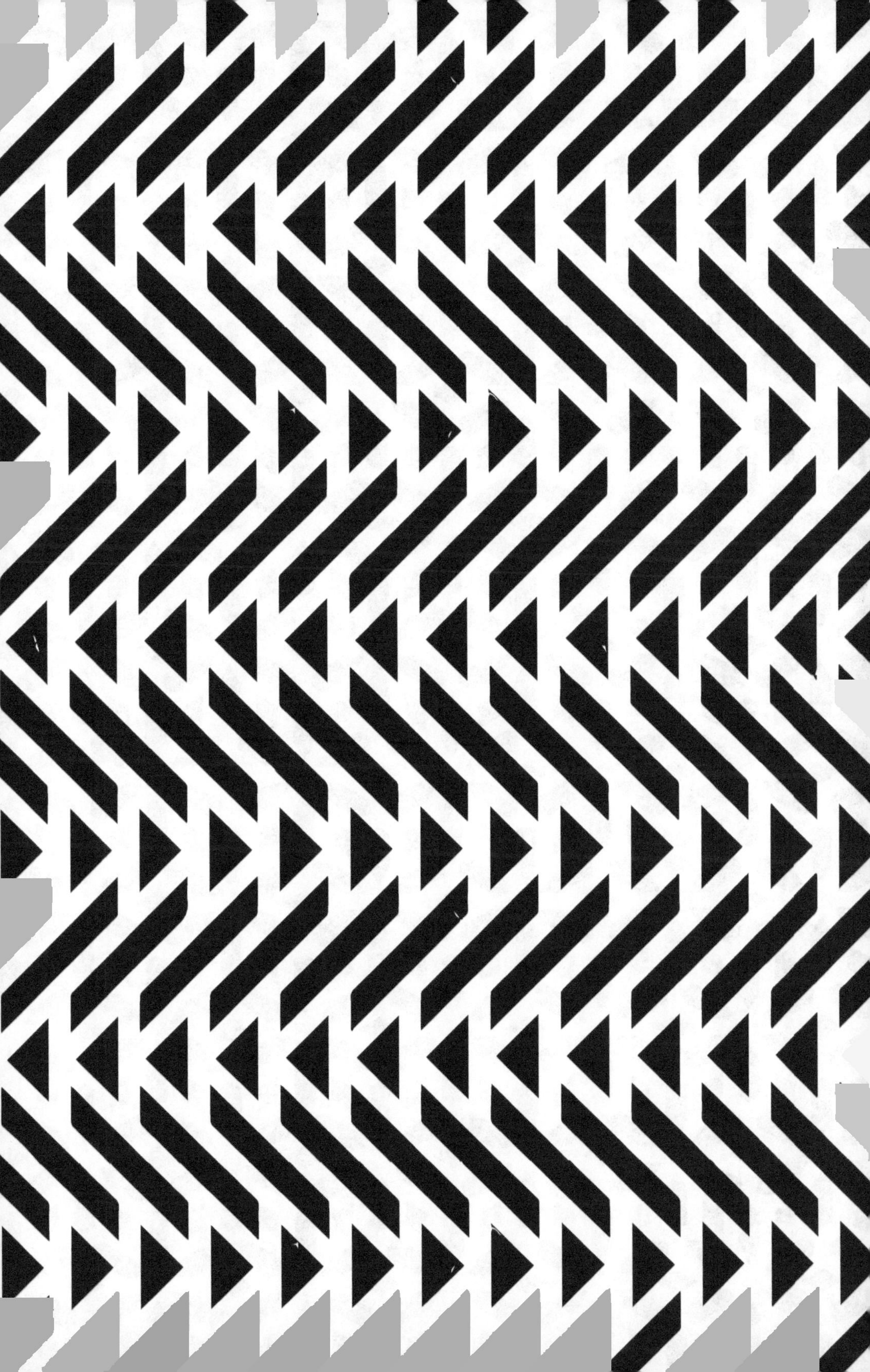

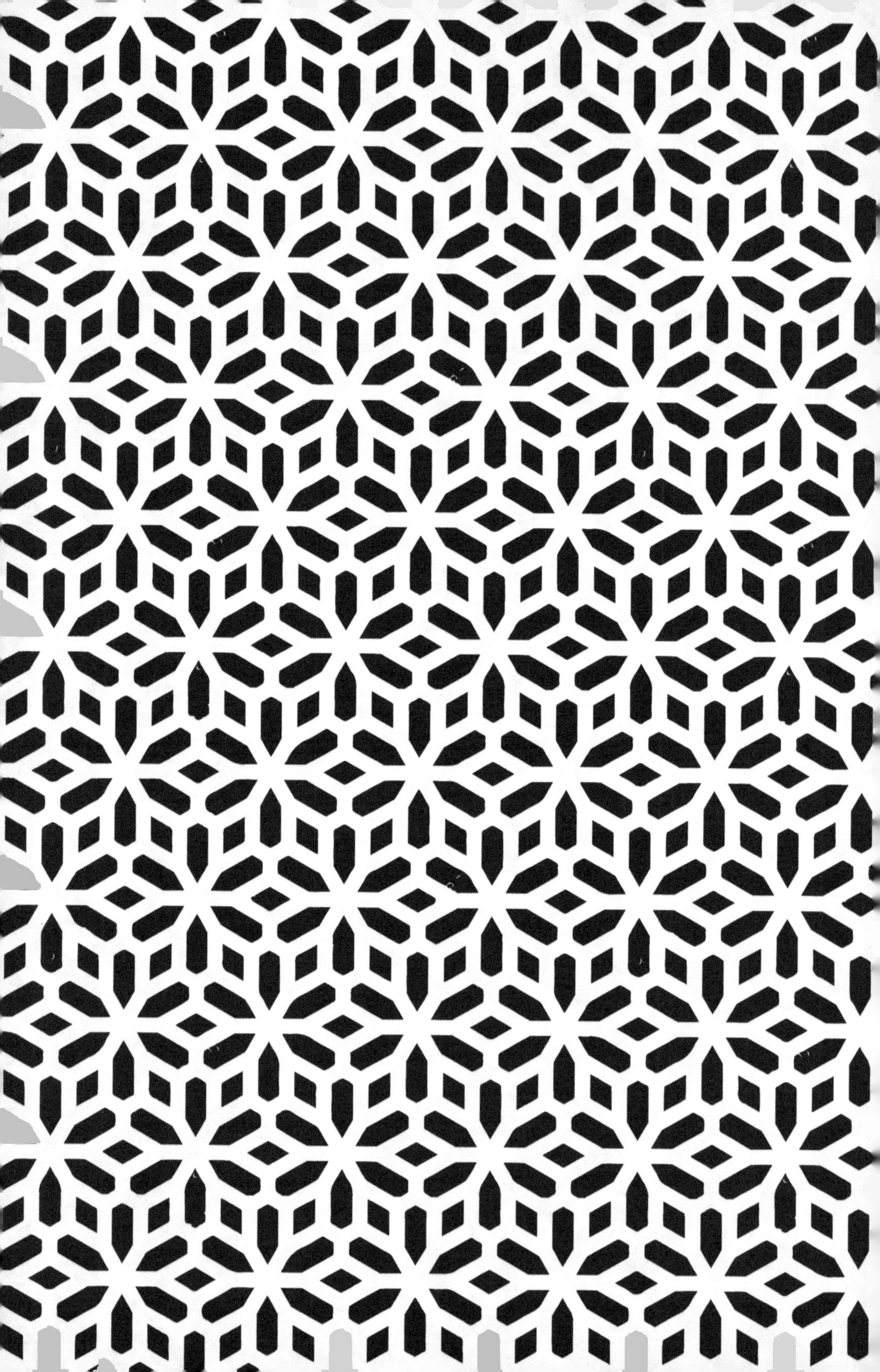

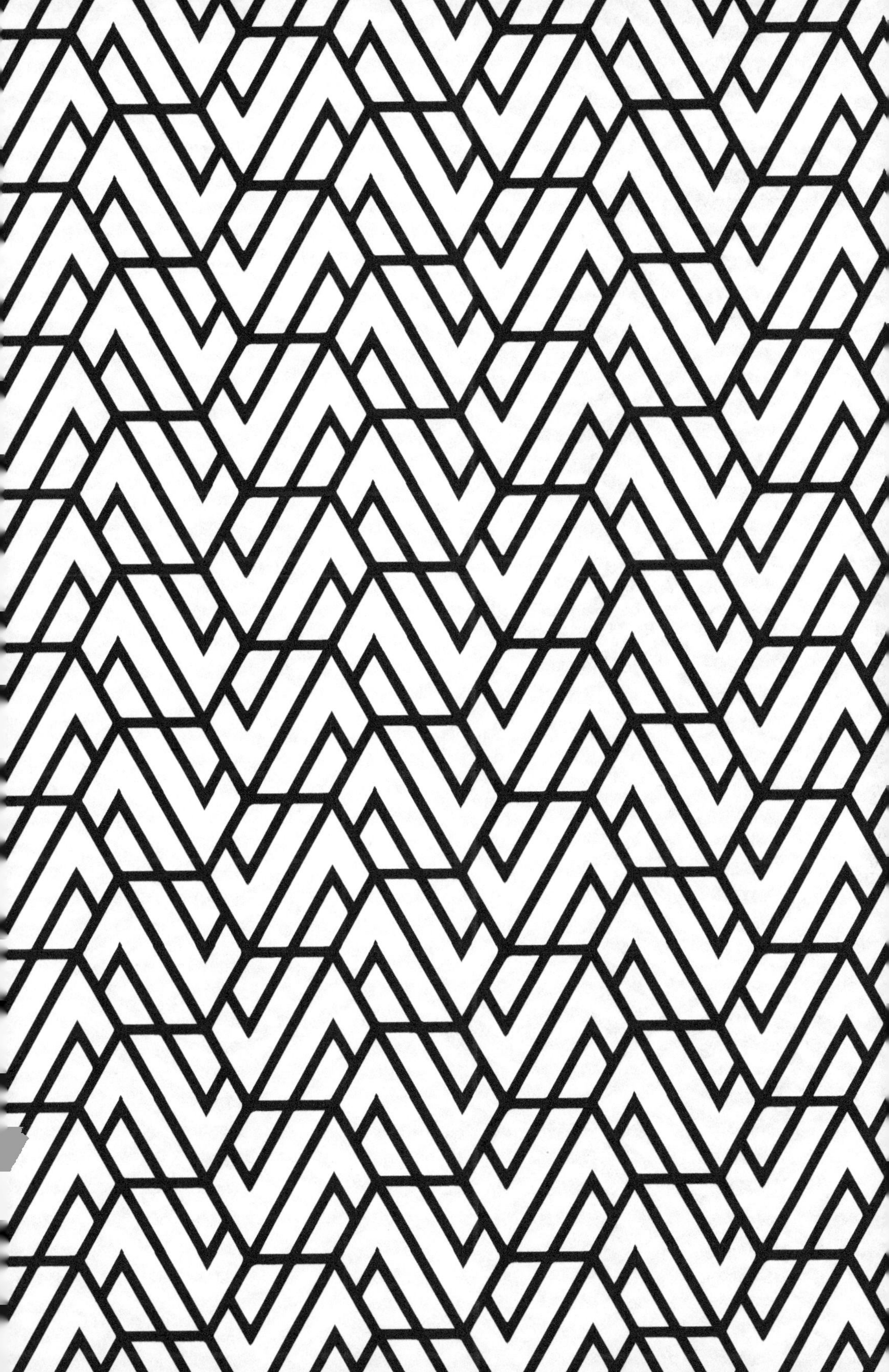

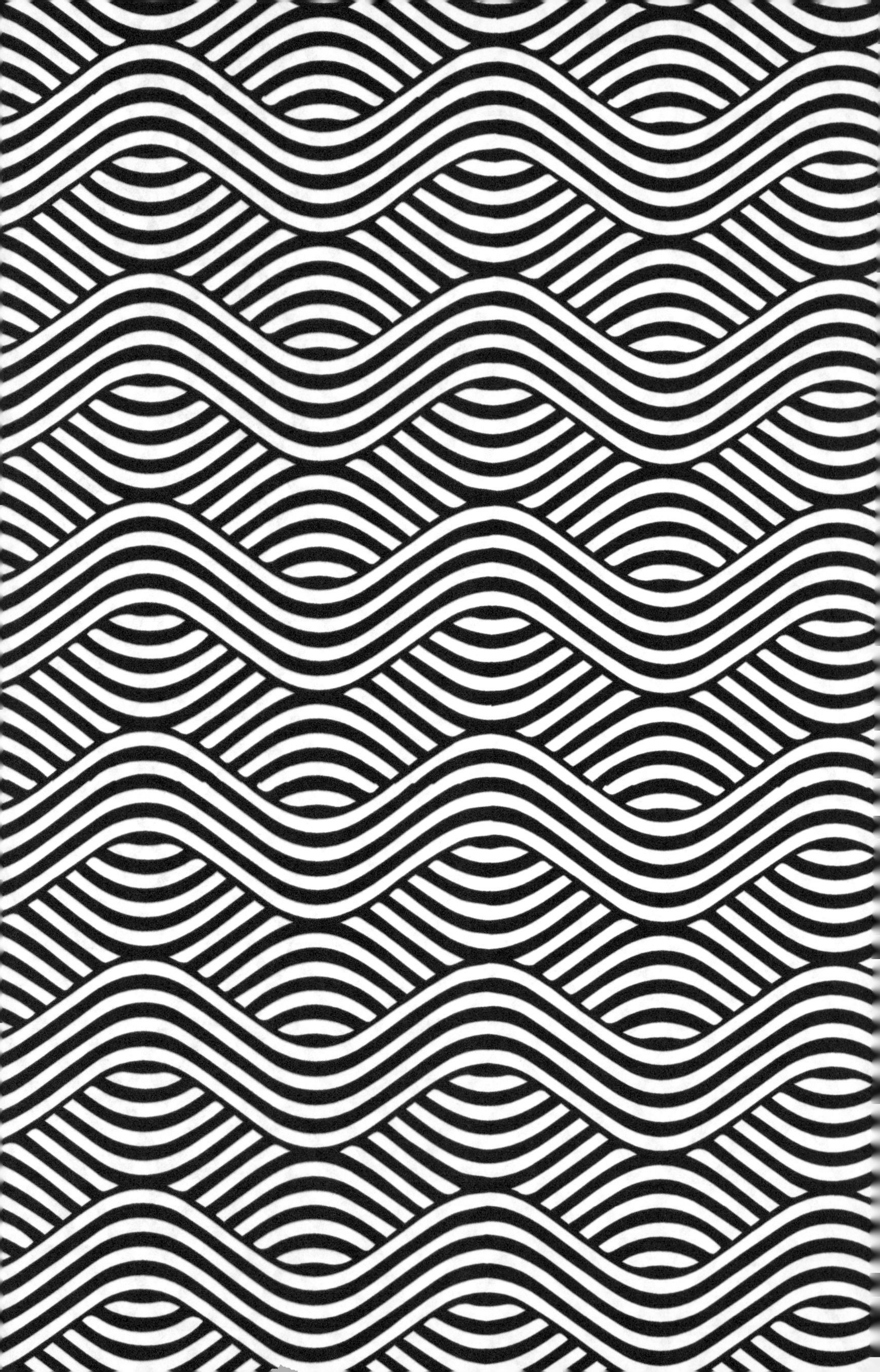

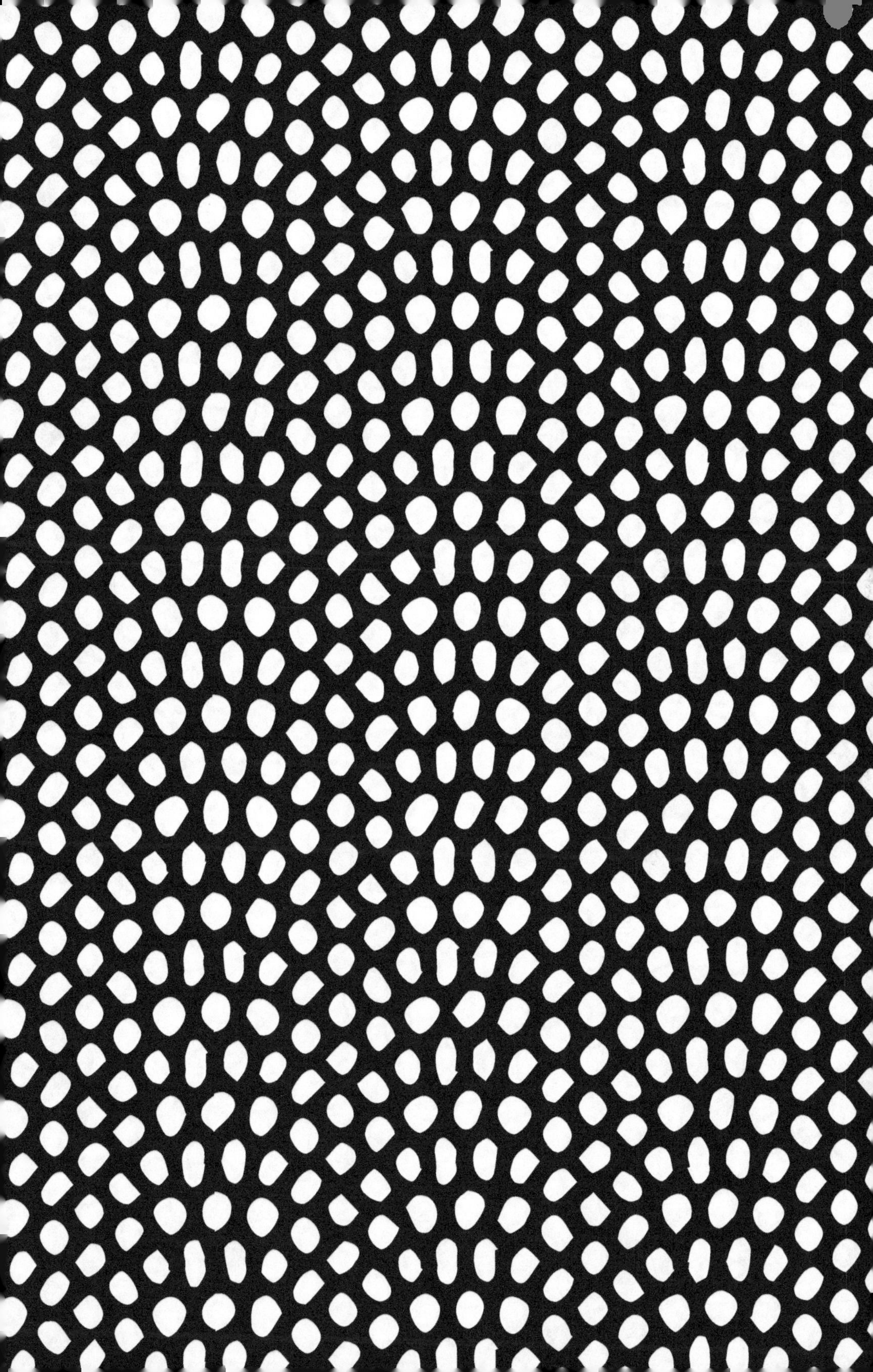

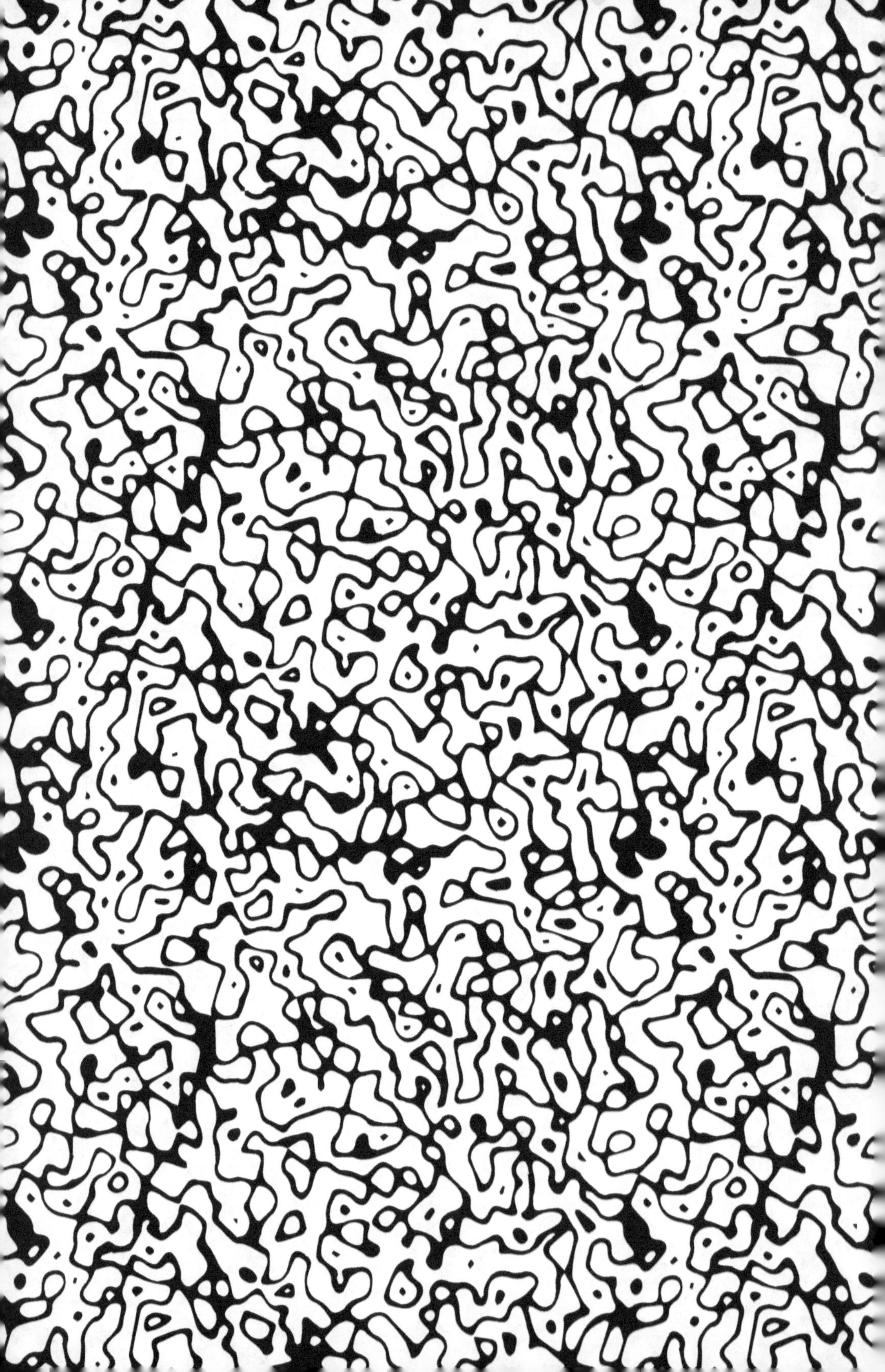

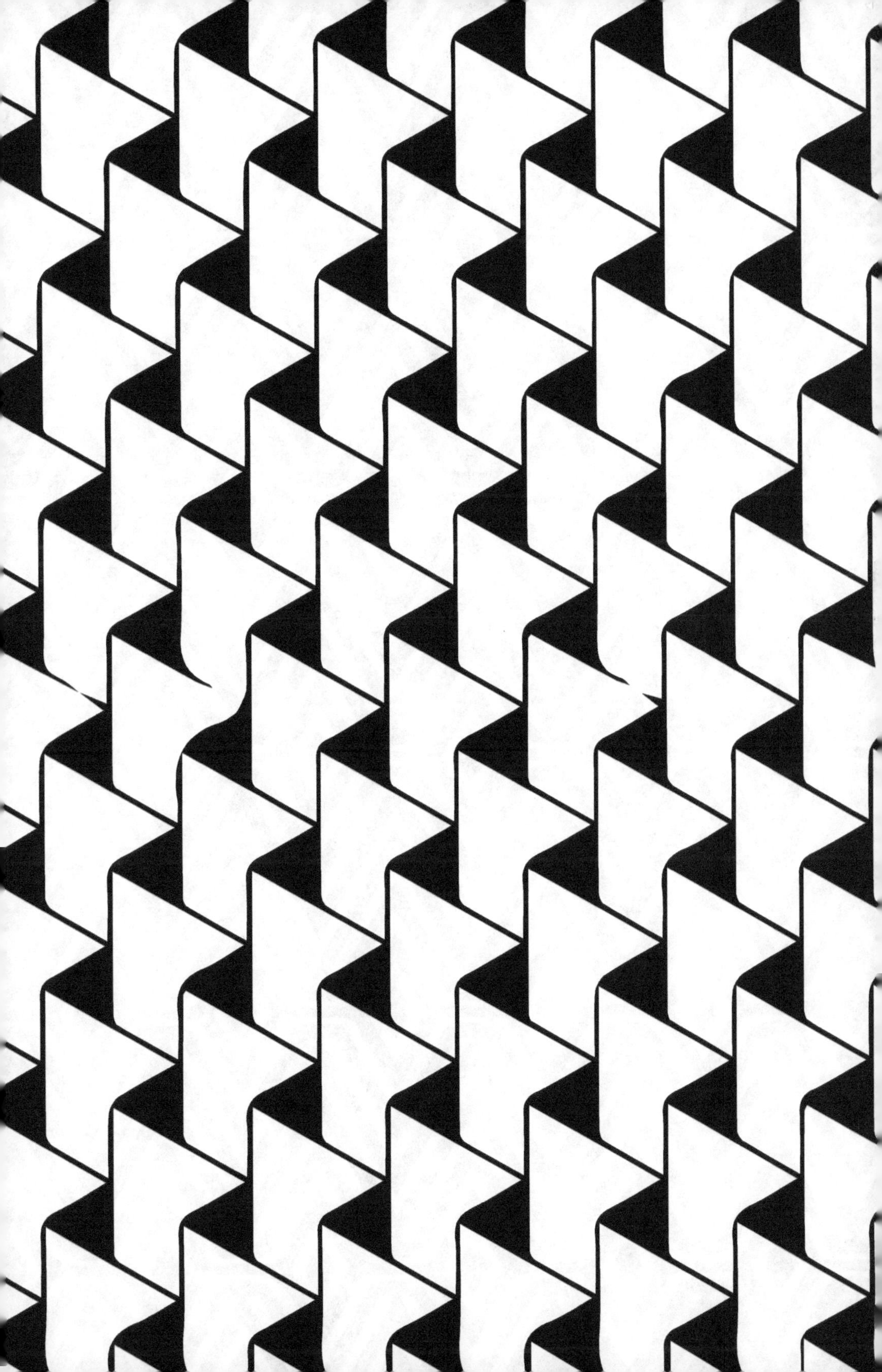

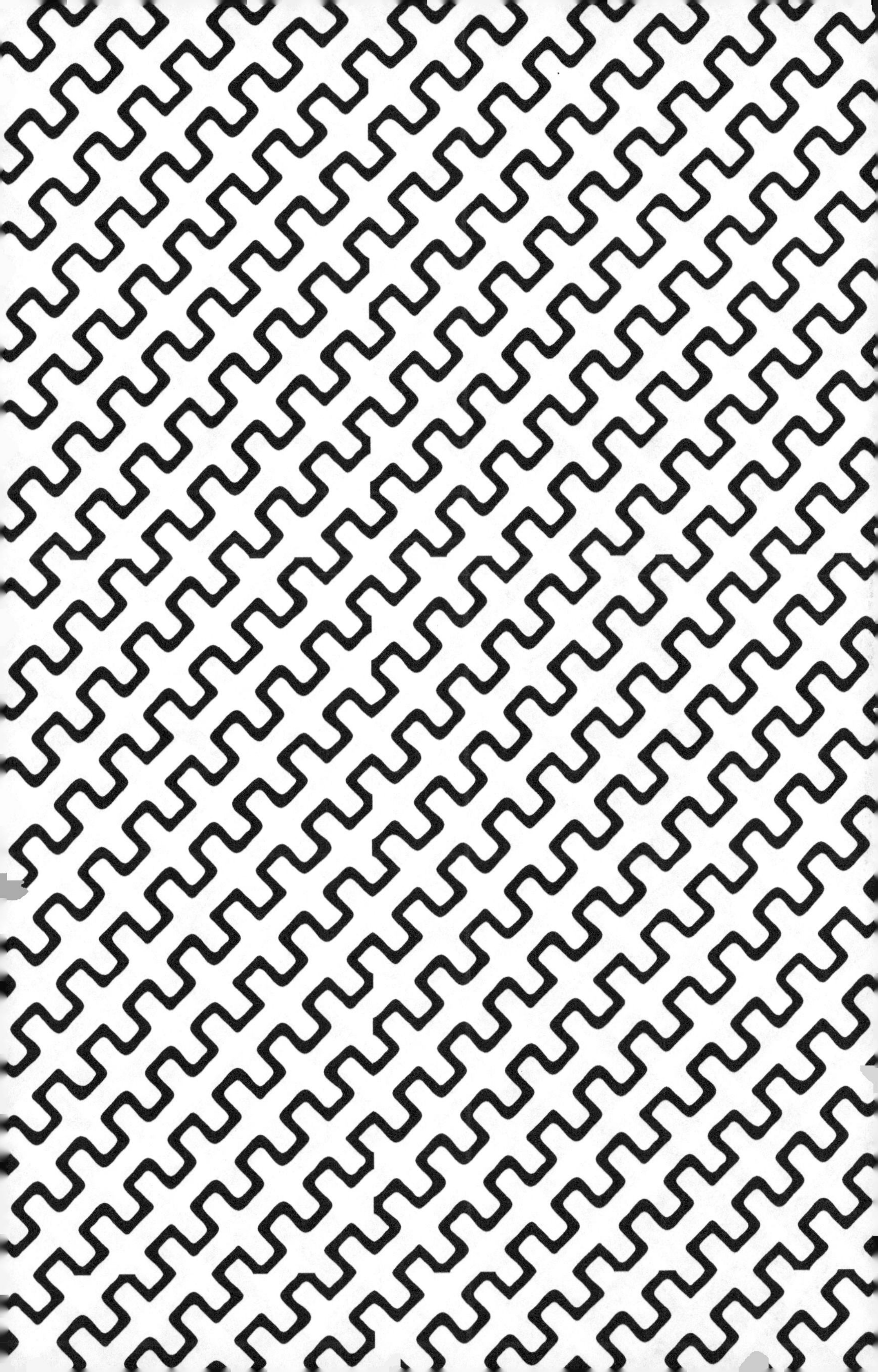

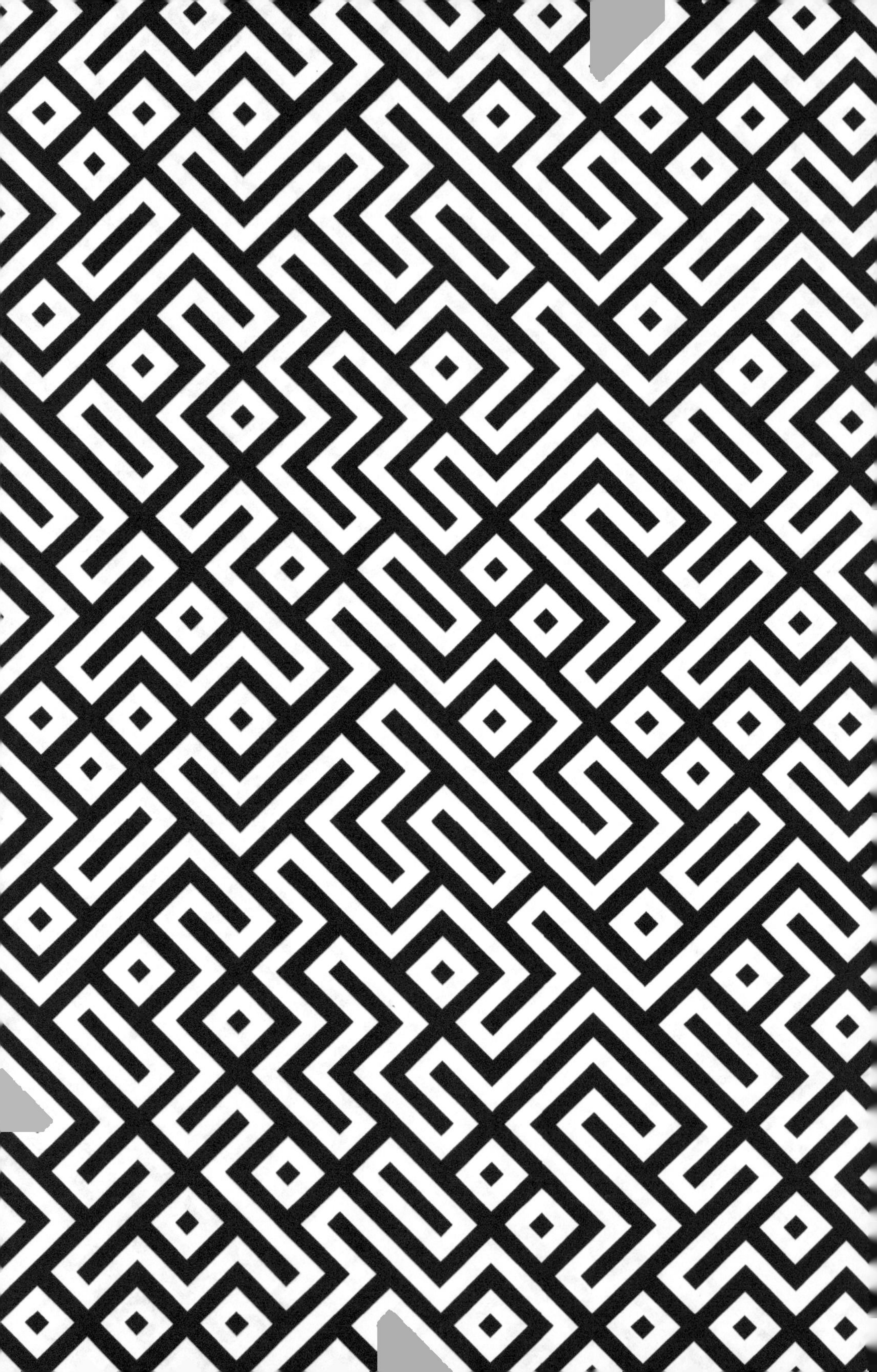

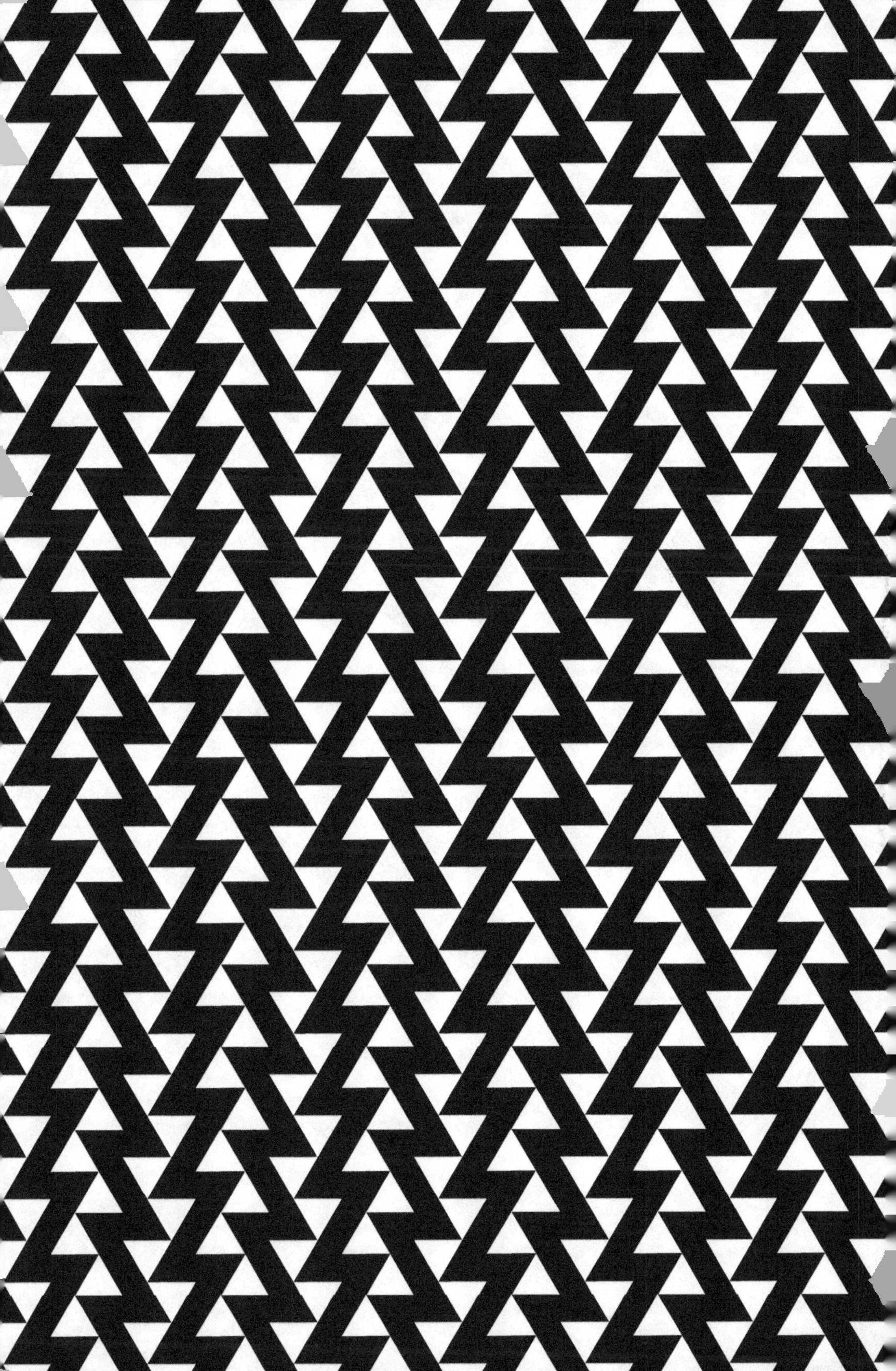

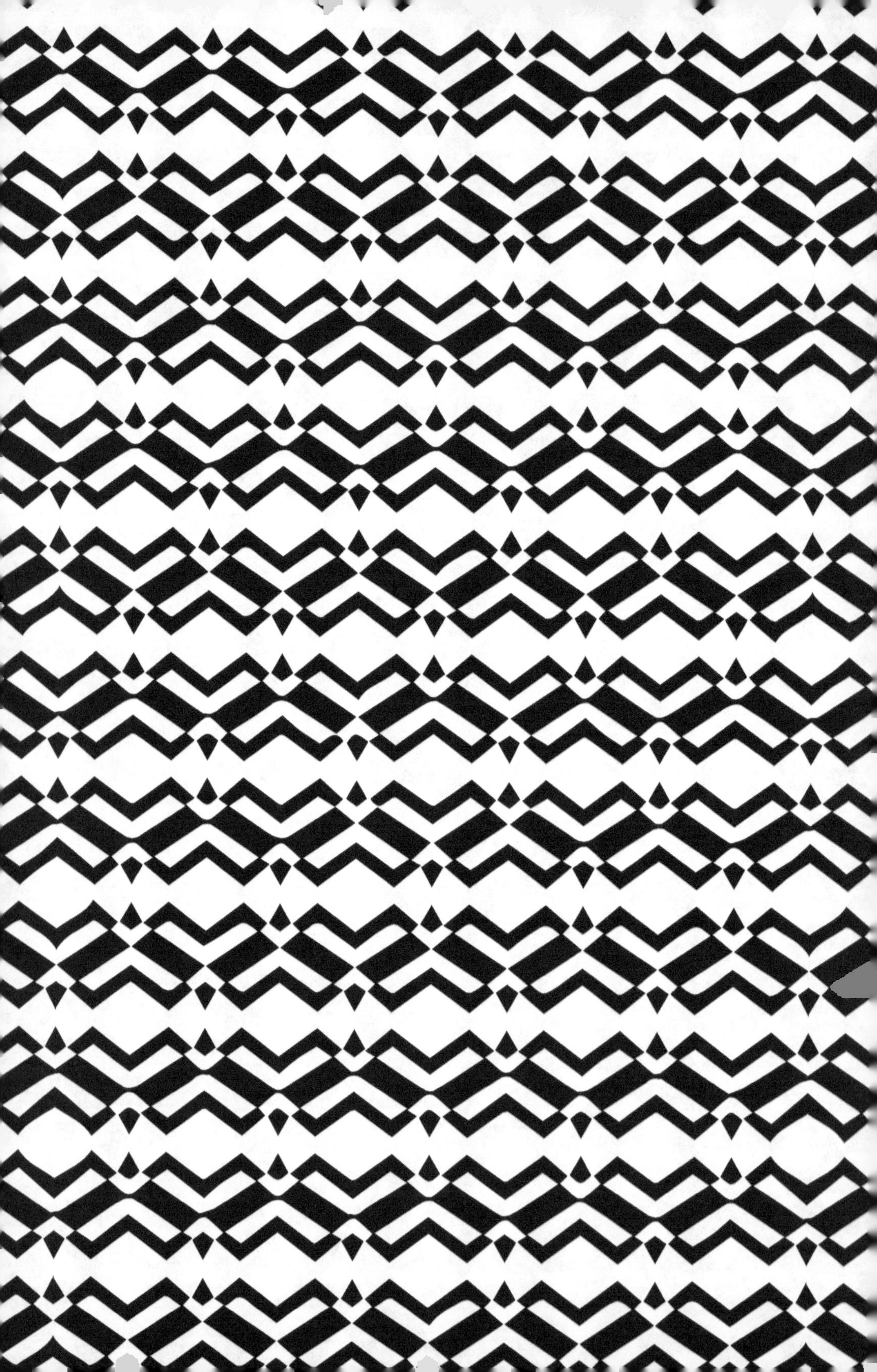

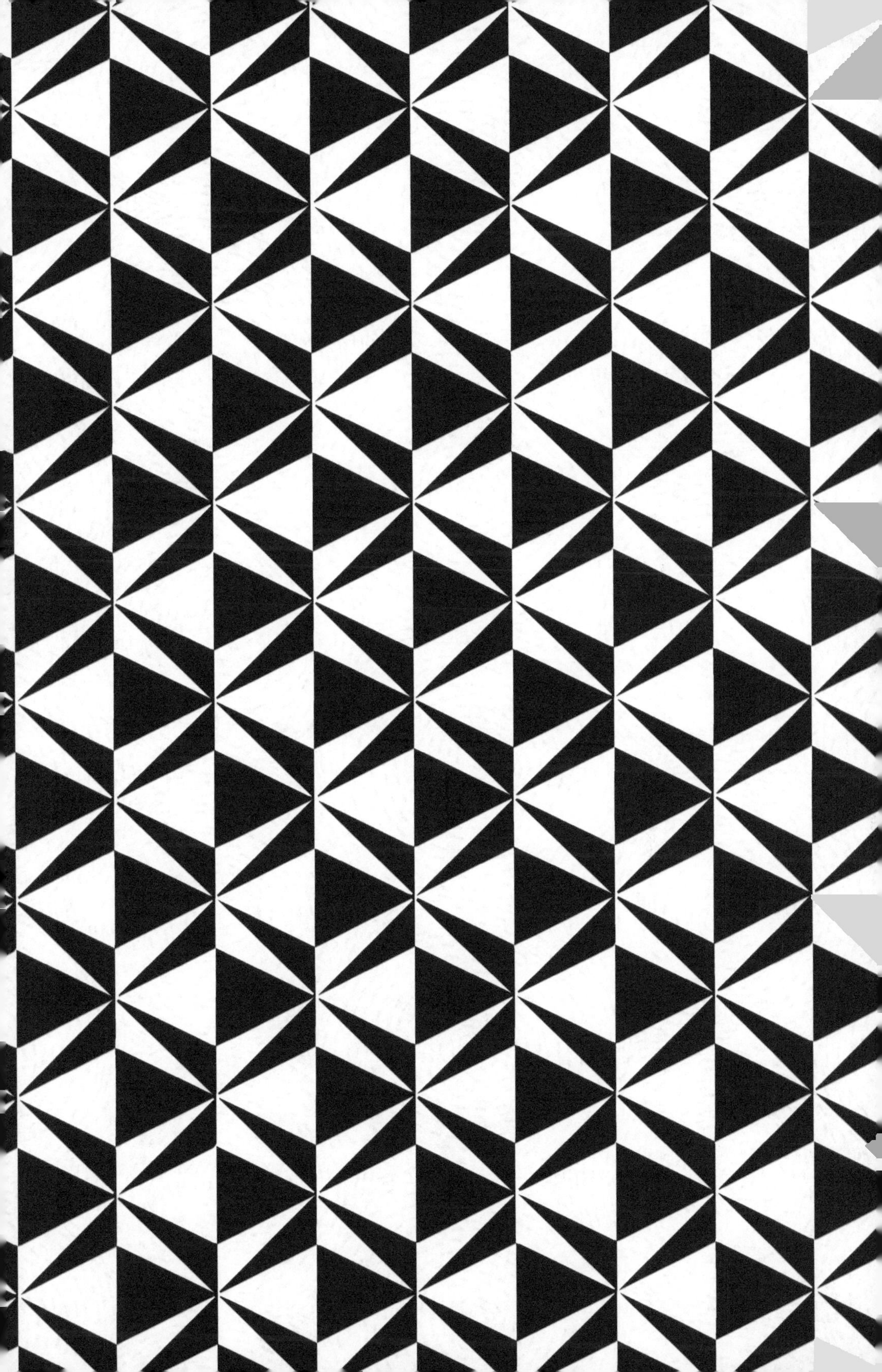

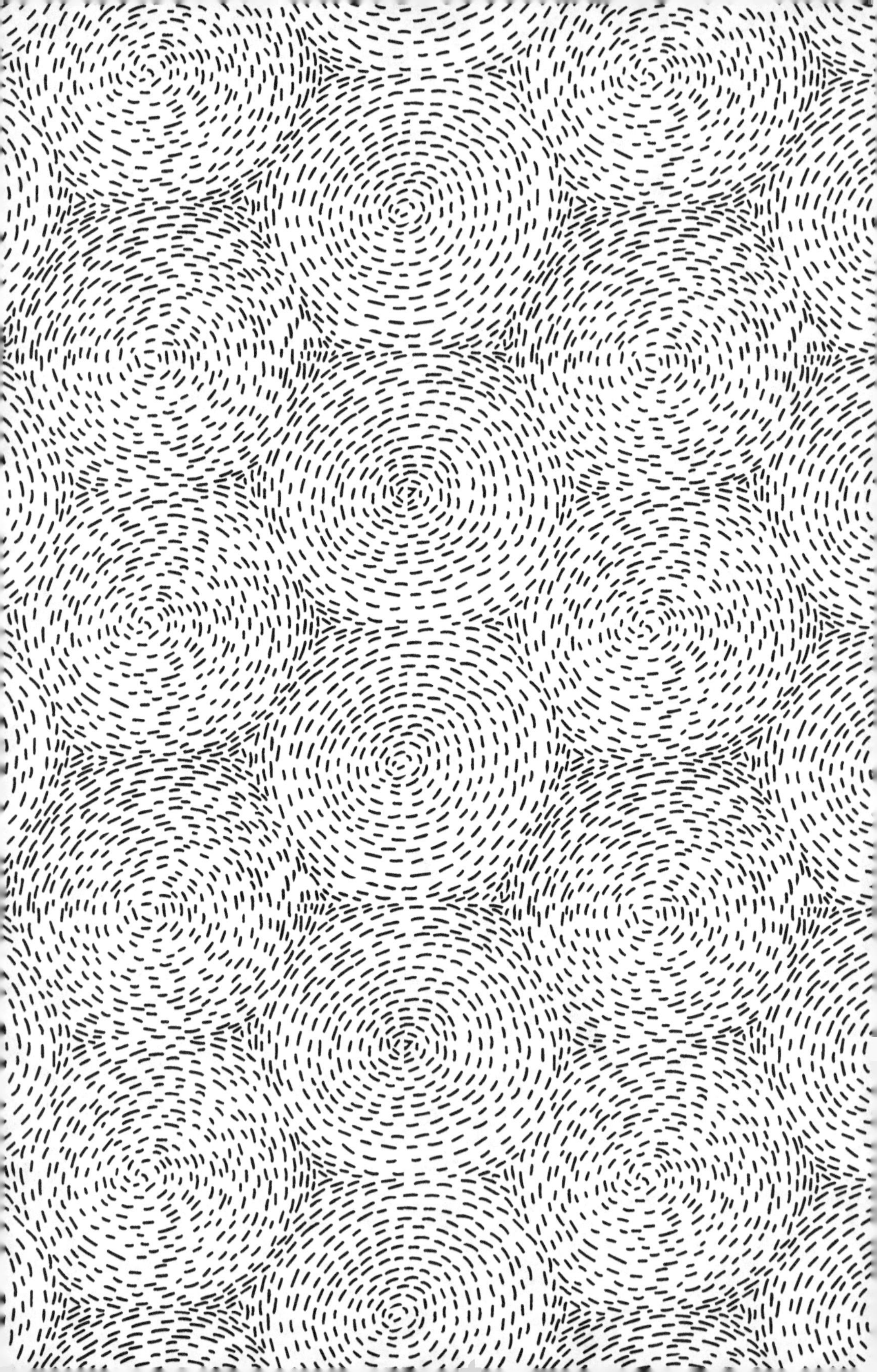

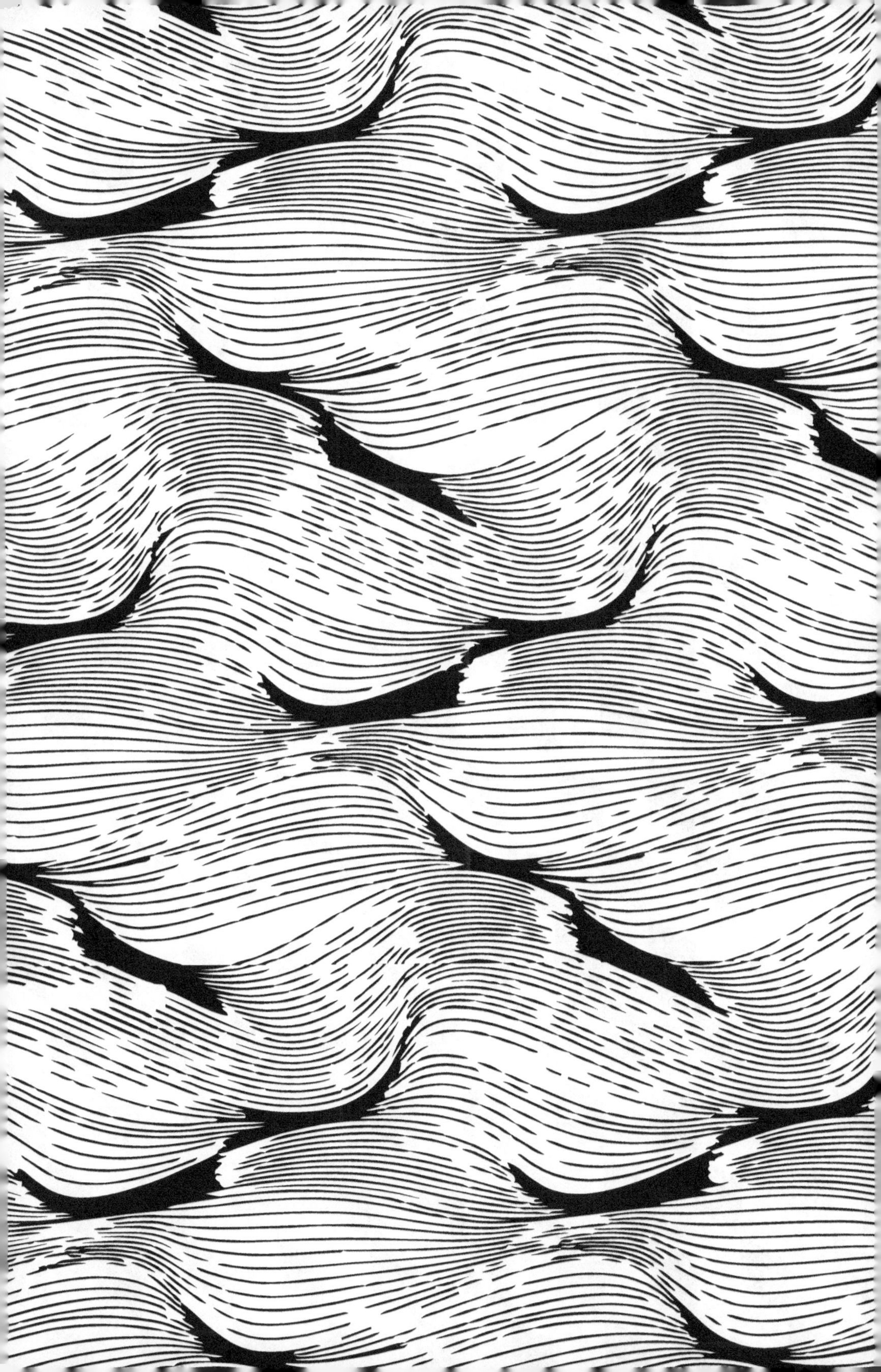

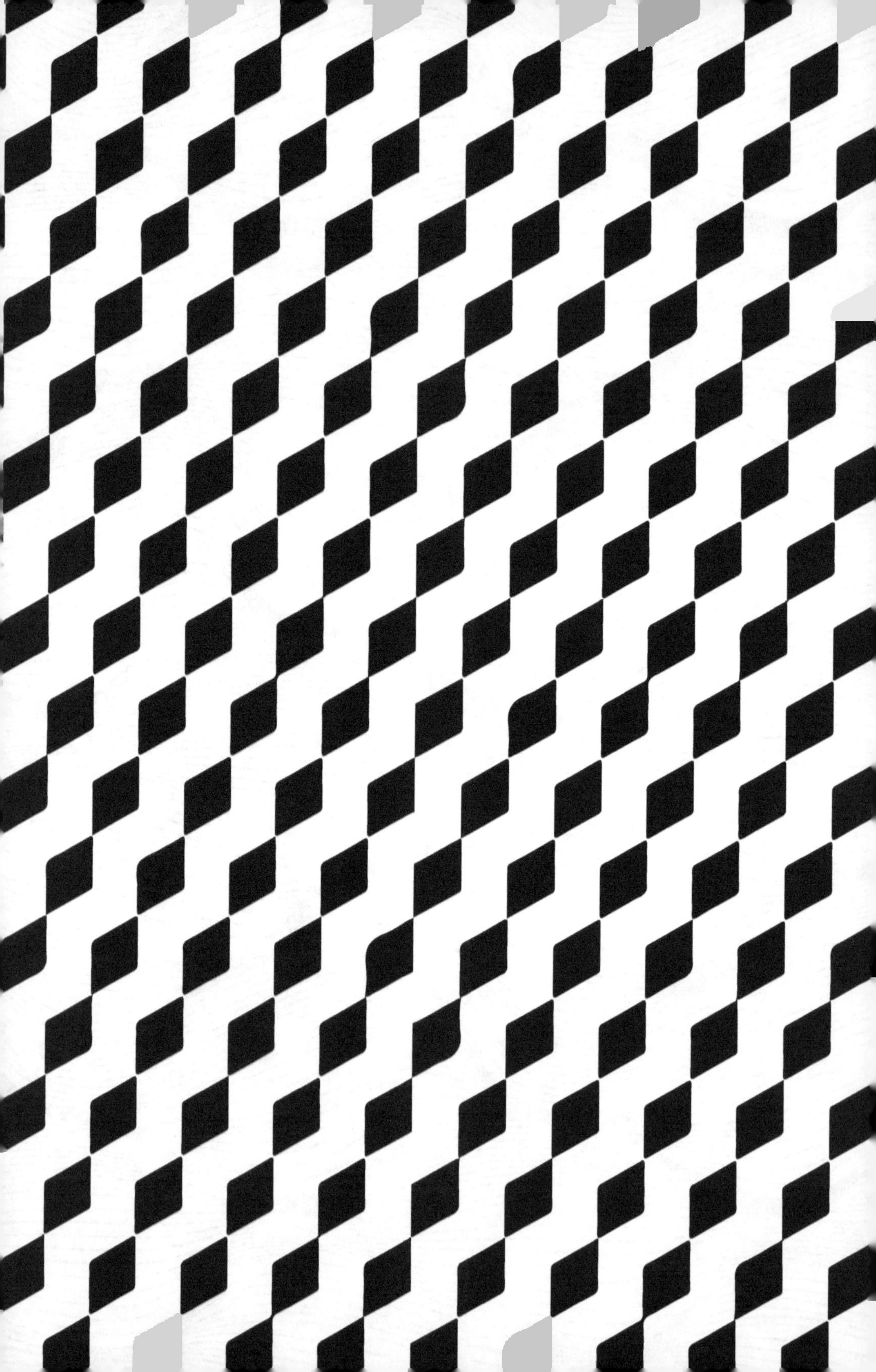